An African Pentecostal Hermeneutics

An African Pentecostal Hermeneutics

A Distinctive Contribution to Hermeneutics

Marius Nel

Foreword by Daryl Balia

WIPF & STOCK · Eugene, Oregon

AN AFRICAN PENTECOSTAL HERMENEUTIC
A Distinctive Contribution to Hermeneutics

Wipf & Stock
An Imprint of Wipf and Stock Publishers
199 W. 8th Ave., Suite 3
Eugene, OR 97401

www.wipfandstock.com

PAPERBACK ISBN: 978-1-5326-6086-3
HARDCOVER ISBN: 978-1-5326-6087-0
EBOOK ISBN: 978-1-5326-6088-7

Manufactured in the U.S.A.   12/27/18

Contents

Foreword

PENTECOSTALISM HAS UNDOUBTEDLY TAKEN the Christian world like a storm, and the scientific contributions of those sharing that tradition to theological studies continue to expand enormously. Hermeneutics might have been a foreign word some decades ago to Pentecostals who, for the most part, regarded the Bible as containing "all the answers to human questions" and—being God's gift—simply to be read, believed, and obeyed! For Carlos Mesters, therefore, the Bible is read such that a "dislocation" occurs since the "emphasis is not placed on the text's meaning in itself but rather on the meaning the text has for the people reading it."[1] Enter Marius Nel into this hermeneutical complexity, within the African context, and, after more than three decades of pastoral practice and serious theological study, we at last have a gem of a book to explain if it is still that way.

In my humble view, pedagogically speaking, the imperative to read the Bible can be taken together with the challenge of an intercultural approach, and, if siphoned from transactional theory, one would arrive at a point where learning is not based on the features of a text or the character of the reader but "on what happens when both come together." This is based on the assumption that learners do not read and then form a worldview but that they do so while they are reading. Understanding the nature of such transactions between text and reader is important in a society where a rich variety of textual temptations can serve to influence the behavioural patterns of impressionable adults. Exactly what happens when text and reader come together can be (and often is) influenced by context. Hence the need for the teaching and learning environments to be subjected to careful scrutiny as we do in the university context generally. Learning as transaction is obviously a dynamic view at variance with seeing science as the (static) study of pre-existing knowledge. It invites

---

1. Mesters, "Use of the Bible," 14.

participation, commitment, and "learning to learn," which cannot be sustained within strict theological boundaries. Hence, of course, my penchant for Pentecostal hermeneutics to be more vigorously interrogated for its utilitarian value, not simply for Christians but for the purposes of learning in general as well.

Notwithstanding the above, I cannot help but ask if we are not living through a time when the "death of the author" has taken place and where reading and interpreting of information occurs predominantly in digital form. Is the burden of interpretation still the same? We know that, traditionally, it was to arrive at the original or intended meaning of a basic text, but that has proved elusive—as many would agree. Today, the reader has become the co-author by decreasing the pressure of the author though the intervention of something called "hyperspace," where the user of the text has now become the one to *organize* its meaning in the absence of a control hierarchy, hegemonic indoctrination, or authentic learning method. This equates to a form of personalized knowledge which, in turn, puts scholars and teachers in an awkward situation, as they can no longer play the role of authoritative interpreter. To perform that function, they have stood in authority over the text with the aim of making the text to *read* the reader or hearer while bringing it under their critical scrutiny, raising questions about its authorship, style, content, and so forth, but deferring commitment or the possibility of making oneself vulnerable to the message of the text. This amounts to a form of "overstanding" as some would say.

With this seminal contribution, Marius Nel seems to be moving us in another direction—one towards appreciating a tradition where the "understanding" of a text which must be preceded by a relationship between text and reader and a disposition of submission before the text, to being open to influence (by the Holy Spirit perhaps) under the interpretation of the text. Instead of making demands on the object of our reading, one risks challenge from the text to one's moral conduct and belief systems, especially if one's positionality and individual agency are not concealed. Put simply, then, my own view would be to welcome this book as a case of old wine being flushed into new wineskins for a generation hungry for new winds of change to our theological imagination. It proves, beyond any reasonable doubt, that Africa has something new to offer on how we on the sub-continent read and interpret the Bible—and how it *reads* us!

Professor Daryl Balia

Executive Dean of Theology

North-West University

Preface

THE PURPOSE OF THIS book is to describe African pentecostal hermeneutics in terms of the direction of interpretation of biblical texts, from the reader anointed by the Spirit, experiencing the revelation of the Spirit in the biblical narrative, and leading to a witness about the experience in terms that remind of the biblical narrative. The experience is formed by the expectation that what people in biblical times experienced with God is to be repeated in the contemporary experience. Most of the academic literature in the field of pentecostal studies in hermeneutics and exegesis is from American or British-European origin. The African context is fairly absent in this discourse, although it is part of the global South where Pentecostalism is growing at such a rate that it is changing the face of African Christianity. The pentecostalization of Africa has been described as the African Reformation. However, African pentecostal theology also presents unique and relevant challenges. This book was written by a theological scholar from Africa, focusing on Africa's need for a well-grounded hermeneutics that will allow Africans to avoid some of the challenges concerned with interpretation of the Bible. African Pentecostals' interpretation of the Bible provides them with the necessary equipment and motivation to contribute to important needed social change because Pentecostals read the Bible with the expectation of life transformation through the Spirit.

This book suggests that, in their hermeneutical labors, Pentecostals should consider emphasizing the centrality of the Spirit, their eschatological lens, and the faith community as normative. The book disseminates original research and new developments in this study field, especially as relevant to the African context because African pentecostal hermeneutics has not been described. In the process, it also addresses the global need to hear voices from Africa in this academic field. It aims to convey the importance of considering Africa's pentecostal voice in theologizing.

The author's varied theological experience—with doctorates in the field of Old and New Testament literature as well as in practical theological and church historical matters of importance to the Pentecostal movement—contributes to the unique and distinct character of the book.

Written from the science of hermeneutics, the book is aimed at scholars across theological sub-disciplines, especially those theological scholars interested in the intersections between theology, pentecostal hermeneutics, and African cultural or social themes. It addresses themes and provides insights that are also relevant for specialist leaders and professionals in this field.

No part of the book was plagiarised from another publication or published elsewhere.

Marius Nel

Unit for Reformed Theology and Development
of the South African Society

North-West University

South Africa

By Way of Introduction: Motivation for Study

Introduction

HERMENEUTICS—THE REFLECTION ON THE principles that undergird correct textual interpretation[1]—is the art of understanding[2] that asks critically what one does when one reads, understands, and applies texts and what the conditions or criteria are that operate to try to ensure responsible and appropriate interpretation while the first order disciplines of exegesis, interpretation, and application concern itself with the actual processes of interpreting texts.[3] "Hermeneutics" carries an obvious relation to Hermes, the messenger god of the Greeks, suggesting that Hermes had to be conversant in the idiom of the gods as well as that of the mortals for whom the message was destined; he had to understand and interpret the message that the gods wanted to convey for himself before he could proceed to translate, articulate, and explicate its intention.[4] Hermeneutics implies linguistic competence, communication, discourse, understanding, and interpretation.[5]

Biblical hermeneutics applies the art of understanding to the Bible and explores how the Scripture of Christians is read and interpreted as

---

1. Oliverio, *Theological Hermeneutics*, 3.

2. Gadamer, *Truth and Method*, 9.

3. Palmer defines "hermeneutics" in terms of three basic notions: to express/to say, to explain, and to translate. Hermeneutics begins and aims to establish the principles, methods, and rules which we need to unfold the sense of what is written, and the task of the interpreter is to make something that is unfamiliar, distant, and obscure in meaning into something real, near, and intelligible. See Palmer, *Hermeneutics*, 13.

4. Zwiep is correct in warning against defining the term "hermeneutics" in terms of its etymological ancestry. To define a term exclusively in terms of its etymology is methodologically incorrect. See Zwiep, "Het Hermeneutische Vraagstuk," 3.

5. Mueller-Vollmer, "Introduction," 1.

1

texts that originated in another time and context of life different from the contemporary world. Hermeneutics is concerned with biblical questions posed by and to the texts; philosophical questions about how one understands and the basis on which understanding is possible; literary questions about types and genres of questions and processes of reading; social, critical, historical, and sociological questions about how vested interests of class, race, gender, prior belief, and political, social, or economic ideology may influence what is read; and linguistic questions about the process of communicating content or an effect to readers or communities of readers, especially when the language of the original and contemporary communication events differ.[6] In biblical hermeneutics, interpretation draws on biblical studies, including the introduction to the Old and New Testament and its exegesis against the background of the "reception" of these texts, as well as Christian theology. The purpose is to develop norms or criteria for a responsible or valid interpretation of Scripture.

"Pentecostal" hermeneutics shares with hermeneutics of other theological traditions those emphases that a consensus of scholars agree are essential to the hermeneutical process, like the importance of reading a text in terms of its genre or literary type; respecting the historical and social context in which the text originated; giving attention to the social context that the original listeners or readers found themselves in; allowing for the distinctive voices of different authors; affirming the overarching narrative, scopus, and fundamental theological unity of the canon as the revelation of the salvation of God[7] to humankind; and identifying ideological elements that protect the powerful in texts. Some traditional principles used for reading the Bible are universal: to read a passage in light of its immediate context; to read it for its function as part of a larger book to which it belongs; and to read it in light of the cultural context that its language, assumptions, and allusions take for granted.[8] The usual way for reading and writing texts has always been in its context, which is common sense. Most Pentecostals read the Bible with a "higher view," or a more conservative perspective on the Bible as authoritative

---

6. Thiselton, *Hermeneutics*, 1.

7. Biological gender cannot be attributed to the transcendent deity and has become a gender-sensitive issue. To accommodate a non-gender view of the deity, I will use language that may seem redundant, referring to God in a gender-less manner by way of necessary, awkward repetition.

8. Keener, *Spirit Hermeneutics*, 117.

and canonical, identifying with a segment of Protestant experience in general.[9]

There are some aspects in pentecostal hermeneutics, however, that are distinctive—although not unique—to the Pentecostal movement. It is further suggested that these elements should characterize all truly Spirit-led hermeneutics by reading from the vantage of the day of Pentecost and the experience of the Spirit and Spirit baptism, and that all readers of the Bible would benefit to some extent to empower themselves from these perspectives. What is being addressed here is an attempt to articulate the distinctive of pentecostal hermeneutics, how the experience of the Spirit that empowered the church on the day of Pentecost (Acts 2) can, should, and does dynamically shape one's reading of Scripture when one is open to the "voice of the Spirit," who interprets and applies Scripture to the context of contemporary believers by way of insights formed in their minds. "Pentecostal theology and hermeneutics are different because they arise not primarily out of rational reflection, but rather out of lived experience."[10] Early Pentecostals thought of the outpouring of the Spirit in the pentecostal revival in ecumenical terms, as a renewal of Christianity as a whole—which justified and defined their origins and existence as a new movement.[11] They were not interested in establishing churches or

9. In interpreting the Bible, pentecostal scholars attend to the following in the same manner as many Protestants: they determine the text, assessing variants and translations; they open up the text, investigating overarching structural features of the text, attending to the context, grammatical and linguistic structure, important word meanings, genre, and comparison with intratextual and extratextual sources; they interpret in a synthetic manner, comparing other revealed texts and the interpretation of previous interpreters, discussing it with the faith community in terms of the challenges of the surrounding world, determining the purpose of the text, and summarizing its theological interpretation and major point (or scopus); and then they communicate their interpretation to the church and world. See Maier, *Biblical Hermeneutics*, 411–12.

10. Ellington, "Pentecostals" 38. "Theology" refers to the second-order affair that proceeds in abstraction from first-hand experience. See Yong, *Spirit-Word-Community*, 2.

11. Hollenweger remarks that Pentecostalism started with a self-perception that it was an ecumenical renewal movement because the experience of Spirit baptism represented a renewal of the day of Pentecost that established the early church, which functioned in unity across boundaries (Hollenweger, *Pentecostalism*, 34). Robeck insists that even "a cursory reading of the earliest pentecostal publications is sufficient to validate [the] claim" (Robeck, "Pentecostals and Ecumenism," 1). Azusa Street was, from the start, an interracial and multidenominational revival movement (Burgess, *Christian Peoples*, 236), an ecumenical melting pot (Vondey, *Pentecostalism*, 49) rather than a church. Oliverio calls original Pentecostalism an ecumenically oriented revival

organizations because they viewed themselves as part of the restoration of the early church by the Spirit who is uniting all Christians in a last outpouring of the Spirit, the "latter rain."[12]

The purpose is not to describe the way how some Pentecostal denominations read and interpret the Bible as such but rather to propose ways of reading the Bible that are faithful to the text—that is, Spirit-inspired while the reader or faith community experience the revelation of the Spirit in their reading act.[13] This is the expectation and experience of

---

movement (Oliverio, "Book Review," 131). Cox implies that the whites who attended the services were mainly unlettered and unrefined as well as unemployed, qualifying them to associate with the blacks that represented the same social class (Cox, *Fire from Heaven*, 46–47). At that time, many American whites would normally not have associated with African Americans on a voluntary basis. Early Pentecostals were optimistic that the outpouring of the Spirit would lead to church unity because the Spirit would unite Christians across the borders of denominations in a new Pentecost. They were open to cooperation with other Christians. Seymour and other leaders of the early movement believed that their experience of Spirit baptism implied the restoration of what happened on the day of Pentecost in Acts 2, including the restoration of the church as the sign that the end of the age has come. The way they interpreted the Bible led many supporters of the Holiness movement to expect that the Spirit would be poured out again like on the day of Pentecost, and they prepared and prayed for it. When this happened on April 9th, 1906, in Los Angeles (Burgess, *Christian Peoples of the Spirit*, 237), their optimism was followed by confrontation and confusion—as Jacobsen, Kärkkäinen, and Robeck illustrate (See Jacobsen, "Ambivalent," 4; Kärkkäinen, "Anonymous Ecumenists?," 14; and Robeck, "Pentecostals and the Apostolic Faith," 65). Instead of renewing and uniting existing historical denominations, the new movement and its experience were rejected, reviled, and booed as a sect and became alienated from mainline churches. Established churches provided stinging condemnation of the movement as a whole (Cox, *Fire from Heaven*, 48).

12. See Burgess, *Christian Peoples of the Spirit* and Barrett, "Appendix" for an extensive discussion of the existence of pentecostal spirituality from the early church to the present. Menzies and Menzies states that, from the time of the apostles and the early church, perhaps two dozen renewal episodes having charismatic overtones related to Spirit baptism can be identified (Menzies and Menzies, *Spirit and Power*, 244). All of these prior movements ended dismally, dissolving into fanaticism and/or heresy.

13. Keener, *Spirit Hermeneutics*, 16. While biblical scholarship has vital contributions to make to global pentecostalism, scholars also have much to learn from humble members of Pentecostal churches who read the Bible in faith, expecting God to move in similar ways in their lives, assemblies and worlds (Keener, "Pentecostal Biblical Interpretation," 280). I agree with Archer that Keener's assertion that what Pentecostals and charismatics need is the best of evangelical exegesis and that a distinctive pentecostal hermeneutic should not be dismissed—although I would add that it is important that its distinctiveness should not stand in the way of ecumenical endeavors to unite the universal church in vision and purpose (See Archer, "Spirited Conversation," 190–91).

Pentecostal communities in general. It is an approach followed by all who read the Bible experientially, hearing God's inspired voice for contemporary people in the Bible, including denomination Pentecostals.[14]

The fact is, pentecostal readings of the Bible are diverse, including widely differing views—such as prosperity teaching[15] and ascetical injunctions—with both a mainstream tradition and diverse local and cultural applications.[16] There is no magisterium for Pentecostals that can decide the case of what is pentecostal.[17] There is no synod, no council,

14. Vondey provocatively states that Pentecostalism at the beginning of the twenty-first century is entering its adolescent years and represents a movement in transition, characterized by a perplexing variety of tensions often found only in the infancy of similar movements (Vondey, *Pentecostalism*, 133). It is a learning movement, where extremes of pluralism, charismatic excessiveness, denominationalism, sectarianism, triumphalism, institutionalism, and anti-intellectualism are confronted by a holistic spirituality, ecumenical ethos, orthodoxy, social engagement, egalitarian practices, and scholarship. As a movement in transition, its critical tensions mark the energy of that transition.

15. Many evaluations of the prosperity gospel of African neo-Pentecostal churches are made from a Western theological perspective. For instance, Grady criticizes neo-prophets for their emphasis on prosperity and argues that it fuels greed, feeds pride, works against formation of Christian character, keeps people in poverty (as it takes the little they have in the name of getting rich), and abuses the Bible (see Grady, "Five Ways"). The phenomenon of the health and wealth gospel in African churches should be analysed and evaluated from the perspective of African people and the values deduced from their worldview. The impact of a prosperity message on the emerging youthful population of Africa with a taste for exotic lifestyles is enormous (see Quaye-si-Amakye, "'Nativizing' the Gospel," 301). Wepener's remark that healing is most probably the main motivation why people go to worship in Africa is also important (Wepener, "Liturgical 'Reform,'" 91). Healing is interpreted in Africa in the holistic sense—that is, the total well-being of the individual, including financial success. Anderson's observations of neo-Pentecostals led to his remark that the neoprophets' primary function is to be healers (see Anderson, "Hermeneutical Processes"). Omenyo concurs and adds that the teaching of prosperity has two dimensions: the prosperity of the soul and material prosperity (Omenyo, "African Pentecostalism," 140). The first emphasis is not lost in the teaching of prosperity and reflects inner peace, satisfaction, contentment, and the maintenance of social networks. Early Pentecostals also emphasized bodily healing and socio-economic upward mobility, with an emphasis on this-worldly rather than exclusively otherworldly sensibilities, which concur with Pentecostals in the Global South (see Yong, "Instead of a Conclusion," 318).

16. Archer emphasizes that Pentecostalism is anything but a monolithic community (Archer, "Spirited Conversation," 193).

17. See, for instance, the magisterium between Lutheran and Roman Catholic churches about teaching authority in the church, as discussed in Chapman, "Spirit and the Magisterium," 268. Magisterium is the authority of the minister of the eucharist in the Lutheran tradition to speak the epiclesis with the confidence that it is accomplished

and no writings by an important leader figure that are viewed as authoritative. While it is true that consensus definitions of pentecostal hermeneutics are elusive because the boundaries are fluid, there is, however, a core spiritual identity that can be identified in the contextualized theological hermeneutical activity of listening to the Spirit within a specific faith community that acknowledges the revelatory activity of the Spirit.[18] There is reasonable consensus among pentecostal hermeneutes about the distinctives of pentecostal spirituality and hermeneutics.[19]

A significant part of the contemporary church probably recognizes the importance of a dependence upon the Spirit in daily life, and interpretation and application of the Bible, and the accompanying spiritual gifts. They may appreciate a discussion of the distinct contribution of pentecostal hermeneutics to the debate of understanding biblical texts[20] since Christianity has entered a new, flat era, where mutual edification has become the rule and Christians from all the world's cultures and regions

---

in their speaking of it, and the whole reality of God in the world is thereby made present and knowable. It is the authority to discern and teach to the community what it means to live in such a way that one's life is a doxology. The Roman Catholic Church accepts the doctrine of infallibility that decides how dogmatic decisions are made, by whom, with what sort of authority, and in what relation to Scripture and to the reception of doctrine by believers in the church. The pope and ecumenical councils have the power to determine such decisions. Pentecostals would accept as their magisterium the authority of the Holy Spirit as the breath of the Father that speaks the words of the Son which makes the Triune God present in and as the community of faith, the body of Christ (Chapman, "Spirit and the Magisterium," 276).

18. Keener, *Spirit Hermeneutics*, 305. Yong defines theological hermeneutics as "the hermeneutics of the divine" (Yong, *Spirit-Word-Community*, 2).

19. Neumann makes the important remark that spirituality is most significant for understanding Pentecostalism since it serves as the primary means for differentiating Pentecostals from other Christian traditions and spiritualities (Neumann, "Spirituality," 196). It should be added that one cannot understand the pentecostal hermeneutic without considering its spirituality because it interprets the Bible as a function of its spirituality. Pentecostal spirituality can be defined as experiential, biblical-revelatory, holistic, and missional-pragmatic. See Albrecht, *Rites in the Spirit*, 13, for a definitive description of pentecostal spirituality.

20. Menzies and Menzies register their amazement at the openness concerning gifts of the Spirit in nearly all established churches, something that twenty years ago would have seemed incredible (Menzies and Menzies, *Spirit and Power*, 181). They emphasize that the hermeneutical climate within evangelicalism (and it should be added, within Roman Catholicism and the high churches) is more conducive now than ever before to the theological contributions of Pentecostals.

have much to learn from one another in a global world ("glocalization"). Global Christianity has become irreversibly more egalitarian.[21]

The hermeneutical approach that is described is consistent with key aspects and emphases of early Pentecostals, which, in some instances, they developed from the holiness revivals that fed the Azusa Street and related revivals at the beginning of the twentieth century (although Pentecostalism did not simply borrow the theological categories of its holiness and Reformed predecessors; it created a new theological tradition as a hybrid between different traditions).[22] Their Bible reading practices distinguished them from the widespread and widely accepted cessationism of the surrounding Protestant mainline churches of their day. They were biblically directed because of their restorationist-primitivistic ethos, justifying their existence as a continuation of the establishment by the Spirit of the early church. They believed that they were living within the larger narrative world of the Bible (establishing a metanarrative for Pentecostals that they lived in), where the supernatural and eschatological determined the apocalyptic worldview that they believed they shared with Jesus and the apostles. They believed their charismatic experiences were in continuity with the early church of the first three centuries and used it as a starting point or pre-understanding (*Vorverständnis*) for engaging with the text.[23] This is their contribution to hermeneutical wisdom—to read the Bible from the perspective of Pentecost and its accompanying experience of Spirit baptism in the same way as, for instance, Anabaptists emphasized caring for the poor as their starting point in reading Scripture and many Protestants used justification by faith.[24]

21. Jacobsen, *Global Gospel*, 13.

22. Studebaker, "Book Review," 376. Early Pentecostals emerged from a wing of evangelicalism that emphasized holiness, divine healing, missions, and social justice. The new movement was rejected by Evangelicals, a part of whom developed into early twentieth-century fundamentalists who excluded and demonized Pentecostals, initially even refusing them entrance into their educational institutions.

23. See Kärkkäinen's remark that, in the first two centuries, charismatic, "enthusiastic" spiritual life was a norm rather than a barely tolerated minority voice in the church (Kärkkäinen, *Pneumatology*, 38). The Montanist movement, emerging in 160 or 170 CE around the Phrygian Pentapolis area, in what is now Turkey, was probably a renewal movement, although it is normally assessed as false and devious. We only know about the Montanists through other people and our assessment is based on the perspective of those opposed to the movement (Kärkkäinen, *Pneumatology*, 41).

24. The Anabaptists are frequently contended as to have devalued Scripture by putting in its place a reliance on the Holy Spirit. Their hermeneutics probably had more to do with how the then-new pentecostal hermeneutics viewed the Bible as a function

Research Question, Aim, and Objectives

The assumption used here is that there is a distinctly pentecostal way of reading and interpreting Scripture that can have potentially useful, normative implications for all Bible believers and practitioners in the third millennium.[25] The way Pentecostals read the Bible is described here specifically in conversation with African pentecostal perspectives. Deep in the soul of Pentecostalism are its African origins—as well as, among others, African-American influences[26]—which, in many places, continue to inform the movement in deep and meaningful ways.[27] After providing a description of African pentecostal hermeneutics, some prescriptives are developed regarding what can and even ought to be done, partly in

---

of the revelation of the Spirit (Kärkkäinen, *Pneumatology*, 55). The Anabaptists saw an integral relationship between the Spirit and the Word. The Spirit was the ultimate authority that first gave authority to the written word of the Bible. They distinguished between the "outer" word—which consists of the mere reading and hearing of the word—and the "inner" word—which consists of the personal appropriation of the word—to emphasize the importance and necessity of the transformative experience of appropriation. The word is broader than the Bible; the word of God can come directly to the heart without an intermediary, for example, through prophecy.

25. See Yong, *Hermeneutical Spirit*, 44.

26. The Pentecostal movement is rooted in the American black slave culture of the nineteenth century and many of its early manifestations were found in the religious expressions of the slaves. These were themselves a reflection of the African religious culture from which the slaves had been abducted. Black Pentecostalism emerged out of the context of the African holistic view of religion with its roots in African religion (MacRoberts, *Black Roots and White Racism*, 77–78).

27. Thomas, "What the Spirit is Saying to the Church," 125. Thomas likens Scripture in a pentecostal hermeneutics to a black gospel choir, where individual notes in rehearsal sound like dissonance but, in its combination, the dissonance sounds beautiful, along with the custom that a single voice may take the lead at the appropriate moment, followed by the choir's participation. In pentecostal hermeneutics, he concludes, the diversity of Scripture may not be forced into an artificial unity that is illegitimate and does the collection a disservice. The intensity of Scripture can only be heard through allowing the dissonance to be heard, and even the smallest and seemingly most insignificant voice should be allowed to take the lead at the appropriate moment. Acceptance of the canonicity of the Bible implies that the essential unifying factor is faith in Jesus Christ, but also that the early church represented a diversity of ways in which faith was expressed (Dunn, "Role of the Spirit," 158). It cannot deny legitimacy to other expressions of Christian faith, worship, or order which can demonstrate legitimacy from the New Testament, nor should it deny the hand of Christian fellowship to such others, strengthening the ecumenical impulse inherent in Pentecostalism (see Nel, "Pentecostal Ecumenical Impulses.")

response to what is perceived as isolated incidences of abuses and misuses of the Bible.[28]

The research question is: what are the distinctives of a pentecostal hermeneutics[29] that characterize the way people interpret the Bible when they have experienced the baptism in the Spirit and the promptings of the Spirit while reading the text? The question is asked against the background of the central problem of biblical hermeneutics: how can the human word of a long-since-vanished time be understood as God's word to the present?[30]

In a first chapter, Bible reading practices of Pentecostals will be discussed to provide a background for the description of their hermeneutics.

In a second chapter, the distinctives of their hermeneutics will be discussed. Three distinctives will be distinguished that summarize the essentials of pentecostal Bible reading practices.

---

28. Although I am an African, I am not a black African. My theological education was primarily a Western one—as is the case of most African Pentecostals—implying that I am limited by my own Western cultural background and education. However, I have been living in Africa for my whole life and my love for and commitment to Africa, its peoples and their cultural heritage, and my identification with their struggle for liberation are all reasons for considering myself an African. I have been actively involved with Pentecostal churches my whole life, serving for the past thirty-six years as a pastor of the Apostolic Faith Mission of South Africa, serving as a leader in the unified church that originated in 1996, and training candidates for the ministry for the past twenty-six years, most of whom were black. I concur with Anderson that, if "African" is meant to signify love for the continent and people of Africa or commitment to an African ideal, then I would certainly include myself in this category (Anderson, *Moya*, 2). For this reason, I consider myself qualified to write about African pentecostal hermeneutics.

29. The use of "a pentecostal hermeneutics" is deliberate, owing to the fact of the diversity of the Pentecostal movement and its hermeneutical practices (see Thomas, "What the Spirit is Saying," 115). The variety of Pentecostalism can be seen in its main "theologies" (Kärkkäinen, *Pneumatology*, 89–90). There are Wesleyan Pentecostals who emphasize the Wesleyan doctrine of "second blessing" instant sanctification, with Spirit baptism as a "third blessing." There are Baptistic Pentecostals who stress gradual sanctification. Oneness Pentecostals teach a Unitarianism of the Son that denies the traditional doctrine of the Trinity and claims that Jesus is Father, Son, and Spirit. The charismatic Pentecostals incorporate aspects of pentecostal practice and theology into the theological frameworks of their own traditions. Independent pentecostal-charismatic theologies and spiritualities have diverse agendas and there are an endless variety of Pentecostal and charismatic movements, especially in the Global South, contributing to the heterogeneity of Pentecostalism.

30. Maier, *Biblical Hermeneutics*, 19.

In the following three chapters, each of these distinctives will be described in more detail and illustrated through pentecostal practice: the experience of the Holy Spirit as the One who inspires and animates Scripture; the eschatological lens that Pentecostals use when they read the Bible; and the faith community as necessary for a normative interpretation of the Bible.

Argument

It is argued that Scripture, by virtue of its textual form, requires to be approached in the same sort of ways in which literary texts are approached due to similarities in, for instance, the occurrence of different genres and the determinative role played by contextualities that influence the origins and interpretations of texts. However, because the biblical text is accorded with authority for the lives of believers, as the "word (or revelation) of God," Christians expect to find illumination and the potential of appropriating the interpreted text when they read and interpret the Bible.[31] Pentecostals believe that the Spirit already generated meaning through the human agents who wrote in contemporary idiom and style for people living in historical contexts that differ from the world in which people live today. The Spirit, however, is also active in the exegetical task through the clear functioning of the Spirit-filled cognitive faculties of the contemporary reader or listener exploring the text because the Spirit acts as one who teaches us everything, and reminds us of all that Jesus told us (John 14:26), as applicable in contemporary contexts.[32] When reading these texts prayerfully, Pentecostals—like the first listeners or readers—also experience the illumination of the Spirit in their minds, as

---

31. "Illumination" consists of hearing the voice of the Spirit in the biblical text. Origen, John Chrysostom, and Augustine described the help of the Spirit in understanding the Bible (see Moberly, "Pneumatic Biblical Hermeneutics," 61–62 and Wyckoff, *Pneuma and Logos*, 13–18). Origen (183–253 CE) was the first Christian theologian who provided a theoretical grounding of a biblical hermeneutics, consisting of a methodology for understanding the Bible (Pollman, "Einführung," 10). In the fifth century CE, the Benedictines developed *lectio divina* to accommodate illumination, while the Eastern Orthodox church defined it as the practice of hesychasm. See Wansbrough, *Use and Abuse of the Bible*, 167–77, for a discussion of *dei verbum* found in *lectio*, *meditation*, *oratio*, and *contemplation*.

32. Contexts are defined as what the text and the interpreter(s) bring with them to the conveying and understanding of meaning (Oliverio, "Book Review," 135).

the successful conclusion of the speech act or perlocution of the text.[33] If the illocution of the text is a command, the perlocution would be obedience. The Spirit's involvement in the perlocution leads to the readers' recognizing and understanding the truthfulness of the text and what it requires from them, empowering them to take the appropriate steps to actualize the intentions that the Spirit initially delivered to the biblical author and applies in the new situation of the contemporary reader.[34] The textual and revelatory meaning of biblical texts adheres to contexts—that is, the original contexts—and the fusion of the contexts of historical and contemporary interpreters are then productive of interpretations whose meanings are accountable to the original texts themselves, which are properly understood only in relation to these original contexts.[35] In this way, the interpreter is accountable to the text's origination.[36] The underlying assumption is that the Bible has a discernible meaning which coincides with God's intention as this is expressed in the biblical texts themselves.[37] The church is competent and obliged to adequately determine their divinely-intended meaning because God reveals Godself through the instrumentality of scriptural writings and because the Bible is sufficient, perspicuous, and a supremely normative standard for Christian faith and living.[38]

33. Keener, *Mind of the Spirit*, 12.

34. See Arrington's remarks on the importance of the Spirit's participation in the act of reading and interpreting the Bible, consisting of: the Spirit-filled believer's submission of the mind to God so that the critical and analytical abilities are exercised under the guidance of the Spirit, a genuine openness to the witness of the Spirit through insights as the text is examined, the personal experience of faith as mediating principle of the entire interpretive process that turns human words into the voice of God, and an appropriate response to the transforming call of God's word (Arrington, "Use of the Bible by Pentecostals," 105).

35. "Meaning" can be defined as the incorporation of real understanding into one's own interpretation of ultimate reality, which influences the way one lives one's life (Archer, "Hermeneutics," 110). Keener mentions that most Christians use Bible verses like sound bites (Keener, *Spirit Hermeneutics*, 113). Rather than reading the Bible meditatively, giving account of the context, they use verses the way they have heard others use them, without relating it to its historical context.

36. Keener, *Spirit Hermeneutics*, 85.

37. Venema, "Interpreting the Bible," 45.

38. N. T. Wright argues that God exercises authority in the Bible through human agents anointed and equipped by the Holy Spirit (see Wright, "How Can the Bible Be Authoritative?," 16). God wants to reveal Godself meaningfully within the space/time universe, not just passing it by tangentially, but in judgment and mercy in a way which will save people. It implies that the church can only be the people of God for the world,

Pentecostal hermeneutics is diverse, reflecting the different backgrounds and theological training of pentecostal readers of the Bible.[39] Some pentecostal scholars embrace postmodern approaches in a qualified sense while others contend for more traditional approaches. While recognizing these differences, it is the contention of this book that it is possible to distinguish a pentecostal hermeneutics by way of certain fundamental distinctives, based on Pentecostalism's primary focus, also representing its contribution to the larger church, which is the present activity of the Holy Spirit.[40] The Spirit also equips God's people for their being and mission in the world through their reading and interpreting of Scripture. Pentecostals view Acts 28 as open-ended, implying the mission's future and requiring the Spirit's power to fulfill it (Acts 1:8) in the same way as they view the Bible as a still unfinished story—a living record of an open-ended history in which they have a part.[41] They view themselves as part of the continuing, postcanonical narrative of salvation history, to which Acts points.[42]

It is true that the Pentecostal movement is diverse, consisting of various parts that are historically related. Half a century ago, David Barrett perceived that African Christianity is transforming "Christianity permanently into a primarily non-Western religion."[43]

Although any classification of Pentecostalism is risky because of its diverse branches, it is customary to speak of three waves.[44] The first is of

---

a city set on a hill that cannot be hidden, when she is constantly being recalled to the story and message of the Bible, without which she will herself lapse into the world's way of thinking (Wright, "How Can the Bible Be Authoritative?," 28).

39. Keener, "Pentecostal Biblical Interpretation," 270. Thomas is correct when he emphasizes that, despite our modern occupation with "readers," whether "actual," "intended," or "implied," for the most part, our attention should be focused on hearers of the Bible (Thomas, "What the Spirit is Saying," 115).

40. Kärkkäinen describes one of the most exciting developments in theology in recent years as an unprecedented interest in the Holy Spirit, shown by both various traditions and mainline denominations (Kärkkäinen, *Pneumatology*, 11). Karl Barth already called the theology of the Spirit the future of Christian theology (Barth, quoted in Kärkkäinen, *Pneumatology*, 13).

41. Cox, *How to Read the Bible*, 8.

42. Keener, "Pentecostal Biblical Interpretation," 276.

43. Barrett, "AD 2000," 50.

44. Due to its diverse nature, there is also a diversity of categorizations of Pentecostalism, but Barrett's proposal for "three waves" is used the most and is probably also the most useful typology of the movement as a whole (see Barrett, "Worldwide Holy Spirit Renewal").

classical Pentecostalism, which looks back for its origins to the beginning of the twentieth century, including Charles Parham's Bible Schools,
William Seymour's Azusa Street Revival in Los Angeles, and similar incidents[45] (not all agree that pentecostal origins in other countries go back
to Los Angeles[46]—sometimes it might have been the result of indigenous
revivals). Today, there is an estimated 200 million people belonging to
these first-wave, classical Pentecostal churches. Secondly, since the 1960s
and 1970s is the charismatic renewal of mainline churches with its openness to the gifts of the Spirit,[47] consisting of a loose worldwide "network,"
which began in California in 1960, started by Dennis J. Bennett, an Epis-
copalian priest, and eventually influencing the Protestant, Roman Catholic, and Eastern Orthodox mainline churches.[48] The movement includes
an estimated 100 million believers in Latin America alone.[49] Thirdly,
there is an independent movement since the 1970s with its synthesis between pentecostal theology and practice, and several other theological

45. Jacobsen calls Azusa Street the Grand Central Station for the Pentecostal movement (Jacobsen, *Thinking in the Spirit*, 57). Menzies and Menzies mention that episodes of isolated outpourings of the Spirit have been chronicled in various parts of the
world, including the United States, as early as the 1850s (Menzies and Menzies, *Spirit
and Power*, 125). Many Evangelicals also employed the language of "baptism in the
Spirit" as part of their drive for sanctification.

46. See Anderson, *Spreading Fires*. Elsewhere, Anderson also remarks that, in
many parts of Africa, indigenous movements arose independently and often prior to
classical Pentecostalism (Anderson, "African Pentecostalism," 28). Something akin to
Pentecostalism emerged in Africa several decades before the Azusa Street meetings,
although it has not been publicized at all, in contrast to the Azusa Street Revival (Jacobsen, *Global Gospel*, 37).

47. Keener, "Pentecostal Interpretation," 271. Some 150 million Catholics are part
of the renewal movement (see Keener, "Pentecostal Interpretation," 272). For instance,
in South Africa, the Vineyard churches quickly grew into a popular independent charismatic church, while St. Charles Catholic Church in Victory Park in Johannesburg
was a leading light in the charismatic movement in the 1970s and 1980s (Frahm-Arp,
"Rise of the Megachurches," 263). Most charismatic theologians view the Spirit baptism in an organic way by identifying it with water baptism, though it is not actualized through spiritual gifts until much later. For charismatics, this view avoids the
problems of the "initial evidence" doctrine, the idea of two baptisms and the dividing
of Christians into two classes—those baptized by the Spirit and those who are not
(Kärkkäinen, *Pneumatology*, 95).

48. Paas, *Christianity in Eurafrica*, 490.

49. Jacobsen, *Global Gospel*, 38.

traditions.[50] This last wave is sometimes denoted as neo-Pentecostalism[51] and it concurs with the pentecostalization of Christian churches, especially in the French-speaking parts of Africa.[52]

Barrett[53] reckons that there are 740 classical Pentecostal denominations, 6,530 non-Pentecostal "mainline" denominations with large organized internal charismatic movements, and 18,810 independent neo-charismatic denominations and networks. Charismatics are found across the entire spectrum of Christianity, within all 150 traditional non-Pentecostal ecclesiastical confessions, families, and traditions. The third-wave phenomenon is found in 9,000 ethnolinguistic cultures, speaking 8,000 languages, and covering 95 percent of the world's total population. In 2000, there were 523 million Pentecostals in total, and in 2025 this total is likely to grow to 811 million. Of these, 93 million will be classical Pentecostals, 274 million will be charismatics, and 460 million will be neo-Pentecostals. Of all Pentecostals worldwide, 27 percent are white and 71 percent are non-white. Members are more urban than rural, more female than male, more children under 18 than adults, more Third World (66 percent) than Western (32 percent), more living in poverty (87 percent) than in affluence (13 percent), and more family-related than individualist. "The growing churches in the non-Western world are mostly

50. Pretorius, "Toronto Blessing," 66–67. Oliverio describes the adherents of the second group—charismatic-Pentecostals—as renewal Christians, adding to the confusion in the terminology surrounding Pentecostalism (Oliverio, "Introduction," 4).

51. Neo-Pentecostals are also referred to as neo-charismatics, Third Wavers, Independents, Postdenominationalists, and neo-Apostolics (Barrett, "Worldwide Holy Spirit Renewal," 404).

52. Ngong, *Holy Spirit and Salvation*, 141. Independent churches are expanding faster than Islam in Africa, at about twice the rate of the Roman Catholic Church, and at roughly three times the rate of other non-Catholic groups. There are now approximately 5,000 independent Christian denominations, all born in the last forty years, all bearing the familiar marks of pentecostal spirituality, and with each church displaying its own distinctive qualities. In South Africa, they embrace about 40 percent of the black population, while in Zimbabwe, 50 percent of all Christians belong to these independent churches (Cox, *Fire from Heaven*, 246–47). In Southern Africa, neo-Pentecostal churches established the International Fellowship of Christian Churches (IFCC) in 1985 under the leadership of Edmund Roepert of the Hatfield Christian Church (Pretoria) and Ray McCauley of the Rhema Bible Church (Johannesburg). There are other associations for neo-Pentecostal churches as well, such as Fred Roberts's "Christian Centres" called Christian Fellowships International, Derek Crumpton's Foundation Ministries, and Dudley Daniels's New Covenant Ministries (Anderson and Pillay, "Segregated Spirit," 237).

53. "Worldwide Holy Spirit Renewal," 383.

Pentecostal-Charismatic, as seen in the Pentecostal movements in Latin America, Independent Churches in Africa,[54] and Charismatic movements in Asia."[55] And while 16.7 percent of Christians lived in Africa, Asia, and Latin America in 1900, it was 63.2 percent by 2010. By 2025, it will be nearly 70 percent.[56] The pentecostalization of African Christianity can be called the African Reformation of the twentieth century. It has

54. Pentecostal-type Indigenous Churches (that is, African Indigenous Churches, African Independent Churches, or AICs) account for more than 40 percent of the South African black population (Anderson and Pillay, "Segregated Spirit," 227, 233). The phenomenon of AICs is notoriously complex; various attempts have been made to classify the phenomenon along diverse lines. Anderson's (*African Reformation*, 15–18) and Oosthuizen's (*Healer-Prophet*, 1–2) classification makes the most sense, with AICs classified as Ethiopian, Zionist, Prophet/healing, and charismatic/Pentecostal or Spirit-churches. In some parts of Africa, Spirit-churches constitute up to 40 percent of the total population (Anderson, *Vision of the Disinherited*, 306). The African expression of the worldwide Pentecostal movement is the Spirit (or spiritual) churches, which forms the pentecostalization of African Christianity. The Spirit AICs, however, are not paradigmatic of African Pentecostalism any longer; they have been overshadowed by the enormous new and independent churches representing the neo-Pentecostal movement which have sprung up in African cities more recently (Anderson, "African Pentecostalism," 29). AICs exist in 60 African countries with 9,300 denominations, 65 million members, and 92 national councils. The continent-wide Organization of African Instituted (formerly Independent) Churches is based in Nairobi, Kenya. The AICs originated in 1864. Previously they were normally classified as "unaffiliated" Christians; today they are described as "independent neo-charismatics" (Barrett, "Worldwide," 405). In southern Africa, the majority of the "churches of the Spirit" are known as Zionists and Apostolics, betraying their respective associations with the Chicago movement of John Alexander Dowie and the Apostolic Faith Mission of South Africa and the Apostolic Azusa Street Revival. AQ NOTE Omenyo and Arthur ascribe the growth of African Pentecostalism to neoprophetism and the popularity of the prophetic movement to the relevance of the phenomenon to the religious context, religious pragmatism, and its compatibility with most sectors of people, the use of a predominantly oral form of communication, providing the youth with the opportunity to exercise their gifts and talents, and phenomena such as dreams and visions in personal and public forms of religion (Omenyo and Arthur, "Bible Says!," 51).

55. Lee, "Future of Global Christianity," 105.

56. Keener and Carroll, "Introduction," 1. Maxwell calls contemporary African Pentecostalism a broad river with currents flowing in different directions, creating contradictions that are continually being worked out (Maxwell, "Social Mobility and Politics," 91). If the so-called African "Spirit" churches are added—in Zimbabwe, Kenya, and Ghana—in 2010, an estimated quarter to a fifth of the population were Pentecostals. In Nigeria, Democratic Republic of the Congo (DRC), Zambia, and South Africa, about a tenth of the population are Pentecostals. More than half of Zimbabwe's population belongs to African Pentecostal churches, 40 percent of South Africa's, over a third of Kenya's, followed by the DRC, Nigeria, Ghana, and Zambia, all over a quarter of the population (Anderson, *Introduction to Pentecostalism*, 114).

fundamentally altered the character of African Christianity. The center of world Christianity has shifted to the Global South,[57] and the dominant theological perspectives have shifted with it.[58] The global church is not invested exclusively in mid-twentieth-century Western biblical scholarship as in the past; the church mushrooming in the Majority World[59] where two-thirds of the world's Christians live[60] is developing its own biblical scholarship in touch with those issues that relate to the global church,[61] and Pentecostalism as a global phenomenon is influencing the

57. When the era of Western colonization came to an end in the middle of the twentieth century, Western Christians began using a new vocabulary, speaking of "older" and "younger" churches. In this rhetorical framework, "older churches" refer to the older established churches in the West, while "younger churches" referred to the recently formed communities and churches in Africa and Asia—such as the mission churches and the African Indigenous Churches. The term "older," however, carried connotations of "wiser," and "younger" implied that these churches still needed supervision and instruction from the more mature Western believers. Now it is fashionable to speak of the Christian movement as consisting of the global Christian North and a global Christian South. North and South do not correspond to the equator but instead to a slanted line that runs from Central America to Siberia, separating Europe and North America from Africa, Asia, and Latin America. Now South enjoys the positive association of being vibrant, growing, alive, and devout, while churches in the Christian North are perceived as soft, flabby, and spiritually stagnant or dying (Jacobsen, *Global Gospel*, 9–10). In 1900, 80 percent of Christians lived in the global Christian North, and only 20 percent in the South. Now, the South is the home of two-thirds of the world's Christians and 35 percent live in the global North. A better description of the Christian church would be that it is flat—in imitation of Thomas Friedman, who describes the world as flat in the sense that, due to the Internet, everyone everywhere competes economically on level ground. Christianity has also entered a flat era, and no single region of the Christian world can claim to be the dominant center (Jacobsen, *Global Gospel*, 12).

58. Laing, "Changing Face of Mission," 165.

59. "Majority World" is the self-designated term that non-Western nations of Africa, Asia, and Latin America prefer. Churches in the Majority World are more sympathetic towards reports about healings and deliverances from evil spirits or demons than Western Christianity in general (Keener, "Pentecostal Biblical Interpretation," 279.

60. Jacobsen, *Global Gospel*, xv.

61. See Castelo's perceptive remark that non-majority voices have a way of accounting for things that majority voices would rather not or, in some cases, cannot account for (Castelo, "*Diakrisis*," 202). Keener emphasizes that Majority World biblical scholars should continue to forge their own ways based on their own convictions and communities of interpretation, not beholden to anyone else's consensus, including that of Western academia (Keener, *Spirit Hermeneutics*, 294).

scholarship.[62] Questions posed to the Bible in the North differ from the liberation questions of the people of the South.[63] The median Christian today is a young woman with limited education from the Global South; her interest is with understanding biblical narrative rather than doctrinal issues, and she is poor.[64]

By the end of the twentieth century, there were already more Pentecostals worldwide than mainline Protestants,[65] accounting for something like 80 percent of evangelical Protestantism's worldwide growth.[66] Some estimate nearly half a billion charismatics worldwide.[67] One report states that there are 614 million adherents, meaning that the charismatic branch is now second in size in Christianity only to Roman Catholicism (with many Roman Catholics being charismatics).[68] By 2050, Charismatics and Pentecostals will likely constitute one-third of Christians and 11 percent of the global population.[69]

62. Keener, "Pentecostal Biblical Interpretation," 274. That the Christian church now exists globally warns of the tendency to regard one's own, sectarian tradition as the only correct way to understand the Bible. The fact is, most Christians function with a de facto canon within a canon, prioritizing some texts and teachings above others. Messianic Jewish believers, for instance, emphasize texts about the Torah and the Jewish people; Chinese and Korean believers highlight the scriptural values of honor and respect due to their exposure to traditional Confucian values; and Latin American Christians may emphasize the justice and liberation that prophetically challenge power structures. Christians need all of these perspectives, requiring them to listen to the global church (as Keener, *Spirit Hermeneutics*, 77–97, correctly indicates, referring to valuable Majority World insights surrounding spirits and miracles that challenge Western skepticism among Christians). Valuing global readings does not equalize all readings; rather, reading texts together with Christians from other cultures and eras can help us to surmount some of our cultural blinders (Keener, *Spirit Hermeneutics*, 279).

63. Bartholomew, *Introducing Biblical Hermeutics*, 544.

64. Harrison, *Introduction*, 21.

65. Mullin, *History*, 211.

66. Berger, "Faces," 425.

67. Keener, *Spirit Hermeneutics*, 83. The topic of pentecostal growth, however, is dependent on who is counting and why, with many demographic sources defining the relevant terms in different ways because there is no consensus about definitional issues of the Pentecostal movement (Yong, "Instead of a Conclusion," 313).

68. Johnson, Barrett, and Crossing, "Christianity 2010," 36; Oliverio, "Book Review: Reading Craig Keener," 130; Wilkinson, "Pentecostals and the World," 373–93.

69. Charismatics share a number of characteristics with their pentecostal friends: a focus on Jesus, an emphasis on praise and worship, a high view of and value for the Bible, belief that God speaks today and reveals Godself in a mediate way, interest in *charismata*, and so forth. Nevertheless, the self-perception of the movement differs

Challenging Hermeneutical Concerns in Africa

Asamoah-Gyadu remarks that Africans generally have opted for pneumatic forms in making choices about their expression of the Christian faith.[70] Pneumatic Christianity enjoys the most support and popularity of all traditions in Africa. Anderson groups together various African movements that he refers to as "Spirit-type churches"[71]—distinguished by their emphasis on a pneumatologically-centered liturgy, proclamation, and ministry and doing a certain type of African theology which is not primarily concerned with clarifying doctrine but rather with helping the African faithful to live Christianity, making the gospel message and Christian doctrines more meaningful to their life situations.[72] African theology comes to life in music and song, prayers and sacramental acts of healing and exorcism, art forms and architecture, liturgy and dress, and church structures and community life. Although they do not place much emphasis on an explicit theology, they have a praxis and a spirituality in which a pneumatologically-centered theology is profoundly implicit.[73] That they do not have a formal theology does not mean that they have no theology at all; the rituals and manifestations of their worship is their enacting of theology.[74] Their interpretation of the working of the Spirit is emphasized in their daily life and practices of spirituality, which reflects their pneumatology. After all, the acting of theology is at least as important as taking it in at a theological seminary or college.[75]

---

from classical restorationist Pentecostals. Charismatics do not view the outpouring of the Spirit so much as a divine restoring of the primitively pure church but rather as a renewal of elements of spirituality present in the church throughout history. They believe that healings, tongues, prophetic utterances, and such had been present at various times and places throughout church history and they were not alone in their sense of living in the Spirit in tension with the surrounding community (Albrecht and Howard, "Pentecostal Spirituality," 247–48).

70. Asamoah-Gyadu, *Contemporary Pentecostal Christianity*, 179.

71. Anderson, *Moya*, 26.

72. Ukpong, "Current Theology," 512.

73. Hastings, *African Christianity*, 54.

74. Charismatic manifestations are described in various ways, with some elements repeating themselves, such as the experience of shocks of power, shaking of the body, involuntary movements, release of extraordinary power, the tangible experience of the presence of God, weeping, joy, words dissolving, the utterance of an unknown language, dancing, and even trances (Anderson, *Moya*, 41–43).

75. Anderson, *Moya*, 33.

Many of the AICs—especially the Zionist and Apostolic types, as well as the three waves of Pentecostalism—belong to these Spirit-type churches. By way of pentecostalization, charismatic manifestations in established or mainline churches qualify these churches to be included as Spirit-type churches. Some large, independent churches in Africa that have arisen independently from the Pentecostal movement—such as the Kimbanguist movement in Zaire, the Harrist churches in the Ivory Coast, and the Maranke church in Zimbabwe—may be considered "Spirit-type" churches in their own right.[76] They share a pneumatological view of the God of Scriptures, envisaged as present through the Holy Spirit. What is important to note is the predominance of religious factors in accounting for the appeal and rapid proliferation of these movements. These factors are largely pneumatological, as Anderson[77] shows, with the adaptation to traditional rituals and customs, the prophetic practices in detecting and removing malignant medicines and wizardry, and the role of healing and exorcism. In Africa, the message that the power of the Holy Spirit can conquer sickness and the oppression of evil spirits impacts on the psyche of indigenous people because they experience the very problems that Spirit-type churches offer a solution to. Their worship satisfies both spiritually and emotionally while the churches established by Western missionaries make them feel "uncomfortable" because of the apparent lack of the Spirit in these churches.[78] Missionaries failed to understand the African worldview and tried to impose Western Christianity on African converts without providing an answer to Africans' concrete physical needs—such as daily misfortunes, illness, encounters with evil and witchcraft, bad luck, poverty, and barrenness. On the contrary, Spirit-type churches provide Africans with more divine involvement than even their traditional religion did with its African God that was predominantly transcendent rather than immanent, a God who did not interfere with or harass humans, and was regarded as "good."[79] Pentecostalism allows the Holy Spirit to work in a particularly African way among Africans.[80]

---

76. Anderson, *Moya*, 29.

77. Anderson, *Moya*, 30–31.

78. As verbalized in Institute for Contextual Theology, *Speaking for Ourselves*, 27.

79. Mbiti, *African Religions and Philosophy*, 43–45.

80. Anderson, *Moya*, 46. Anderson emphasizes that the Holy Spirit has a specifically "African" way of revealing the Spirit to Africans, implying that the encounter with the Spirit will necessarily be colored and influenced by the receiver's culture. This African way of working by the Spirit has often been misunderstood by the missionaries who

The reasons indigenous Christians rejected historic mission Christianity were mainly that the missionaries' religion did not have pneumatic elements and was not biblical enough.[81] Historic mission Christians were perceived as neglecting or diluting biblical teachings to suit their liberal lifestyles and their indifference to such truths as the experiences of Spirit baptism and the practice of the *charismata*. Their religion did not attract Africans because it did not solve their daily existential challenges. In African Pentecostalism, the Bible speaks to everyday, real-world issues of poverty and debt, famine and displacedness, racial and gender oppression, state brutality and persecution. In the words of David Wesley Myland, an early Pentecostal, when the Spirit enters one's life, it is like swallowing "God liquidized."[82]

The Bible is also used in ritualistic ways, as a book of supernatural power. It is holy because it is the vehicle through which the gospel of Christ is communicated. As a rule, African Christians handle the Bible with care and reverence because of its supernatural import. The words of the King James Version are considered more powerful by many African Pentecostals in countries where English is one of the languages being used; the archaic English and weighty words of the KJV carry for users a certain supernatural import that is not found in modern English versions.[83]

South Africa has at least 6,000 Pentecostal churches, comprising some 10 million people, that emphasize the Holy Spirit and the practices of divine healing, exorcism, prophecy, revelation, and speaking in tongues.[84] In the past few years, the press in South Africa has repeatedly reported stories of "Pentecostal" pastors ordering their church members to do things that the pastors seemingly derive from the Bible but endanger their members' lives. These pastors are representative of neo-Pentecostal (independent) churches, some of which are growing phenomenally in

---

brand these manifestations as excesses, manifestations of demons or of the "flesh," and a groping back to traditional religion. Africans' ecstatic experiences are by no means confided to Africa, although they may differ in different contexts.

81. In the opinion of Asamoah-Gyadu, *Contemporary Pentecostal Christianity*, 161.

82. Myland, quoted in Jacobsen, *Thinking in the Spirit*, 1.

83. Asamoah-Gyadu, *Contemporary Pentecostal Christianity*, 162.

84. Anderson & Pillay, "Segregated Spirit," 227. LeMarquand states that South Africa may be the most biblically literate society on earth (LeMarquand, "New Testament Exegesis in (Modern) Africa," 13).

Africa, at the same time influencing churches from the classical Pentecostal and charismatic fold.[85]

To give a few example of these stories, in May 2015 it was reported
that Pastor Lesego Daniel of Rabboni Centre Ministries in Garankuwa,
north of Pretoria, made his congregation eat grass to "be closer to God."
He asserted that the Bible taught human beings that they could eat anything to feed their bodies; their faith would change the natural substances
of what they eat into solid and healthy food. He told his congregation that
by eating grass they would rid themselves of their sins and heal them of
any ailments they might have had. Photos on the Rabboni Centre Ministries Facebook page showed the followers eating the grass as well as Pastor Daniel walking across them as they lay spread out on the floor. Under
the instruction of the pastor, dozens of followers dropped to the floor to
eat the grass provided in the church. "Yes, we eat grass and we're proud
of it because it demonstrates that, with God's power, we can do anything,"
one of the members, Rosemary Phetha, told journalists. The 21-year-old
law student said she had been battling with a sore throat for more than
a year, but it was healed after she had eaten the grass. Doreen Kgatle, 27
years old, of Garankuwa suffered a stroke two years ago. "I could not
walk but soon after eating the grass, as the pastor had ordered, I started
gaining strength, and an hour later, I could walk again," Kgatle testified.
Photos showed dozens of people getting sick in the toilets; an image of
the bathrooms showed women clutching their stomachs, while the men
were vomiting in the sink. A few days later, it was revealed that dozens of
church members were now ill as an aftermath of the experiment.[86]

The *Times Live* reports that during a service of at least 1,000 people
in a marquee, Daniel screamed, "Sleep!" and six people went to sleep. He
ordered other congregants to slap those that were asleep and trample on
them, but the sleepers did not react and remained rigid and unresponsive
until he ordered them to wake up. "You can leave them like this for six
months. I love this, I don't want to be bored. You can even make police go
to sleep when they come to arrest you," he is alleged to have said. Daniel

85. These independent churches are expanding in Africa faster than Islam, at about
twice the rate of the Roman Catholic Church, and at roughly three times that of the
other non-Catholic groups. There were over 5,000 independent Christian denominations and groups in South Africa that bore the familiar marks of pentecostal spirituality when Cox wrote his book in 1995 (Cox, *Fire from Heaven*, 245–46). In South Africa,
they embraced 40 percent of the black population, and in Zimbabwe, 50 percent of all
Christians belonged to such independent churches.

86. Banjo, "Aftermath."

did not respond to the negative publicity his behavior caused except for flatly stating on Facebook, "God is at work and His people are testifying right now at the farm. TO GOD BE THE GLORY." The pastor's actions during the service prompted a series of online complaints.[87]

Next, the same pastor made his congregation drink petrol, telling them that it tasted sweet, like pineapple juice. In YouTube footage, members of his congregation were seen clamoring desperately to have a drink of the petrol as the pastor instructed and encouraged them. The members exclaimed how "sweet" and "nice" it tasted, comparing it to "Iron Brew" and "pineapple juice." Some of them even begged the pastor to "please give us some more." A few of the followers who consumed the petrol ended up collapsing on the floor, displaying symptoms such as breathing difficulties, throat pain, burning in the esophagus, abdominal pain, vision loss, vomiting with blood, bloody stools, dizziness, extreme fatigue, convulsions, body weakness, and unconsciousness. The video clearly showed how several members of the congregation displayed some of these symptoms.[88] Daniel also reportedly fed members of the church flowers, and one happy flower eater declared, "They tasted like mint chocolate." "I felt fresh and good," testified another. The different kinds of flowers had different tastes and they were nothing short of delicious, said some members. In pictures published by a newspaper, one man eating the yellow chrysanthemums looked a bit anxious, but he did not defy the pastor. He bit the flower, ended up with petals in his mouth, and then swallowed. It was not immediately clear from the pictures whether eating the flowers gave him a surge of spiritual power.

The pastor motivated his unusual practices to treat his members with several kinds of dangerous and poisonous media by explaining that it was necessary for their healing process. It was the only way that members could be helped with their problems. He had also been captured on video praying in tongues and he interpreted it as the authoritative source for his controversial demands.

In 2015, he told the South African Commission for the Promotion and Protection of the Rights of Cultural, Religious, and Linguistic Communities Rights Commission (CRL), a legal commission set up by the South African Parliament after it had received several complaints of

---

87. Reilly, "Lawn again Christians."

88. Sethusa and Mathebula, "Pastor's Supporter Drinks Petrol."

religious abuses, "When I do things, it is no longer me, but me and my Master. I was led by the Holy Spirit."[89]

Other examples abound. In May 2015, a pastor of the Soshanguve branch north of Pretoria of End Times Disciples Ministries, Penuel Mnguni, allegedly suggested that his congregation members stripped and then he stepped on them when he preached. His sermon was—appropriately—about Adam and Eve in the Garden of Eden walking around naked and enjoying communion with God. On the following night, May 21st, 2015, Mnguni commanded the "temperature to decrease into snow atmosphere," according to the church's Facebook page. "The congregation started to feel coldness in their [bodies] and covered themselves with blankets," the post stated. According to the paper, Mnguni is the understudy of Rabboni Ministries leader, Prophet Lesego Daniel, mentioned above, who made headlines for making his congregation eat grass and drink petrol. Later, he also encouraged churchgoers to drink petrol, pouring some of the petrol into a bucket before dropping a match into it and setting it alight to prove that it really was petrol. He then told them that it had been turned into pineapple juice and persuaded people to sip from a bottle of the liquid.[90] He also encouraged church members to strip themselves of their clothes in order to enjoy communion with God. Images that were posted to the church's Facebook page in the course of 2016 went viral on social media and across the Internet. In the images, members of the church can be seen stripped down to their underwear and the pastor is seen stepping on some. There is an image of a church member licking the pastor's boots and a picture of the pastor allegedly jumping on members of the congregation without them getting hurt. In a caption for the image of the pastor jumping on members, it is implied the congregants felt no pain as God was with them. The caption reads, "Total Demonstration of God's Power. No Pain felt in them, meaning God is with us. To God be the Glory." The page has since deleted some of the pictures and the pastor could not be reached by journalists for comment.[91]

Mnguni was reported to have been beaten up by some angry South African youths in Mmakaunyane Village in the North-West Province. In the course of the attack, the youths—led by the far-left political party, the Economic Freedom Front (EFF) and its leader, Julius Malema—burnt

---

89. Molobi, "Pastor: Grass to Flowers!"

90. Craven, "Beware All Prophets of Doom."

91. CNS Reporter, "Pastor Penuel Mnguni Makes Congregation Strip."

down his church and tied him and a member of his church up with ropes.[92] Police officers, however, came to their rescue. The controversial pastor had reportedly been lying low for some time before he set up his church inside a bush in Mmakaunyane community. Members of the community eventually caught him in the act and did not allow him to continue with the building. A resident, who identified himself as Johanna Baloyi, said the pastor and his congregation were not welcome in their area any more, asking, "How can a person eat a rat and claim it tastes like chocolate? That's evil." A lady who reportedly spoke on condition of anonymity said, "I am one of the church members," insisting that, "We have the right to attend any church we want." According to her, "The rats have healed and saved them (members) from suffering." These controversial methods have drawn criticism from thousands of people, but members of the congregation swear by their pastors' methods—he is said to have claimed that humans can eat anything to feed their bodies and survive on whatever they choose to eat.[93]

Meanwhile, in Tanzania, police authorities arrested a pastor after two people he was baptizing in a river drowned on July 16th 2017. The local deputy police commandant, Hamisi Selemani Issa, told the BBC that the two drowned in the River Ungwasi after being overwhelmed by strong currents while being immersed in the water as part of the baptism ceremony conducted by the pastor of the Shalom Church in the Rombo area.[94] The irresponsible act of baptizing people in a flooded river reputed for its currents has been widely criticized.

A Kenyan pastor, Reverend Njohi of the Lord's Propeller Redemption Church in Dandora Phase 2, an eastern suburb in Nairobi, ordered all his female congregants to attend church services without panties and bras to allow Christ to enter their lives.[95] Another incident that was publicized widely is Pastor Lethebo Rabalago of Mount Zion Christian Assembly (MZCA) in Zebediela in Mpumalanga, South Africa. He is no stranger to controversy as he had claimed to have been elected already in his mother's womb to become a great prophet of God. He also claimed that thousands of people received healing through his ministry. In November 2017, he sprayed a toxic pesticide, Doom, on people seek-

92. "Notorious Pastor Penuel Mnguni."
93. Ogbeche, "Youths Burn Down Church."
94. Adeseun, "Tanzanian Pastor Arrested."
95. Banjo, "Pastor Orders."

ing miraculous healing during a church service. The pastor asserted that, in his experience, Doom was extremely useful for driving out demons. He called upon members of the church who were ill. A woman by the name of Mrs. Mitala was one of those who came forward. "She went to the forth and told the Prophet that she suffers from ulcer. The Prophet sprayed doom (sic) on her and she received her healing and deliverance. We give God the glory," stated the post on the church's Facebook page. Pastor Rabalago told a broadcaster that those who believe in Jesus's name were given the authority to pick up snakes and be sprayed with Doom and it would not do anything to them, according to Mark 16.[96]

Rabalago's practice of spraying pesticide on his congregants, claiming to heal them from a variety of illnesses, received the attention of several South African government departments and other organizations, including the South African Council of Churches, which stated publicly that the pastor was being abusive. He was warned from several quarters that his actions were not only criminal and could lead to prosecution but that he was causing damage to the reputation of Christianity in South Africa. The company that produces Doom also warned of the risks of spraying the substance on or near people, while a government commission (Commission for the Promotion and Protection of the Rights of Cultural, Religious, and Linguistic Communities) urged anyone affected to lodge complaints. However, church members of other controversial South African neo-Pentecostal churches said they were standing behind the pastor who sprayed the toxic pesticide on people seeking miraculous healing during church services. One of them stated that he (the pastor) "stands tall before the Goliath of this world, the media."[97]

Later, the Limpopo High Court granted an interdict against the controversial pastor, effectively barring him from using hazardous materials for so-called "healing purposes."[98] Department of Health Member of the Executive Committee of the Limpopo Province, Phophi Ramathuba, welcomed the Limpopo High Court ruling of the presid-

---

96. The reference is to the so-called longer ending of the Gospel that, according to scholars' consensus, was not part of the original manuscript. The pentecostal *Wirkungsgeschichte* of Mark 16:9–20 takes a more holistic view of the passage, concluding that, while this text may be clearly non-Markan, it is, at the same time, part of the canonical witness confessed by the church (Thomas, "What the Spirit is Saying to the Church," 119).

97. "Church Members Defend Pastor."

98. Zaimov, "Doom-Spraying Pastor."

ing Judge, George Phatudi in March 2017, extending an earlier ruling, made at the end of 2016, that Rabalago may not spray any congregant or visitor to his church with the insecticide Doom, use any form of harmful substance, administer orally any harmful liquid, or give instructions that such an act must be performed. Pastor Blessing Selepe, President of the Limpopo Ministers' Fraternal (LMF), said the organization was delighted about the verdict issued by the judge and said it had campaigned since 1999 for a system to be created to hold religious leaders and their entire membership accountable for weird and dangerous doctrinal practices. He referred to various examples of religious extremism and expressed his appreciation for the Department of Health for taking the matter to court. The Department of Health asked for an interdict against Rabalago and other congregants towards the end of 2016 after photos of him spraying his congregants with Doom went viral on the Internet and in the media.[99] The Limpopo Health Department also warned that the practice posed a serious health risk. They have since recommended that Rabalago's mental state be evaluated.[100]

Rather than just attacking the users of snakes and oil, it is time to re-open the important debate on the way neo-Pentecostal (and other) churches abuse the Bible to justify some of their practices.[101] Detached from scholars' safeguards and attention to historical context, some popular charismatic interpretation of the Bible is undisciplined and badly in need of correction.[102] Keener provides several examples where popular interpreters link biblical interpretations without regard for context, for instance, in producing phrases like, "We are the will of God, and because Jesus is God's righteousness and so are we, resulting in us being Jesus."[103]

99. Erasmus, "Judge Extends Ruling on 'Doom' Pastor."

100. Faeza, "Pastor Sprays Congregants with Doom," and Kimmie, "Court Orders Pastor to Stop Spraying Doom."

101. For an instance of such abuse, see Keener, *Spirit Hermeneutics*, 13, who relates the true story of a woman who explained to her therapist that God had told her to divorce her husband and marry another man with whom she was romantically involved. God had told her to "put on the new man" (Eph 4:24) as the key to her "divine guidance"!

102. Keener, *Spirit Hermeneutics*, 269.

103. This observation leads to Keener's generalizing remark that, on average, one will get a better exposition of the Bible from traditional evangelical media preachers than from many charismatic media preachers. This is true when the former focus on Bible exposition while the latter often focus on instant cures for felt needs. Appealing to felt needs is a proven way to gain a hearing for the gospel in an overcrowded, secular

The problem is that these figures sometimes achieve success; they are followed and financially supported by many people, including young believers and biblically illiterate persons who thrive on a few proof-texts as the content of their beliefs. Keener refers to two more examples of influential contemporary teachings that qualify as malpractices because it does not regard the context of biblical texts when these texts are used: the movement that promotes the breaking of generational curses, and the teaching of popular Word of Faith teachers like Kenneth and Gloria Copeland, Charles Capps, and Kenneth Hagin.[104]

These malpractices and abuses in South Africa led to the establishment of the Commission for the Promotion and Protection of the Rights of Cultural, Religious, and Linguistic Communities (CRL), a Chapter Nine Institution of Parliament, to investigate "fake pastors" feeding on the superstitious beliefs of some believers and allegations that certain Christian churches use religion to make money illegally, with religion being commercialized.[105] CRL Chairperson Thoko Mkhwanazi-Xalavu's remark has often been quoted, that "Churches cannot be spaza shops selling holy water and prayers for a profit," echoing sixteenth-century Martin Luther's criticism of the church of his day's sale of "relics" and "indulgences." In responding to criticism by commission members, some church leaders told the CRL that they were acting in accordance

---

market. While it is true that Jesus provided in the needs of his listeners by healing and delivering them, he also demonstrated his character by what he taught and the way he treated the needy. Jesus knew and used Scripture in context and his message was in keeping with the heart of the Bible. See Keener, *Spirit Hermeneutics*, 270.

104. Keener, *Spirit Hermeneutics*, 270–73.

105. See also the problem raised by Christian Action, an organization that, since 1991, has been mobilizing and equipping Christians to make a positive difference in society from an evangelical Protestant perspective. They refer to the Hate Speech Bill of the South African Parliament, particularly its extremely broad definition of hate speech under section 4, which "includes in its scope any communication which is considered 'abusive or insulting' and intended to 'bring into contempt or ridicule' a person or group of persons on the basis of their gender, sex, sexual orientation, gender identity, etc. This includes email or social media communications as well as teachings from a pulpit or in a Bible study." Most religions have a long history of intolerance and hate speech, mostly against each other, from the brutal Christian crusades up to the Islamic State of today. In football matches between "Protestant" Rangers and "Catholic" Celtics, for instance, tens of thousands of fans utter hate speech in the name of "religion." Christian Action is clearly worried that their members could be dragged before the courts for only repeating what they have been saying for years about heathens, infidels, and other religions (See Christian Action, "Threats to Freedom of Speech in South Africa").

with their religious beliefs, that they did nothing illegal since their congregants participated willingly, and that they based their controversial
practices on "the Bible," posing hermeneutical challenges that need to be
faced.[106] For the moment, the South African Parliament is of the view that
religious freedom ensconced in the Constitution allows churches to act
independently although they are also required to act within the bounds
of the law, but the behavior of some neo-Pentecostal church leaders
might eventually compel the government to regulate and oversee church
bodies.[107]

Methodology

In discussing distinctive pentecostal hermeneutical aspects and principles, the discussion will be descriptive, based on intra-biblical or
Spirit-inspired readings as discussed in publications of early Pentecostals as well as later pentecostal scholarship in order to define what is
distinctive in pentecostal hermeneutics. Many Pentecostals of the past
sixty years borrowed and utilized the hermeneutical models provided

106. Craven, "Beware All Prophets of Doom."

107. A tragic example that underlines the reality that the State might deem it necessary to regulate churches is the Ngcobo Killings of 21 February 2018, where five
policemen and an off-duty soldier were shot during an attack on a police station in
Ngcobo, between Mthatha and Komani (previously Queenstown) in the Eastern Cape.
During the attack, ten firearms and a police van were stolen from the police station before an ATM a short distance from the police station was robbed (See "Five Policemen
Dead"). Seven suspects were eventually killed and ten others arrested after a shootout
with police at the town's Mancoba church, including one of the church's leaders. His
brother confirmed his involvement with the gang who killed the policemen. Their
motive was presumably to access funds because of the dire financial straits that the
church found itself in. The South African Council of Churches responded by stating
that it had lodged a complaint with government over the Seven Angels Church but was
ignored. Commission for the Promotion and Protection of the Rights of Cultural, Religious, and Linguistic Communities (CRL) chairwoman Thoko Mkhwanazi-Xaluva
reacted to the events at eNgcobo by stating that the church was probed already in 2016
and authorities were alerted to children living at the church and not attending school.
The committee suggested that the government should regulate church leadership
by way of registration. The co-operative governance and traditional affairs portfolio
committee of Parliament responded to the committee's report by stating that the state
could not prescribe when it came to beliefs and religious convictions because of the
value of religious liberty ensconced in the Constitution of the Republic but it unani-
mously condemned the abuse of vulnerability by religious leaders. See "Parliament
slams CRL."

by conservative evangelicalism with some smaller modifications. This is especially the case in the United States, where Evangelicals strongly outnumber Pentecostals. The tenor of pentecostal theology is different in Europe, Africa (including South Africa), Asia, and, to some extent, Latin America; historically, the movement in the rest of the world has not been so strongly influenced by conservative evangelical concerns.[108] Other Pentecostals utilized socio-political contextual theologies while, within the movement, there also developed certain distinct pentecostal models, such as the Kenyon-Hagin-Copeland group and (post-)modern literary theory, while a few pentecostal academicians also developed hermeneutical models, such as Arden C. Autry, John C. Thomas, Gerald T. Sheppard, Rickie D. Moore, Larry R. McQueen, and Mark J. Cartledge.[109]

Early Pentecostals read the Bible not merely in terms of understanding a text that originated in an ancient culture but as a faith community that are today living in the biblical experience—that is, living by the same Spirit who guided God's people in the Bible—while using language derived from the Bible when they witness about the encounters with God generated by their reading of the Bible with the help of the Spirit, bringing together the ancient and contemporary horizons of understanding in a unique manner.[110] Their narrative world coincided with that of biblical figures. This noncessationist or continuationist approach to the Bible is based on the Pentecostal community's identity founded on their experience of Spirit baptism that formed them into a prophetic-eschatological people of God (Joel 2:28–32; Acts 2:21).[111] Being pentecostal means that one is committed to a Spirit-centered, miracle-affirming, praise-oriented version of Christian faith.[112] They read the Bible not primarily to gain knowledge about ancient history or ideas, but because they expected to share the same kind of experiences and the same kind of relationship with God that the Bible witnessed to. This implies that they read and un-

---

108. Clark, "Investigation," 54.

109. See Clark, "Investigation," 53–90 and 166–78, for a fuller discussion.

110. Gadamer states that the peculiar function (*eigentliche Leistung*) of language is to bring about the fusion of the horizons of the interpreter and of the historical object, which characterizes the act of understanding (Mueller-Vollmer, "Introduction," 39).

111. Keener, *Mind of the Spirit*, 231. Martin explains that the outpouring of the Spirit gave Pentecostals an alternative vision of God's plan, which was supported by a new understanding of Scripture (Martin, "Introduction to Pentecostal Biblical Hermeneutics," 1).

112. Jacobsen, *Thinking in the Spirit*, 12.

derstood texts according to their purposed function but also as "sources" by which one addresses other questions,[113] allowing for the unique revelation of the Spirit, the "voice of God," who applies a specific passage to a new situation as well.[114] In the Bible, people heard from God, they spoke God's words and experienced miracles of deliverance and healing, establishing patterns that lead contemporary Pentecostals to expect that God would repeat similar interventions in their lives and circumstances, including supernatural wonders and miracles, so that the "supernatural" element within the community forms the essence of Pentecostalism.[115] Pentecostals' worldview is more holistic than the average Westerner's, incorporating "natural" and "supernatural" without any qualms. They operate their worship gatherings on the assumption that God can, and will, do exactly what God wants, and reject formal liturgical structure to provide God that opportunity.[116] Their worship services need to keep the spontaneity where the Spirit may at any time intervene as the Spirit wills. They read the Bible dynamically, as a description of how God acts in the world and age they are living in. It is posed that the entire church must be experiential in the same sense if it wishes to be biblical. While some conservative interpreters might study the Bible to satisfy their historical curiosity about events of salvation history or liberal scholars might read it to assess historical ideas, Spirit-filled people read the Bible in the power of the Spirit in service of their relationship with God, to verbalize their expectation of how God might intervene in their lives based on biblical examples, and in order to implement moral virtues proposed in the Bible. In this way, a descriptive approach toward pentecostal hermeneutics flows into a prescriptive approach.

Historical information of Scripture's narrative world, socio-economic and cultural context, and languages enriches one's reading of the Bible and is necessary for a full understanding of the text. Biblical texts need to be heard first in their own cultural setting before translating them into

113. Bultmann, "Problem of Hermeneutics," 79.

114. Van der Geest remarks that the two main ingredients of participant observation are that one sees a person's life and takes part in it, and it only makes sense when it is accompanied by speaking and listening (Van der Geest, "Participant Observation," 40). When one speaks of the "revelation of God," such participant observation is involved, with a reciprocal relationship consisting of give and take by the two parties. In a cerebral reading of the Bible—with accompanying rational evaluation of "truth"—such a relationship seems to be impossible.

115. Archer, "Pentecostal Hermeneutics," 131.

116. Davies, "What Does it Mean to Read?," 253.

fresh contexts that reflect the contemporary situation.[117] In their desire to hear from God, Pentecostals might forget the importance of reading the ancient text in terms of its historical horizon. However, although they know that understanding a text's grammar is important, they also acknowledge that it differs from understanding, welcoming, and embracing its message with faith. Pentecostals have been subjected to the criticism of drowning in a sea of excessive subjectivity in their spirituality,[118] and with right.[119] While serious study of the Bible can help them counter such unbridled subjectivism, however, their study must always also lead to living out (and living out of) biblical experience in the era of the Spirit who animates the words of the Bible. It may never degenerate into a Spirit-less Word or lifeless rationalism.[120]

Concept Clarification

It has become the custom in many academic circles to distinguish between "Pentecostal," which refers to pentecostal scholars, members, and denominations (including charismatics in mainline churches, members of neo-Pentecostal churches, and others who share similar spiritual experiences) and "pentecostal," referring to a basic pentecostal experience, theology, and hermeneutics. *Pentecostal* is uncapitalized here except when used as a noun or when it occurs within proper names; "pentecostal" is thus used adjectivally, referring to the work of the Spirit and a basic pentecostal experience or ethos more than it does to a specific denominational and traditional theological undertaking.[121] The same also applies to the terms "Evangelical/evangelical" and "Holiness/holiness."

117. Keener, "Pentecostal Biblical Interpretation," 281.

118. Pinnock, "Work of the Holy Spirit," 233. Keener argues that the individual spiritual experience is necessarily subjective, but it can and must be balanced with something objective—that is, by tested past revelation, corporately affirmed by God's people in all times and places since the Bible's acceptance (Keener, *Spirit Hermeneutics*, 112). See discussion in chapter 5.

119. For a sympathetic discussion of the challenges of subjectivity in charismatic experience with positive suggestions for interpreting it, see Middlemiss, *Interpreting Charismatic Experience*, 194–236.

120. Moore, "Pentecostal Approach," 29–30.

121. There are widespread differences in the custom to un/capitalize "pentecostal" and I follow two of the most prominent pentecostal theologians, Yong and Keener, in this regard (see Yong, *Hermeneutical Spirit*, xii and Keener, *Spirit Hermeneutics*, 7–8).

Definitions of terms pose several problems. In the Western context, charismatic movements are normally renewal groups operating within older and more firmly established historic mainline denominations.[122] In sub-Saharan Africa, however, the expression "charismatic" is used more in reference to the new wave of independent Pentecostal movements, indicated in Western Christianity as "neo-Pentecostal." These churches in Africa are also mostly inspired by North American, neo-Pentecostal, televangelistic movements with their high-profile leaders, mega-church philosophies, world-dominating agenda for Christianity, and religious entrepreneurial (and capital-generating) ambitions.[123] The use of these terms are not consistent in Africa, with many variations. For this reason, and with the eye on international readers, the terms will be employed as follows: "Classical Pentecostal" refers to the movements and churches which take their origins back to the events around the beginning of the twentieth century,[124] "charismatic" refers to the renewal movement within established churches that originated around the 1960s and 1970s, and "neo-Pentecostal" refers to the concept of independent churches with charismatic features that originated in the 1980s and 1990s.

Charismatic Christianity has turned into a global culture and it can be predicted that eventually the result would be a blurring of categories to such an extent that it may become necessary to refer to the movement as a whole, without trying to impose any typologies. At the same time, (especially in—but not limited to—the African continent) many established "mainline" churches are applying pentecostalizing recipes to their practices, such as accepting a pentecostal way of worshiping, singing the same type of culture-friendly songs as among Pentecostals, and even using pentecostal language such as "outpouring, baptism, and fulfilment with the Spirit."

---

122. Menzies and Menzies distinguish between three distinct phases in the charismatic renewal movement: The first phase, which began in 1955, was impacted by high-church Protestantism and influenced by South African David du Plessis, who led many of his World Council of Churches friends into a pentecostal experience; a second phase started in 1967 with Roman Catholic laypeople seeking charismatic renewal; and a third wave, starting in 1985, with some Evangelicals experiencing their "own Pentecost" (Menzies and Menzies, *Spirit and Power*, 447–82).

123. Asamoah-Gyadu, *African Charismatics*, 1.

124. In parts of Africa as well as Asia, the classical Pentecostal movement is not causally linked to the origins of North American Pentecostalism, which began in the early years of the last century (Asamoah-Gyadu, *African Charismatics*, 1–2).

"Pentecostal experience" or "charismatic experience" refers to an encounter with God modeled and based on the description of Spirit baptism in Acts 2 and also references the functioning of the *charismata* in 1 Corinthians 12–14, Romans 12:6, and 1 Peter 4:10.[125]

125. Pentecostalism presupposes a point of contact between the divine and the human. The mediating key is pneumatological and the foundational events are pneumatic encounters between the divine *pneuma* and human *pneuma*, resulting in a blurring of the boundaries between divine and human spirit throughout the Bible (Yong, *Spirit-Word-Community*, 41). Keener's remark that spiritual experience can seem insane to those who do not share it is relevant here (Keener, *Spirit Hermeneutics*, 174). Those with worldviews that rule out some sorts of divine action will question even their own spiritual experiences. Only believers look at the cross and see the resurrection; faith is necessary as a precondition for understanding the testimony of someone who witnesses a spiritual experience. Faith is a worldview, a perspective that allows access to its truth, provided it is directed toward divine truth. This worldview accommodates belief in divine intervention in a continuationist sense as in biblical times.

CHAPTER 1

Bible Reading Practices of Pentecostals

Introduction

IN RESEARCH ABOUT MEMBERS' Bible reading practices, completed by the Apostolic Faith Mission of South Africa (AFM of SA)[1] in 2016, it was found that 96 percent of respondents have a Bible: 72 percent read it in printed form and 24 percent on an electronic device.[2] A total of 98 percent indicated that they read the Bible: 74 percent of them on a daily basis, 41 percent read more than one chapter a day, and 30 percent read a chapter a day. The implication is that 70 percent of participants spend time with the Bible on a regular basis, while 35 percent indicate that they read the Bible on a daily basis together.

While 33 percent of respondents use a commentary along with the Bible and 23 percent a devotional, no less than 47 percent read only the Bible. Approximately 33 percent indicate that they have read all of the New Testament and 35 percent that they have read all of the Old Testament while 30 percent indicate that they attend a weekly Bible study group and 30 percent indicate that they are not part of any formalized Bible study.

---

1. The Apostolic Faith Mission of South Africa is the first and largest classical Pentecostal denomination in South Africa, with 1.4 million members.

2. Nel, "Bible Reading Practices in the AFM." In the research, samples of respondents from inner-city, suburban, rural, and far rural areas of all nine provinces (Western Cape, Eastern Cape, Northern Cape, North West, Free State, Kwazulu Natal, Gauteng, Limpopo, and Mpumalanga) were used.

Of those involved in the research, 75 percent indicated that they are Spirit-filled and the same percentage indicate that they pray more than once during the day.

When asked about the historical situatedness of the Bible, only 30 percent believe it is important that the Bible is interpreted in terms of the context and culture of its time, 66 percent believe everything that the Bible says is true, and 67 percent believe that the entire Bible is the inspired Word of God. It seems that many members use the Bible in a biblicist-literalist or concordist way that differs from the way early Pentecostals read the Bible.[3] To understand the discrepancy between Bible-reading practices of early and contemporary Pentecostals, it is necessary to discuss the history of hermeneutical development within the Pentecostal movement.

There are many researchers that identify Pentecostalism as a variant of fundamentalism[4] in terms of its hermeneutics although fundamentalism is younger than the Pentecostal movement and was and is its most bitter opponent.[5] In this view, Pentecostalism is an expression of conservative Christian protest against modern theological trends that deny *inter alia* the divinity of Christ and the authority of Scriptures to define doctrine and ethics for contemporary Christians,[6] in conjunction with similar groups like the Association of Fundamental Baptist Churches, parts of the Presbyterian church, the Association of Independent Methodists, Conservative Grace Brethren Churches, and the Fellowship of Fundamental Bible Churches.[7] The success of the Pentecostal movement

3. Anderson, *Introduction to Pentecostalism*, 223.

4. This chapter is partly based on Nel, "Fundamentalism and Pentecostalism." The fact is, pentecostal diversity allows some to be fundamentalists, others rationalists or liberals, and others every shade of opinion in between (see McKay, "When the Veil is Taken Away," 62). The fact that Pentecostal denominations are not normative, expecting believers to read and understand in a prescribed way, accommodates the postmodern need for a personal understanding and experience of spirituality.

5. Hollenweger, "From Azusa Street to Toronto," 6.

6. Thus Green characterizes modern biblical criticism with the term "autonomy," explaining that one is expected to peel off all allegiances, whether they be to certain theological formulations or institutions, and remove oneself from social locations, before engaging with biblical texts (Green, "Pentecostal Hermeneutics," 160). Pentecostals, in contradistinction, surrender some of their autonomy as readers in order to acknowledge their dependency on the Spirit (Pinnock, "Work of the Holy Spirit," 241).

7. See Kennedy, *Modern Introduction to Theology*, 11. Some of the most vocal opponents of Pentecostals are the cessationists, who claim that the charismatic functioning of the church—in terms of Spirit baptism and spiritual gifts—ended with the death

in reaching two-thirds of the world (the Global South)[8] and providing a spirituality acceptable to many postmoderns (or late-moderns) is then ascribed and linked to Pentecostalism as the resurgence of conservative fundamental faith around the world.[9]

Early Pentecostalism, however, should rather be comprehended in terms of the line of antecedents and movements from which it sprang and the hermeneutical angles they used, namely evangelical Protestantism, especially the Wesleyan Methodist variety (with its notion of a "second blessing," a crisis experience subsequent to conversion called "sanctification"); the American Holiness movement[10]; the Reformed revivalism of

---

of the last apostle, and liberal theologians, who, in their skepticism that nothing can happen that is not scientifically explainable that may destroy believers' faith in regular divine interventions in the lives of contemporary people and their churches. It is my submission that Pentecostalism, in historical terms, should rather be evaluated as a reaction against the institutional church's perceived formalism, spiritual deadness, slackness, and lifeless worship, as a restorationist and primitivistic urge to regain (something of) the enthusiasm and life of the earliest church (see also McClung, "Introduction," 4).

8. The phrase "Global South" refers broadly to the regions of Latin America, Asia, Africa, and Oceania. The division is sometimes interpreted as the Brandt Line, a visual depiction of the north/south divide, proposed by West German Chancellor Willy Brandt in the 1980s. It encircles the world at a latitude of approximately 30 degrees north, passing between North and Central America, north of Africa and the Middle East, climbing north over China and Mongolia, but dipping south, so as to include Australia and New Zealand in the "Rich North." It is made up of Africa, Latin America, and developing Asia, including the Middle East. The South—with three quarters of the world populations—has access to one-fifth of the world income. It is one of a family of terms, including "Third World" and "Periphery," that denote regions outside Europe and North America, mostly (though not all) low-income and often politically or culturally marginalized. The use of the phrase "Global South" marks a shift from a central focus on development or cultural difference toward an emphasis on geopolitical relations of power. The term Global South functions as more than a metaphor for underdevelopment. It references an entire history of colonialism, neo-imperialism, and differential economic and social change through which large inequalities in living standards, life expectancy, and access to resources are maintained (Dados and Connell, "Global South," 12–13).

9. The resurgence of conservative, fundamental faith may be linked to the worldwide trend to the right that, in 2016, resulted *inter alia* in Brexit, followed by the election of Theresa May as prime minister of Britain, and Donald Trump as the president of the United States. It is linked to the return to conservatism as a way to close ranks against the perceived new enemies, the needy immigrants from conflict-riddled parts of the world, especially from Muslim countries, perceived as "overflowing" developed countries.

10. There were three distinct groups of holiness adherents: the Wesleyan Holiness position, typified by Phoebe Palmer, who described "entire sanctification" or "perfect

Jonathan Edwards and the "Oberlin Perfectionism" of revivalists Charles Finney and Asa Mahan; the Keswick movement with Dwight L. Moody, Reuben A. Torrey and Andrew Murray; and the healing movement of Christoph Blumhardt, Dorothea Trudel, Charles Cullis, A. B. Simpson, Carrie Judd Montgomery, and Maria Woodworth-Etter.[11] These movements share a view of themselves as being the product of God's historical action in the same way as the nation of Israel viewed itself in the Hebrew Bible and the church of Acts thought of its origin and mission.[12] Pentecostals also stress their continuity with the personal dynamic action of the saving and revealing God through the intervention of God's Spirit in human history. Through a called and empowered priesthood (and prophethood) of individual believers—by way of personal discipleship— God establishes God's kingdom on earth through the church. They see themselves as the continuation of the early church; God must be seen to have a people, the new "Israel." The aim of the church was not to compile dogma, confessions, and lectionaries but rather to live and act the gospel of Jesus Christ.[13]

A further prerequisite for understanding the phenomenon of the early Pentecostal movement is that its hermeneutics be comprehended in terms of its early adherents who mainly came from the marginalized and socially and economically disadvantaged.[14] Anderson asserts that most Pentecostal converts came from peasant roots and their religious heritage differed from that of evangelical-pietistic Protestantism.[15] Their spirituality consisted of mystical, supernatural, and even animistic and

---

love" as the "second blessing" or Spirit baptism, identified with moral purity; the Reformed and Keswick position, exemplified by R. A. Torrey and South African Andrew Murray, who held that Spirit baptism was an enduement with power for service; and the "third blessing," a radical fringe position, which distinguished between the "second blessing" of sanctification and a "third blessing" or "baptism with fire." What links these groups together is their dedication to mission service as their highest priority (Anderson, "Keswick Movement," 129–30).

11. Anderson, *Introduction to Pentecostalism*, 25–34; see Synan, *Holiness-Pentecostal Movement*. Pentecostal churches and movements can be divided according to their distinctive theological themes, to those teaching a doctrine of sanctification in the Wesleyan Holiness tradition with "three works of grace," those reducing this pattern to "two works of grace," and those holding a "Oneness" or "Jesus Only" view of the Godhead (Dayton, *Theological Roots of Pentecostalism*, 18).

12. Clark, "Investigation into the Nature," 39.

13. Clark, "Investigation into the Nature," 40.

14. Keener, "Pentecostal Biblical Interpretation," 274.

15. Anderson, *Vision of the Disinherited*, 135.

magical notions common to those who live close to the soil, although the quite human element in spirituality was always eminent, leading many to dismiss charismatic Christianity as counterfeit.[16] The answer to such criticism is not to reject the Spirit's work but rather to sift through and discern what is of God and hold on to that (1 Thess 5:19–21), separating what is from God and what is from oneself.[17] Pentecostal spirituality has several sensibilities, habitual attitudes, or predispositions that characterize its relationship with God. It is hardwired to perceive and respond to the influences of the Spirit, oriented to experience and attend actively to the Spirit's guidance, and is characterized by a sense of conflict in the spiritual realm, indicated as spiritual warfare. Pentecostals perceive themselves as part of a movement, rather than a denomination, organization, or religious society, as participants in a work of the Spirit on earth. In their world, the supernatural and the "power" of God is important; they value restoration, renewal, and the democratic participation of all believers and mission.[18] They see themselves as a fellowship of congregations seeking to follow God's will, and their anti-organizational and anti-hierachical rhetoric led to their being even more decentralized and disorganized than Protestantism.[19] They seek to remain open to the movement of the Spirit and want their churches to be flexible in responding to God's call.

Asamoah-Gyadu's typology of African spirituality is useful to understand the psyche of African Pentecostals.[20] Their spirituality affirms

16. Anderson supports Weber's argument that artisan classes generally share the same religious notions, consisting of animism and spiritism (Weber, *Sociology of Religion*, 80–84). Jacobsen argues that spirituality needs religion to keep it from simply dissipating into thin air, and religion needs spirituality to keep it from becoming hollow (Jacobsen, *Thinking in the Spirit*, 2).

17. McKay, "When the Veil is Taken Away," 67. The Spirit of God is unpredictable; the Spirit is like the wind that blows wherever it wants. Religious experience attributed to the Spirit may not occur in any systematic way, leading to Asamoah-Gyadu's remark that care should be taken in sitting in judgment over those whose experiences do not follow known patterns, for they could be as genuine as those stipulated as the norm (Asamoah-Gyadu, *African Charismatics*, 243). The Spirit does not need to follow human logic in completing the Spirit's course.

18. Albrecht and Howard, "Pentecostal Spirituality," 240–43.

19. Jacobsen, *Global Gospel*, 20 and 35.

20. Asamoah-Gyadu, *African Charismatics*, 235–41. It should be remembered what the institution of slavery contributed to the African identity. People threatened or victimized by slavery found comfort in the liberation stories of the Bible, especially the Old Testament (Zwiep, "Bible Hermeneutics," 997). Cone identifies five sources

God's existence, presence, and involvement in the daily lives of believers. The Western atheist debate seems strange in an African context, where a striking feature of Africans is the intense conviction with which spirituality is being expressed by people who have encountered the reality of God in a personal sense. They find it difficult to understand how someone can argue that God does not exist when God is an integral part of their daily lives. The attention is drawn to the importance of experience in Christian faith and life; they know God because they have experiences with God. African Pentecostals consistently affirm that the God in whom they have come to believe is not a figment of someone's imagination. They have experienced God as real because God fulfills God's promise of rebirth for those who trust in Jesus, and Jesus gives them new tongues to speak in, heal their sick, and deliver the demonically possessed and oppressed. Out of their experience with God, they also "know" that there is a transcendent dimension to life. There is no area of life that God cannot touch with God's liberating and transforming power. Further, in African spirituality, the living God authenticates God's power and presence in "signs and wonders," especially healing. Healing is interpreted in its wider connotation as a response to physical, social, and spiritual disorder, and its ministry forms a central activity in indigenous pentecostal renewal. Evidence of its result is provided by the testimonies through which participants point to dramatic transformations in personality, recovery from ill-health, restoration of relationships that had gone awry, and restoration of human dignity as a result of receiving the grace of cessation of alcoholism, womanizing, drug abuse, prostitution, neglect of family, and general aimlessness in life.[21]

Vondey adds that Pentecostals operate at the limits of speech and are more comfortable with testimony, story, song, proclamation, testimony, *glossolalia*, and praise than with the definitions, concepts, propositions,

---

in *Black Theology*: Black experience, black history (in which slavery played an integral part), black culture, revelation, and Scripture (Cone, *Black Theology of Liberation*, 24–37). Mosala criticizes black theology for not recognizing that the biblical text itself is a product of class struggle. He focuses his attention behind the text, looking for clues to the ideology which gave rise to the text. In his exegesis of Luke, he acknowledges that the writer treats the poor as a subject but warns that the text is written by and addressed to the rich. What is needed is that the Bible first be "liberated" by exposing not only its expediency to but also its origins in the class struggle. LeMarquand explains that Mosala writes within an explicitly Marxist paradigm (LeMarquand, "New Testament Exegesis," 13).

21. Asamoah-Gyadu, *African Charismatics*, 237.

theses, systems, philosophies, and methodologies that characterize and dominate the world of Western writing, publishing, scholarly conversation, and even worship services and spirituality.[22] African Pentecostalism also affirms the restoration of the *charismata*, not just in an ontological sense but also as a functional reality.[23] The Spirit equips some believers with the necessary *charismata* to become "ministers," "pastors," or "evangelists," by filling them with power and faith.[24] This leads to conflict with established clergy who may feel scandalized and threatened that ordinary "lay people" may become respected church leaders, while previously they counted for nothing. In many instances, these gifted leaders do not even have the necessary theological training required by established denominations for ordination.[25] Their emphasis is placed on worship, witness, and mission rather than preparation, training, and study. With the experience of the baptism with the Holy Spirit, Pentecostals feel sufficiently equipped to do the work of the Spirit, which consisted of saving, delivering, and healing lost people.[26] Anderson notes that the mass involvement of the so-called "laity" in the African Pentecostal movement is undoubtedly one of the reasons for its phenomenal success.[27] In African Pentecostalism (as in early Pentecostalism), there is a diminished need for theologically articulate clergy, because cerebral and clerical Christianity had—in the minds of many Africans—already failed them. What is needed, rather, is a demonstration of power by indigenous people to whom ordinary people could easily relate. A last characteristic of African spirituality, described by Asomoah-Gyadu is the affirmation of worship as an authentic encounter with God, resulting—in some cases—in the non-deliverance of the sermon because the congregants start worshiping

---

22. Vondey, *Pentecostalism*, 121.

23. The difference between African and Western Pentecostalism lies in the African churches' orientation to the spirit world. They agree with a close affinity regarding the Holy Spirit and the *charismata* (Anderson, *Moya*, 34); they link the world of the Spirit and the world of spirits in a holistic sense.

24. In Pauline thought, *charisma* is synonymous with *diakonia* (Asamoah-Gyadu, *African Charismatics*, 239). See also 1 Cor 12:4–6.

25. Charles Parham, founder of the two Bible Schools where baptism in the Spirit was emphasized, remarked that, precisely because he lacked any educational preconditioning, he could read the Bible in an "entirely unbiased" manner (Jacobsen, *Thinking in the Spirit*, 20).

26. Vondey, *Pentecostalism*, 118, and King, *Regeneration*, 2:510–23.

27. "Global Pentecostalism in the New Millennium," 222.

in an emotive, expressive, and spontaneous manner, resulting in miracles and conversions.[28]

When African Pentecostals confess that they believe in the Holy Spirit, it is because, during their Christian pilgrimage, they have, in some way, experienced the Spirit first-hand, and they identify with the experiences of the charismatic community to which they belong. Peter L. Berger asserts that the human experience could also contain theologically relevant data.[29] For that reason, he is of the opinion that "inductive faith" holds the greatest promise of "new approaches" to religious truth.[30]

Anderson defines Pentecostalism in terms of a unique response to the common problems of the working poor, consisting of the notion that religion was a matter of the "heart" rather than the intellect, and that miracles and wonders held a central place.[31] The poor thrived in the emotionalistic and supernaturalistic outlook that also characterized the Holiness movement, in contradistinction to evangelical-revivalistic Protestantism. Anderson argues that because they were frustrated with their low social position in society and could not adjust to the challenges presented by urbanization, their social discontent became the root source of Pentecostalism.[32] However, most pentecostal researchers do not accept this explanation and instead depict the movement's self-understanding

28. Asomoah-Gyadu, *African Charismatics*, 240.

29. Berger, *Rumour of Angels*, 100.

30. Inductive faith refers to "a religious process of thought that begins with facts of human experience," unlike deductive faith, which begins with ideas (Berger, *Rumour of Angels*, 100). Inductive faith proceeds from human experience to statements about God. For African Pentecostals, faith is born from their experiential encounter with Jesus through the mediation of the Spirit.

31. Anderson, *Vision of the Disinherited*, 228.

32. Anderson, *Vision of the Disinherited*, 240. If social depravity explained the attraction of pentecostalism then one would expect that in the contemporary Pentecostal movement the poor would still form the majority of members, which is not the case, at least not in Western churches (Hine, "Deprivation and Disorganization Theories," 656). Hine adds that the characteristics associated with the "sect type" and "socially and economically disinherited people," such as emotionally charged religious experiences, lay leadership, a confessional requirement for membership, a high degree of participation by members, and reliance on the guidance of the Spirit occur in contemporary Pentecostal churches consisting of middle and upper class converts as well. By 1950, Pentecostalism was no longer solely a religion of the poor and the marginal (Peel, "Post-Socialism" 184). Although Pentecostalism still draws people from the lower socio-economic classes, many from other economic classes also join the movement. Today, Pentecostalism is mainly an urban religion, the faith of choice for tens of millions of city-dwellers on five continents (Cox, *Fire from Heaven*, 11).

in terms of its quest for a deeper and developing relationship with Jesus through his Spirit. Individuals were primarily attracted to Pentecostalism through its attention to people's religious quest, serious consideration of spiritual growth, and the way they respected and interpreted the Bible.[33] The vast majority of recruits came from the Holiness movements, both the Wesleyan Holiness movement[34] and the Keswickian Higher Life movement.[35] Pentecostal identity was established by the preaching of the full gospel message[36] in a restorationist-revivalistic manner with

33. *Contra* Miller ("Pentecostalism as a Social Movement," 114). Asamoah-Gyadu makes the important observation that while most if not all Pentecostals respect the Bible, African Pentecostals regard the Bible itself as holy, mediating holiness from the supernatural realm to the natural realm of existence, containing a divine and supernatural status, as the last word on any matters of belief or behavior (Asamoah-Gyadu, *Contemporary Pentecostal Christianity*, 166–67). It is a symbol of sacred power, able to protect the believer from adverse effects of evil because, in the African imagination, that which is holy exudes power that could even be dangerous (Asamoah-Gyadu, *Contemporary Pentecostal Christianity*, 171).

34. This movement serves as Pentecostalism's immediate predecessor and provides the new movement with several important characteristics, such as: a form of literal-minded biblicism, emotional fervor, a puritanical ethical code of living, enmity toward established denominations due to its rejection by these churches, and a belief in the "second blessing" in Christian experience, resulting in sanctification. The Church of God in Christ under the leadership of Charles Mason and the Church of God (Cleveland) had been, at first, holiness denominations, and now they accepted a third work of grace, the baptism of the Holy Spirit, usually accompanied by speaking in tongues. Sanctification consists of moral perfection, attainable in this life through the baptism of the Spirit with the resultant eradication of inbred sin (Anderson, *Vision of the Disinherited*, 289–90).

35. Archer, *Pentecostal Hermeneutic*, 12. Higher Life movements advocated a second work of grace called the baptism of the Spirit consisting of an enduement of power, enabling one to become an effective winner of souls (*contra* Wesleyan Holiness groups). Sanctification is, for them, a progressive process instead of an immediate experience (see Waldvogel, "Overcoming Life.") The Keswick Convention recognized two distinct experiences, the "new birth" and the "fullness of the Spirit," with sanctification seen as a possible but progressive experience (Anderson, "Keswick Movement," 128). "Fullness of the Spirit" was interpreted in terms of "holiness" in the Holiness movement and the "higher Christian life" in the Keswick Convention (Anderson, "Keswick Movement," 128). By the end of the nineteenth century, however, Spirit baptism was primarily understood in Keswick and elsewhere as empowerment for mission service, and not only as individualistic holiness (Anderson, "Keswick Movement," 129).

36. Pentecostals seldom have an elaborately worked-out theology (Anderson, *Moya*, 32–33). Their theology comes to life in song, music, prayers, sacramental acts of healing and exorcism, art forms, architecture, liturgy, dress (especially important in Africa), church structures, and community life. Although they have little of an explicit theology, they have a praxis and spirituality in which their theology is implicit. "It is of

an emphasis on millenarian theology, ecstatic charismatic experiences, the expectation that miracles would occur, and the experiential celebrative worship—consisting of participatory expressiveness of tongues and prophecy.[37] Hollenweger[38] describes the aspects that form pentecostal theology as: maximum participation at the level of reflection, prayer, and decision making, forming of community that is reconciliatory; inclusion of dreams and visions into personal and public forms of worship, functioning as a kind of icon for the individual and the community; and an understanding of the body/mind relationship that is informed by experiences of correspondence between body and mind, with the most striking application the ministry of healing by prayer.

People did not become Pentecostals because they were deprived, disorganized, and defective, but because of their religious concerns and their acceptance of a pentecostal hermeneutics, specifically its continuationist sentiment. This hermeneutics also draws their attention to Jesus's predilection for the marginalized, transforming them into agents of change in the poorer parts of society,[39] allowing Gerlach to define Pentecostalism not as a "reaction to change" but rather as a "cause of change."[40] Pentecostalism is not a reactionary but a revolutionary movement.[41] It resides in the margins, set apart from the larger Christian community by its distinct doctrines of Spirit baptism and speaking in tongues.[42] While

---

the essence that the believer interpreting the Spirit-inspired Scriptures be in submission to the Holy Spirit through prayer in order that he might be filled with the Holy Spirit (Eph 5:18), walk by the Holy Spirit (Gal 5:16–25), and live by the Holy Spirit (Rom 8:1–11), so that his sinful nature might not quench the Holy Spirit's work (1 Thess 5:19)" (Seaman, *Illumination and Interpretation*, 167).

37. Archer, *Pentecostal Hermeneutic*, 32. The Full Gospel was understood by early Pentecostals to be a restoration of the New Testament presentation of the gospel of Jesus Christ, a complete gospel that emphasized the importance of Jesus's redemptive ministry for humanity (Archer, "Full Gospel," 89). Salvation, baptism in the Spirit, divine healing, and the second coming are the four cardinal doctrines commonly referred to as the Full Gospel. There was a shared belief and proclamation of the four- (or five-) fold understanding of the work of Jesus as savior, (sanctifier), Spirit-baptizer, healer, and soon coming king, and of tongues as the initial evidence of Spirit baptism (Purdy, *Pentecostal Hermeneutic*, 33).

38. Hollenweger, "After Twenty Years," 6.

39. Hine, "Deprivation and Disorganization Theories," 652, and Gerlach, "Pentecostalism," 671.

40. Gerlach, "Pentecostalism," 672.

41. Archer, *Pentecostal Hermeneutic*, 36.

42. Archer, *Pentecostal Hermeneutic*, 209. Most scholars accept that the "languages"

Evangelicals equated Spirit baptism with conversion, most Pentecostals insist that the Spirit came on the disciples at Pentecost not as the source of new covenant existence but rather as the source of power for effective witness. This experience is analogous to Jesus's experience of the Spirit at the Jordan. As Jesus's experience at his baptism serves as a model for the experience of the disciples on the day of Pentecost, so does the disciples' experience at Pentecost also serve as a model for subsequent Christians.[43] Spirit baptism is an experience that is logically, if not chronologically distinct from conversion, which unleashes a new dimension of the power of the Spirit for service.[44]

Pentecostalism provided people with a democratic worship event where all and sunder might participate as equals, allowing everyone to live out their ministry and spiritual gifts with emotional support from like-minded people in a group interaction characterized by equality between its members. Involvement was a key component of pentecostal worship and its equality included all races and genders as well as age groups (at least, initially).[45] Therefore, ordinary, untrained people were able to participate in public worship in a variety of ways, including the exercise of spiritual gifts, for example, bringing a message (sermon)[46] or

---

in Acts 2 refer to genuine foreign languages (see Chance, *Acts*, 49, and Schnabel, *Acts*, 115), breaking down—for the moment at least—the barriers of human languages as the essence of the curse of Babel (Thomas, *Acts*, 30–31). Speech was confounded at the Tower of Babel; understanding was restored at Pentecost (Cox, *Fire from Heaven*, 38), although Keener contends correctly that the text in Acts 2 gives no indication that Luke made the connection (Keener, *Spirit Hermeneutics*, 50). Babel and Pentecost stand like two great mountains at either ends of the Bible, demonstrating the value of language to separate and unite (Bartholomew, *Introducing Biblical Hermeutics*, 543). This is Scripture's seminal language miracle (Keener, *Spirit Hermeneutics*, 60). At the same time, scholars accept that the Corinthian languages refer to a different category of languages, of unknown languages.

43. Menzies, *Pentecost*, 30.

44. Menzies and Menzies, *Spirit and Power*, 744. See also: "They have received the Holy Spirit just as we have" (Acts 10:47).

45. Cox, *Fire from Heaven*, 246. Early Pentecostalism was, in fact, the only portion of Protestantism that was integrated racially, referring to the situation in the United States (Marsden, "Everyone One's Own Interpreter?," 83). This is true for South Africa as well, at least initially (Burger and Nel, *Fire Falls in Africa*, 384).

46. Early Pentecostals avoided using the term "sermon" because of its association with established churches and the ministy of preaching confined to the professional pastorate, and preferred to speak of "a message from the Lord," supposing that any Spirit-filled believer might be used to bring the message.

giving a personal testimony.[47] In their testimonies, they made theological sense of their participation by describing it as a gift of the Spirit who had now become present in the new creation of the believer and church as an abiding, empowering presence, a term which primarily means "participation in," in Fee's opinion.[48]

Early Pentecostals moved along the fringes of established denominations; their theological preferences of eschatological urgency to evangelize the whole world before the end of the age would occur had already marginized them from these mainline churches.[49] That they were successful is seen in the fact that they reached fifty nations within the first two years of the existence of the Pentecostal movement with the message of "Pentecost."[50] They voiced a lack of patience at the prospect of forsaking or postponing the spread of the gospel due to the possible requirements of a formal theological education that conflicted with the eschatological urgency of their expectation of Christ's imminent return.[51] Their revivalistic, experience-oriented worship was appealing to those who were often shunned by mainline congregations and sidelined by society.[52] Pentecostal preachers, energized by their eschatological fervor, preached wherever they could find space and, due to financial restraints, their locations were often storefronts, warehouses, etc., making them both accessible and appealing to marginalized and disenfranchised persons.[53] Pentecostalism was the faith of the underclass.[54] They often worked along the fringes of

47. Purdy, *Distinct*, 46.

48. Fee, *To What End Exegesis?*, 259. Gordon Fee is a preeminent scholar whose commentaries are widely read and respected in evangelical circles (Oliverio, *Theological Hermeneutics*, 168).

49. Dempster, "Search for Pentecostal Identity," 1.

50. Anderson, *Moya*, 27.

51. Vondey, *Pentecostalism*, 118. Vondey states that even when Bible schools and institutes became more prominent in the 1920s and 1930s, many Pentecostals went into the mission field without credentials and formal studies. In Africa, it is still the custom that a believer would move to a new neighborhood, start a prayer meeting in their home, and, before long, would serve as the leader of a small assembly. In most cases, they do not have any formal theological training, and, in some instances, they eventually become respected leaders of successful churches.

52. Purdy, *Distinct*, 45. See Keener's (*Spirit Hermeneutics*, 46) provocative remark that most of the places experiencing profound spiritual revival are situated among the poor and marginized.

53. Cox, *Fire from Heaven*, 24.

54. Davies, "What Does it Mean to Read?," 249.

the established churches since their message appealed to those who had been turned off (or turned away) by the cold, cerebral religion of mainline denominations.[55] Their reading of the metanarrative with its latter rain motif[56] and primitivistic impulse[57] was driven by their passionate desire for an unmediated experience with the Spirit, developing into a deeper, personal relationship with Jesus, and their restorationist views, molding the subculture in which Pentecostalism flourished.[58] Their attitudes toward the world were shaped by their conviction that current cultural values necessarily opposed true faith and they interpreted persecution and discrimination against them as a measure of spiritual strength and a sign of the correctness of their beliefs.[59] They volubly opposed much of their culture, and the sense that they offered a viable, satisfying alternative to this-worldliness was instrumental in attracting new adherents.[60]

55. Purdy, *Distinct*, 46.

56. The use of the motif in the Pentecostal movement should be distinguished from the New Order of the Latter Rain, a revival serving as a precursor of the charismatic movement of the 1960s and originating at the Sharon Orphanage and Schools in North Battleford, Saskatchewan, Canada in 1947. George Hawtin, a pastor of the Pentecostal Assemblies of Canada, clashed with colleagues due to his controversial statements, prophetic utterances, and "heavenly revelations," leading to an organizational schism and a new movement (Mittelstadt, "Latter Rain Movement," 135–36). Hawtin's ministry was precipitated through the ministry of the controversial healing evangelist William Branham. The movement was driven by strong expectations of the imminent return of Christ and re-established apostles, prophets, evangelists, pastors, and teachers (Eph 4:11–12) as present-day ministers that would herald the final days (Mittelstadt, "Latter Rain Movement," 137).

57. Archer, *Pentecostal Hermeneutic*, 136 and 150.

58. The charismatic movement that eventually originated within established mainline churches does not adhere to classical pentecostal primitivistic restorationism; it is more open to also appreciate the Spirit's work in and through the historical church tradition, which classical Pentecostals traditionally viewed with deep suspicion (Neumann, "Spirituality," 198).

59. Early Pentecostals were certain that God had called them despite the fact that they were poor and unlettered. They also perceived that God had called them because of their poverty and their resultant dependence upon the power and care of God (Cox, *Fire from Heaven*, 254).

60. Blumhofer, *Assemblies of God*, 19. Cox emphasizes the necessity of reading the Bible also "from below," calling conventional readings into question (Cox, *How to Read the Bible*, 219). The excluded and disinherited in any society include those mistreated for a variety of reasons, such as color, physical makeup, gender, language, religion, sexual orientation, or disability. It is critically important that people who read the Bible from a more comfortable position in society need to check their impressions against those who read it from a less secure point of view.

The Pentecostal movement represents diverse phenomena and view-points, and it cannot be brought together under one rubric. For instance, further study is necessary to ascertain the way African neo-Pentecostal groups look at the Bible and what their relation is to the fundamentalist paradigm. The conglomeration of groups forming part of the charismatic renewal in traditional historical denominations, another part of the Pentecostal movement, read the Bible with the hermeneutical angle that their different churches use. This dissertation is not concerned with the view of Scriptures held by these diverse groups.

There may be some historical reasons for viewing pentecostal hermeneutics as, to a certain extent, fundamentalist—as some researchers have characterized it. What is then added in Pentecostalism is the speaking in tongues as initial proof (or as a sign, or one of the important signs) of Spirit baptism. This is, however, for several reasons, a misinterpretation that does not represent the genius and genesis of Pentecostalism, and certainly not the whole Pentecostal movement, as will be argued here.[61]

Historical Survey of Pentecostal Hermeneutics

At first, early Pentecostals generally separated themselves from "the world" as part of the drive to holiness that was viewed as incompatible by believers with a lower socio-economic status.[62] Before, during, and directly after the Second World War, however, it became important for socio-economically upwardly-mobile Pentecostals to change to acceptable and respectable status; their status as cult and sect became an albatross around their neck.[63] Starting in the 1930s and lasting to the 1960s, Pentecostals' perspective shifted gradually—but also crucially—from the viewpoint that the anointing with the Spirit was all one needed in order to understand and interpret the Bible and proclaim its message effectively, to the realization of the need for (some kind of) theological training in order to meet the challenges that reading an ancient document and proclaiming its message to people living many centuries later poses for the believer and pastor. At the same time, and as no coincidence, the Pentecostal movement slowly shifted its theological stance of the church

61. Jacobsen, *Thinking in the Spirit*, 355.
62. Nel, "Pentecostalism and the Early Church," 158–59.
63. Anderson, *Vision*, xi, and Burger and Nel, *Fire Falls in Africa*, 389.

as the body of Christ, with each member taking responsibility for its edification, to the professional pastorate taking up more and more of the responsibilities of the ministry.[64] Although more and more requirements were set for the training of pastors, it is true that most of them did not receive any professional teaching in exegetical methods and hermeneutics. Even today, most Pentecostal pastors probably read the Bible without subjecting either the text or their reading of it to critical analysis. In Africa, one also seldom finds a tradition of academic use of the text from a distinctively pentecostal perspective.[65] There is historically no formal pentecostal academic tradition.[66] Most pastors employ a pre-critical and, in some senses, a fundamentalist hermeneutics within their sermons and Bible instruction.[67]

It is also possible to describe the development of pentecostal hermeneutics in other ways, depending on one's perspective. Archer, for instance, thinks of three stages: of an early pre-critical period, from its origin until the 1940s; a modern period, from the 1940s to the 1980s; and the contemporary period, from the 1980s to the present.[68] The first stage in his typology was characterized by the Bible reading methods and interpretive procedures that Pentecostals inherited from the holiness traditions, with inductive reasoning, which focused on the text, and deductive reasoning, which required all available biblical data on a particular topic to be examined and compared on the same level. This approach was thoroughly popularistic as a pre-critical, canonical, and text-centered approach from a revivalistic-restorational biblicist perspective.[69] Such

---

64. Menzies, *Pentecost: This Story*, 129. In the AFM's research into Bible Reading Practices of its members, referred to above, 61 percent of respondents indicated that they think their pastor knows the Bible well, while only 58 percent think that the Bible is taught well at their local church. A meager 52 percent think that their pastor's sermons are based on the Bible, while 51 percent indicate that no reference is made in these sermons to the Bible (Nel, "Bible Reading Practices"). The research shows that all is not well with the sermonizing of the professional pastorate, at least within this particular African denomination.

65. Davies, "What Does it Mean to Read?," 249–50.

66. Because God is, for Pentecostals, so far above and beyond their grasp, they perceive that anything they can assimilate intellectually cannot be from God; hence their skepticism about academic theology *per se* (Davies, "What Does it Mean to Read?," 253).

67. Cargal, "Beyond," 170.

68. Archer, "Hermeneutics," 111–15.

69. As typified by Archer, *Pentecostal Hermeneutic*, 91–92.

an approach assumed that the Bible could be read in a straightforward manner and understood by the common reader or listener. The inductive approach focused on the literary context of the biblical text, interpreting single words. Then, the verse was to be understood in the larger literary context, such as the paragraph, chapter, and book, Old or New Testament, and the whole Bible. The deductive method was then utilized in order to develop a biblical doctrine based on the comparison of all texts related to the theme. It required that all the biblical data about a subject or topic be examined and then harmonized into a cohesive synthesis. The method was not unique to Pentecostals; other emerging evangelical groups were also using the method.[70]

The second stage saw a shift away from the Bible reading method to historical-critical methodologies, with a focus on the world behind the text, although Pentecostals rejected the naturalistic worldview of modernity.[71] These readers used an interpretive approach called the historical-grammatical method, an adaptation of historical criticism, with the aim to identify the socio-historical influences on the author and possibly some of the circumstances that led to the production of the text.[72] The goal was to arrive objectively at the author's intended meaning, as communicated through the text, in order to apply the meaning of the text to the current situation, based on the deductive principle.[73] However, no reader can be totally objective and free of presuppositions which profoundly influence their interpretation. We need help to move from our language and culture into the different biblical languages and cultures of the authors without changing or distorting their meanings.[74]

70. Archer, "Pentecostal Biblical Interpretation," 169.

71. Keener describes the Western worldview as mechanistic and naturalistic, a product of the Enlightenment (*Aufklärung*) that is currently culturally and historically idiosyncratic (Keener, *Spirit Hermeneutics*, 97).

72. The method is concerned with the grammatical principle of words and sentences, analyzing etymological, historical, cognate, and comparative word studies, figurative language, and genre; as well as with the historical principle, analyzing the key people, societies, geography, and topography (Tolar, "Grammatical-Historical Method," 21–37).

73. The modern academic interpretive methods moved some pentecostal scholars to abandon tongues as initial evidence for Spirit baptism because the book of Acts was interpreted as simply a historical narrative (Archer, "Hermeneutics," 113), leading to further hostility and anti-intellectualist sentiment from the side of more conservative classical Pentecostals towards academic theology.

74. Tolar, "Grammatical-Historical Method," 21.

One of the products of the modern Western worldview—resulting from the Enlightenment, with its mechanistic and closed view of the universe—was the development of historical-critical methods applied in reading historical texts, comprising of textual criticism, source criticism, form criticism, redaction criticism, and tradition criticism, whose main focus was the relationship between the text and the source. Ansberry and Hays acknowledge that historical criticism can be dangerous because it was traditionally fuelled by atheistic hostility to the authority of the Bible and an over-weaning skepticism.[75] Instead of rejecting these methods in a wholesale manner, like most Pentecostals do (at least in practice), the authors make the meaningful and significant proposal that exegesis should sail like Odysseus's ship, driven by the winds of knowledge and history, towards the Scylla of sincere but anti-intellectual sectarianism and the Charybdis of rigorous but apostate criticism. What is necessary is that the exegete be both critical and confessional because historical criticism can provide the exegete with exciting and significant resources, especially when the insights generated by criticism are harnessed by the perspective of faith. What is needed to interpret the revelation of God is a combination of rigorous historical inquiry, humble self-examination, and exultant faith.[76] A majority of Pentecostals rejected historical criticism because it was perceived as a dead-zone, irradiated and left lifeless by atheistic historiography (in the metaphor of Ansberry and Hays)[77]; I suggest that the issue should be revisited and these methods recaptured and utilized in a manner that is conducive to the pentecostal ethos. Their robust spirituality will help Pentecostals to practice a critical faith and faithful criticism.

The third stage embraces more post-critical and postmodern approaches, including literary approaches (what the text is communicating and how it is communicating it), reader-response approaches (what impact the text has upon the reader community), and advocacy hermeneutics (how the socio-economic and ethnic makeup of interpreters leads to "seeing" and "hearing" things in the text that others miss).[78] Methodolo-

75. Ansberry and Hays, "Faithful Criticism," 205.

76. Ansberry and Hays, "Faithful Criticism," 207.

77. Ansberry and Hays, "Faithful Criticism," 221.

78. Western pentecostal scholarship experiences a tension between those who utilize a historical-critical hermeneutic, emphasizing historical context, and others who favor a postmodern hermeneutic, playing down the importance of the original historical horizon. The first group is caricatured for an illusory goal of pure objectivity,

gies that focus on the final form of the text have proved to be especially beneficial to pentecostal academic studies and are more in step with the pentecostal pre-critical stage of Bible reading. It also emphasizes the importance of the interpretive community that is reading and listening to the biblical text and the role of the Holy Spirit. Interpretation always takes place in an interpretive community that channels the "correctness" of interpretation; hence, interpretation cannot, in a certain sense, be right or wrong. There is no single way of reading that is correct or natural, only "ways of reading" that are extensions of community perspectives, necessitating comparison of one's interpretation with the insights of other interpretive communities. There are limits to what one can make reasonably of a text, however. These limits are established by an informed reader with a certain literary competence within an interpretive community.[79] Today, pneumatological interpretation, human experiences, the importance of Luke-Acts as guiding pentecostal theology, the scopus of the fourfold or fivefold Full Gospel, and theological methodology are contemporary concerns of a pentecostal hermeneutics.[80]

Many Pentecostals still experience a certain tension between the working of the Spirit and academic training and endeavors, a sentiment that was even more accentuated in earlier times.[81] The pursuit of scholar-

---

the second that they are falling into an abyss of unconstrained relativism. However, limiting the choice to ancient or modern meaning is invalid as both the ancient and modern horizons have historical contingency. Culture makes a difference on both ends or horizons of interpretation, in understanding the ancient context as well as in relating it to the interpreter's context. Interest in ancient meaning is demanded by the shape of the texts themselves (Keener, *Spirit Hermeneutics*, 132). What is needed is a balance between the ancient and contemporary horizon, necessitating a both-and approach (Keener, *Spirit Hermeneutics*, 142–51). Contemporary readers need ancient as well as modern meanings; the horizons need to be fused before significant meaning is generated. Once we understand what biblical texts communicated in their first context, we must hear their challenge or comfort in our own settings as well.

79. For a discussion regarding the insights of Stanley E. Fish in his texts about response criticism, see Zwiep, "Bible Hermeneutics from 1950," 986.

80. Archer, "Hermeneutics," 115.

81. As expressed, for example, by Cronjé ("AGS Teologiese Kollege," 46). Resistance to long-term intellectual pursuits was often supplanted by the more direct and negative perception that an intellectualization of the Christian faith was resisting or suppressing the work of the Holy Spirit (Vondey, *Pentecostalism*, 118). The division in Pentecostal churches between academic and church worlds has led to a kind of theological schizophrenia, where the Pentecostal community practices one form of theologizing in its proclamation and worship, and a quite different form when pentecostal academicians discuss faith with those who do not claim the same set of charismatic experiences

ship is often still considered a hindrance to the determination shared by Pentecostals that the gospel of salvation is to be proclaimed to a world facing the imminent second coming of Christ and the kingdom of God.[82] Pentecostals perceive themselves as in discontinuity with the institutionalized and intellectualized church that has displaced the power of the Spirit. The established church, in Pentecostals' perception, had driven the Spirit out of the church and replaced the Spirit's presence with a reliance on the intellectual and rational abilities of human beings evidenced in speculative thinking, creeds, doctrines, theories, and criticisms that paralyze the believers with skepticism.[83]

Since the 1950s and 1960s, however, Pentecostal denominations required more proper theological training as a prerequisite to be ordained as an official pastor, at least in the developed countries.[84] And while previously women were treated as equals to men—because ministry was derived from the gifts of the Spirit and the Spirit endowed many women with leadership and ministry gifts—now women, in most instances, were

---

(Ellington, "Pentecostalism and the Authority of Scriptures," 169). The result is that some scholars "park their faith" at the doorstep of academia and "park their brains" at the church's doorstep, as described by Masenya ("Foreign on Own Home Front?," 393). This practice is unacceptable because of its logical implication that Pentecostalism and biblical scholarship are incompatible. Compare also the remark of McKay ("When the Veil is Taken Away," 39) that the kind of scholarship practiced today in most religious academic institutions is incompatible with a charismatic understanding of the Bible. Modern scholarship interprets theology in terms of doctrines, assumptions and hypotheses about the nature of Scripture and revelation, while charismatics practice theology in the light of their experience of Spirit baptism. Pentecostal theology is fundamentally different from other models of theology, requiring from pentecostal theologians to articulate their theology in terms of their experiences of encountering God in dynamic and powerful ways, rather than out of rational reflection. Modern pentecostal scholarship has expanded its horizon from a church-dominated audience to a dialogue partner with diverse publics in the church, academy, and society (Vondey, *Pentecostalism*, 131). It is not concerned with Pentecostalism as such, but with Pentecost, or more precisely, the renewing work of the Spirit across all boundaries, taking pentecostal scholarship to the frontiers of religion, science, technology, politics, economics, and other fields (Vondey, *Pentecostalism*, 132).

82. Vondey, *Pentecostalism*, 117.

83. Vondey, *Pentecostalism*, 119.

84. See Nel, "Hundred Years of Theological Training," 108–26; Nel, "Development of Theological Training and Hermeneutics," 191–207; and Nel and Van Rensburg, "Integrating Spirituality and Rationality," for a discussion of theological training in South African Pentecostal churches (with emphasis on the AFM of SA).

disqualified from the teaching and preaching ministry, except to children, other women, and prison inmates.[85]

Some Pentecostals are worried that theological expertise might serve as a substitute for and eventually replace the direct revelation and guidance of the Spirit in a church where theological training is being made conditional to entry into the ministry.[86] This view is supported by the perception that they share with early Pentecostals, that some historical churches with excellent theological training for their ministers are lacking the "revivalistic spirit." Their "learning" presumably made them immune to the direct revelation of the power of the gospel demonstrated in signs and wonders. What Pentecostals value is revelation knowledge or a direct revelation of the Spirit through what is read in the Bible but also sometimes of an extra-biblical nature, supported by the working of the Spirit's power in the form of miracles of healing, deliverance, and provision.[87] They believe that revelation does not end with the Bible.[88] Revelation knowledge (sometimes called a *rhema* word) was viewed as superior to knowledge attained through theological study or the labor of informed exegetical investigation of Scriptures.

Pentecostals must acknowledge that revelation knowledge was at times used without recourse to any evaluation against theological knowledge or scientific Biblical exegesis, resulting in several heretical teachings that led to schisms within the Pentecostal movement.[89] To overcome this problem, many Pentecostal denominations from the 1960s on chose purposefully to provide training for their pastors in "Bible Schools" where the training was characterized as "spiritual" (that is, driven and initiated by the Spirit), Bible-centered and Bible-oriented—with the Bible serving

85. Since its inception, the Pentecostal movement recognized the ministry of women as legitimate and as equal with that of men, based on the perception that experience showed that the Spirit used women in all ministries. This was an important witness over claims by cessationist fundamentalists, Evangelicals, historic Protestants, Catholics, and Orthodox alike, that women are simply to be "silent in the church." See Robeck, *Azusa Street*, 25.

86. For example, see Fee, *Gospel and Spirit*, 84.

87. Some argue that such a revelation always undermines the full and final revelation contained in Scriptures (Cartledge, "Locating the Spirit," 252). Pentecostals would respond that the Spirit as the source of the revelation is the Spirit of Christ, who reveals Christ to them as the full and final revelation of God. See Omenyo and Arthur, "Bible Says!," 52.

88. Kinyua, *Introducing Ordinary African Readers' Hermeneutics*, 301.

89. Burger and Nel, *Fire Falls in Africa*, 389–94.

as the main (and in many instances, the only) textbook, and committed to the "fundamentals of the faith."[90]

The drive for acceptance by the second and third generation of Pentecostals, referred to above, led to Pentecostals seeking an alliance with the broader conservative Protestant tradition, requesting to cooperate with Evangelicals,[91] playing a particularly significant role in the establishment of the National Association of Evangelicals (NAE) in the United States,[92] leading to the "evangelicalization" of Pentecostals (and, eventually, also the "pentecostalization" of Evangelicals).[93] Pentecostals largely abdicated

90. Anderson and Pillay, "Segregated Spirit," 236, and Archer, *Pentecostal Hermeneutic*, 393.

91. The Pentecostal movement originated in the United States and American missionaries' work in South Africa from 1908 led to the establishment of the classical Pentecostal denominations in South Africa. The decisions and tendencies of the American Pentecostal movement to a large extent determined the history of the movement in South Africa, an influence that is still forming the liturgical and theological development of the South African Pentecostal movement along with the direction provided by the successful neo-Pentecostal churches, which, in some instances, draw crowds of thousands of interested persons. Missionaries from Azusa Street arrived in Liberia and Angola in 1907 (Anderson, *Introduction to Pentecostalism*, 114).

92. In Britain, the revival led by John Wesley (1703–1791) gave birth to an evangelical awakening, eventually forming the Evangelical Alliance in London in 1846, affirming nine doctrinal affirmations (among which are the inspiration of the Bible, the Trinity, and the mediation of the divine Christ). In New England, the evangelical awakening led by Jonathan Edwards led to "Old School" orthodox theology with its emphasis on the Bible as inerrant and the only source of divine revelation deductively discerned as objective truth. Charles Finney—together with the Princeton theologians, B. B. Warfield, A. A. Hodge, and Charles Hodge—converged with the older movements to produce the impetus of the fundamentalist movement (see Oliverio, *Theological Hermeneutics*, 86; Daunton-Fear, "Deliverance and Exorcism," 75; and Anderson, "Fundamentalism," 230). At the St. Louis, MO meeting of the National Conference for United Action Among Evangelicals in 1942, about 10 percent of the 150 delegates were Pentecostals. The meeting formed the NAE, and, by the end of the twentieth century, Pentecostals formed the majority, the Assemblies of God with more than 2 million members and the Church of God as well as the Church of the Nazarene with half a million members each respectively. Full participation did not come easily, but it was important for American Pentecostals to gain visibility and respectability among their evangelical peers, leaving behind their reputation as sectarians. The rival organization established by Carl McIntire in 1942, the American Council of Christian Churches (ACCC)—the conservative alternative to the Federal Council of Churches of Christ in America and succeeded by the National Council of Churches of Christ in the United States—never accepted Pentecostals, applying to them the epithet of "the tongues group" (see Robeck, "National Association of Evangelicals," 634–36, and National Association of Evangelicals, "History").

93. Ellington, "Pentecostalism and the Authority of Scriptures," 151.

their theological agenda to evangelical academic leadership; pentecostal Bible schools now even employed evangelical textbooks wholesale and uncritically.[94] In South Africa, acceptance by Evangelicals did not come easily; some Reformed faculties of theology at state-operated universities did not even welcome students from the pentecostal fray who were interested in furthering their theological studies. When Pentecostals did attend these theological faculties, they were exposed to textbooks from the Reformed perspective and paradigm with no sympathy or understanding for their unique paradigm.

Acceptance by and participation in the evangelical community, however, came at a cost to Pentecostals.[95] Because they accepted the hermeneutical angle of the Evangelicals with which they formed an alliance, creating a hybrid hermeneutics of their own,[96] they started interpreting the Bible differently in terms of several important issues. For instance, prior to the Second World War, most Pentecostals were pacifists, pledged to nonviolence, declaring that, in accordance with Scripture and Jesus's example, they could not participate in war and armed resistance which involved the destruction of lives.[97] Because Jesus teaches his disciples to turn the other cheek, they would not retaliate wrongs done to them but would try to love their enemies. This viewpoint was changed without much discussion, and, in the case of the AFM of SA, without taking any resolution at a representative council of the church, in accordance with the norms of evangelicalism that support patriotism and nationalism. Its initial support for women in ministry was also superseded by evangelical values that do not allow women to partake in the teaching ministry, as already stated.[98] The involvement of the laity and their democratic participation in worship services and ministry was also sacrificed for the establishment of a professional pastorate and orderly worship services

94. Menzies and Menzies, *Spirit and Power*, 495.

95. Bebbington describes Evangelicalism as a subset of Protestantism, which emphasizes conversionism, that is, the transformation of lives; activism, in spreading the gospel; biblicism, by which is meant a particularly high regard for the Bible; and crucicentrism, that is, a stress on the sacrifice of Christ on the cross, as central to the gospel message and soteriology (Bebbington, *Evangelicalism in Modern Britain*, 3).

96. Oliverio, "Introduction," 3.

97. Robeck, "Assemblies of God and Ecumenical Cooperation," 107–50. See Nel, *Pacifism and Pentecostals*.

98. Poloma, *Assemblies of God*, 119, and Daniels, "Everyone Bids You Welcome," 235.

in accordance with evangelical practices.[99] Pentecostalism also shed its early restorationist and premillennialist fervor and became more like longer-established denominations,[100] all because many Pentecostals now accepted the evangelical viewpoint of the verbal inerrancy and propositional infallibility of Scriptures, aligning itself, to some extent, with the fundamentalist use of the Bible and creating a hybrid between evangelicalism and fundamentalism,[101] with a particular pentecostal flavor.[102]

According to Christian Smith, the biblicist-literalist viewpoint consists of ten mutually interrelated beliefs that can be summarized as follows: that the Bible, in all its details, consists of and is identical with God's very own words, written inerrantly in human language; that the Bible represents the totality of God's communication to and God's will for humanity; that the divine will about all the issues relevant to Christian belief and life is contained in the Bible and applicable to the contemporary situation without fail; that any reasonably intelligent person can read the Bible in his or her own language and correctly understand the plain meaning of the text as its first listeners or readers understood the intended meaning of the author, and that all that is needed to interpret the Bible is common sense and the ability to read; that the best way to understand biblical texts is by reading them rigidly in their explicit, plain, most obvious, and literal sense, as the author intended it to be read[103]; that the significance of any given biblical text can be understood without reliance on creeds, confessions, historical church traditions, or other forms of larger theological

---

99. Clark, "Contemporary Pentecostal Leadership," 16.

100. Blumhofer, *Assemblies of God*, 15.

101. Oliverio, *Theological Hermeneutics*, 85.

102. For fundamentalists, the Bible is a reliable guide to life, containing systematic rules for living that have been proven over "6,000 years" of human history (in line with most fundamentalists' creationist viewpoint). Everything in Scripture is true, and, if they have questions about a specific Scripture—such as, its condoning of slavery, polygamy, or the use of excessive violence to subject enemies in the Old Testament—they believe that prayer, study, and the pastor's wisdom will provide an answer (Ammerman, "North-American Protestant Fundamentalism," 61). Keener, in his normative work on pentecostal hermeneutics, *Spirit Hermeneutics*, does not emphasize "inerrancy" when he writes about the Bible as authoritative and inspired. A pentecostal hermeneutics holds a high but also realist view of Scripture (see Archer, "Spirited Conversation about Hermeneutics," 186).

103. Early Pentecostals' operative principle of interpretation was the conviction that exegesis is best when it is as rigidly literal as credibility can stand (Wacker, "Functions of Faith," 365).

hermeneutical frameworks[104]; that all related passages of the Bible on any given subject fit together almost like puzzle pieces into single, unified, internally-consistent bodies of instruction; that what the biblical authors taught God's people at any point in history remains universally valid for all Christians at every other time, unless explicitly revoked by subsequent scriptural teaching; that all matters of Christian belief and practice can be learned by sitting down with the Bible and piecing together through careful study the clear "biblical" truths that it teaches[105]; and that the Bible teaches doctrine and morals with every affirmation that it makes, so that together those affirmations comprise something like a handbook or textbook for Christian belief and living.[106]

Hauerwas and Willimon explain that fundamentalist biblical interpretation and the phenomenon it reacts to, that is, higher criticism or modernism, are actually two sides of the same coin.[107] Fundamentalism is rooted in the Scottish Common Sense school of philosophy in a synthesis with the Baconian method, which asserted that propositions are accessible to any thinking, rational person. It led to two fundamental premises concerning knowledge: that God's truth was a single, unified order, and that all persons of common sense were capable of knowing that truth.[108] It implies that any rational person ought to be able to see the common sense of the assertion that God created heaven and earth. All that is needed is that a Christian asserts these kind of propositions which, because they are true, are understandable to anybody with common sense.[109] Fundamentalists and modernists shared the philosophical

104. The contention of early fundamentalists was that creeds divided Christians and thus hindered the mission of the church (Hunt, "Dispensationalism," 63).

105. In contrast, for early Pentecostals, the Bible was not a past, static deposit of truth, but a present primary source book for living a charismatic life (Byrd, "Paul Ricoeur's Hermeneutical Theory," 214, and Oliverio, *Theological Hermeneutics*, 42). Their testimonies proved to Pentecostals that God was still working miracles in the present, as in biblical days. The testimony not only served to provide evidence of God's miraculous power but also aided in the process of interpreting the Bible. It helped to shape the understanding and expectation of those attending the worship service. In this manner, the Pentecostal community participated in the hermeneutical process.

106. Smith, *Bible Made Impossible*, 4–5.

107. Hauerwas and Willimon, *Resident Aliens*, 163.

108. Marsden, *Fundamentalism*, 12–13.

109. Hauerwas and Willimon are also of the opinion that the church has no stake in the utilitarian defense of belief as belief based on the assumption that the Christian religion is a system of belief (Hauerwas and Willimon, *Resident Aliens*, 22). The Bible's concern is whether or not we shall be faithful to the gospel of Jesus Christ—the truth

conviction that only what was historically and objectively scientifically verifiable could be considered "true" and thus meaningful.[110] Faith was based on objective historical evidence.[111]

On the other hand, the historical-critical method as higher criticism denies the fundamentalist claim and asserts that the Bible is the product of a long historical process, requiring the application of sophisticated rules and tools of historical analysis to a given biblical text because one could not understand the text without understanding its true historical context.[112] It asked the who, what, where, when, and why questions of ancient writings, uncovering the original setting and original meaning of

---

about the way things are now that God is with us through the life, death, and resurrection of Jesus Christ—and not with whether it is still possible for modern people to believe. This leads Hauerwas and Willimon to assert that the theological task is not merely the interpretive matter of translating Jesus into modern categories but rather to translate the world to him (Hauerwas and Willimon, *Resident Aliens*, 24).

110. Torrey, *Fundamentals*, 83. However, one should distinguish between different kinds of truth at each level (Keegan, *Interpreting the Bible*, 153). Some things are historically true, others are true expressions of the preaching, teaching, and worshiping needs of the early Christian community, while still others are true expressions of the theological perspective of the specific author of a biblical book.

111. Keegan makes the interesting remark that fundamentalism is actually fundamentally an Islamic view of inspiration, although it is not possible to prove a historical link (Keegan, *Interpreting the Bible*, 156–57). According to Islam, the prophet Mohammed had a kind of mystical experience in which the angel Gabriel revealed to him that God's word was inscribed on his heart. He was commanded to recite the word of God that was on his heart ("Koran" means "recitation"). His recitation was written down by others since he could not read or write. Islam is based on this inspired word, coming directly from God without any human interference, reminding us of Jer 1:9, Jer 2:1, and Ezek 2:9–3:3. During the late seventeenth century, the dominant explanation of inspiration in Protestant orthodoxy became the notion of verbal dictation, with the Spirit dictating the words of Scripture to the authors.

112. The starting point of classic "historical criticism" is skepticism and doubt. Descartes introduced the principle of universal doubt into modern thought. The fundamental presupposition of historical criticism of the Bible is systematic doubt, toppling the Bible as the authoritative source of all human knowledge and critical understanding (Maier, *Biblical Hermeneutics*, 281 and 284–85), with Christian theology as the queen of all sciences. For instance, Spinoza regarded the Bible as a human book, Lessing accorded truth actual authority (and not the Bible), and Kant integrated revelation into reason in a fundamental manner. Scripture and revelation is separated in historical criticism: "Holy Scripture and Word of God are very much to be distinguished, because we know the difference" (J. S. Semler in Maier, *Biblical Hermeneutics*, 298). Historical criticism is intended to be criticism of the content of the Bible, leading to a basic incompatibility between historical criticism and revelation.

these documents,[113] although it also often led to speculative conjectures concerning the material and their meaning.[114] It frequently asked questions that were seldom the ones on which human lives hinged, as Wink asserts, and it was married to a false objectivity, subjected to uncontrolled technologism, separated from a vital faith community, implying that it has outlived its usefulness.[115] It implied that anybody who applies the correct historical tools will be able to understand the text.

Both the fundamentalist and the higher critic assume that it is possible to understand the biblical text without training, without moral transformation, and without the forgiveness and confession that come about within the church. In an unconscious manner, both try to make everyone religious and able to understand and appropriate the Bible, without everyone's being a member of the community of which the Bible is the sacred Scripture.[116] In contrast, Pentecostals regard the authority of Scripture not as a theological proposition but rather as a transformational experience of the Holy Spirit[117] which happens every time when one is seized by the text. Texts change people through personal engagement.

---

113. The practice of interpretation in ancient Greek times used a typology of seven questions: Who (is the author) (*quis/persona*)? What (is the subject matter of the text) (*quid/materia*)? Why (was the text written) (*cur/causa*)? How (was the text composed) (*quomodo/modus*)? When (was the text written or published) (*quando/tempus*)? Where (was the text written or published) (*ubi/loco*)? By which means (was the text written or published) (*quibus faculatibus/facultas*)? (Detel, *Geist und Verstehen*, 84–97).

114. Efird, *How to Interpret the Bible*, 10.

115. Wink, *Bible in Human Transformation*, 15.

116. Hauerwas and Willimon, *Resident Aliens*, 163.

117. Formal doctrinal statements on the authority of Scripture among conservative churches arose out of debates which were not immediately important or relevant within the Pentecostal movement. When they adopted statements of scriptural authority, Pentecostals did so to gain a wider acceptance among Evangelicals and the conservative Christian community. Actually, the authority of Scripture is secondary in importance for Pentecostals to the experiences of an authoritative God in and through the Bible. Where Evangelicals use "proofs" for inspiration to support a sagging argument for biblical authority, Pentecostals begin with an authoritative encounter with God and then seek to describe biblical inspiration in the only terms available to them, those of conservative evangelicalism, with a limited amount of success (see Ellington, "Pentecostalism and the Authority of Scriptures," 152). Pentecostals experience miracles and the mystery of personal experiences of God's presence, experienced and mediated through the biblical text (among other ways), and, therefore, value knowing by perception over knowing by proof. As a result, they prefer to interpret Scripture by encounter more than exegesis (Davies, "What Does it Mean to Read?," 254).

And while exegesis is important (or even indispensable) for working on the text-horizon, grasping the text's significance is another matter and just as important. The Spirit makes the knowledge of God a possibility in and through an "I-Thou" encounter.[118] It is the transformative experience of conversion, that inner work of the Spirit in one's life, and a daily life lived in the power of the Spirit that bears witness to the power and authority of Scripture.[119]

While the doctrine of the premillennial rapture of the church taught by many fundamentalists who supported dispensationalism with its pessimistic and apocalyptic premillenarian tendencies[120] had already been admired and accepted by Pentecostals,[121] a major difference be-

118. Pinnock, "Work of the Holy Spirit," 240.

119. Solivan, "Sources," 137.

120. Dispensationalism is related to a wider culture of despair brought about by the global conflict, revolutionary upheavals, and economic disasters that characterized the nineteenth century (Hunt, "Dispensationalism," 62).

121. Dispensationalism accepts that God is pursuing three distinct programs: one for the Jews, one for the church, and one for the nations. This distinction is based on 1 Cor 10:32, implying separate economies for the different groups. God's dealings with Israel are totally different and separate from his dealings with the church and the nations. God administered law to Israel, grace to the church, and punishment to the world. Scripture never mingles the principles of law and grace. The law of Moses—the Torah—is a unity, meant for a distinct people, Israel, and for a distinct period, from Sinai (Exod 19:1), and for a distinct place, the promised land (Deut 6:1), until it was nailed to the cross and was canceled by the death of Christ (Col 2:14). The church, established by grace, began at Pentecost and will cease at its rapture to the millennial reign of Christ (premillennialism) (Waltke, *Dance*, 486). A large part of early Pentecostalism adapted the premillennialism of dispensationalists in their eschatological expectations. Another feature of dispensationalism is that it separates church and state and regards states as being governed by the eternal moral law, which they do not equate with the Ten Commandments. Though the nations are part of God's unified kingdom, they belong to the "world," which stands in black-and-white opposition to the church and is under the rule of Satan (Luke 4:5–6) (Waltke, *Dance*, 487). Dispensationalists are concerned with saving the church out of the world before the imminent rapture rather than with transforming culture. Pentecostalism also inherited this ecclesiology and practice of separation from the world (see Nel, "Pentecostalism and the Early Church"). After the church is raptured, God will again restore Israel to their rightful position as the people of God, and they will live in the promised land for a thousand years while the church will reign with Christ over the Jews, the subjects of the kingdom. The kingdom will be administered according to the provisions of the new covenant, which consist of the substance of the unified Mosaic law, including its ceremonies and food regulations, but differing in terms of it containing better promises and provisions. In the millennial kingdom, the nations will subject themselves to the rule of perfected Israel (but note the distinction between the nations and the

tween fundamentalists and Pentecostals was concerned with Pentecostals' claim that miracles and supernatural interventions still happen in contemporary times.[122] Fundamentalists and dispensationalists revered the appearance of miracles described in the Bible as one of the bedrock fundamentals of the faith, but they limited it to a sub-dispensation of the church age in which the *charismata* and supernatural interventions occurred, which ceased with the closure of the canon of the New Testament at the end of the apostolic era (the so-called "cessasionist viewpoint" that opposes the noncessationist or continuationist view).[123] For Pentecostals, the reappearance of the *charismata* was perceived as a sign of the restoration of the apostolic era and the early church; a sign that the latter rain would herald the rapture of the church before the end of the age. Keener questions early Pentecostals' allegorization of Joel's "latter rain" (Joel 2:23) to refer to the contemporary outpouring of the Spirit, although their eschatological expectations as such rang true.[124] The idea was that the showers of spring were followed in Palestine by the showers of autumn, the latter rain, which were greater than the showers of spring.[125] According to Acts 2:17–21, Peter recognizes that Jesus's followers now live in a special, biblically promised time—the "last days"—when God would pour out God's Spirit and save all who call on the name of Jesus, restoring the church of the last days.[126] "Restoration" is then interpreted

---

church) (Waltke, *Dance between God and Humanity*, 488).

122. Kärkkäinen, "Pentecostal Hermeneutics," 76–115.

123. Keener, *Spirit Hermeneutics*, 54. Continuationism means that interest in biblical texts is not simply for what they teach about ancient history or ideas, even though it may be intriguing, but rather because contemporary readers expect to share the kind of relationship with God and spiritual experience discovered and described in Scripture (Keener, "Pentecostal Biblical Interpretation," 274). Hard cessationists posit radical discontinuity between biblical miracles and the present day, despite periodic "special providences," as cessationists describe events that look like miracles (Keener, "Pentecostal Biblical Interpretation," 275). Most cessationists rule out only regular supernatural giftings, not special divine activity. This viewpoint rules out a contemporary practice of prophecy, interpretation of tongues, and other *charismata* of powers and miracles (Keener, *Spirit Hermeneutics*, 321). That most Protestants are no longer cessationists is a tribute to the effectiveness of the Pentecostal movement (Keener, "Pentecostal Biblical Interpretation," 275). Many cessationists argue that they believe miracles could happen but they have not seen any.

124. Keener, "Pentecostal Biblical Interpretation," 277.

125. Torrey, *Fundamentals*, 138.

126. Pentecostals rightly grasped the sense of eschatological existence and anticipation that characterizes the church age, the period between the first and second comings

in terms of a number of characteristics: a longing for the revelation of the power of God as a sign with eschatological significance; the importance of the biblical significance of Pentecost as described in Acts 2; tangible evidences such as conversions, powerful experiences of sanctification, and moving experiences of being filled with the Spirit; a tension with traditional Christianity; and the expectation of the unity of the church, with God recollecting God's people from all denominations and walks of life.[127] The latter rain motif provided the Pentecostal movement a sense of having a key role in the approaching climax of history as a means by which God was preparing the "bride" of Christ to meet her Lord.[128]

To define fundamentalism is not straightforward. Evangelical fundamentalism is the result of the Protestant denial of any institution, including pope, prelate, church, or synod to interpret the Bible for others, and the right of the individual reader to interpret Scriptures, necessarily placing weight on the text itself to instruct readers. Martin Luther responded to Pope Leo XXIII's bull, *Exsurge Domine*, which claimed that he interpreted Scripture otherwise than the Holy Spirit demanded because he was inspired by his own sense of ambition, by declaring that Scripture ought to be interpreted in the most certain, simple, and clear way, with Scripture interpreting itself (*sui ipsius interpres*), testing, judging, and illuminating all things.[129] Vanhoozer paraphrases Luther's meaning by arguing that the meaning of Scripture is clear for those who attended to the grammar of the text and to the leading of the Spirit.[130] Obscure passages should be read in the light of clearer ones. John Calvin, in the same spirit, argued that the meaning and authority of the Bible did not depend on the church. The presupposition is that the Bible is clear in its meaning and that any reader can understand it if it is read in translation

---

of Christ, as attested to by, *inter alia*: Rom 12:2; 1 Cor 2:9–10; 10:11; 2 Cor 1:22; 5:5; Gal 1:4; Heb 1:2; 6:5; 1 Pet 1:20 (Keener, "Pentecostal Biblical Interpretation," 277).

127. Albrecht and Howard, "Pentecostal Spirituality," 245–47. See Nel, "Pentecostal Ecumenical Impulses."

128. Dayton, *Theological Roots of Pentecostalism*, 28. Pentecostals were drawn to premillennial aspirations by two factors: first, the spiritual condition of the mainline denominations (described by John Nelson Darby) as apostate churches that conservative Christians should leave as soon as possible, and second, the persecution they experienced at the hand of the Christians associated with mainline churches, including fundamentalists, enhancing pentecostal apocalyptic tendencies and identity of the "true church" (Hunt, "Dispensationalism," 62).

129. Starling, *Hermeneutics as Apprenticeship*, 8–9.

130. Vanhoozer, *Is There a Meaning?*, 171.

and with common sense. However, this does not adequately discount the diverse literary forms that the Bible contains, requiring different reading strategies, or that translations are, to a certain extent, already interpretations, transposed onto the text by the translator. Extreme Protestants do not possess a "church" to govern interpretation because they deny institutional authority, "all the while possessing a *de facto* institutional structure which is all the more powerful for being hidden."[131] It should also be kept in mind that Bible translation is already an exercise in power and control, especially in colonial Africa.[132]

The fundamentalism discussed here refers to a movement among theologically conservative[133] Protestant churches that organized themselves into the American Bible League in 1902 and the World's Christian Fundamentals Association in 1919, based on information published between 1910 and 1915 in twelve pamphlets entitled *The Fundamentals*, edited by A. C. Dixon and R. A. Torrey.[134] The movement is grounded in five points: the verbal inerrancy of Scriptures,[135] the virgin birth and deity of Jesus Christ, the substitutionary atonement, the physical resurrection of Jesus, and his bodily return to the earth in the near future.[136] It found strong support among laypersons and in revivalist circles, but, at the same time, it was a scholarly movement from the beginning, typical of the history of theology in the United States (and, indeed, partially even of the intellectual interchange between North America and Europe). It

131. Boone, *Bible Tells Them So*, 18.

132. Kinyua, *Introducing Ordinary African Readers' Hermeneutics*, 6–7.

133. It must be emphasized that "fundamentalist" is not synonymous with "conservative." Fundamentalists share with conservative Christians support for "traditional" doctrines like the virgin birth of Christ, the reality of Jesus's miracles and his resurrection, and his eventual return. However, fundamentalists are also found among the Evangelicals, who are defined as those who accept that only an individual decision to follow Jesus will suffice for salvation and who seek to "win souls for Christ," testifying to the necessity of a life-changing decision to become a Christian, leading to a sense of a personal and intimate communion with Jesus (Ammerman, "North-American Protestant Fndamentalism," 57).

134. Synan, "Fundamentalism," 324. It influenced Christian churches in other parts of the world, including South Africa.

135. There exists a range of conventional, modern evangelical positions within and beyond inerrancy (see Merrick, Garrett, and Gundry, *Five Views on Biblical Inerrancy*). When they joined evangelicalism in the 1940s, some Pentecostals defined their belief more narrowly as "inerrancy," and not simply inspiration, an intrinsically pentecostal-friendly concept (Keener, *Spirit Hermeneutics*, 364).

136. Synan, "Fundamentalism," 325, and Ellington, *Evangelical Movement*, 49–72.

served as an act of defense and therefore possessed a basically defensive and apologetic character. It worked mainly on systematic-theological premises and was therefore inclined toward deductive procedure.[137] In a sense, it is the most persistent surviving example of reformational-pre-critical Scripture interpretation.

An eschatological schema that interprets history and prophecy in terms of seven periods or "dispensations" according to the different methods of God's dealings with humankind also became integral to the fundamentalist movement.[138] Dispensational theology was imported from the Plymouth Brethren movement in England through the teaching of John Nelson Darby, where it thrived as part of the American revivalist movement.[139]

Dispensationalists use a distinctive method of textual division and classification whereby seven dispensations, or ages, are distinguished in the biblical material. The dispensations are the following: of innocence or freedom, prior to Adam's fall (Gen 2:8–17; 25); of conscience, from Adam's fall to Noah (Gen 3:10–18; Rom 2:11–15); of government, from Noah to Abraham (Gen 9:6; Rom 13:1); of patriarchal rule or promise, from Abraham to Moses (Gen 12:1–3; 22:17–18; Gal 3:15–19); of the Mosaic Law, from Moses to Christ (Exod 20:1–26; Eph 3:1–9); of grace in the current church age (Rom 5:20–21; Eph 3:1–9); and of a literal, earthly, thousand-year millennial kingdom that has yet to come but soon will be inaugurated (Isa 9:6–7; Isa 11:1–9; Rev 20:16). The church age is the age of grace ending with the rapture of the church and the second coming of Christ. Each of the dispensations represent a different way in which God deals with humankind, specifically a different testing of human-kind. Its beliefs about Israel are also important in order to understand dispensationalism. There is a fundamental distinction between Israel and the church; they represent two peoples of God with different destinies, underlying a fundamental distinction between the law and grace that are mutually exclusive. The New Testament church is a parenthesis in God's plan which was not foreseen by the Old Testament. And there is a distinction between the rapture and the second coming of Christ; the rapture

---

137. Maier, *Biblical Hermeneutics*, 362.

138. Initially developed by A. C. Gaebelin (1861–1945) and C. I. Scofield (1843–1921).

139. Anderson, "Fundamentalism," 231.

of the church at Christ's coming in the air (1 Thess 4:17) precedes the second coming to the earth by seven years of tribulation.[140]

Apparent intertextual contradictions are often resolved by identifying dispensational differences.[141] Fundamentalists believe the Bible to be perspicuous and its meaning deducible by the common reader.[142] In most cases, the meaning the plain person gets from reading the Bible is the correct one. This method of biblical interpretation is called literalism. If the meaning of the Bible contradicts known facts or flies in the face of logic, then the facts are to be disregarded and the logic ignored.[143] The Bible is given a central position, signifying the high status of the text. To demonstrate its centrality, the pulpit stands high, in the center of the sanctuary, and sermons are expository, based on a primary text that is cross-referenced with other scriptural passages.[144] Fundamentalists are anti-scientific and anti-intellectual in the sense that they are unwilling

---

140. See Hunt, "Dispensationalism."

141. Boone, *Bible Tells Them So*, 13.

142. If believers are encouraged to read the Bible in a devotional sense, there must be a presumption that the words of the Bible are perspicuous—that is, clear enough that all can understand what they say without needing the counsel of a scholar at their elbow to instruct them (Kaiser and Silva, *Introduction to Biblical Hermeneutics*, 215). Martin Luther especially affirmed the principle, although he admitted that many texts in the Bible were obscure and abstruse. However, these texts in no way hindered a knowledge of the essential subject matter of the Bible, and there existed no need of anyone's history of tradition to interpret those things that were necessary for salvation and growth in Christ. The Bible was clear and perspicuous on all these things. In the words of the Westminster Confession of Faith (1647), "All things in Scripture are not alike plain in themselves; yet those things which are necessary to be known, believed and observed for salvation, are so clearly propounded, and opened in some place of Scripture or other, that not only the learned, but the unlearned, in a due use of the ordinary means, may attain unto a sufficient understanding of them" (quoted in Kaiser and Silva, *Introduction to Biblical Hermeneutics*, 216–17). It demonstrates the basic intelligibility and non-contradictory nature of Scriptures (Mueller-Vollmer, "Introduction," 2).

143. Whalen, "Literalism," 280–81. Keener relates the remark of a visiting pastor that, after forty days of fasting, had achieved a particular eschatological view that pretribulational Christians would escape the tribulation while posttribulational Christians would stay behind to evangelize the world. Keener retorted that even forty days of fasting would not coerce from the Spirit something that contradicted the biblical text and that the Spirit had already inspired (Keener, *Spirit Hermeneutics*, 101).

144. Boone, *Bible Tells Them So*, 13. Fundamentalists prefer the *Schofield Reference Bible* (1967) and the more recent *Ryrie KJV Study Bible* (1978), which contains extensive footnotes explaining "the true intent" of each passage of Scripture (Ammerman, "North-American Protestant Fundamentalism," 62).

to accept the principal assumptions and conclusions of recent science, although they accept Francis Bacon's principles of careful observation and classification of facts, but with an accompanying underdeveloped historical consciousness.[145] They wed these principles to "common sense" which affirms the ability to apprehend the facts clearly ("Scottish Common Sense Realism"), requiring them to harmonize "facts" drawn from the Bible and scientific data, forming the unspoken assumptions of fundamentalist thinking, along with their faith in the Bible.[146] With the Bible as the only textbook for interpreting the events of history and as a manual for developing true faith and doctrine, dispensationalist-fundamentalist theology holds an inerrant and infallible view of Scripture and utilizes grammatical-historical exegesis.[147] The original documents of the Bible had no errors whatsoever, and all parts of the writings are absolutely, literally true, not only religiously but also in historical and scientific detail.[148]

After the Scopes trial in 1925,[149] American fundamentalists retreated from the seminaries and universities and built their own Bible institutes, where their faith was shielded from modernist theological "heresies" and where, in many instances, they developed forms of political radicalism, supporting either anti-Semitism or pro-Zionism, radical anti-communism, separatism, and several conspiracy theories.[150] The

145. It states unequivocally that science could uncover nothing that contradicts the Scripture and Scripture is a "storehouse of facts" (Charles Hodge, quoted in Ammerman, "North-American Protestant Fundamentalism," 72). Unfortunately, it is true that much of contemporary Christian fundamentalism is ignorant, populist, and hostile to intellectual theology, in contrast to its original roots. It is only loosely connected with institutional churches and effectively functions through individual organizations on their own (Barr, "Fundamentalism," 364).

146. Ammerman, "North-American Protestant Fundamentalism," 64, and Marsden, *Fundamentalism*, 7–8. They argue that the only thing necessary for proper understanding of God's word is the implementation of common sense while reading it (Cherok, "Common Sense Philosophy," 107).

147. Poythress, *Understanding Dispensationalism*, 142, and Hutchison, "Bible Study," 63–64. Historical-cultural investigation is concerned with the author and intended readers, the time period of the writing, the occasion for the writing, social-cultural customs and religious beliefs of the period, societal structures, religious and political centers of power, geographical and physical features, economic structures, and the historical referential meaning of words (Archer, "Pentecostal Biblical Interpretation," 180).

148. Efird, *How to Interpret the Bible*, 5.

149. Russell, "Biological Science and Christian Thought," 51–56.

150. Fundamentalism has become "a worldwide reaction against many of the mixed offerings of modernity" (Marty, *Religion and Republic*, 299) and appeals to

Pentecostals followed suit and established Bible Schools, as will be described in the next section.

After 1960, the term "fundamentalist" is reserved for separatist groups, excluding conservatives in most mainline denominations.[151] Fundamentalists find their strongest ally in the pietistic tradition and revivalist movement, where it receives popular support in the grassroots evangelicalism that revivalism produces.[152] Today, the term is used in the United States mostly to refer to Baptist dispensationalists and some churches forming the Holiness movement.[153] They view cultural factors as subversive of biblical faith and strongly reject the world with its secularism and humanism as antithetical to God's revealed truth in the Bible. They are active in mounting campaigns against pornography, abortion, and those contemporary forces which break down and undermine the traditional family.[154] Another semantic shift in the word "fundamentalism" encompasses "fundamentalisms" in other religions. The term "fundamentalism" is increasingly being applied to phenomena found in other faiths, notably Islam, but also Judaism, Hinduism and aspects of Roman Catholicism.[155] The semantic shift has led to many people perceiving "fundamentalism" in these extreme terms (Islamic or Hindu fundamentalism), equating it with "Christian fundamentalism," a notion that clouds any discussion of the term. These forms of fundamentalisms have nothing to do with the original Christian movement of the early 1920s and their identification by way of the term "fundamentalism" is causing a lot of semantic and pragmatic confusion.

---

those looking for "authoritarian solutions." Fundamentalists are less motivated by religious belief as such than by psychological disposition, social forces, and historical circumstances. It is best defined as "militantly anti-modernist Protestant evangelicalism" (Marsden, *Fundamentalism and American Culture*, 4). Its present resurgence is partially due to contemporary fundamentalists' skilful use of the mass media (Marty, *Religion and Republic*, 300). The history of fundamentalism contains many instances of the persecution of denominational leaders and theologians suspected of "modernist" tendencies (Anderson, "Fundamentalism," 230).

151. Many conservatives became disillusioned with the negative and separatist stance of the fundamentalists and started formulating a new approach to defining the theological agenda, exemplified by *inter alia* Carl F. Henry and Harold J. Ockenga with their "new evangelicalism" (Marsden, *Reforming Fundamentalism*, 243).

152. Anderson, "Fundamentalism," 231.

153. Marsden, *Understanding Fundamentalism*, 4.

154. Anderson, "Fundamentalism," 232.

155. Barr, "Fundamentalism," 365.

What is important is to distinguish between fundamentalism as an epithet and as a phenomenon. When it is used as an epithet, theological groups brand each other with it. As a phenomenon, fundamentalism refers to the attitudes of individuals and groups that, in an exclusivist and sectarian manner, consider their position as the only standard of truth, rejecting all other viewpoints and perspectives in advance, without any further discussion.[156] This attitude is not confined to theology or religion but can even occur in scientific endeavors and includes people from diverse viewpoints, from extremely conservative to liberal.[157]

In conclusion, fundamentalism can be defined for purposes of comparison with the Pentecostals as a religious attitude in conservative circles that display the following characteristics: it views the Bible as the absolute source of authority[158] and focuses on the verbal inerrancy of the Bible[159]; it is negative toward and feels threatened by modernist theology, especially German higher critical views, and science, especially the theory of evolution[160]; it is highly exclusivist and sectarian and functions with the supposition that its theology contains the whole and full truth. The basis of faith (and truth) is something given; it does not lie in the church as an institution (*contra* Roman Catholicism) and it is neither a matter

---

156. "Sectarian" refers to the claim that one holds the exclusive right to be doctrinally correct. "Truth" was, at times, seen as supposing the view that it represents autonomous, value-free research. Postmodernism has rightly helped us to see that such a view is a myth, that all of us approach the world in particular ways and with particular foundational commitments. True progress can only be made if scholars bring their foundational commitments out into the open and foster a genuine pluralism in which different foundational commitments are allowed to come to expression and real, in-depth dialogue can begin (Bartholomew, *Introducing Biblical Hermeneutics*, 5). Keener agrees and argues for global readings (see Keener, *Spirit Hermeneutics*, 67–98). Pentecostal foundational commitments include that the Bible contains the word of God when the Spirit reveals the truth to the praying, meditating believer. In studying the Bible, the aim is not to gain knowledge but rather to encounter the One who is the truth, the life, and the door (John 14:6 and 8:32). One needs the interpretations of other faith communities to compare with one's own interpretation in order to ascertain the validity of one's reading.

157. See Barr, "Fundamentalism."

158. "The one unifying factor in all these movements, without a doubt, is their common adherence to the basic authority of the Scripture as the only dependable guide for faith and practice" (Falwell, *Fundamentalist Phenomenon*, 53). For a brief but informative outline of the crisis of biblical authority, see Goldingay, *Models for Scripture*, 117–21.

159. Packer, *Fundamentalism*, 32.

160. Ammerman, "North-American Protestant Fundamentalism," 56.

of reasoned or dispassionate discussion nor something to be worked out or discovered, but something already known and to be proclaimed with certainty, clearly exemplified in the Bible, and which must be accepted without question or qualification.[161]

As stated, the moderate fundamentalists who distanced themselves from Carl McIntire and his ACCC, establishing the NAE in 1943, accepted the Pentecostals, marking the beginning of a new era of cooperation with evangelicalism that replaced the reputation of the previous, discredited movement. In the process, it influenced the way Pentecostals interpreted the Bible, as they adopted evangelical statements about the inspiration of Scripture uncritically, based on 1 Timothy 3:15–6, 2 Peter 1:20–21, John 10:35, and Matthew 5:17. Land emphasizes that, for Pentecostals, Scripture is always "Spirit-Word"—that is, the dynamic interaction of written text and the Spirit.[162] The same Spirit who inspired and preserved the Bible still illuminates, teaches, guides, convicts, and transforms people when they meet the word, Jesus Christ, in the pages of the Bible through the working of the Spirit. The word is alive, quick, and powerful because of the Spirit's ministry. The relation of the Spirit to the Bible is based on that of Spirit to Christ; as the Spirit formed Christ in Mary, so the Spirit uses the Bible to form Christ in believers (and vice versa). The authority of the Spirit stands above the authority of the Bible; the Spirit was prior to the Bible, and without the Spirit, there would have been no word, incarnate or written. Without the word, there would have been no church.[163] If the Bible is to become the word of God in the lives of contemporary readers, the letter is going to have to become alive by means of the Spirit.[164] In other words, the Bible is not of itself the word of God, but becomes the word of God to the reader or hearer through the action and participation of the Holy Spirit in a continuation of inspiration, introducing the reader to the word in an encounter that is transformative.[165] Pentecostals agree

161. Barr, "Fundamentalism," 363–4.

162. Land, *Pentecostal Spirituality*, 100.

163. Land, *Pentecostal Spirituality*, 106.

164. Pinnock, "Work of the Holy Spirit in Hermeneutics," 4.

165. The Spirit serves as the ultimate arbiter of meaning and significance, the self-authenticating key in the hermeneutic process (Anderson, "Hermeneutical Processes of Pentecostal-type," 3). In discussing inspiration, Keegan distinguishes between inspiration located in the author of the text, in the text itself, or in the reading of the text (Keegan, *Interpreting the Bible*, 153). The last option—inspiration in the reading of the text—is supported by reader-response criticism which maintains that the text is a virtual entity that comes into being in the act of reading when the reader actualizes

that the Bible is divinely inspired, but they do not stop there in relation
to inspiration. Rather, the community has a role within the interpretive
process, and the Holy Spirit works through that community by inspiring
it to make right decisions, in accordance with how Pentecostals interpret
Acts 15.[166] The Bible is the authoritative word of God because the same
Spirit who inspired its writers meets us today in its pages. Biblical authority does not rest in the text but rather in the God that we meet and know
in and through the text.[167] Scripture is not viewed in the static sense of
received, true propositions, simply to be believed and applied, but as the
locus of God's continuing act of revelation.[168] The Bible does not merely
describe believers' experiences of God; it enables them to have experiences with God, implying that the Bible is the primary reference point for
community with God.[169]

If Scripture contains the word of God, no one can stand before it
as a mere spectator. It must be read and interpreted in the light of the
same Spirit by whom it was written.[170] Following the secularization of
academic biblical studies as a part of Western academics, it has become
acceptable to divorce biblical interpretation from a spiritual, prayerful,
and meditative reading. Pentecostals accept that the obedience of faith
cannot be confined to the cultic sphere alone; the practice of Christian
scholars who inhabit two unrelated worlds—the world of the church and
the world of the lecture room—is incompatible with faithful living. In
the first, a close walk with Christ is acknowledged while in the other,
Christ is unwelcome, where reason and neutrality reign.[171] Pentecostal

---

the literary text. I suggest that pentecostal practice finds its connection here, with Pentecostals supporting the inspiration of the Bible in terms of its text, but hearing the
word of God only when the text is actualized and appropriated to their contemporary
situation. The word of God happens or takes place at the nexus of text and context
with the canonical text becoming the word of God over and over again—as situations
change and as the Spirit wills (Keegan, *Interpreting the Bible*, 155).

166. Cartledge, "Text-Community-Spirit," 133.

167. Ellington, "Pentecostalism and the Authority of Scriptures," 157.

168. Cartledge, "Text-Community-Spirit," 134.

169. The role of the Spirit is to use the witness of the original meaning of the Bible,
that is, what is and does not change, in new ways and ever new settings, creating significance for contemporary readers and working out salvation in history (Pinnock,
"Work of the Holy Spirit in Hermeneutics," 16).

170. As verbalized by Jerome, *St. Jerome: Commentary on Galatians*, 207.

171. Bartholomew, *Introducing Biblical Hermeneutics*, 45.

hermeneutics requires an integration of ecclesial and academic interpretation, both rooted in a profound sense of Scripture as God's word.

From the 1970s, new developments led to the change from "Bible School" training to proper theological training and the establishment of theological colleges, later called seminaries.[172] The movement accepted that its leaders and pastors should be sufficiently trained to lead believers in a responsible manner, leading to an integrated, pentecostal liberal education[173] and a pastorate consisting of full-time professional pastors.[174] Eventually, theological training was made compulsory for anyone considering to enter the ordained ministry and, as a result, the gap between the "clergy" and "laity" broadened.[175]

It is necessary to discuss the period between 1940 and 1970, and the development of pentecostal hermeneutics.

172. See, for example, Reddy, "Apostolic Faith Mission of South Africa," 160, and Chinappan, In Covenant Bible College, 4.

173. See Turnage, "Early Church and the Axis," 4–29, especially 21.

174. Burger and Nel, Fire Falls in Africa, 393.

175. Goff, Measuring the Clergy/Laity Gap, 91.

How Pentecostal Hermeneutics Developed

Early Pentecostalism's spirituality was charismatic with an emphasis on the participation of every believer due to an acceptance of the prophethood and priesthood of every believer, implying that, through the Spirit, each one was endowed with unique equipment for the edification of the body of Christ (1 Cor 14:26) and eschatologically driven by an urgency to reach the world with the gospel before the imminent second coming.[176] Their spirituality determined how they interpreted the Bible, with an emphasis on supernatural interventions and the expectation of the rapture that could occur at any moment.[177] The Bible was read in order to experience Christ's presence, empowering and allowing all believers to preach and witness.[178] Everyone participated in the proclamation of the message and through personal testimonies.[179] Members would affirm their approval with what was said in their meetings by saying, "Amen" and "Hallelujah," and, in many instances, someone listening would be moved to stand up and participate in the service. The worship service was not the responsibility of a professional.[180] Sermons—and even some testimonies—ended with an altar call,[181] and interested parties would be

176. The early Pentecostals saw the soon coming of Christ as the prime motivation for the urgent task of preparing the world for the cataclysmic event, and prophecies and interpretation of tongues as well as visions affirmed this expectation (Anderson, *Spreading Fires*, 221). The Azusa Street Mission's magazine, *Apostolic Faith*, writes in 1908: "'Jesus is coming very soon,' is the message that the Holy Ghost is speaking today through nearly everyone that receives the baptism with the Holy Ghost. Many times they get the interpretation of the message spoken in an unknown language and many times others have understood the language spoken. Many receive visions of Jesus and He says, 'I am coming soon.' Two saints recently in Minneapolis who fell under the power were caught up to Heaven and saw the New Jerusalem, the table spread, and many of the saints there, both seeing the same visions at the same time. They said Jesus was coming very soon and for us to work as we had little time."

177. Land, *Pentecostal Spirituality*, 3, and Kärkkäinen, *Spiritus Ubi Vult Spirat*, 77.

178. Sandidge, *Roman Catholic-Pentecostal dialogue*, 141.

179. In terms used by Karl Barth, proclamation is defined here as human language in and through which Godself speaks, which is meant to be heard and apprehended in faith as the divine decision upon life and death, as the divine judgment and the divine acquittal, the eternal law and the eternal gospel both together (Barth, *Kirchliche Dogmatik*, 1.1:57).

180. Archer, *Pentecostal Hermeneutic*, 67.

181. See Moore, "Altar Hermeneutics."

accompanied by believers who shared prayer with them. The message[182] was pragmatic and directed to listeners' needs.[183]

Oliverio bases the ethos of early Pentecostalism upon four core interpretive assumptions, that, in his opinion, explain its orientation.[184] The first is that the Protestant Scriptures were the sole, ultimate authority for Christian belief and living, which functioned dialogically with the religious and general experiences of early Pentecostals to form a theological understanding of their world and circumstances. Second is the restorationist beliefs, centering on the narrative of God's plan for humankind coming to pass with the outpouring of the Spirit in the latter rain. Third is the fourfold or fivefold "Full Gospel," which served as the doctrinal grid, which oriented pentecostal beliefs and living, and as doctrinal hypotheses, which explained Scripture and spiritual experiences. And lastly, a

---

182. In its early days, Pentecostals did not refer to a "sermon," as explained above. The term was limited to the formal mode of speech they connected with established denominations and professional ministers. Pentecostals expected that the preacher would bring a charismatic "message from the heart of God," often found in a deeper significance of the biblical text's meaning, which can only be perceived by the help of the Spirit (Anderson, *Introduction to Pentecostalism*, 223). In order to receive the message, it was not as important to exegete a text from the Bible than to pray, experience the anointing of the Spirit, meet God in an encounter, and hear directly the voice of the Spirit. The historical-critical approach to reading the text was held as especially suspicious because it was perceived to reflect human efforts to interpret God's word (Byrd, "Paul Ricoeur's Hermeneutical Theory," 203–5), and the uncritical adoption of these methods leads to a denial of the theological insights of early Pentecostalism (Studebaker, "Book Review," 376). Oliverio discusses the use of historical-critical methods by some Pentecostals, leading to his distinction of a "contemporary evangelical-pentecostal hermeneutic," with proponents like James Railey, Benny Akker, Stanley Horton, Gordon Anderson, David Bernard, Gordon Fee, and, to a certain degree, Roger Stronstad and William and Robert Menzies (Oliverio, *Theological Hermeneutics*, 133–84). It includes a range of approaches, such as those that affirm the inerrancy of the Bible as the starting point for interpreting God, the self and the world, those who affirm the authority of the Bible but who are more philosophically engaged in the hermeneutical debates over meaning in the biblical texts, and those who find a crucial place for the presence of the Spirit for the proper interpretation of biblical texts. The first looks to the texts as the word of God, the second to the authors (and editors) of the biblical texts for their intention, and the third to the reader's relationship to the Spirit in interpretation. It is an open question whether a distinction (such as Oliverio makes) for a contemporary evangelical-pentecostal hermeneutic is justified in terms of the proponents that he identifies.

183. Wacker, *Heaven Below*, 10.

184. Oliverio, *Theological Hermeneutics*, 231–34.

pragmatic, naive realism formed early pentecostal rationality, integrated with an understanding of the primacy of the supernatural.[185]

For them, the Bible served as the inspired Word of God, determining doctrine and lifestyle through the mediation of the Spirit. Scripture had epistemic primacy and merited epistemic priority over doctrinal statements, serving as the optimal resource for verifying or falsifying its claims.[186] When they read the Bible, in most instances, they probably did not recognize the historical distance between contemporary believers and the text. They did not read the text in terms of its social-cultural and historical setting but as though it were written for their situation. It was important to read the Bible as literally as possible, taking it at face value.[187] In the process, the distance between the original context of Scripture and the context of the reader was collapsed.[188] They searched the Bible for all scriptural references to a particular subject and then synthesized those references into a theological statement. It is a harmonizing and deductive method.[189]

Difficult texts were given a new lease on life and applied to their own context by way of allegory, anagogy, typology,[190] or tracing hidden,

185. The tacit realism that presupposes direct correspondence between early Pentecostals' theological views and the realities to which these articulations pointed led to an absolutism which, in the decades following the Azusa Street Revival, resulted in the splintering of the movement into many groups and denominations (Oliverio, *Theological Hermeneutics*, 32). Oliverio discusses the classical Pentecostal hermeneutic at the hand of four early Pentecostal leaders: Charles Fox Parham, William Joseph Seymour, Charles Harrison Mason, and Garfield Thomas Haywood (Oliverio, *Theological Hermeneutics*, 51–77).

186. Keener, *Spirit Hermeneutics*, 104. What is important is that Christians grant epistemic priority to what the exegesis of Scripture reveals rather than to the church's tradition.

187. Archer, *Pentecostal Hermeneutic*, 65–66. To read the Bible literally implies that "it means what it says" (Boone, *Bible Tells Them So*, 13).

188. Martin, "Introduction to Pentecostal Biblical Hermeneutics," 3, and Carson, *Exegetical Fallacies*, 127.

189. Archer, *Pentecostal Hermeneutic*, 102.

190. Spittler, "Scripture and the Theological Enterprise," 75–77. Thomas Aquinas refers to the anagogic power of Scripture, that is, its capacity to edify and inspire (Davies, "What Does it Mean to Read?," 254). Luther was not impressed with the allegorical meaning of Scripture and described allegories as empty speculations, the scum of Holy Scriptures, awkward, absurd, invented, obsolete, and loose rags. Calvin called it a contrivance of Satan and emphasized the need that an interpreter should let the author say what he does say, instead of attributing to him what we think he ought to say (Kaiser and Silva, *Introduction to Biblical Hermeneutics*, 270).

spiritual meanings in the text.[191] What was important was not to provide believers with a lot of information about God; what was more essential was that people experienced an encounter with God in the same terms as described by biblical witnesses. Believers learned how to verbalize their experience of encounters with God in order to become witness to the pentecostal truth by way of biblical witnesses. They learned the vocabulary of their testimonies from the Bible.[192] To know God was to stand in a relationship with God rather than to have information about God. When you witnessed about God, you talked about your encounter with God in your testimony.[193] They also understood history in a positivist sense; historical (and scientific) "facts" provided in the Bible were undeniably true because it was contained in the Bible, the word of God.[194] That it was written in the Bible guaranteed its truth. They utilized a specific scopus to interpret the Bible, either the fourfold Full Gospel pre-understanding

191. McKay, "When the Veil is Taken Away," 63. See Tenney, *New Testament Survey*, for how to read the Bible in a devotional way: with a spirit of eagerness, which seeks the mind of God, a spirit of humility, which listens to the voice of God, a spirit of adventure, which pursues earnestly the will of God, and a spirit of adoration, which rests in the presence of God (Kaiser and Silva, *Introduction to Biblical Hermeneutics*, 214).

192. Plüss, "Azusa and Other Myths," 191. It should be emphasized that the Bible contains a record of testimonies of the relationship between God and God's creation. Therefore, the Bible is ideally positioned to serve as a corrective for experience (Ellington, "Pentecostalism and the Authority of Scriptures," 162).

193. Ellington, "Pentecostals and the Authority of Scriptures," i–viii. Cartledge mentions that a testimony has a coordinating function that brings together other sources of knowledge (perception, memory, introspection, and reason) and expresses them in a narrative shape. It is an auto-ethnographic description of observations and experiences (Cartledge, "Locating the Spirit," 259).

194. The positive side is that history is taken seriously as history by a pentecostal hermeneutic. Because the present age can share in the experience and power of that of the first century CE, it is relevant to inquire what actually happened then. Correlation between then and now became significant enough to read the text closely to understand its socio-political and economic realities. Identification was not total and absolute and Pentecostals recognized the many real and challenging discontinuities between the New Testament era and the present day. In essence, Pentecostals strove for closer identification with the One propagated by the early church, as attested by the texts they left behind. Commonality was of discipleship and experience rather than of historical coincidence (Clark, "Investigation into the Nature," 181). Pentecostals described church history in terms of a progressive restoration, leading from Wycliffe and Luther, who restored Scripture and justification by faith, through Wesley, who restored the doctrine of sanctification, and on to the present pentecostal revival, which was understood to have restored the doctrine of Spirit baptism and the *charismata* (Albrecht and Howard, "Pentecostal Spirituality," 246–47).

of Jesus—as savior, baptizer, sanctifier, and soon coming king[195]—or the fivefold Gospel of Christ—as savior, healer, sanctifier, baptizer, and coming king—that forms the central defining characteristic of the Pentecostal movement.[196] Jesus at the center of pentecostal theology was the theological grid that provided a firm interpretive lens for the fluid Pentecostal community and their reading of Scripture.[197] In the early worship services, most participants were uneducated and poor, functioning at the edge of society and experiencing revilement and rejection for what many perceived as their emotionalist ways of worshiping,[198] functioning primarily as an oral culture.[199] They did not do theology in a standard Western mode but rather through their songs, poems, testimonies, and dances.[200]

However, as argued before, early Pentecostals did not interpret the Bible in fundamentalist manner[201] because they did not ascribe authority to the Bible due to its inerrancy or infallibility but rather its utility of showing the way to a personal encounter with God.[202] Pentecostal theol-

---

195. Menzies, "Methodology of Pentecostal Theology," 14, and Tomberlin, *Pentecostal Sacraments*, 35–53. The five theological motifs are: justification by faith in Christ; sanctification by faith as a second definitive work of grace; healing of the body as provided for all in the atonement; the premillennial return of Christ; and the baptism in the Holy Spirit, evidenced by speaking in tongues (Kärkkäinen, *Pneumatology*, 91). Kärkkäinen suggests that the "prophethood of all believers" should be added as a sixth motif (see Land, *Pentecostal Spirituality*, 18).

196. Lewis, "Reflections of a Hundred Years of Pentecostal Theology," 1–25, and Nel, "Pentecostals' Reading of the Old Testament," 526–27.

197. Archer, *Pentecostal Hermeneutic*, 137.

198. Spittler, "Scripture and the Theological Enterprise," 75. Pentecostals were rejected by fundamentalists, the holiness bodies from which they came, and all the established denominations of their day, forcing them to carve out their own path in isolation (Menzies and Menzies, *Spirit and Power*, 328).

199. Martin, "Hearing the Voice of God," 219.

200. Hollenweger, *Pentecostalism*, 269–72.

201. See Hollenweger, "From Azusa Street," and Lewis, "Reflections of a Hundred Years," 8.

202. Ellington, "Pentecostals and the Authority of Scriptures," 17. Cox agrees that it is a serious mistake to equate Pentecostals with fundamentalists (Cox, *Fire from Heaven*, 15). While fundamentalists attach unique authority to the letter of the verbally inspired Scripture, they are suspicious of the Pentecostals' subjective stress on the immediate experience of the Spirit of God. While the beliefs of fundamentalists are enshrined in formal theological systems, Pentecostals embed their beliefs in testimonies, ecstatic speech, and bodily movement. But Pentecostals do practice theology, with a full-blown religious cosmos and an intricate system of symbols that respond to the

ogy was a theological trajectory that emerged from nineteenth-century evangelicalism rather than from twentieth-century fundamentalism.[203] Cox's definition of pentecostal theology is correct, stressing general worldview over systematic comprehension and rightness of logic.[204] He includes moral and emotional values alongside cognitive matters, suggesting that pentecostal theology ought to be conceived of in terms of the symbolic cosmos of the Pentecostal movement. Pentecostal theology flourishes in the context of song, prayer, sermon, and testimony, and not in the format of lengthy treatises.

Early Pentecostals embodied the trajectory of American evangelicalism that emphasized the spiritual exercise of experience and piety, an innovative process of resourcing tradition and constructing a new and hybrid theological foundation.[205] They viewed the Bible as a single, unified narrative of God's redemptive plan, a grand, unified story that led them to utilize intertextuality as a justifying mark of a faithful reading.[206] They appreciated the narrative quality of Scripture because it allowed

---

perennial questions of human meaning and value. The difference is that Pentecostals sing and pray their theology, put it in pamphlets to distribute on street corners, and proclaim it enthusiastically. For instance, Pentecostals refer to the Spirit in terms of the symbols of wind, water, and fire, symbols that are typologically revealed in the cloud which sat over the people of Israel in the wilderness (Exod 13:21–22). These elements are, however, not only life-giving and preserving; they also have a destructive capacity (Yong, *Spirit-Word-Community*, 44).

203. Studebaker, "Book Review," 375.

204. Cox, *Fire from Heaven*, 201.

205. Archer notes the type of questions that early Pentecostals typically asked from the Bible during their spiritual exercises: What does the Spirit intend with the passage in light of the redemption provided in Christ? How are we to appropriate or embody a particular theological practice as a faith community or as individuals? What kind of spiritual practices are necessary in order to carry out the message? How does this passage challenge or affirm other passages that address similar concerns, beliefs, and practices? And how am I being impacted by the biblical narrative? See Archer, "Pentecostal Biblical Interpretation," 180.

206. Green, "'Treasures Old and New,'" 15. Maier's remarks about faith as an aid to understanding is relevant here (Maier, *Biblical Hermeneutics*, 51–53). It is "thoroughly unnatural," in his opinion, to deny the Christian faith in the process of interpreting the Bible. To divest one of the encounter with Christ and prior Christian background in order to do critical research is unscientific. The scientific way is to examine one's own pre-judgments and pre-decisions and to render them fruitful. It is also not desirable to detach faith and love for God's word from the person doing biblical research. A distinction should therefore be made between the regenerate and unregenerate interpreter. The theologian needs to be familiar with the *oratorio-meditatio-tentatio* (prayer-meditation-struggle) sequence.

them to become part of the biblical story of God's involvement in the world.[207] For that reason, I proposed elsewhere that Pentecostals should develop literary perceptivity in interpreting the Bible because of their interest in biblical narratives.[208] They should read these narratives not only as "literature" or as texts that should be analyzed; rather, they should read them looking for insights and encouragement in their ongoing campaign for the sake of the kingdom.[209] They should further develop skills to read narratives as literature in order to enable them to read and reflect critically.[210] The skills of structural analysis and narratological synthesis can be helpful.

Early Pentecostals did not look at the Bible from the outside; they had entered the world of the Bible, and the world of the Bible shaped their world.[211] It is in the nature of narratives that they have the potential to engage and change readers. Their daily charismatic experiences altered their epistemology, giving them existential awareness of the miraculous in the biblical worldview and appreciating the influence of the Spirit.[212] Their own experiences of the supernatural affirmed and supported the truthfulness of the supernatural components of the biblical story and suggested a broader approach to knowing the truth; the Spirit who had inspired the Bible moved in them to reveal the meaning of Scripture as

207. Because the central message of Christianity is the epic story of redemption, the bulk of Scripture consists in the form of narrative (Pinnock, "Work of the Holy Spirit," 245).

208. Nel, "'He Changes Times and Seasons,'" 15–21.

209. Cox, *How to Read the Bible*, 10. Cox's remark here is motivated by his observation that academically trained biblical researchers often try to distance themselves from any personal stake they might have in what they discover in the Bible, arguing that, to be objective, their personal life should not have any bearing on their research (Cox, *How to Read the Bible*, 11). Any pretense of total objectivity should be set apart as illusory and self-serving. See also Green, "'Treasures Old and New,'" 15.

210. Interest in the narrative aspects of biblical texts goes back a long way in the history of interpretation, and, in recent years, there has been a rediscovery of narrative and story in both biblical studies and theology (see Frei, *Eclipse of Biblical Narrative*). This is part of a wider cultural movement, demonstrating a disenchantment with things abstract, rationalistic, cerebral, didactic, intellectualist, structured, prosaic, scientistic, and technocratic, with a new appeal of the concrete, affective, intuitive, spontaneous, and poetic, which contribute to the story focus (Fackre, "Narrative Theology," 342). The remarkable growth of Bible study groups on a grassroots level may be connected to this trend, as part of a protest against the separation of expert and layman, theological scholar and church member (West, *Biblical Hermeneutics of Liberation*, 63).

211. Pinnock, "Work of the Holy Spirit," 246.

212. Ervin, "Hermeneutics: A Pentecostal Option," 24.

well.[213] Their view of the Bible as lived story allowed them to utilize narrative parts of the Bible for theologizing; some biblical narratives became examples that the church should follow (supported by their interpretation of 1 Cor 10:11, 1 Pet 2:21, John 12:14, and 1 Pet 2:21).[214] Narratives were understood literally, taken to be repeatable, and the experience of biblical characters were seen as something to be emulated.[215] For Pentecostals, the biblical story had its beginning, center, and goal in Jesus Christ. The Old Testament was read Christologically, often using allegory and typology to find Christ in the ancient texts. Early Pentecostals also believed that the work of the Spirit was to restore the last-days church to its primitive capacity, and that the activity of the Spirit, including interpreting the Bible for contemporary readers, occurred in the church. God's presence legitimated the community as the people of God; it was not feasible to belong to God without belonging to God's people. The eschatological expectations of early Pentecostals compelled them to an urgent pursuit of world evangelization. For them, the Bible functioned primarily to form and equip the church for its mission of evangelization, providing the content of their message to the world. They read the Bible with an end result in mind.[216]

Although the Bible served for them as the standard to define faith and practice,[217] their angle to define doctrine was on the basis of their ex-

213. Their view of "illumination" goes beyond the Reformed concept to allow for an element of divine revelation. It is also true that Pentecostals do not acquiesce to the evangelical doctrine of *sola Scriptura* because the revelation of God is not transmitted to new generations by Scripture alone, but by the work of the Holy Spirit (Waddell, *Spirit of the Book of Revelation*, 127). Kaiser and Silva calls the doctrine of *sola Scriptura* the formal principle of the Protestant Reformation, while *sola fide* and *sola gratia* constituted the material principles (Kaiser and Silva, *Introduction to Biblical Hermeneutics*, 270).

214. Narrative texts are notoriouosly difficult to interpret theologically. See Dayton, *Theological Roots*, 22.

215. Nel, "Pentecostals' Reading," 527. Although Pentecostalism did not invent anything which was completely new and unique, few, if any, other Christian churches today take the New Testament accounts of experiences of a lived relationship with God and empowerment by the Spirit for ministry so literally as the Pentecostals (Ellington, "Pentecostalism and the Authority of Scripture," 153).

216. See Martin, "Introduction to Pentecostal Biblical Hermeneutics," 4–8, for a description of the early pentecostal hermeneutical paradigm.

217. Reading the biblical narrative with faith means reading it as true, making the boundaries between the narrative world and one's own world permeable. The God of the Bible is one's God. Especially early Pentecostals saw themselves as living in the continuation of "Bible days." Charles Parham and others in the movement assumed that

periences with the God who utilized the Bible to reveal Godself through God's Spirit.[218] Doctrine was defined experientially in terms of the Bible. Canonical texts were "measuring sticks" and not texts to be exploited for ideological agendas.[219] A pentecostal hermeneutics denied a variety of readings that seek to use Scripture in ways that run contrary to its implied design, such as irresponsible readings that seek to abuse the authority of biblical texts instead of honoring them.[220]

There is a consensus that early pentecostal hermeneutics is characterized as oral, charismatic, largely ahistorical and minimally contextual, literal in its interpretations, morally and spiritually absolutizing, pragmatic, and pastoral. It differs from fundamentalism in several other ways as well.[221] Kraus helpfully outlines the major distinctions as follows: Pentecostalism is charismatic while fundamentalism is didactic; Pentecostalism is Wesleyan/Arminian while fundamentalism is Calvinistic; Pentecostals emphasize the *charismata* that provide assurance while, for fundamentalists, inerrant Scripture provides assurance; Pentecostalism is experience-centered while fundamentalism is theology-centered; in Pentecostalism, non-rational elements are recognized while, for fundamentalists, the rational message is emphasized; for Pentecostals, the church serves as a community while, for fundamentalists, the church serves as a non-denominational fellowship; Pentecostals make a separation between

---

Christian experience today should match that reported in Acts (see Nel, "Pentecostal Movement's View of the Continuity.")

218. Pentecostals understand and utilize doctrine in a fundamentally different way from most other traditions which are grounded in rationalist models of considering the question of the authority of Scripture. For Pentecostals, doctrine is not essentially *generative* in function; it is rather descriptive, because they utilize doctrine to describe and verbalize lived experience. Formal deductive doctrinal statements are for Pentecostals an attempt to organize and understand described experience and not an attempt to serve as proof for those things which lie completely outside the realm of experience (Ellington, "Pentecostalism and the Authority of Scriptures," 150). Pentecostals base their faith first on the God that they have met and only then do they attempt to articulate their experiences in normative, doctrinal ways.

219. Keener defines "canon" as the minimal revelation that all of us agree on as the measuring stick for testing other claims to revelation (Keener, *Spirit Hermeneutics*, 107–8). If Scripture is our measuring stick, then it does matter what God inspired it to mean, implying that Christians would take the trouble to understand its intended meaning. Especially if the divinely commissioned and inspired message of Jesus is to be valued (Keener, *Spirit Hermeneutics*, 111).

220. Keener, *Spirit Hermeneutics*, 188–89.

221. Oliverio, *Theological Hermeneutics*, 51.

church and state while, for fundamentalists, the Christian nation and church are cognate; and Pentecostals, with their holiness ethic, strive for separation from the world, while fundamentalists, with their born-again ethic, see themselves as justified within the world.[222]

What is also important to note is that, while fundamentalists accept the cessasionist view that the supernatural should be ensconced in the past and bracketed off from the present, the essence of pentecostal spirituality is the charismatic experience of Spirit baptism, leading to the expectation of the miracle-working intervention of God in the present-day church.[223] Pentecostal spirituality is hardwired to perceive and respond to the influences of the Spirit.[224] Ironically, fundamentalism shares with modernism the elimination of the supernatural from the contemporary experience of faith[225]; fundamentalists affirm the supernatural in theory

222. Kraus, "Great Evangelical Coalition," 58–59.

223. Pentecostals do not think to replicate every kind of experience found in Scripture. Many events described in Scripture are one-time events, such as the experience of David, Mary (the mother of Jesus), or the prophets. That does not imply that we cannot learn lessons from their lives and characters. In cases of supernatural interventions described in the Bible, Pentecostals do not expect that God would intervene in their situations in exactly the same way, but the biblical narratives encourage them to expect that God will intervene in some or other immediate way.

224. Albrecht and Howard, "Pentecostal Spirituality," 240.

225. It is ironic because modernist Bible interpretation in the form of the historical-critical methods generally practices a functional atheism, separating the text from the streams of existence and objectifying it, making the biblical text into an abstract object without any ready applications to practical situations or daily use (Ellington, "Pentecostalism and the Authority of Scriptures," 164). The historical-critical method functions on the premise that outside interference and arbitrary divine intervention is unconditionally excluded. These and other observations about contemporary Western methods of biblical interpretation illustrate the bankruptcy of biblical scholarship, which is founded largely or entirely on a rationalist understanding of faith and God. As long as "objective distance" implies the objectification of the Bible, it must remain non-relational in nature and therefore limited in its application (Ellington, "Pentecostalism and the Authority of Scriptures," 169). Pentecostal scholarship is to counteract what it perceives to be the bankruptcy of a biblical scholarship based exclusively on cerebral cognition (Vondey, *Pentecostalism*, 125–28). Pentecostal scholarship is experiential, and an encounter with the Spirit is of central importance for the Christian life. It is an attempt to articulate this normative encounter with God in the diverse forms, methods, and vocabulary of the scholarly and scientific communities. It operates on the principle of play, of "pure means" or "pure self-presentation," rather than performance-oriented and utilitarian categories of traditional scholarship under the tyranny of rationalism and seriousness. In an important sense, pentecostal scholarship is also always embodied, going beyond the mere intellectual pursuit of knowledge to include holistic modes of learning and being. Finally, pentecostal scholarship is based

and in events described in the Bible, but deny its present-day revelation in practice. "Pentecostalism, as a whole, was just too physical and too lacking in philosophical rationality for most fundamentalists to give it a positive look."[226]

Fundamentalists view God's relation to the world in constant, unchanging terms; Pentecostals experience the relation as dynamic and progressive. For fundamentalists, the truth was delivered in the Bible and the Bible represents a closed canon; Pentecostals expect that God would reveal the truth in the present moment on an ongoing basis. The primary task of fundamentalists is to defend the absolutely essential foundation and criterion of truth given once and for all in the Bible[227]; Pentecostals accept that God's character is unchanging and constant, however, God is passionately involved in the history of human affairs, representing the apocalyptic worldview favored by the Jesus of the Gospels.[228] Truth is still unfolding because the Spirit reveals Christ in new situations and contexts at the hand of the biblical testimony. While Pentecostals respect the Bible as the fount of revealed truth, the Bible also functions as the road sign, showing the way to meet God in God's ongoing revelation of truth. They are not primarily concerned with the truth found in the Bible but in encountering the truth described as the word of God that reveals the Father, Jesus Christ; biblical witnesses testify to the truth and show the way to meet God, through God's Spirit. At the same time, however, it is important to state that what the Spirit has to reveal to the church is not new doctrines or new revelations which go beyond and add to what Jesus said. The Spirit will never lead the church into "new" truths but into "all" truth. The Spirit leads the church forward in history.[229] What Christ says today will not contradict what his witnesses said in Scripture. Some matters, however, need to be made more explicit and developed, and, in

---

on a comprehensive hermeneutic that, in the broadest sense, can be characterized as analogical, as a "this-is-that" hermeneutic, with interpretation of the present in terms of the past, the Christian life in terms of biblical texts, and the charismatic experience in terms of the story of Pentecost. It is this principle of analogy that defines and correlates the pentecostal interpretation of Scripture and of the contemporary world.

226. Jacobsen, *Thinking in the Spirit*, 357.

227. Barr, "Fundamentalism," 363.

228. Menzies, *Pentecost*, 13. See also discussion in chapter 4.

229. Pinnock, "Work of the Holy Spirit," 238.

this way, go beyond the text, but never contradicting the spirit/Spirit of the Bible.[230]

The Bible is viewed and respected as inspired and preserved by the Spirit with the purpose of illuminating, teaching, and transforming the lives of contemporary believers. Their purpose in reading the Bible is to find something there that can be experienced as relevant to their felt needs.[231] The Bible becomes the word, as Luther emphasized, because of the Spirit's ministry; the authority of the Spirit comes before and determines the authority accorded to the Bible.[232] The expectation is that a modern-day believer can experience existentially what the earliest apostles experienced through the working of the same Spirit[233] and accompanied by the same charismatic phenomenology that also characterized the earliest church.[234]

Early Pentecostals viewed creedalism as a sign of the petrification of historical mainline denominations where truth only existed in a historic sense[235] because they did not enjoy the Spirit baptism and the resultant Spirit's illumination when reading the Bible, while fundamentalism greatly valued the historic confessions of faith as founding the church's proclamation of biblical truth. For Pentecostals, the Bible was viewed as the all-sufficient source of God's self-revelation, and an encounter with Scripture was perceived as an encounter with God, requiring no need of any creedal formulation.[236] In the words of early pentecostal pioneers,

230. Pinnock, "Work of the Holy Spirit," 241.

231. Anderson, *Introduction to Pentecostalism*, 222.

232. Land, *Pentecostal Spirituality*, 100, 106, and Welker, "Word and Spirit," 52–79. According to John 10:35, Jesus says that Scripture cannot be loosed, unbound, unfastened, or annulled.

233. According to Martin, the apostles' hermeneutics changed when they were confronted by four new contextual factors that supplemented their standard Jewish exegetical practices: The life, teachings, and resurrection of Jesus; the gift of the Spirit poured out on the day of Pentecost; the mission of spreading the gospel, which demanded that the disciples hasten to reach the ends of the earth; and the eschatological nature of God's kingdom, which required the disciples to wait patiently for the return of Jesus (Martin, "Introduction to Pentecostal Biblical Hermeneutics," 2).

234. Ervin, "Hermeneutics," 22.

235. In the words of the early Pentecostal Bible School principal, Charles F. Parham, "The best of creeds are but the sawdust of men's opinions, stuffed in skins and feathers of truth to give them a pleasing and attractive appearance; to draw people into the support of an organized ecclesiasticism, or an individualistic propaganda" (Parham, *Kol Kare Bemidbar*, 67).

236. Arrington, "Hermeneutics," 380–81. Arrington also makes the important

theological endeavors in mainline, established churches were viewed by Pentecostals as a fence of words that prevented Christians from having to confront the living God as the One who surpasses all the church's neat formulas—and sometimes even contradicts it.[237] Theology, in part, represented the long night of theological dryness that was characterized by people being fed on the theological chips, shavings, and winds. But now, with the new pentecostal light that dawned in 1906 at Azusa Street, it had passed.[238] Dogmas and doctrine were viewed as the worn-out shells of yesterday, idols of ink and paper,[239] thankfully discarded after holding Christians in bondage for so many years.[240] Dogmas were viewed as essentially reductionistic and impersonal because they were cast in the form of inflexible doctrine.[241] What was important was not to defend truth but to advance it, through the power of the Spirit.[242]

Harvey Cox divides the population into four large spiritual or ideological blocks: scientific modernists, conventional (mainstream) religious believers, fundamentalists,[243] and proponents of experimentalism.[244] He places most Pentecostals in the last group rather than among the funda-

---

observation that a methodology that tries to make either Scripture or experience chronologically (or even logically) prior to the other should be rejected. They are always in dialogue with each other. Just the same, Scripture is prior in a normative manner. Experience is improperly used by Pentecostals when they wrongfully confuse their own spirit with the Spirit of God; Scripture and the faith community properly hold pneumatic interpretation accountable. And it is improperly used when experience becomes the basis for theology—even though it has its proper place in one's presuppositions and in confirming theological conclusions (Arrington, "Hermeneutics," 384). Fee and Stuart's remark that Scripture is to be considered the penultimate authority is more in line with pentecostal hermeneutic (Fee and Stuart, *How to Read the Bible*, 32); God is the ultimate authority, although the Bible carries its own authority since God communicates and reveals Godself through it.

237. Parham, *Kol Kare Bemidbar*, 66.

238. Spurling, *Lost Link*, 22.

239. Pinnock, "Work of the Holy Spirit," 247.

240. Kenyon, *Identification*, 63.

241. Ellington, "Pentecostalism and the Authority of Scriptures," 162. By building faith on doctrine rather than personal experience one builds on a singularly unstable foundation.

242. Jacobsen, "Knowing the Doctrines of Pentecostals," 104.

243. The fact is that Pentecostalism was, for the better part of its history, largely ignored by mainstream scholarship and neglected as a subject matter. It was even ridiculed as a dialogue partner by scientific modernists, conventional religious believers, and fundamentalists alike (Vondey, *Pentecostalism*, 122).

244. Cox, *Fire from Heaven*, 81.

mentalists, arguing that Pentecostalism enjoys its current phenomenal growth[245] because it has somehow reached beyond the levels of creed and ceremony, cognizant of a cerebral religion, into the realm of "primal spirituality," defined in terms of the search for connection with the pre-cognitive core impulse of human life that had been evident in several influential cultural movements during the last century.[246] Pentecostals have a penchant for experience combined with the rejection of the notion that a coherent and comprehensive vision of God, themselves, and the world may exist. Faith is rather a spiritual bricolage, an eclectic, pulled-together bundle of ideas and practices that helps people to traverse the spiritual journey pragmatically.[247] Their faith reaches beneath, around, and beyond currently available language to help people deal with deep human experiences that defy translation into rational speech. *Glossolalia* fulfills the function in terms of their spirituality to verbalize the relation-ship with God who is unknowable. Pentecostal spirituality places equal value on the affective, moral, and doctrinal (or cerebral) dimensions of faith—that is, feeling, action, and belief.[248] Scripture is read not only with the mind but also with the affective-spiritual dimensions of existence. It is only through exegesis of the Spirit of God of the spirit of believers that true understanding and appropriation of Scripture is possible, leading

245. Pentecostalism is often treated by sociologists and other scientists as an anom-aly rather than the religious future. As a practical religious reality, however, Pentecos-talism has countered the three modes of secularity spelled out by Charles Taylor in *Secular Age*, consisting of secularization in the public place of religion, actual religious belief, and plausibility conditions of religious belief (see also Oliverio, "Book Review," 131). Pentecostalism has provided a counternarrative to the mainstream stories of Western secularization concerning all three modes of secularism.

246. Cox, *Fire from Heaven*, 117. Cox defines "primal spirituality" in terms of three dimensions: primal speech, the ecstatic utterance of "speaking in tongues," or "pray-ing in the Spirit"; primal piety, consisting of phenomena like visions, healing, dreams, dance, and other archetypal religious expressions; and primal hope, as the millennial outlook consisting of the insistence that a radically new world age is about to dawn.

247. Cox, *Fire from Heaven*, 304–5.

248. See the critique of Johns that, for a pentecostal service to be successful, there are two prerequisites: The Holy Spirit needs to be present in a palpable and emotional way, and there has to be some form of seizure—God has to take control. Johns is correct in the sense that Pentecostals' religion is concerned with affection; however, the worship service is still mostly driven by rational elements. The term "seizure" is used by the author as a synonym of "ecstasy," without qualifying the relation between "seizure" and some psychiatric illnesses (Johns, *Pentecostal Paradigm*, 18). Pentecos-tals do not typically emphasize loss of consciousness or self in the divine (Neumann, "Spirituality," 197).

to the desired transformation.[249] Theology is defined as more than the intellectual, an option that many postmodern people find attractive.[250]

As stated already, after 1945, it became imperative for Pentecostals to improve their status. When the Evangelicals accepted them,[251] they established Bible Schools to train pastors in Evangelicals' fundamentalist-literalist way of reading the Bible and utilizing the textbooks written by conservative Evangelicals.[252] They rejected any criticism of the Bible, ascribing the lax morals in some churches to the influence of modern theologians in destroying the faith of ordinary Christians.

Since the 1970s, more and more Pentecostals ventured into the academy of theology,[253] eventually leading to the establishment of theological colleges, seminaries, and a debate about pentecostal hermeneutics with a strong pneumatic element in order to authentically account for the pentecostal ethos and tendencies.[254] Oliverio confides how he and many of his fellow pentecostal scholars found the original classical pentecostal hermeneutics to be a hermeneutics that interprets Scripture and the rest of life anew in a manner that could create a new Christian tradition of classical Pentecostalism.[255] In describing the pentecostal method of interpretation as essentially pneumatic or charismatic, the necessity is emphasized that the interpreter relies on the Spirit's illumination of the biblical text in order to come to the fullest understanding of the biblical text.[256]

249. Martin, "Spirit and Flesh in the Doing of Theology," 5–31.

250. Jacobsen, *Thinking in the Spirit*, 362.

251. Jacobsen, "Knowing the Doctrines of Pentecostals," 90–107.

252. Jacobsen, *Thinking in the Spirit*, 356.

253. It is true that many pentecostal scholars who entered the academy were required to abandon their ethos, oral culture, and emphasis on experience to adopt the modes of logic, reason, and linear thought that characterized Western biblical scholarship. Those who accepted the Western Enlightenment model either forsook their pentecostal tradition entirely and remained in the Pentecostal church—but aligned themselves with evangelical fundamentalism or a rationalistically framed reaction against "liberalism," accepting an evangelical hermeneutic and separating their scholarly life from their spiritual life—or adopted an elitist mentality of "enlightened" Pentecostalism, attempting to retain their connection to Pentecostalism but no longer embracing its ethos (Martin, "Hearing the Voice of God," 220).

254. Lewis, "Reflections of a Hundred Years of Pentecostal theology," 10, and Oliverio, "Introduction," 3. For a survey of the debate surrounding the issue of pentecostal hermeneutics, see the Fall 1993 and Spring 1994 issues of *Pneuma*, the journal of the Society of Pentecostal Studies.

255. Oliverio, "Book Review," 1.

256. Arrington, "Pentecostal Identity," 16.

This method reaches beyond the literal meaning of the text. Arrington explains in what way the pneumatic interpreter relies on the Spirit to come to a full understanding of the biblical text: a personal experience of faith as part of the entire interpretive process; submission of the mind to God so that the critical and analytical abilities are exercised under the guidance of the Spirit; a genuine openness to the Spirit as the text is examined prayerfully; and a relevant response to the transforming call of God's word is necessary.[257]

The meaning of the biblical message for contemporary people cannot be explained apart from the Spirit. 1 Corinthians 2:9–10 explains at the hand of a quotation, "What no eye has seen, nor ear heard, nor the human heart conceived, what God has prepared for those who love him," that God has revealed such things to contemporary readers through the Spirit, for the Spirit searches everything—even the depths of God. While anyone with sufficient rational faculties and skills can glean truth from the Bible, real insights that transform the lives of present-day readers come from faith and the Spirit.[258]

A significant part of members and pastors of the classical Pentecostal movement, however, still read the Bible in fundamentalist fashion.[259] For that reason, they prefer to use the King James Version,[260] and, in South Africa, the Afrikaans Ou Vertaling, leading to a divergence between members, pastors, and some theologians.[261]

Very early in pentecostal history, a turn to an evangelical-pentecostal hermeneutics developed—even before the 1940s—when Pentecostals looked for alliances with Evangelicals due to an uneasy relationship between Pentecostals and fundamentalists-dispensationalists.[262] Oliverio identifies three major subtypes of this hermeneutics: one focusing on the principle of inerrancy, another on author-centered hermeneu-

257. Arrington, "Pentecostal Identity," 18. See also Cox, *How to Read the Bible*, 217.

258. Arrington, "Pentecostal Identity," 18.

259. See, for instance, the results of research into the Bible reading practices within the AFM of SA discussed in chapter 1, which found that 66 percent of those who completed the questionnaire believe everything that the Bible says is true and 67 percent believe that the entire Bible is the inspired Word of God. See Nel, "Bible Reading Practices in the AFM."

260. The King James Version is still the most read English translation in the twenty-first century (Zylstra, "Most Popular," 1); see also Altany ("Biblical Criticism," 64).

261. Lederle, *Treasures Old and New*, 162; Cargal, "Beyond the Fundamentalist-Modernist Controversy," 179; and Lewis, "Reflections of a Hundred Years," 10.

262. Oliverio, *Theological Hermeneutics*, 317.

tic theory, and another on a pneumatic version.[263] Oliverio divides the hermeneutical developments since the 1970s in different streams: the contemporary evangelical-pentecostal hermeneutics, the contextual-pentecostal hermeneutics, the postmodern contextual-pentecostal critique, and the ecumenical-pentecostal hermeneutics.[264] The contextual-pentecostal hermeneutics is a critique of the evangelical-pentecostal hermeneutics and engagement with current concerns in philosophical hermeneutics such as the issues of the author's intention, the force of the interpreter's own context, and what counts as a text (associated with the work of Martin Heidegger, Hans-Georg Gadamer, Jacques Derrida, Richard Rorty, and Paul Ricoeur).[265] Pentecostal scholars such as Richard D. Israel, Daniel E. Albrecht, Randal G. McNally, Timothy B. Cargal, Joseph Byrd, Jean-Daniel Plüss, Murray W. Dempster, Samuel Solivan (and his development of an ethnic contextual-pentecostal theological hermeneutics), John C. Thomas and Kenneth J. Archer[266] (with their narrative and communitarian approaches to pentecostal hermeneutics), Amos Yong (with his trinitarian-pneumatological approach), and James K. A. Smith (with his creational hermeneutics participated in the conversation). A last major hermeneutics in Oliverio's typology is the ecumenical-pentecostal hermeneutics, in continuity with the ecumenical impulse and sentiment that characterized the early Pentecostal movement,[267] whose charismatic spirituality included believers from diverse Christian traditions,[268] but was in discontinuity with the institutional forms of classical Pentecos-

---

263. These subdivisions seem to me to be subjectivistic, inviting researchers rather to keep the hermeneutic type together.

264. Oliverio, *Theological Hermeneutics*, 133–34. Oliverio acknowledges that his typology—based on and inspired by Henry May's typological interpretation of the four forms the Enlightenment took in America (Studebaker, "Book Review," 375)—is not the only legitimate categorization of or the only proper angle for approaching the development of pentecostal theology, nor that it is comprehensive. Rice is correct in stating that Oliverio works almost exclusively from the view of historiography of North American classical Pentecostalism, although it might be true that there are interfaces with other traditions such as African Pentecostalism due to globalization and glocalization (Rice, "Book Review," 1).

265. Oliverio, *Theological Hermeneutics*, 186.

266. Yong refers to the Cleveland School, with the contributions of Moore and Thomas of the Pentecostal Holiness Church in Cleveland, TN, who established the *Journal of Pentecostal Theology* and write about pentecostal hermeneutics and spirituality (Yong, *Hermeneutical Spirit*, 8).

267. See Nel, "Pentecostal Ecumenical Impulses."

268. Studebaker, "Book Review," 376.

talism that emerged and became dominant throughout the twentieth century, associated with the work of Ernest S. Williams and Cecil M. Robeck, Frank D. Macchia (with an expansion of the boundaries of Spirit baptism, Veli-Matti Kärkkäinen (with his development of consensual doctrines), Simon Chan (with a call for pentecostal "traditioning"), and Koo Dong Yun (with a dialectical approach to Spirit baptism). Williams (1885–1981) experienced Spirit baptism at Azusa Street and became a dialectician in the tradition of David du Plessis and Donald Gee with his three-volume *Systematic Theology*, while Robeck served as co-chair of the Fourth (1990–1997) and Fifth (1998–2006) Phases of the International Roman Catholic-Pentecostal Dialogue, affirming an ecumenical orientation.[269] The assumption is that the Spirit has been present in the past, is doing new things in the present, and will do so in future, and, although tradition is differentiated from Scripture in its role as a source for theology, pentecostal hermeneutic tradition must always still be corrected by the Bible.[270]

In his contribution to the development of a pentecostal hermeneutics, Oliverio emphasizes that a "text" is anything that is interpreted theologically, including, *inter alia*, the Bible, the world of nature, special religious experiences, general human experience, the human self, rationality, and tradition.[271] His hermeneutics is ubiquitous and necessary for offering cogent theological accounts of our world, in line with the "linguistic turn" in twentieth-century Anglo-American analytic philosophy and a similar turn in the phenomenology of the Continental tradition.[272] It should be understood in terms of holistic paradigms, which provide, in his opinion, the best theological accounts of reality and which intertwine the ontologies implicit in hermeneutics, the specific discernments made concerning the truths of historical existence, and what has come to be the structures of the hermeneutics themselves. The pentecostal experience of God and a fruitful pentecostal theological hermeneutics draw

---

269. Oliverio, *Theological Hermeneutics*, 264–65 and 272–74.

270. Oliverio, *Theological Hermeneutics*, 311.

271. Oliverio, *Theological Hermeneutics*, 319–60.

272. Though certain universal principles were to be found in all languages, each language constituted through its grammatical form a unique manner and way of perceiving the world, leading to the Swiss Ferdinand de Saussure's distinction between language as a system (*langue*) and language as speech or utterance (*parole*). Understanding is grounded in language as the correlative of speaking (Mueller-Vollmer, "Introduction," 13–14).

upon Word, creation, culture, and tradition in the manner that and to the degree which each are graced by God. In doing so, the Spirit serves as the guide. Spirit baptism does not imply that we relate to God as an object of reflection but rather that we are baptized into God as a powerful field of experience, which opens up wonders and joys as a daily experience, requiring theological reflection.[273] It implies that Christianity is not essentially based exclusively on revelations of timeless truths, though it does include such revelations. A good hermeneutics draws together a framework that includes the history of the text, recognizes the role language plays in regard to author, text, and interpreter, and acknowledges the existence of time (and thus the contextuality and finitude of the interpreter, who operates in a tradition of interpretation), but still keeps on looking at the experience of transcendence and a transcendent God, which is the subject matter of theology, while also being aware of the communal nature of all interpretation.[274] An adequate pentecostal interpretation is not simply cognitive but also can be found in the reader's encounter with a transcendent God through the text because people do come to know God in life-transforming ways, and Scripture promotes and enables such encounters in the service of the Spirit.[275] The experience of God is the hermeneutical goal in pentecostal hermeneutics, and it is the result of careful listening to and for God's word.[276] While Protestants tend to be word-oriented, emphasizing the cognitive content of the biblical revelation and its logic-based interpretation, Pentecostals, by contrast, emphasize spirit/Spirit and the experienced reality of God in one's life and in the world, even though Protestantism and Pentecostalism also share many other similarities, such as: the priesthood of all believers, with every believer having direct access to God; the singular authority of the Bible, in contrast to tradition or church hierarchy; and salvation based on grace alone through faith alone, apart from any human effort.[277] For Protestants, the center of gravity is the word, with doctrine and scriptural teaching being central; Pentecostalism's center of gravity centers on experience, expecting the felt presence of God in a person's life as normative for a Christian life, and their experience is their creed. Although they

273. Macchia, *Baptized in the Spirit*, 56.

274. Autry, "Dimensions of Hermeneutics," 32–47.

275. Autry, "Dimensions of Hermeneutics," 50.

276. Autry, "Dimensions of Hermeneutics," 44.

277. Jacobsen, *Global Gospel*, 18–19.

embrace the message of the Bible and believe its words, they read the Bible in order to live like people whose stories are told in the Bible rather than to define doctrine or theologize about biblical issues.[278]

The role of culture, in Oliverio's view, is also important.[279] Culture consists of the cultivation of language, action, habits, gestures, and thoughts, forming the context for doing theology. The hermeneutical task is not only to recognize that culture provides the context for interpretation but also that it provides the venue of God's revelation and the place of constructive interpretive action. This always occurs in language, as illustrated in the wonderful works of God, heard in the many languages of the people who heard the disciples speaking in their own languages (Acts 2:5–11). Christianity is a translating and translated religion because of its essential task of interpretation for different cultures. At the same time, a pentecostal hermeneutical paradigm also draws upon sources from the deep well of the larger Christian tradition (see 1 Cor 11:23; 15:3; 2 Thess 2:15), consisting of the variety of ways the faith has been passed on and the ways Christian faith communities are continuing to form traditions and pass on the faith. A viable pentecostal hermeneutics should also be ecumenical, making it imperative to recognize the role of tradition. In this sense, Yong argues for a hermeneutics of ecclesial tradition that consists of tradition as past history (which is needed for a historical consciousness), tradition as present location, and tradition as the act of traditioning (which directs actions toward forming the future).[280]

Pentecostal faith is, in some sense, flexible and "postmodern," but that does not and should not mean that anything goes in a relativistic fashion. Pentecostals agree that the Bible—as the word of God—should remain the bedrock of truth, even if they allow for ongoing revelation. Extra-biblical revelation should always be measured against the guidelines provided in Scripture, and the community of faith should remain the center of discernment to protect it against the risks inherent to its subjectivism.

---

278. Jacobsen, *Global Gospel*, 35–36. William Seymour frequently told seekers that they could not be filled with the Spirit when they were caught up in "thinking thought"; they had to become like "little babes" to get the blessing. They had to set their "adult minds" aside (Jacobsen, *Global Gospel*, 36).

279. Oliverio, *Theological Hermeneutics*, 359.

280. Yong, *Spirit-Word-Community*, 265–73.

Concluding Remarks

Although the Pentecostal movement is diverse, as demonstrated by the diverse movements from which it originated, it is possible to define a valid pentecostal hermeneutical approach already functioning in its earliest days in terms of four aspects.[281] First, the Bible becomes a living word when it interprets the believer in ways that cannot be predicted or determined, leading to a transformation of the reader's life. That is the work of the Spirit and cannot be predicted. Secondly, when the believer stands in a relation with God, it leads to knowledge about God that is based on the Bible and mediated through their experiences with God; knowledge about God comes from Scripture and practical experience with God. Pentecostals do not primarily compile information about God in the Bible; the Bible anticipates what happens when God meets people. Thirdly, pentecostal hermeneutics is characterized by a democratic reading and interpretation of the Bible, where all believers witness to the truth of the Bible as it is reflected in their encounters with God. In their testimonies about their encounters with God, they utilize the vocabulary provided by biblical witnesses.[282] Lastly, the church serves as a corrective influence to discern truth and prevent individual interpretation that may lead to heresy. Believers equipped with the gift of discernment (1 Cor 12:10) protect the church from the influence of spirits foreign to Christ.

Although Pentecostals allow that each believer may interpret the Bible in terms of its common sense[283]—as do fundamentalists—they believe that the core of truth lies in an encounter with God which leads to life transformation.[284] Scripture forms a fixed reference point for the encounter with God; this is the core of pentecostal identity.[285] Their pre-critical Bible reading approach, initially shared with the Wesleyan Holiness and Keswickian movements, was an adaptation of the proof-text method, which consisted of stringing together a series of scriptural

281. Moore, "Pentecostal Approach," 12–13.

282. Some recent contributions to pentecostal hermeneutics even includes the element of testimony in the hermeneutical process; see Moore, "Deuteronomy and the Fire of God," 12–23. Moore allocates the larger part of his article to this topic and McQueen, making much of the realization of the message of Joel, particularly in terms of lament, in his own interpretation of that book (McQueen, *Joel and the Spirit*).

283. "In ninety-nine out of a hundred cases, the meaning that the plain man gets out of the Bible is the correct one" (Torrey, *Fundamentals*, 34).

284. Martin, "Pentecostalism: An Alternate Form," 59–60.

285. Johns, "Pentecostalism and the Postmodern Worldview," 75.

passages on a given topic in order to understand what God has said about the topic under investigation.[286] The focal point and primary concern of the Bible Reading Method was to synthesize the data into a doctrinal statement and thereby produce a biblical understanding concerning the topic under investigation.[287] The only textbook used was the Bible and the primary method was to read and study the Bible by taking a subject, looking up the references on that subject, and then praying for the anointing of the Spirit to open up the message in such a way as to bring necessary conviction to the students of the Bible.[288] Bible doctrines are to be believed, experienced, and practiced. Pentecostal interpretation of Scripture was always done with praxis being the goal.[289] It had three basic characteristics: it was pneumatic, experiential, and its focus was primarily on historical narratives.[290] Since the Holy Spirit had guided the writers of the Bible, so should the interpreter also seek to receive such guidance and inspiration. As there was only one true God as the embodiment of truth, so there was only one truth and, therefore, one correct interpretation of the Bible—a perspective that had the potential for causing numerous disputes and factions among Pentecostals. The relationship between experience and the interpretation of the Bible operated in a dialogical

286. Archer, *Pentecostal Hermeneutic*, 62. Brookes explains how this method of studying the Bible should be applied in a group Bible study: "Have your reader select some word, as faith, repentance, love, hope, justification, sanctification and, with the aid of a good concordance, mark down, before the time of the meeting, the references to the subject under discussion. These can be read as called for, thus presenting all the Holy Ghost has pleased to reveal on the topic" (Brookes, "Studying the Bible," 314). The assumption of proof-texting is that the Bible was equally inspired throughout (Archer, *Pentecostal Hermeneutic*, 64). Popular users of proof-texts often do not give attention to the text's contexts. However, some conservative readers did advocate inductive Bible study as well, emphasizing the need to read each book of the Bible as a whole (Keener, *Spirit Hermeneutics*, 378n4).

287. Torrey, *Fundamentals*, 102.

288. D. Wesley Myland, an early pentecostal pioneer, teaches that Scripture ought to be interpreted in a dual manner (Myland, *Latter Rain Covenant*, 3). First, Scripture should always be interpreted literally and historically, and then it should be applied spiritually and typologically. Some portions, however, require a threefold interpretive approach, moving from the literal-historical understanding through the typological-spiritual application into the prophetic-dispensational understanding of God's redemptive plan. The "latter rain covenant" is ranked third among the seven great covenants of God's purpose, and is relevant for this Gospel age.

289. Torrey, *Fundamentals*, 108.

290. Arrington, "Hermeneutics," 382–83. See also Oliverio, *Theological Hermeneutics*, 43.

manner and not as the result of linear progression. At every point, experience informed the process of interpretation, and the fruit of interpretation informed experience.

Proof-texting assumes that the Bible is equally inspired throughout and timeless in its teachings ("plenary" refers to the Bible being "fully inspired").[291] Thus, any verse of Scripture could be used as a proof to support a doctrinal position.[292] They believed in the harmony of Scripture with a gradual and progressive unfolding of truth. They accepted that the Bible cannot contradict itself on any given subject. It was possible to harmonize Scripture because everything in the Bible is in agreement with everything else, for the reason that the whole Bible was built in the thought of God. Its unity displayed the unity of the divine plan and supreme intelligence.[293]

The preferred Bible study method was the inductive-synthetic model, stressing that the Bible should be understood as a unified book before breaking it down into its individual parts.[294] The syntax, grammatical structure, and repetition of words and ideas in the text in the translated version of the Bible should receive the reader's close attention. One needed to form an overview or panoramic view of the Bible before one started investigating its different parts. The basic premise was that the Bible was an objective body of literature and one should approach it in an objective manner, consisting of objective, impartial induction. Deduction was viewed as too subjective and pre-judicial.

Pentecostal hermeneutics differs from fundamentalism in several ways. Fundamentalists believe that the supernatural should be bracketed off from the present, while Pentecostals' experience of the Spirit baptism leads them to expect supernatural intervention in their daily lives. The truth was delivered in the closed canon of the Bible for fundamentalists,

291. Efird, *How to Interpret the Bible*, 3.

292. Archer, *Pentecostal Hermeneutic*, 64.

293. Torrey, *Fundamentals*, 97–98.

294. Wilbert W. White developed the inductive method of Bible study and influenced many Bible readers. His principal goal was to train readers of the Bible in developing for themselves a way that they could independently apply to get original ideas from the text of the Bible that would help them to grow in the grace and knowledge of Jesus (Kaiser and Silva, *Introduction to Biblical Hermeneutics*, 213). Arrington emphasizes that it was inductive Bible study that led to the doctrine of the baptism of the Spirit at the turn of the twentieth century in the Parham Bible School in Topeka, Kansas and students responded to the insight by setting themselves apart in prayer for a similar experience (Arrington "Pentecostal Identity," 18).

while Pentecostals expect that God would reveal the truth in the present moment. The primary task of fundamentalists is to defend the absolutely essential foundation and criterion of truth given for once and for all in the Bible, while Pentecostals accept that God is involved in the history of their daily lives as well. They respect the Bible for its revealed truth but add that the Bible serves as the road sign showing the way to meet God. The Pentecostal movement lives in the tension of two opposing ways of viewing the Bible—a fundamentalist and pentecostal hermeneutics.

CHAPTER 2

Defining A Pentecostal Hermeneutics for Africa

Introduction

THE QUESTION IS, WHAT is distinctive about Pentecostals' reading of the Bible? In what way do Pentecostal people read the Bible so that they reach different conclusions than believers of other denominations? Is it possible to speak of a pentecostal hermeneutics? In what way does it differ from the hermeneutics found in other theological traditions, such as the Catholic, Eastern, and Reformed traditions? And how does their hermeneutics inform Pentecostals' practice?[1]

In the previous chapter, the way Pentecostals read the Bible in the early days of their existence and today was described. It was shown that, although it may seem as if Pentecostals read the Bible in a fundamentalist-literalist way, this observation is only partly correct.

In this chapter, the theme of a pentecostal hermeneutics is further developed in order to describe the distinguishing factors that define its ethos. The most significant observation is that Pentecostals' religious consciousness expects an experience or encounter between God and human beings through God's Spirit. This is supposed to happen not only in the worship service but also in the practice of Bible reading, whether individually or collectively, as well as in the part of the worship service where a message is proclaimed. They read and proclaim the message in the light of their experience of the repetition of the day of Pentecost.

---

1. The chapter is partly based on Nel, "Attempting to Define a Pentecostal Hermeneutics."

Because they have received the gift of the Spirit, Pentecostals read the Bible prayerfully and with the expectation that the Spirit will explicate and apply the word to their lives.[2] The pentecostal presupposition is that the word is revealed in the Bible only when people experience God, and the existential precondition leads to a pentecostal emphasis on narratives describing similar encounters in the Bible, appreciating narratives for their theological value.[3]

Underlying the distinctive existence of different theological traditions is a specific way of reading and interpreting the Bible (hermeneutics), serving as the justification for traditions existing separately from the rest of the Christian church.[4] These different traditions have also been produced by their specific ways of reading and interpreting the Bible because the interpretation of biblical texts leads to "sense-making with existential consequences,"[5] resulting in different theologies informing the different denominations.

Hermeneutics is the unavoidable activity of interpretation, an intellectual quest to discover meaning driven by a governing question: "What does the process of interpretation involve and can it even uncover indubitable meaning?"[6] The Greek *hermeneuein* was deployed by the Greeks to refer to three basic meanings: to express aloud in words (or to vocalize), to explain, and to translate. Palmer argues that, in all three cases, something foreign, strange, and separated in time, space, or experience

---

2. This is the reason why Keener, in his important work, describes Pentecostals as reading the Bible in light of Pentecost (see Keener, *Spirit Hermeneutics*).

3. Keener, "Pentecostal Biblical Interpretation," 274.

4. See Porter and Stovell, *Biblical Hermeneutics*, for a description of five such views, comprising the historical-critical or grammatical view, the literary or postmodern view, the philosophical or theological view, the redemptive-historical view, and the canonical view. The Pentecostal movement would find itself at home somewhere on the continuum between the discussion of the last two views. The canonical hermeneutic focuses on interpreting the Bible as a Christian text, gathered together by the church and for the church (Yong, *Spirit-Word-Community*, 3) while a redemptive-historical hermeneutics emphasizes the corpus of the gospel message of Jesus Christ as summary of the Bible. Canonical exegesis is based on an understanding of the Christian Bible, including a particular canonical shape, which functions as an authoritative witness to God and God's workings in the world, and a reading of the Bible in the context of the Christian faith and the faith community (Smit, *Canonical Criticism*, 10–11).

5. Lategan, "New Testament Hermeneutics (Part I)," 13.

6. Kennedy, *Modern Introduction to Theology*, 164.

is made familiar and comprehensible.[7] It is interpreted and explained in order that the unfamiliar becomes familiar.[8]

Hermeneutical Problem

A wide variety of theoretical approaches characterize the modern hermeneutical debate,[9] summarized by Thiselton as the hermeneutics of understanding, the hermeneutics of self-involvement, the hermeneutics of metacriticism and the foundations of knowledge, the hermeneutics of suspicion and retrieval, the hermeneutics of socio-critical theory, the hermeneutics of liberation theologies and feminist theologies, the hermeneutics of reading in the context of literary theory, and the hermeneutics of reading in reader-response theories of literary meaning.[10] In discussing a pentecostal hermeneutics, it should probably be classified in the terms developed by Thiselton's categories in terms of a hermeneutics of metacriticism, where the foundations of knowledge, the basis of understanding the biblical text, and the modern reader's possible relation to the text's message are addressed.[11] Because Pentecostals read the Bible with faith that its message is true, Keener typifies it as a hermeneutics of trust.[12] The God of the Bible is their God; the Jesus of the Gospels is their risen Lord; the angels and demons that inhabit the New Testament exist in their world; and the Bible's verdict on human moral failure is what they see reflected around them continually. "Pentecostal rituals exhibit a worldview that presupposes that worship is about encountering God, including a faith in an all-powerful God," writes Anderson.[13] Reading with faith means reading biblical narratives with the expectation that God will speak or act in some way related to God's revelation in the narrative world of the Bible; it is the same God who is active in our world. "Jesus Christ is the same yesterday and today and forever," (Heb 13:8) is a text Pentecostals love to quote that underlines this sentiment. Expecting God

7. Palmer, *Hermeneutics*, 14.

8. Kaiser and Silva, *Introduction to Biblical Hermeneutics*, 37.

9. See, for example, Kaiser and Silva, *Introduction to Biblical Hermeneutics*, 275–93 for a summary of the debate.

10. See Thiselton, *New Horizons*. See also Kaiser and Silva, *Introduction to Biblical Hermeneutics*, 34.

11. Gräbe, "Hermeneutical Reflections," 14.

12. Keener, "Pentecostal Biblical Interpretation," 276.

13. Anderson, *Ends of the Earth*, 138.

to act today as God did in the Bible is closely related to what the Bible calls "faith."[14]

A pentecostal hermeneutics emphasizes three elements: the interrelationship between the Holy Spirit as the one animating Scriptures and empowering the believing community[15] with the purpose that members are equipped for ministry and witness in culturally appropriate ways.[16] In the rest of the chapter, these three elements—Spirit, Scriptures, and believing community—will be discussed in order to analyse the way Pentecostals interpret the Bible to define the distinctives of their hermeneutics.

Before it can be discussed, the hermeneutical challenge should be described. While the *Aufklärung* of the eighteenth century demanded understanding to be objective and that truth could be found by rigorous methodical exercises, the modern consensus is that all understanding is necessarily based on preconceptions or presuppositions determined by prior understanding (pre-understanding) engendered by being engaged with the matter involved.[17] Readers' prior experiences and presuppositions are all a part of the horizon within which they interpret what is read with the last influencing the present horizon (Lategan calls it the reader's "personal backpack,"[18] containing past experiences, preconceived ideas, understanding of how the world works, personal prejudices, fears, and expectations). It is necessary to be critically aware of the role played by pre-understanding although it is not necessary (or possible) to rid oneself of one's past or prejudices (*Vor-urteil*) before one can partake in the act of understanding. What is necessary, rather, is to take our prejudices— an outgrowth and function of one's historical existence[19]—into account and place them in balance, leading to the conscious act of the fusing of horizons.[20] To understand is, according to Gadamer, to confront the text

---

14. Keener, "Pentecostal Biblical Interpretation," 276.

15. See Archer, *Pentecostal Hermeneutic*.

16. Rance, "Fulfilling the Apostolic Mandate," 8.

17. Gadamer, *Wahrheit und Methode*, 278.

18. Lategan, "New Testament Hermeneutics (Part II)," 81.

19. Mueller-Vollmer, "Introduction," 38. Prejudice, according to Gadamer, is a necessary condition of all historical (and other) understanding. Acts of understanding or interpretation always involve two aspects: The overcoming of the strangeness of the phenomenon to be understood, and its transformation into an object of familiarity in which the horizon of the historical phenomenon and that of the interpreter become united.

20. Gadamer, *Wahrheit und Methode*, 289.

with the conscious awareness of one's necessary pre-understandings or one's own "horizon of expectation"[21] in order to validate or correct one's pre-understandings through the text.[22] "The ongoing cyclic process of pre-understanding—challenge—rejection or acceptance—adjustment—new self-understanding—new pre-understanding is what is understood as the 'hermeneutical circle.'"[23] The image of the hermeneutic circle has been modified and reconfigured by Osborne into a spiral,[24] which explains the hermeneutical process in a clearer way because it represents an open-ended movement from the horizon of the text to the horizon of the reader.[25] The process of interpretation consists of spiraling nearer and nearer to the text's intended meaning, as the text is allowed to continue to challenge and correct alternative interpretations, guiding the delineation to its significance for the situation today.[26] But the spiral is also a cone, not twirling upward forever with no ending in sight but rather moving ever narrower to the meaning of the text and its significance for today. It also emphasizes that the reader must be concerned not only with discovering "what Scripture means" but also experience "what the word does," with the two tasks of the hearer never to be divorced.[27] Experiencing what the text does goes hand in hand with determining what Scripture means. We need to pay attention not only to the way in which Scripture interprets *us* but also the way in which Scripture interprets *itself.*[28] Keener[29] adds that authorial intention (*Absicht) is* necessarily conditioned by probability; we often make probable inferences about the implied author from the text's literary strategies in their originating contexts.[30] Bruns makes the impor-

21. "Horizon of expectation" is a term coined by Thiselton, *New Horizons,* 61.

22. See Gräbe, "Hermeneutical Reflections," 17.

23. Lategan, "New Testament Hermeneutics (Part II)," 81.

24. Osborne, *Hermeneutical Spiral,* 22.

25. Oliverio, "Book Review," 134.

26. Carson, *Exegetical Fallacies,* 126.

27. O'Day refers to the generativity of the Bible, its capability for producing new meaning in new contexts (O'Day, "'Today this Word is Fulfilled,'" 357). Scripture does not remain static. It generates new life and meanings for itself in a community's appropriation of it.

28. Starling, *Hermeneutics as Apprenticeship,* 13.

29. Keener, *Spirit Hermeneutics,* 140.

30. Authorial intention implies that words and sentences, if used correctly, would always convey the meaning which the author intended. If a text appears obscure or ambiguous, this is because the writer did not succeed in the correct use of language, the correct explanation of terms, or in the proper construction of his arguments

tant observation that the beginnings of scriptural interpretation are to be looked for within the Bible itself.[31] The making of Scripture was a hermeneutical process in which earlier biblical material was rewritten in order to make it intelligible and applicable to later situations, implying that the Bible can be read, despite its textual heterogeneity, as a self-glossing book. One learns to study it by following the ways in which one portion of the text illuminates another, explains Bruns. In his opinion, the scribes who shaped and reshaped the biblical texts appear to have designed it to be studied in this way.

Starling[32] suggests that the metaphors of the hermeneutic circle and spiral can be supplemented by the image of a snowball, explaining the interpretive relationship between Scripture's constituent parts. The hermeneutical statement that Scripture is a unity should be qualified; it is a weighty, complex, and multi-layered unity because the Bible did not fall from the sky like a single snowflake but rolled down the hill of salvation history, adding layers as it went. Each new layer of this accumulating collection presupposes what comes before and wraps itself around it, and, in so doing, offers direction in how to read it, asking to be interpreted in light of it.[33] The existence of a fuller sense is many times revealed when one studies a text in the light of other texts.[34] One gains meaning from reading the Bible by circular movements between analysis and synthesis, pre-understanding and disclosure, from spiralling toward the text but also by realizing that the text came into existence through a history in which it was already approaching the reader, rolling down the hill for hundreds of years, accumulating layers of self-interpretation on its way. The progressive revelation that believers accept in faith when they read the Bible (*progressio revelationis*), however, is not a simple and one-dimensional model, leading from the old to the new and from good to bad, as Hebrews 1:1–2 might suggest. The process of interpreting progressive revelation also did not stop when the canon was closed because the process of interpretation is still going on. The Bible's reception history did not end when the canon was declared closed (whenever and

---

(Mueller-Vollmer, "Introduction," 5).

31. Bruns, "Midrash and Allegory," 626–27.

32. Starling, *Hermeneutics as Apprenticeship*, 14.

33. Hebner, "Introduction," 2–3. Each text presents different historical layers for interpretation and with each historical layer, different possibilities for theological meaning are conveyed.

34. Pinnock, "Work of the Holy Spirit," 242.

if that happened at all as the termination of a specific historical event); rather, the contemporary church should regain an "evangelical *ressourcement*," in the words of Williams,[35] that includes a renewed acquaintance with Protestantism's patristic[36] and medieval heritage as a corrective to an ahistorical, sectarian, and modernist tendency in exegesis and theology. This does not deny the canonical boundary that sets the Bible apart among human writings and the uniquely authoritative role played by inner-biblical interpretation.[37] Croatto, a Latin American liberation theologian, outlines the three aspects of the discipline of hermeneutics: as the "privileged locus" of the interpretation of *texts* (first aspect), while all interpreters condition their reading of a text by a kind of *pre-understanding*, arising from their own life context (second aspect), and where the interpreter also *enlarges the meaning* of the text being interpreted (third aspect).[38] Pentecostals dislocate the text by placing emphasis not on the meaning of the text in itself but rather on the meaning the text has for those people reading it.[39] Croatto also contends that the Bible must not be viewed as a fixed deposit that has already said everything; it is not so much that the Bible "said" but rather that the Bible "is saying." In committing their message to writing, the biblical authors themselves disappeared, but their absence means semantic richness. The "closure" of

35. Williams, *Tradition, Scripture, and Interpretation*, 7–8.

36. Exegesis in the patristic era was founded in the philosophical schools of Platonism and Stoicism. Platonism interpreted reality in terms of an ideal and incorporeal reality of which this world was a shadowy copy. To understand the true nature of reality, one had to turn one's gaze away from the visible world and begin an ascent into the ideal world of forms, which was not material at all, but changeless, eternal, and truly real. Stoicism differed from Platonism by denying a gulf between the intelligible and visible world; all that existed was material. Ultimate reality, which was essentially rational, was itself material and permeated the entire universe. This universe is governed by natural law and is rationally organized. Human beings as rational creatures could understand the natural laws, leading to the development of allegorical interpretation (Bernard, "Hermeneutics of the Early Church Fathers," 91). For the school of Alexandria, the combination of Platonism and Stoicism formed a framework for interpreting the Scriptures. The school of Antioch, on the other hand, had no use for allegorical interpretation but considered the historical text in terms of its literal meaning, grammar, and historical context. They emphasized insight or *theoria* into spiritual truth to be gained from the Bible, insisting that such insight was rooted in the literal meaning of the text (Bernard, "Hermeneutics of the Early Church Fathers," 94).

37. I will be discussing the canonical boundaries and its implications for Pentecostalism later in this chapter.

38. Croatto, *Biblical Hermeneutics*, 1.

39. Mester, "Use of the Bible," 124.

authorial meaning results in the "opening" of new meaning. The reader's responsibility is not exegesis, consisting of bringing out a pure meaning, but rather eisegesis, the entering of the text with new questions so as to produce new meaning.[40]

A precondition to understanding is the consciousness of one's participation in the effective histories of the text where the different variations of historical criticism (text criticism, source criticism, form criticism, tradition criticism, and later variations such as redaction criticism and social-scientific criticism)[41] can help to explain the origins of phenomena and plotting their development.[42] Bultmann already emphasized that understanding implies a living relationship between the interpreter and the text,[43] based on "fore-understanding" because it is already presupposed and not attained through the process of understanding. When reading the Bible, the Christian believer utilizes a necessarily Christian existential fore-understanding[44] because the New Testament originated within and was specifically intended for the Christian community.[45]

40. Croatto, *Biblical Hermeneutics*, 17 and 66. See also Kaiser and Silva, *Introduction to Biblical Hermeneutics*, 279.

41. Green, "Modern and Postmodern Methods," 189.

42. Jeanrond, "Biblical Interpretation as Appropriation," 4, and Lategan, "New Testament Hermeneutics (Part II)," 83.

43. As explained by Gadamer, *Truth and Method*, 295, and Lategan, "New Testament Hermeneutics (Part I)," 35.

44. Gadamer, *Truth and Method*, 196.

45. Kasper, "Prolegomena zur Erneuerung," 523. Kruger asks the provocative question whether the authors of the Gospels, letters, and other writings that later formed the New Testament were aware that they were contributing to authoritative documents, even though the canon was only formulated much later (Kruger, "Modern and Postmodern Methods," 155 and 202–203). Most scholars have settled on the end of the second century CE as the point at which much of the transition into a canonical decision took place. Kruger then argues that the people in Irenaeus's own time period already perceived many of the New Testament books as Scripture (as illustrated in the Maratorium Fragment, Clement of Alexandria, and Theophilus of Antioch), but this trend can be traced even further back into the second century, with Justin Martyr seemingly knowing of four canonical Gospels, and Papias, Ignatius, Polycarp, *1 Clement*, 2 Peter, and 1 Timothy, regarding a number of Christian writings as Scripture or as possessing apostolic authority (Kruger, "Modern and Postmodern Methods," 202). The conclusion is that Christians began to view some books as Scripture much earlier than Irenaeus, perhaps even by the turn of the first century in to the second. The canon was thus not a late development but had grown naturally and innately out of the earliest Christian movement. The authors of the New Testament appeared to have some awareness that they were writing Scripture. In this way, Kruger challenges the "big bang" theory of canon that argues that the canon was forcibly planted within the

Postmodern biblical interpretation traverses ambiguous boundaries that are not easily mapped. It began as a reaction to modernity's assumed objectivity and the new approaches are held together by a common commitment by critical sensibilities rather than a common method.[46] Postmodern interpreters argue that we have no objectively determined ledge of truth on which to stand in order to make value-free judgments in the work of creating meaning. Truth does not exist as an abstract reality apart from human knowing. Meaning is not a property of the text that readers must discover or excavate but rather is the product of the interaction of readers with texts. Critical tools are not neutral[47] and their underpinnings may require reconfiguration in relation to the epistemic priority of one's theological stance.[48] Several interpretive strategies have been formulated and there is no such thing as abstract exegesis.[49] Some approaches address the text as a window through which to access and examine the deposit of meaning (behind-the-text approaches). Others recalibrate their focus on the qualities of the text itself, its architecture and texture (in-the-text approaches), and a last group orients themselves around the perspective of various readers of the text, communities of interpreters, and the effects of these texts on readers (in-front-of-the-text approaches), leading to narrative criticism, rhetorical criticism, feminist

---

soil of the church by later ecclesiastical powers (whether by Irenaues or others) with the purpose of refuting the existing heresies. Kruger suggests that the canon began like a seed present in the soil of the church from the very beginning (Kruger, "Modern and Postmodern Methods," 203). It might have happened that the earliest church did not see any necessity for a canon of writings since they had the apostles who taught them the words of Jesus, and they awaited the imminent second coming of Christ in their generation. Only when some of the apostles died did the early church realize its need for Scriptures that contain the apostles' teaching.

46. Archer defines "modernity" as Descartes's autonomous, rational substance encountering Newton's mechanistic world, forming a humanistic (mastery of all naturalistic and supernaturalistic forces), positivistic (science and instrumental reasoning as sole arbiter of truth), and naturalistic-mechanistic universe (material universe is the sum total of reality) (Archer, Pentecostal Hermeneutic, 43).

47. It is never neutral because interpretation always betrays and perpetuates certain biases on behalf of both the sender (which is embedded in the text) and receiver (who determines the true meaning of the text) (Archer, "Hermeneutics," 109).

48. Bartholomew, Introducing Biblical Hermeneutics, 10.

49. Davies, "What Does it Mean to Read?," 262.

criticism, African American criticism, intercultural or contextual criticism, postcolonial criticism, womanist criticism, and Latino/Latina criticism, to name a few.[50]

The Bible cannot be understood adequately only in terms of an individual's self-understanding based on their participation in the world but also from faith's self-understanding, determined by the fact that faith is a gracious act of God that happens to the one who has faith.[51] Faith is a pneumatological reality[52] and, from a pentecostal perspective, the Bible is interpreted as the product of an experience with the Spirit which the Bible describes in phenomenological language,[53] leading to the expectation by modern-day Pentecostals that the Spirit would apply biblical truth and promises to their every-day experiences and circumstances.[54] "The experience of the presence and involvement of the Spirit in the be-

---

50. See Green, "Modern and Postmodern Methods," 196–201.

51. Gadamer, *Philosophical Hermeneutics*, 54.

52. Schütz, *Einführung in die Pneumatologie*, 3–4.

53. Ervin, "Hermeneutics: A Pentecostal Option," 33. Castelo thinks that a proper "first theology" would be pneumatology, the doctrine of the Spirit, constituting a "*Theology of the Third Article*" *contra* a "*Theology of the First Article*," associated with Roman Catholicism's emphasis on grace perfecting nature, and a "*Theology of the Second Article*," associated with Protestantism's focus on the disruption implied by the fall and the restoration provided by Christ (Castelo, "*Diakrisis* Always *En Conjunto*," 200). This is not the case for most textbook discussions of theology; see, for example, Klein, Blomberg, and Hubbard, *Introduction to Biblical Interpretation*, 635–36, who spend little more than a page at the very end of their monumental work describing the role of the Holy Spirit in Bible interpretation. See also Yong's argument that to begin with the Third Article rather that the Second opens up towards a trinitarianism that is much more robust than that which has to date emerged from a christological starting-point (Yong, *Spirit-Word-Community*, 8–9). A pneumatological starting-point is both christological and patriological, the Spirit being the Spirit of Christ and the Spirit of the Father (*filioque*). The question is where to start theology, with the divine or the human, descent or ascent, of God as always in and around us (Schleiermacher) or who is the "wholly Other" (Barth). The benefit of a Theology of the Third Article over the others is that it is not a theology from above (Barth) or from below (Schleiermacher) because pneumatology stresses that God is, in a sense, both and neither from above and below; God is a relational God who is beyond *and* in the midst of creation. The Spirit is not subjective or objective but rather transjective. Castelo's work follows Dabney, "Why Should the Last be First?," 240–61.

54. Some researchers accuse Pentecostals of an overemphasis on pneumatology at the cost of a developed Christology. In the heart of pentecostal theology, however, as already explained, one finds Jesus as healer, savior, baptizer, and sanctifier. Christ is not relegated to the periphery; in fact, the focus on the Spirit is continually interspersed with and amplified by clear-sighted visions of Jesus (Daneel, *Quest for Belonging*, 259).

liever's life enables one to come to terms with the apostolic witness in a truly existential manner,"[55] leading to a continuity with the original faith community for whom the epistle or Gospel was intended, as well as the modern-day community.

Luke-Acts and Paul: A Different Pneumatology

Pentecostals engaged in a debate about the pneumatology of Luke and Acts. Initially between Dunn and Menzies, the debate raged in the *Journal of Pentecostal Theology* of 1993 and 1994, with Menzies charging Dunn[56] that he does not give Luke enough credence for a view of pneumatology that is distinct from Paul.[57] Traditionally, "cessasionists" interpreted the Spirit baptism in terms of conversion and identified it with incorporation into the body of Christ as the representation of the new covenant.[58] It is what makes a person truly a Christian.[59] Following John Wesley's (1703–1791) eighteenth-century contribution to the discussion on sanctification in contrast to the Lutheran dialectic of the Christian existing as simultaneously sinner and saint (*simul iustus et peccator*),[60] Spirit baptism was brought by some in relation to sanctification.[61] As a synthesis between nineteenth-century dispensational and holiness theology, twentieth-century Pentecostalism identifies baptism with an ecstatic experience characterized by speaking in tongues, powerful equipment for

55. Gräbe, "Hermeneutical Reflections on the Interpretation," 19.

56. James D. G. Dunn was one of the first scholars to take Pentecostalism seriously enough to write a major scholarly critique of its understanding of Spirit baptism. Dunn is not a Pentecostal or charismatic in popular terms, although his rigorous dialogue with Pentecostals was always characterized by a conciliatory and friendly spirit (Keener, *Spirit Hermeneutics*, 23). Dunn affirms the continuance of the *charismata*.

57. See Byrd, "Paul Ricoeur's Hermeneutical Theory," 204–8, for a summary.

58. See, for example, Stott, *Baptism and Fullness*, 23, and Peerbolte, "'Do not quench the Spirit!'" 4.

59. Menzies and Menzies, *Spirit and Power*, 744. Paul was elevated above all other canonical writers due to Luther's and Calvin's emphasis on Pauline epistles, which supported their respective doctrines of justification by faith and the sovereignty of God. The privileging of Paul was further encouraged by German scholarship critical of the historical reliability of Acts. Until recently, Evangelicals viewed Luke as a historian rather than a theologian (Menzies, *Pentecost*, 26). Pentecostals accept that Luke wrote history with a theological purpose in view, utilizing his own vocabulary and style as he presented the material.

60. Oliverio, *Theological Hermeneutics*, 23.

61. Dayton, "Holiness Movement," 475.

both service and witness.[62] From the Sixties of the last century, the charismatic movement that was born from the marriage between traditional Lutheran, Catholic, and Reformed theology and charismatic experience reinterpreted Spirit baptism as an actualization of the Spirit.[63] "Although there is a consensus among renewalists on the noncessationist interpretation of Scripture, most other elements of the renewal tradition hold to a broader view of pneumatology in Luke/Acts than classic Pentecostals."[64]

At the heart of the difference about the interpretation of Spirit baptism lies fundamental hermeneutical methodological differences related to different literary genres.[65] Paul's theology is derived from letters; Luke writes what role the Spirit has fulfilled in history in narrative form. The difference between letter and narrative leads to a fundamental methodological difference in how the work of the Spirit is described.[66] Pentecostals accept continuity between the events that Luke writes about in his Gospel and events in the earliest church in Acts.[67] In the process, they tend to emphasize the theological character of the narratives at the expense of their historical uniqueness, while "cessasionists" again highlight the historical character of the narratives at the expense of their

62. Holdcroft, *Holy Spirit*, 120. See also Vondey's provocative remark that *glossolalia* is the flagship of the pentecostal resistance to the dominance of the human language and the discourse of meaning (Vondey, *Pentecostalism*, 122). Where the intellect fails to grasp meaning and purpose, Pentecostals rely on the affections and imagination to allow the utterances to stand.

63. McDonnell, "Holy Spirit and Christian Initiation," 82. As a worldwide phenomenon, the charismatic movement adds a number of important dimensions to the global temperament of Pentecostalism (Vondey, *Pentecostalism*, 23–25). The most significant is the ecclesial connectedness of the movement that integrates pentecostal spirituality and practices in the liturgical and ecumenical contexts of the established "mainline" traditions. A second dimension is the widespread social acceptance of pentecostal and charismatic spirituality often connected with church leaders, councils, well-known personalities, and representatives of the intellectual elite. A third element is their intellectual and academic dimension. Another element is its establishment of a global character also in its theological dimensions. Fifthly, the movement has significantly expanded the ecumenical sensitivities of Pentecostals, with "allies" now found among the Evangelicals.

64. Spawn and Wright, "Emergence of a Pneumatic Hermeneutic," 17.

65. Fee, *Gospel and Spirit*, 110–11.

66. Zwiep, "Luke's Understanding of Baptism," 134.

67. *Contra*, e.g., Conzelmann, *Theology of Saint Luke*, 150; Minear, "Luke's Use of the Birth Stories," 124; and Gasque, *History of the Criticism*, 294, who assume theological homogeneity.

theological character.[68] This leads to Farrell's judgment that the historical narratives in Acts offer "a flimsy foundation" on which Pentecostals build their teachings of Christian life so that he can assert that "no directives for normative Christian experience are contained in these passages."[69] Doctrine cannot be rooted in narrative alone, for narrative is too slippery, elastic, and imprecise.[70] Against this argument stands the viewpoint of Pentecostals that "the events that occurred on the day of Pentecost are held to be the pattern for centuries to come."[71]

Paul's own theological way of working undermines a clear dichotomy between narrative and literary writing, using historical narratives to draw didactic conclusions: "For whatever was written in former days was written for our instruction, so that by steadfastness and by the encouragement of the scriptures we might have hope" (Rom 15:4). If Paul uses the historical narratives of the Old Testament to motivate didactic statements, it is logical to assume that Luke would use the stories of the church for didactic reasons, as he bases his historiography deliberately on Old Testament historiography.[72] Marshall asks whether history and theology stand opposite each other and answers that Luke regards his task to provide a description of historical events, colored by his theological viewpoint.[73] He uses history to illustrate his message of the gospel of Jesus Christ. The implication is that his narratives contain more than descriptions or facts because it is subordinate to his theological interests. A dichotomy between historical and didactic material in Luke-Acts is therefore artificial and arbitrary. Luke-Acts represents history with a

---

68. Stronstad, *Charismatic Theology*, 6.

69. Farrell, "Outburst of Tongues," 5. Fee agrees, stating that Pentecostals wrongly use historical portions of the Bible to justify their doctrinal claims rather than the didactic (Fee, *Gospel and Spirit*, 86). They mistakenly take the descriptive history of the primitive church and attempt to make it normative for the contemporary church. Stronstad and Menzies replied to Fee's objections to the distinctive pentecostal doctrines by denying a simple dichotomy between descriptive historical portions of Scripture and didaction portions, aiming to establish the thesis that Luke is a theologian in his own right—and a charismatic one at that—and that one should move from biblical theology to systematic theology (an approach advanced by Robert Menzies). See also discussion in Stronstad, *Charismatic Theology*; Menzies, "Synoptic Theology," 14–21; and Keener, *Spirit Hermeneutics*, 252.

70. Menzies and Menzies, *Spirit and Power*, 585.

71. Holdcroft, *Holy Spirit*, 110.

72. Marshall, *Luke*, 56, and Atkinson, "Angels and the Spirit," 51–52.

73. Marshall, *Luke*, 52.

purpose, history written with a theological agenda in view.[74] That is why Luke's narratives provide an important and valid source for his teaching of the Spirit that has normative implications for the church's mission and religious experience.[75]

To interpret Luke's historical narratives about the work of the Spirit in Pauline terms is an "illegitimate identity transfer."[76] This happens when didactic passages enjoy preference above historical narratives and the book of Acts is read and interpreted from 1 Corinthians.[77] 1 Corinthians 12:13 describes Spirit baptism as initiation and incorporation into the body of Christ[78]; Stott interprets Luke 3:16, Acts 1:5, and Acts 11:16 in the same terms, interpreting Luke with a Pauline interpretation.[79] The conclusion then is that the Spirit baptism does not represent a second-phase experience but refers to the initiation experience.[80] And Luke's terms ("filled with the Spirit," for example, in Luke 1:15) is then interpreted in terms of Ephesians 5:18, so that Paul's single use of the phrase is made normative for Luke's nine references.[81] Against this viewpoint, Pentecostals hold that Luke was a historian and theologian in his own right who deliberately and independently developed his teaching about the Spirit. Luke's charismatic, prophetic pneumatology[82] thus exists next to and independent of Paul's soteriological theology of the Spirit.[83]

74. Menzies and Menzies, *Spirit and Power*, 623.

75. Rudolf Otto refers to "religious experience" as the non-rational element in religion (Otto, *Idea of the Holy*, 3). It may be correct in a general sense to assert that religious experience has largely been jettisoned out of the idea of the "holy." At the same time, modern Africa has become "totally inconceivable apart from the presence of Christianity" (Forrester, "Christianity in Europe," 40), and Pentecostalism is the area in which the growth in African Christianity has been most conspicuous (Asamoah-Gyadu, *African Charismatics*, 7–10),

76. Barr, *Semantics of Biblical Language*, 222.

77. Dunn, *Baptism in the Holy Spirit*, 15, and Green, *I Believe in the Holy Spirit*.

78. Dunn, *Baptism in the Holy Spirit*, 129–30.

79. Stott, *Baptism and Fullness*, 23.

80. Green, *I Believe in the Holy Spirit*, 141–42.

81. Stott, *Baptism and Fullness*, 43–51.

82. Turner, "Does Luke Believe Reception," 8.

83. Menzies, "Luke's Understanding of Baptism," 112. Luke writes much later than Paul, probably around 70 CE, and could possibly be seen as a reversal of and correction on Pauline pneumatological trends (Atkinson, "Angels and the Spirit in Luke-Acts," 89). From South African ranks, pentecostal scholars wrote two dissertations on 1 Corinthians 12–14: Möller, *Diskussie oor die Charismata* is about the *charismata* as it is practiced in the Pentecostal movement in comparison with what the Corinthian

Paul's pneumatological perspective is not irreconcilable with that of Luke. On the contrary, Menzies and Menzies argue that the pneumatologies of Luke and Paul are different but not incompatible, and these differences should not be blurred.[84] Both perspectives offer valuable insights into the dynamic work of the Spirit. Paul has the more developed view, for he writes about the full richness of the Spirit's work. For Paul, the Spirit is the source of the Christian's cleansing (Rom 15:16; 1 Cor 6:11), righteousness (Rom 2:29; 8:1–17; 14:17; Gal 5:5; 5:16–26), intimate fellowship with God (Rom 8:14–17; Gal 4:6), as well as the source of power for mission (Rom 15:18–19; Phil 1:18–19). Fee[85] emphasizes that the Spirit plays an absolutely crucial role in Paul's Christian experience and his understanding of the gospel. Crucial to the Spirit's central role is the thoroughly eschatological framework within which Paul both experienced and understood the Spirit. Equally crucial to the Pauline perspective is the dynamically experienced nature of the coming of the Spirit in the life of the individual and community.[86] Paul attests to both the soteriological and charismatic dimensions of the Spirit's work, while Luke's view is less developed and more limited, only bearing witness to the charismatic dimension of the work of the Spirit. But Luke also has an important contribution to make, reminding us that the church is a prophetic community empowered for a missionary task by virtue of its reception of the pentecostal gift.

That is the reason for Luke adding a unique text to his Gospel, in his account of the sending of the Seventy (Luke 10:1–16). The three Synoptic Gospels record Jesus's words of instruction to the Twelve as they are sent out on their mission. Only Luke records a second, larger sending of disciples, either "seventy-two" or "seventy," a number that cannot be determined with confidence.[87] The number might have symbolic significance. As the number "twelve" clearly symbolizes the reconstitution of Israel (Gen 35:23–26) with the twelve tribes of Israel as basis, the background

---

letter teaches about it, and Bezuidenhout, "Pauliniese Kriteria" is on Pauline criteria regarding the practice of *charismata*. In both cases, exegesis is done on Paul's description of the *charismata* without investigating Paul's view of the baptism of the Spirit, a subject examined by later pentecostal scholars in more detail.

84. Menzies and Menzies, *Spirit and Power*, 931.

85. Fee, *God's Empowering Presence*, 896–99.

86. Kärkkäinen, *Pneumatology*, 34.

87. Metzger, "Seventy or Seventy-Two Disciples?," 321.

for the reference to the "seventy" is to be found in Numbers 11:24–30.[88] Numbers 11:25 describes how YHWH took of the Spirit (spirit) that was on Moses and put the Spirit on the seventy elders. They started prophesying for a short duration. Two of the elected elders, Eldad and Medad, did not attend the meeting but remained in the camp. When they started prophesying and Joshua heard about it, he rushed to Moses with the request that he should stop them. Moses replied, "Are you jealous for me? I wish that all of the Lord's people were prophets. And I wish that the Lord would put his Spirit on them" (Num 11:29). This accounts for the two textual traditions underlying Luke 10:1, in Menzies's view, because of the interplay of seventy and seventy-two prophets. It also finds explicit fulfilment in the narrative of Acts and it ties into one of the great themes of Luke-Acts, the work of the Spirit. Menzies then finds the significance of the symbolism in the expansion of the number of disciples into mission from twelve to seventy (or seventy-two), actualizing the wish of Moses that all YHWH's people would be prophets. This wish was fulfilled throughout Acts, including the people of Samaria (Acts 8:14–17), the man from Africa (Acts 8:27–40), the Roman officer Cornelius's house (Acts 10:44–48), and Ephesus (Acts 19:1–7). Luke wishes to state succinctly that every member of the church is called (Luke 24:45–49; Acts 1:4–8; Isa 49:6) and empowered to be a prophet (Acts 2:17–21; 4:31). The prophetic enabling experienced by the disciples at Pentecost is available to all of God's people, realizing Moses's wish. Luke anticipates the fulfilment of this reality (Luke 10:1).[89] Pentecost then represents the fulfilment of Moses's wish that all believers would be prophets, rather than the disciples' entrance into the new age.[90]

The Reading Community

The results of a pentecostal encounter with the Bible are: a deepening respect for the witness of the Scriptures, especially the apostolic witnesses

88. Menzies, *Pentecost*, 33.

89. Menzies, *Pentecost*, 35.

90. As argued, only by reading Luke-Acts through the lens of Pauline theology can Pentecost be construed as the moment when the disciples enter into the new age (Menzies, *Pentecost*, 36). Twelftree argues that, for Luke, the beginning of the church must be traced back to Jesus's selection of the Twelve, and the ministry of the church is not seen as distinct from but continues the ministry of Jesus (Twelftree, *People of the Spirit*, 30).

concerning Jesus contained in it[91]; a denial that all passages should be read and interpreted literally, as though the truths contained in the passage are transferred in a mechanistic or automatic way; and the interpretation of Scriptures within the pneumatic continuity of the faith community through all ages.[92] The community is defined in terms of being Spirit-driven, Spirit-led, and Spirit-empowered to accomplish God's purposes for and through the community—a community that is to be Spirit-governed, Spirit-supported, and Spirit-propagated.[93] Pinnock adds that a genuinely Spirit-led reading will be consistent with the apostolic witness, which he deems an important check and that matches the restorationist motif that helps to determine pentecostal self-identity.[94] The preference for "Apostolic" in the title of many Pentecostal groups and movements, going back to the self-designation of the Azusa Street group, testifies to the importance for Pentecostals that their teaching and practice should be in accord with the witness of the first apostles.[95]

If understanding is defined as the fusion of horizons conditioned by effective historical criticism, the important question remains: how does one validate one's experience with the text? Ricoeur is concerned about text comprehension and shows that the relationship between interpreter and text should be approached methodically in a critically accountable way.[96] He contends that one should distinguish between the relations of speaking-hearing and writing-reading. In spoken discourse, the meaning of the discourse overlaps the intention of the speaker. However, with written discourse, the author's intention and the meaning of the text cease to coincide. What the text means now matters more than what the author meant when he wrote it.[97] The interpretive process is dialectical, progressing from an initial, naive understanding, to an explanation of the

---

91. Gee, *Pentecost*, 8.

92. Gräbe, "Hermeneutical Reflections," 19.

93. Rance, "Fulfilling the Apostolic Mandate," 9.

94. Pinnock, "Work of the Holy Spirit," 241.

95. See Yong, *Hermeneutical Spirit*, 12–13.

96. Jeanrond, *Text Und Interpretation als Kategorien*, 27.

97. Kaiser and Silva, *Introduction to Biblical Hermeneutics*, 279. John Wyckoff, a pentecostal scholar, devoted his dissertation to addressing pneumatic hermeneutics, contending that Scripture is the final authority only if the author's original intended meaning, as opposed to the perspectives of the readers, is determinate for all other possible valid meanings, in which he includes what many prefer to call "applications." His view that denies authorial intention is, however, a minority view among Pentecostals (see Wyckoff, "Relationship of the Holy Spirit").

text, a deeper understanding of the text, and a methodological validation of the results of the first or naive understanding.[98]

I contend that although the meaning of a biblical passage need not (and cannot always) be identified completely with the author's intention—there will always be uncertainty about the intention of a specific author—authorial meaning can never be secondary or dispensable. In certain cases, the task of identifying what the biblical author meant is not the only legitimate way of proceeding in interpreting the text, but such a task is always necessary and must continue to function as an essential goal of the hermeneutical process. Before further considerations are brough to the text, one must always listen to the author in terms of language, historical, social and economic context, and genre. In order not to read into the text one's own ideas and meaning, one should take the trouble to hear the text speaking on its own terms. No modern author would be happy with readers interpreting the text in a way that reflects their own ideological ideas without listening to the arguments in the text.[99] The stated primary purpose of the Bible is to communicate an intelligible message that requires a response, and the Bible is read in a spiritual manner by believers with the purpose to hear the voice of God, despite the Bible also being a literary and artistic work.

True understanding always includes the act of application.[100] An important part of the application of texts consists of the personal involvement of the reader or listener with the word, as the author of Jeremiah declares: "Your words were found, and I ate them, and your words became to me a joy and the delight of my heart; for I am called by your name, O Lord, God of hosts" (Jer 15:16). "I am called by your name" literally reads, "Your name was upon me," evoking the language of Deuteronomy 12:5 and 11, which refers to the place where YHWH would choose to put his name and habitation (eventually in Jerusalem). YHWH inhabits the prophet; Jeremiah has to "become" Jerusalem in order to proclaim God's message to Jerusalem. He needs to be "with God" in order to receive and proclaim God's word.[101] This is not an objective, neutral, distant reading or hearing of God's word; the interpreter must be owned by God,

---

98. Jeanrond, "Biblical Interpretation as Appropriation," 5, and Jeanrond, *Text Und Interpretation als Kategorien*, 42.

99. See Kaiser and Silva, *Introduction to Biblical Hermeneutics*, 291.

100. Gadamer, *Truth and Method*, 270.

101. Bartholomew, *Introducing Biblical Hermeutics*, 539.

obedient to God, confident in God, and at God's disposal in order to be God's prophet.[102]

The text that is understood historically is always forced to abandon its claim that it is uttering something true, argues Gadamer, and the acknowledgment of the otherness of the other involves the fundamental suspension of its claim to truth, leading to the dilemma of theology when Scripture is applied in an edifying way in Christian preaching.[103] Here, understanding involves the application of the text to be understood to the present situation of the interpreter and the listeners.[104]

The relation between interpreter and text consists in "understanding"; the methodological activity taking place between interpreter and text leads to "explanation"; a last element consists in "assessment," consisting of the reader's personal responsibility towards the meaning of the text that opens up before them.[105] Assessment of biblical texts consists of discovering the claim(s) made by the text and making a personal ("altar") response to it.

What does it mean, then, that the interpreter should rely upon the Holy Spirit in interpreting the text? Arrington suggests the following ways in which the interpreter relies on the Spirit: submission of the mind to God, so that the critical and analytical abilities are exercised under the guidance of the Holy Spirit; a genuine openness to the witness of the Spirit as the text is examined; the personal experience of faith as part of the entire interpretative process; and response to the transforming call of God's word.[106] The Holy Spirit enables the interpreter to bridge the historical and cultural gulf between the authors of the Bible and the present readers. Pentecostals ascribe their strong emphasis on the Spirit to Scripture which emphasizes the role of the Spirit in revealing God and God's will to God's people. "But, as it is written, 'What no eye has seen, nor ear heard, nor the human heart conceived, what God has prepared for those who love him'—these things God has revealed to us through

102. To be a true prophet would thus always include that one meets opposition, hatred, and persecution because one shares in God's holiness and separatedness. The prophet may become a lonely person and appear to be a failed and therefore false prophet (Bartholomew, *Introducing Biblical Hermeutics*, 539–40).

103. Kaiser and Silva, *Introduction to Biblical Hermeneutics*, 329.

104. Gadamer, *Truth and Method*, 274, and Kaiser and Silva, *Introduction to Biblical Hermeneutics*, 328.

105. Jeanrond, *Text Und Interpretation als Kategorien*, 70 and 125.

106. Arrington, "Use of the Bible," 105.

the Spirit; for the Spirit searches everything, even the depths of God" (1 Cor 2:9–10).

The two dimensions of the interpreting process—the experiential-pneumatic (or spiritual) and the exegetical elements—should be kept in balance. By overemphasizing the experiential and pneumatic at the cost of the work of the mind can lead to a subjectivizing interpretative process. Scripture should always stand as the objective standard to which all interpretation must submit. Unless it can support its case biblically, it has no compelling reason to exist.[107]

Pentecostals believe that God still speaks today, and when God speaks, God has more to say than just Scripture. Yet what God says will never be in contradistinction to what Scripture teaches because it is the same Spirit who inspired the authors of the Bible who reveal God to contemporary believers.[108]

By way of concluding, faith does not render scientific methodologically controlled interpretation of biblical texts impossible but rather forms the framework that makes the enterprise meaningful.[109] However, the ceaseless movement of biblical interpretation begins and ends in the risk of a response, which is not exhausted by commentary.[110] Faith forms the necessary and unique precondition from which believers orient themselves in all their choices. Hermeneutics reminds that biblical faith cannot be separated from the movement of interpretation, which elevates it into language.[111] From a pentecostal perspective, faith is interpreted as a transforming and empowering encounter with the divine, as described in Acts, leading to a Christian community eager to bear witness to the power and love of God that they experienced[112] and a consciousness of the real presence and power of the Spirit.[113]

The Pentecostal movement believes that the Spirit has manifested again as in the days of the early church when the Spirit gives the *charismata*

---

107. See Bruner, quoted in Thomas, "Women, Pentecostals, and the Bible," 49.

108. Archer, "Pentecostal Hermeneutics," 148.

109. Stuhlmacher, *Vom Verstehen des Neuen Testaments*, 204.

110. Ricoeur, "Philosophical Hermeneutics," 31.

111. Kaiser and Silva, *Introduction to Biblical Hermeneutics*, 56, and Gräbe, "Hermeneutical Reflections," 23.

112. Schnackenburg, *Belief in the New Testament*, 81–82.

113. Pentecostals find that God is so intrusively real that their subjective experience is constantly being challenged and proved (Ellington, "Pentecostalism and the Authority of Scriptures," 154).

of *glossolalia*, prophecy, miracles of healing, and other signs in contemporary times. Pentecostals now read the Bible in order to understand themselves,[114] a mode of subjectivity which responds and corresponds to the power of the New Testament to display its own world, radiated by the living Lord and present among God's people, the community of faith, through the Holy Spirit and leading to the transformation of the lives of the readers.[115] They also expect these same signs and wonders to occur in their ministry; they prioritize spectacular displays of celestial power, such as healing and deliverance from sinful habits and Satanic bondage, to authenticate the preaching of the Word and build the faith of listeners to expect the miracle they need in faith, leading to faith in the word.[116]

Canon of the Bible?

Pentecostals are part of the Protestant tradition and mostly accept without question the canon of the Reformation. However, the different lists of canonical books found in Catholic, Protestant, and other Christian Bibles necessitate that the issue of the boundaries of the canon should still be attended to. Canonical criticism shows the fluidity of the canon throughout the first few centuries of the Christian church's existence which, at times, experienced intense canonical debates.

The Reformation used the criterion of apostolicity for determining the canon of the New Testament *contra* the Roman Catholic Bible. For determing the canon of the Old Testament, the reformers, in their rejection of the Catholic Bible, accepted the Jewish canon. For that reason, the Protestant Old Testament has the same books as the Jewish Old Testament, although it follows the same order of the books as most Septuagint manuscripts (the Greek translation of the Old Testament).[117]

114. Ricoeur, "Philosophical Hermeneutics," 30.

115. In this regard, Schüssler Fiorenza refers to "self-conscious relativity" as a necessity in reading the Bible effectively (Fiorenza, *Bread not Stone*, 104). This requires our being quite explicit about where we are coming from, who we are, what our tradition is, and what we hope to find in the Bible. The past does not reveal itself to a supposedly detached, objective, and value-free spectator. Christians claim that God continues to "speak" to us from the Bible, but the Bible speaks to us only when we come to it with our honest questions and real hopes, not as distanced outside observers (Cox, *How to Read the Bible*, 13).

116. Anderson, "Towards a Pentecostal Missiology," 35.

117. The order of the Jewish canon is important, consisting of the Torah (or Instruction of Moses), the Nebi'im (or Prophets), and the Ketubim (or wisdom writings). The

Western Christianity has generally accepted what is now the Catholic Old Testament as canonical from at least the fourth century onward.[118] There were some conflicting voices, however, such as Jerome, the translator of the Bible into Latin, who found many discrepancies between the Hebrew text and the Septuagint translation. However, Augustine, the influential bishop of Hippo, and several ecclesiastical synods declared the longer list to be canonical.[119]

The Reformers decided to follow the Jewish canon rather than the canon decided upon by the synods of the early church since the Hebrew Bible originated among the Jews and the Christian religion comes out of Judaism.[120] A complication is that the determination of the Jewish canon is later than the Christian Old Testament. It is clear that the canon of the Hebrew Bible was not established at a supposed Synod of Jabne or Jamnia at the end of the first century CE, as many scholars accepted during the twentieth century. The synagogue at Jamnia served as the center of later rabbinic Judaism but there is no clear documentary evidence that it took a decision that was binding on all Jewish communities.

Prior to Christianity, all Jews and Samaritans recognized the Torah or Pentateuch as the foundation of their religion. Some of the prophets were also revered, interpreted, and accorded authority by many Jews, but not all. The Sadducees, for instance, only accepted the Torah, even in Jesus's day (Matt 22:23; Mark 12:18; Luke 20:27; Acts 23:6–8).

First-century Christian believers were at first Jews but, at least since the destruction of Jerusalem in 70 CE by Roman forces, most Christian believers were non-Jews, using mostly Greek as *lingua franca*. They read

---

Torah served as the main canon while the Prophets served to interpret the Instruction, and the Wisdom writings served to interpret the Prophets, showing a distinction in the authority and value of the different parts of the canon (Collins, *Introduction to the Hebrew Bible*, 2–10).

118. Their canon also contains 1 Esdras (Vulgate 3 Esdras); 2 Esdras (Vulgate 4 Esdras); Tobit; Judith; Rest of Esther (Vulgate Esther 10:4—16:24); Wisdom of Solomon; Ecclesiasticus (also known as Sirach); Baruch and the Epistle of Jeremiah (all part of Vulgate Baruch); Song of the Three Children (Vulgate Daniel 3:24–90); Story of Susanna (Vulgate Daniel 13); The Idol Bel and the Dragon (Vulgate Daniel 14); Prayer of Manasses; 1 Maccabees; and 2 Maccabees (Collins, *Introduction to the Hebrew Bible*, 5).

119. Keegan, *Interpreting the Bible*, 150.

120. However, the Reformers allowed that the apocryphal books (as they called the Roman Catholic "deuterocanonical" books) be read for personal upbuilding but not for the formulation of doctrine. John Wesley relied much on the Apocrypha in his sermons (Wansbrough, *Use and Abuse of the Bible*, 129).

the Scriptures in Greek, using the Septuagint, with the thirty-nine books of the Hebrew Bible and a further fifteen writings composed in Greek. "The Septuagint, not the Old Testament in Hebrew, was the Bible of the early church."[121] This is important to remember. The early Christian writings that were later accorded authority were also written in Greek. Since the Septuagint contained books that eventually would not be included in the Jewish canon, the Christian synods accepted these books as part of their Bible; since they had been using the Septuagint since the establishment of the church, it was not a matter of discussion for them which books to allow into the canon. First-century Christians saw themselves as the implied readers of these books; it spoke to their life situations.[122]

Prior to the first century CE, the technology for binding books did not exist, and different books were found on different scrolls, making the question of which books should be bound together in the Bible a question that was not (and could not be) asked or considered. When the Christian church eventually did answer the question, it was based on the practice of the early church and on the book selection of the Septuagint.

In its eventual answer to the question of the boundaries of the canon, Judaism, at a later stage, decided to leave out such books as Maccabees with its apocalyptic militarism that had resulted in the destruction of the Temple. Their decision to leave out some books was also probably related to their reaction to Christians' utilization of the Septuagint.[123] Their decision was determined by their new self-understanding, as a post-temple rabbinic faith community.[124] Whatever the case, the Jewish canon was shorter, excluding some of the books that early Western Christians accepted.

---

121. Soulen, *Sacred Scripture*, 20.

122. Keegan, *Interpreting the Bible*, 151.

123. The most contentious point was the Septuagint's rendition of Isa 7:14, which referred to a "virgin" (Greek *parthenos*) who would conceive and bear a son. The more ancient Hebrew version of Isaiah reads "young woman" (Hebrew *alma*), not "virgin." By rejecting the Septuagint and reverting to the Hebrew texts, the rabbinic movement sought to counter the scriptural grounds Christians employed to defend Jesus as the Messiah as foretold by the Jewish prophets (Soulen, *Sacred Scripture*, 21). The Hebrew Bible came into existence (*inter alia*) as a defensive reaction to the rise of Christianity and its decision to reject the Septuagint was determined by Christians' acceptance of the Greek translation of the Hebrew Bible (along with and including the apocryphal writings). Under the leadership of Rabbi Akiba, the Jews condemned the Septuagint in 130 CE.

124. Keegan, *Mind of the Spirit*, 152.

It is suggested that Pentecostals should revisit their unquestioning acceptance of the Reformed canon of the Bible. The question to be asked is whether the Protestant tradition was correct in following the Jewish canon, ignoring the practices of early Christians. The question seems to be especially relevant for Pentecostals with their restorationist urge.

Perhaps Pentecostals should reconsider introducing the Apocrypha to their churches but then the conception should be emphasized that the apocryphal books are to be read only in terms of the guidelines provided in and under the standard of the other, unquestionably canonical books (as deutero-canonical books, with the Bible books serving as *norma normata*). The inner boundary of the canon is the minimal canon of the Reformation churches and does not admit of further reduction; and specifically in pentecostal thinking, the outer boundary, on the other hand, is not fixed.[125]

Africa's Contribution

Christianity was introduced to Africans on the day of Pentecost, with people from Africa present where Peter provided his first sermon, emphasized by the events that Acts 8 witnesses to. In Acts 8, Philip's ministry proleptically fulfills two of the three points of mission in Acts 1:8, to Samaria and the ends of the earth, when he advanced the gospel north, to the Samaritans, and south,[126] to the Africans.[127] Philip, in obedience to an angelic command and the Spirit's voice, encounters a God-fearing African official who is not yet a full proselyte.[128] He is reading a primary messianic text for the Jesus movement and invites Philip to interpret the passage for him. The unnamed official becomes the forerunner of the

---

125. Maier, *Biblical Hermeneutics*, 159.

126. The term "South" in Acts 8:26 can also be translated as "midday." "South" fits the context of a road "from Jerusalem to Gaza" better. Perhaps Nubia refers to a black African kingdom between Aswan and Khartoum. Its leading cities were Meroë and Napata and since the early third century BCE had ruled from its capital in Meroë. Some scholars think that the intention of the reference should rather be interpreted as that the man comes from "far away," from an exotic destination (Keener, *Acts*, 1552).

127. Keener, *Acts*, 1464.

128. Because/if the man is a eunuch he does not qualify to become a full proselyte. The term "eunuch" can refer to a eunuch or a high official. Keener is of the opinion that the arguments in favor of the man's being a eunuch and hence merely a God-fearer are stronger than those favoring his being a full proselyte (Keener, *Acts*, 1567).

African mission, as the first non-Jewish convert, and the forerunner of the gentile mission in general.[129]

By the second century, Christians could be found all across the northern coast of the continent, as part of the Roman Empire. The Bible was known to the Africans as early as the second and third century, mainly in the North African cities of Carthage, Hippo, and Alexandria.[130] Despite the growing influence of the Christian church, however, the use of the Bible in Africa remained elitist and confined only to the latinized minority, largely disconnected from the local population. Even though the Greek New Testament had been translated into Coptic, Ethiopic, and Nubian languages, serious biblical studies were lacking.[131] Soon, Christianity also spread southward, and Africans who were not part of the extensive Roman Empire accepted the gospel. In Axum (Ethiopia), Christianity soon became the official religion of the state in the fourth century, and nearby Nubia (Sudan) was Christianized in the sixth century. The successful evangelization of a region showed a pattern across continents: a charismatic nun or monk would visit the region, preach the gospel, and perform miraculous acts that challenged pagan deities, demonstrating the power of the Christian God. Then, the local king and/or queen would embrace the gospel and require everyone in their realm to do the same.[132]

African Christianity began to decline in the mid-600s when Islam started taking over much of the region. By the year 1000 CE, Christianity had practically been eliminated from much of North Africa, except for the Coptic church in Egypt and the Ethiopian church. By 1400, Africa was religiously divided, with Islam dominant in the north and African traditional religions (ATR) continuing to flourish in the south. In 1491, Portuguese missionaries arrived in the central African region. There were many other European Christian forays into the continent. Until 1800, these expeditions were led by Catholics, but in the early nineteenth century, Protestants began joining the ranks of Catholic missionaries, just when the African slave trade was finally ending.[133]

129. Keener, *Acts*, 1545.

130. Kinyua, *Introducing Ordinary African Readers' Hermeneutics*, 12.

131. Metzger, *Text of the New Testament*, 68.

132. Jacobsen, *Global Gospel*, 5. Conversion was generally a group phenomenon, especially in Africa.

133. Jacobsen, *Global Gospel*, 44.

When the industrial age dawned, the nations of Europe unilaterally decided to take control of the continent in order to exploit its resources and inhabitants as cheap natural resources. Between 1885 and 1915, Belgium, France, Germany, Britain, Italy, Portugal, and Spain engaged in dividing Africa between them, with Abyssinia (Ethiopia) and Liberia as the sole exceptions.[134] At the Conference of Berlin in 1884–1885, most of the continent was carved up between France—who acquired almost a third of the continent—and Britain, with Portugal retaining two large countries in southern Africa, Belgium taking a large part of central Africa, and Germany, Spain, and Italy also receiving large parcels of land.[135] At the beginning of the colonial era, roughly 5 percent of the African population was Christian. By the time colonialism ended, in the 1960s, almost a third of Africa's population was Christian, including 45 million Catholics, 35 million Protestants, 20 million members of the AICs, and 20 million members of the old Orthodox churches of Egypt and Ethiopia.[136]

The Bible reached Africa through what West calls the sometimes uncomfortable—but nonetheless successful—partnership between colonialism and the Christian missionary enterprise.[137] Either the missionary enterprise used colonialism as an effective and readily available vehicle to reach the religious heart of the "dark continent," or it was colonialism that used the missionary enterprise to soften the hearts and minds of Africans. There is a thin line between the missionary intention and the intent of the colonizer, explaining the negative reputation earned by missionaries.[138] In the words of Mofokeng: "When the white man came to our country he had the Bible and we had the land. The white man

134. Jacobsen, *Global Gospel*, 48.

135. Anderson, *Spreading Fires*, 151–52.

136. Jacobsen, *Global Gospel*, 51. Kinyua defines colonialism and its discourses as the representation and categorization of the African identities produced and reproduced by various colonial rules, systems, and procedures in order to create and separate the Africans as "other" (Kinyua, *Introducing Ordinary African Readers' Hermeneutics*, 2).

137. West, *Biblical Hermeneutics of Liberation*, 52.

138. It should be stated, however, that not all missionaries cooperated with the colonizing powers, and some of the missionaries and missionary organizations served as highly critical of the behavior of white people. LeMarquand states that, in his research, most African Christians are grateful for the work of the missionaries that was many times accompanied by great suffering, although they are also aware of the cultural blindness and racial prejudice of much mission activity (LeMarquand, "New Testament Exegesis in (Modern) Africa," 8).

said to us, 'Let us pray.' After the prayer, the white man had the land and we had the Bible."[139] The remark illustrates the central position occupied by the Bible in the ongoing process of colonization, national oppression, and exploitation, the incomprehensible paradox of being colonized by a Christian people and yet being converted to their religion and accepting their Bible, their ideological instrument of colonization, oppression and exploitation. It expresses a historic commitment that is accepted solemnly by one generation and passed on to another, a commitment to terminate exploitation of humans by other humans.[140]

In 1971, John Gattu of the Presbyterian Church in East Africa called for an immediate moratorium on all missionary activity in Africa, demonstrating the shift of emphasis away from Western-style reason and orderliness toward a more free-wheeling focus on the Spirit.[141]

The translation of the Bible into African languages aided the spread of Christianity more than almost any other factor. These vernacular translations gave the Bible a degree of independence from the European missionaries' worldview and gave Africans a source of Christian authority external to the missionary. Now they could hear (and read) the Bible

---

139. Mofokeng, "Black Christians," 34.

140. Mofokeng, "Black Christians," 34. Barbara Kingsolver wrote a novel, *Poisonwood Bible*, about the poisonous effect that the Bible—or rather, what it represents for a certain fanatical mentality—could have under certain circumstances, in this case on people who live precarious subsistence-economy lives in the African jungle of what used to be the Belgian Congo (later Zaire, after independence, and more recently designated as the Democratic Republic of the Congo). "Poisonwood," in the Congo, is a plant that leaves horrible, suppurating sores on the hands and arms of people who touch it inadvertently; hence, as an adjective qualifying the Bible as symbol of Western culture, it makes the Bible a metonymy of the poisonous effects that Western culture has had on those cultures unfortunate enough to have it imposed on them (see Olivier, "Kingsolver's Narrative Indictment"). It is the story of a fiery Baptist preacher from Bethlehem, Georgia, overflowing with evangelical fervor, his wife, and his four daughters, who arrived in the Belgian Congo in 1959—just before independence—to replace the former minister of religion (a Catholic) in the village of Kilanga. The preacher tries his best to convince the village Congolese of the advisability to switch from the worship of their local gods to that of "Tata Jesu," and, moreover, of the importance of being baptized in the nearby river—an ill-advised thing to do, considering that there were dangerous, human-eating crocodiles there. Small wonder that the indigenous people regard Nathan with suspicion. The Price family suffers to survive through the misery of the drought, the threat brought by independence (and the father's refusal to leave the Congo, despite their sponsors' urgent advice to do so), the disastrous "mass hunt" to provide food for the starving villagers, and the subsequent flight of the mother and her surviving three daughters from the village in torrential rain.

141. Jacobsen, *Global Gospel*, 52.

on its own terms, leading to the enormous growth of AICs and other organizations, effectively merging African culture and tradition with their own readings of the Bible. In translating the Bible, however, the missionaries and other scholars also interpreted it. Their translation and reading of the vernacular Bible was filtered through cultural lenses which were not always congenial to African traditional life and they rejected many traditional African customs without considering its possible value for a Christian worldview.[142] Africans saw the discrepancy between what missionaries said and what the Bible stated in terms of an issue like polygyny and polygamy; African readers noted that many of the great "heroes of faith" had more than one wife. And while missionaries did not "hear" aspects of the New Testament message concerning divine healing, African Christians did, because they had traditionally been accustomed to asking God for healing.[143] Missionaries accepted that only by becoming less African could one become Christian; Africans were required to accept the customs of Western civilization before they were qualified to become "Christians." At times, missionaries described their task of bringing the gospel to Africa in terms of "carrying the light of civilization" into Africa. LeMarquand states that Western biblical interpretation is still pervasive in mission-founded churches in Africa.[144] Most published material in African Christian book stores, and those exegetical and other theological material used and prescribed in facilities training African candidates for the ministry use the paradigm of Western theology.[145]

Some hold the opinion that Africans feel more at home with the Old Testament than with the New; they show a predilection for the Old Testament. While it is probably true that they use the Old Testament more frequently in their preaching than what happens in other parts of the world—because concepts and philosophies contained in the Old Testament are more readily comprehensible in African contexts—it is not true that the African and New Testament worlds do not contain many continuities as well.[146] While Africans find many similarities between their context and the Old Testament world in terms of, for instance, sacrificial

142. Some of these customs, like female circumcision, were not acceptable on moral terms.

143. LeMarquand, "New Testament Exegesis," 15.

144. LeMarquand, "New Testament Exegesis," 8.

145. This is especially the case in South Africa, where the debate about decolonized syllables for theological and other studies is raging.

146. LeMarquand, "New Testament Exegesis in (Modern) Africa," 7.

rituals and their proverbial tradition that links to the Old Testament wisdom literature, the New Testament is considered to be more "powerful" by many Africans and it is often used in a magical way to combat evil. New Testament texts also play an important role in the identity formation of some African congregations and preachers.

The most profound and widespread social transformations in Africa in the twentieth century were religious in character, with a meager 18 percent of the African population belonging to either Christianity or Islam in 1900, and more that 80 percent of the 1.2 billion Africans today being either Christian or Muslim.[147] Africans are "notoriously religious," with no separation between the worlds of play and prayer, market and miracle. A staggering 84 percent of Africans say that religion is very important in their lives, compared to Europe, where only 21 percent say that religion is of importance in their lives (see also North America, with 57 percent, and Latin America, with 66 percent). About 80 percent of African Christians attend worship at least once a week, and many attend more frequently—double the reported attendance of North American Christians—and more than half of African Christians say they have been born again. Most believe the Bible should be interpreted literally, word for word.[148] About 45 percent of Africans are Christians (more Africans are Christian than Muslim), and Pentecostal Christianity in Africa is estimated at about 31 percent (up from 11 percent in 2004),[149] leading Asamoah-Gyadu[150] to call Africa a "hotbed of Pentecostal/charismatic activity."[151] Pentecostalism is big business in Africa. Omenyo and Atiemo[152] use a typology of African Pentecostalism that takes into account historical and theological categories, making sense of the diversity of Pentecostal denominations, independent groups and movements within Africa: The Africa Initiated (Instituted, Independent, Indigenous) Churches (AICs) or Aladura Churches are the oldest type, established at the turn of the twentieth century by African Prophets and considered to be the first stream of African

---

147. Ukah, "Deregulation of Piety in the Context," 362.

148. Jacobsen, *Global Gospel*, 60. This is also reflected in the survey concerning Bible reading practices within the AFM of SA, referred to above. See Nel, "Bible Reading Practices in the AFM."

149. Jacobsen, *World's Christians*, 50.

150. Asamoah-Gyadu, *Contemporary Pentecostal Christianity*, 32.

151. In Africa, there are 126 million charismatics or members of mainline churches with a charismatic experience (Barrett, "Worldwide Holy Spirit Renewal," 409).

152. Omenyo and Atiemo "Claiming Religious Space," 58.

Pentecostals[153]; the classical Pentecostal movements, some of which had roots in William Seymour's Azusa Street revivals; transdenominational fellowships such as the Full Gospel Business Men's Fellowship International (FGBMFI), Women Aglow Fellowship International, and others[154]; charismatic renewal groups in the mainline churches, the independent neo-Pentecostal churches and ministries which started as a result of local initiatives, and neo-prophetism, which is an amalgamation of forms of ministries of the AICs and neo-Pentecostal churches. Africa is also a diverse continent with more than three thousand ethnicities and distinct languages.

African scholars trace the origin of biblical interpretation on their continent to the cities of Alexandria in Egypt and Hippo Regius (modern-day Annaba) in Algeria, where hermeneutical models were formed in a ferment of theological endeavors in the first four centuries CE. Important names in these debates are Clement of Alexandria (150–215), Origen of Alexandria (185–254), Cyprian (200–258), Tertullian (155–240), Athanasius (296–373), Augustine of Hippo (354–430), and others who lived in North Africa.[155] Alexandrian theologians perfected the allegorical method that influenced the Western church until the *Aufklärung*, when it became the fashion to refer to allegorization as pre-modern and uncritical.[156]

153. Omenyo, "African Pentecostalism," 136.

154. Collins, "Deliverance and Exorcism," 93.

155. Katho, "African Biblical Interpretation," 284, and Quayesi-Amakye, "'Nativizing' the Gospel," 292.

156. Maier refers to the positive aspects of pre-critical methods of interpreting the Bible that have been discovered in more recent hermeneutical discussion, such as its emphasis on the material unity of Old and New Testament, the integrity of the biblical canon, and the identity of Scriptural doctrine and systematic theology (Maier, *Biblical Hermeneutics*, 333–36). It was strongly realistic, at once historical and literal, with an emphasis on philology and history, with an openness to a spiritual meaning in Scripture. Pre-critical exegesis sought to work with philological precision, historical realism, and multidimensionality as a result of its conviction regarding inspiration. The renewal of the Christian interpreter through the Spirit was presupposed, implying no distinction between life and doctrine of the interpreter. Interpretation aimed ultimately at preaching and instruction and served a salvation-historical view of the events described in the Bible. It is also characterized by a methodologically reflected interpretation, a self-awareness of one's own procedure, testability, feasabililty, understandable, and learnable presentation (Maier, *Biblical Hermeneutics*, 342–43). The Bible was read as self-interpreting and the hermeneutical rule of comparing Scripture with Scripture was commonplace. It was directed by its adherence to the "rule of faith," as a story that could only be read in a trinitarian manner. Interpretation was primarily

The eighteenth century saw the development of the historical-critical method, which determined biblical scholarship until the middle of
the twentieth century, when literary approaches became the fashion, only
to be gradually supplemented by social-scientific criticism.[157] The historical-critical approach to the interpretation of the Bible treats biblical
texts primarily like any other texts that function as historical sources. It
does not proceed from the conviction that the canonical Bible is a unified
whole or that the different books can be understood best by reading them
in canonical context. It focuses on the *Sitz im Leben* as it is historically
reconstructed and authenticated by scholarly methodology, aiming to
establish what the text originally meant and not what it might now mean
for the contemporary reader, creating a "historical distance" between the
ancient biblical text and the contemporary interpreter. It drives a wedge
between the narrative recounted in the biblical narratives (*Geschichte*)
and the actual history (*Historie*) that is ascertained by the methods of a
scientific historiography.[158] Karl Barth describes the critical deficiency of
much historical-critical interpretation of biblical texts as the failure to
read the Bible as a realistic narrative of God's self-revelation in the history

---

the task of the faith community and not isolated individuals (Venema, "Interpreting
the Bible," 27–29).

157. Traditionally the Bible was primarily the church's book. For many centuries,
Western Christians did not read the Bible themselves but rather listened to its interpretation by the church. The Reformation handed the Bible back to ordinary believers,
allowing them to interpret it for themselves, and running the risk that they might
misinterpret or misappropriate it. Then, Enlightenment scholarship took the Bible out
of the church's lectern and placed it in the scholars' study (Keegan, *Interpreting the
Bible*, 145). The Enlightenment paradigm offered historical-critical approaches such
as textual criticism, source criticism, form criticism, redaction criticism, and tradition
criticism, whose main focus was the relationship between the text and the source.
Kinyua emphasizes that biblical scholarship in Africa must realize that the Enlightenment scientific paradigm has run its course (Kinyua, *Introducing Ordinary African
Readers' Hermeneutics*, 295). Kinyua argues further that the Reformation churches
read the Bible in solidity because they did not allow church tradition to interpret the
Bible. Enlightenment scholarship purposed to make the Bible something solid and
objective, on which Reformation Christianity could stand. In the process the Bible
was separated from the community and its faith, contributing to a skepticism against
"theologians" from the side of some believers. The believing community is bracketed
out in biblical scholarship, and faith is bracketed out from the consideration of the
scholar, allowing the scholar to be "objective." Keegan asserts that one who does not
participate in the faith community that is presupposed of the implied reader of a given
text cannot read that text in a sensible way (Keegan, *Interpreting the Bible*, 147).

158. Venema, "Interpreting the Bible," 31–32.

of Jesus Christ.[159] For Barth, religion is a human, cultural phenomenon, or, even more negatively, reflecting human hubris, an attempt to avoid the true God with idolatry. For that reason, it is important that exegesis must not serve the ends of religion, for the Bible is not about religion. It is about God, God's action, and God's revelation.[160]

The historical critical approach to biblical exegesis did not impact African scholarship to a significant extent. The emergence of formal biblical interpretation in modern Africa is linked by Kinyua[161] to John Williams's *Hebrewism of West Africa*, published in 1930. Willliams draws linguistic parallelism between the Ashanti and Hebrew languages as a vilification of African traditions and religions. The major works in African biblical studies were those of Harry Sawyer (1968), Kwesi Dickson (1968, 1969), Byang Kato (1975), Leonidas Kalugila (1980), Kofi Appiah-Kubi (1977), John Mbiti (1971 and later), Daniel Wambutda (1978), Charles Nyamiti (1984), and Johnson Kimuhu (2008). Mbiti's works were especially influential as he pioneered the idea of integrating the biblical world with that of the traditional African world through African theology.[162] This trend was later called "inculturation theology" (intercultural exegesis or intercultural hermeneutics)[163] by African theologians such as Zablon N'thamburi and Douglas Waruta. Its purpose was to consciously and explicitly subject biblical texts to a socio-cultural analysis and relate it comparatively to African socio-cultural perspectives while acknowledging the sacred status of the Bible and its normative value for Christian life.[164] African religions, culture, and metaphors became the hermeneutical keys through which the texts were engaged.[165] Justin Ukpong[166] explains that inculturation theology is not a theological discipline but

---

159. Barth, *Kirchliche Dogmatik*, 1.2:620.

160. See Topping, *Revelation, Scripture, and Church*, 11.

161. Kinyua, *Introducing Ordinary African Readers' Hermeneutics*, 11–12.

162. See, for example, Mbiti, "Biblical Basis in Present Trends," 122. African theology can be described as an attempt to give African expression to the Christian faith within a theological framework (Ukpong, "Current Theology," 501). Mbiti argues (along with other African theologians) that African theology should stay within the orbits of an African worldview in order to traditionalize Christianity within African culture.

163. Loba-Mkole, "New Testament and Intercultural Exegesis," 7.

164. Loba-Mkole, "New Testament and Intercultural Exegesis," 11.

165. Kinyua, *Introducing Ordinary African Readers' Hermeneutics*, 12.

166. See Ukpong, "Current Theology."

rather a way of doing theology which cuts across disciplines, characterized by consciously and explicitly seeking to interpret texts from the
socio-political perspectives of different people. It reads the Bible in light
of the needs, hopes, cultural values, religious aspirations, political, social,
and economic realities of human beings.[167] Four issues from the African world appear to command the most attention from African biblical
scholars, according to LeMarquand: mission and colonialism; suffering;
faith; and African traditional religion and culture.[168] From the perspective of inculturation biblical hermeneutics, however, African context and
people are not just used as a field of applying "exegetical" conclusions
but they stand as the subject of interpretation, equipped with genuine
epistemological privilege.[169]

In the process, the historicity of biblical texts was at times sacrificed (as far as its content was concerned) to transfer African meaning to
the passage. What is notable is that these efforts represented a conscious
rejection, defiance, and interruption of the patronizing and hegemonic
Western biblical hermeneutics that have silenced Africa for years. However, Ituneleng Mosala[170] warns that African hermeneutics can easily fall
into ideological captivity to the hermeneutical principle of a theology
of oppression. The "inculturation" theology is represented by an over-
whelmingly male-dominated and patriarchal group, criticized for being
patronizing to women by ignoring their voice.[171] What is needed is an
African theology that represents all voices, including those of women
and children, as well as the working class and poor peasant culture, in
order to define its hermeneutical starting point. Hermeneutics must be
accountable to the marginalized and not just to academia.[172] It is not
enough to read the Bible "for" the poor and marginalilzed; these communities themselves have insights which must also be brought to the table to
discover the liberating potential of biblical texts.[173]

In post-*Aufklärung* Africa, Western biblical scholarship determined
the way African pastors and theologians functioned until the 1930s when

---

167. Ukpong, "Current Theology," 524.

168. LeMarquand, "New Testament Exegesis in (Modern) Africa," 14.

169. Loba-Mkole, "New Testament and Intercultural Exegesis," 24.

170. Mosala, *Biblical Hermeneutics and Black Theology*, 16–20.

171. Kanyoro, *Introducing Feminist Cultural Hermeneutics*, 13.

172. Kinyua, *Introducing Ordinary African Readers' Hermeneutics*, 16.

173. LeMarquand, "New Testament Exegesis in (Modern) Africa," 13.

an "African" scholarship originated.[174] What is indicated by "African" in biblical interpretation is the integration of the specific context of Africa— socio-political, religious, philosophical, and economic—in the theologizing of African theologians. The distinctive character of African biblical interpretation is the focus of the interpreter on the interaction between the biblical text and the context against which the text functions, and the situation of the contemporary interpreter with its unique challenges.[175] In the Western context, theologizing invariably involves rational, systematic analyses of the "contents of faith," that is the nature, purposes, and activity of God in relation to the world. The purpose is to formulate propositional statements that are valid for all people and all times. African Pentecostals also theologize, but their emphasis is on the center of their Christianity, their encounter with Christ through Christ's Spirit, experienced as the heartbeat of their faith. Therefore, Asamoah-Gyadu[176] makes the sensible remark that it is more appropriate in the oral African tradition to speak of pentecostal beliefs and practices rather than of pentecostal theology, which might give the impression of a rational systematic reflection of what faith entails. African Pentecostalism is concerned with spirituality and life much more than with theology. The articulation of their beliefs is based on believers' experiences of the Spirit, which can be better expressed as their theological orientation or spirituality. The codification of pentecostal theology also has the distinct disadvantage that it does not take account of the prominence of particular beliefs in specific cultural contexts that continuously change within an oral world.[177]

The development of African biblical interpretation can be described in three stages.[178] The early period, from the 1930s to the 1970s, saw the focus on legitimizing African religions and cultures *contra* Western missionaries' wholesale rejection of indigenous cultures and religions. Afri-

---

174. Today, the people of Africa refer to Western civilization as WEIRD: Western, Educated, Industrialized, Rich, and Democratic. WEIRD people see themselves as self-sufficient and independent, in contrast to the African notion of being rooted in communion (Jacobsen, *Global Gospel*, 62).

175. African scholarship provided several experts on different issues, although Asamoah-Gyadu correctly emphasizes that to function as an authority in Pentecostal circles, one should prove that one's theology is based not exclusively on ideas but on experience, and that these ideas are translatable on the ground (Asamoah-Gyadu, *African Charismatics*, 244).

176. Asamoah-Gyadu, *African Charismatics*, 7.

177. Asamoah-Gyadu, *African Charismatics*, 8.

178. See Katho, "African Biblical Interpretation," 285–89.

can scholars described what they perceived as the similarities between Hebrew and African cultures and worldviews, with related values such as the importance of community life and the omnipresent nature of religion in everyday life, through comparative methods.[179] In this way, African Christians claimed their unique identity that accompanied the experience of achieving independence for most African nations in the 1950s and 1960s. Theologians contributed to national development in political, economic and cultural sense.[180] African theological scholarship is almost always confessional in its ethos. Most African biblical scholars find Western skepticism underlying all scientific endeavors unacceptable. While in North America, God has become marginalized, in Africa, God is acknowledged as a living reality, not bracketed out in the illusion of being objective.[181]

A middle period of African theology, from the 1970s to the 1990s, was dominated by inculturation (or indigenization), in an attempt to understand the relationship between the Bible and African culture and to facilitate understanding and communication of the message of the Bible in Africa with the hope that a new understanding would introduce a Christianity that is both biblical and African, and by a liberation hermeneutics, reflecting the African continent's relatively poor, oppressed and

179. See the remark of Asamoah-Gyadu that perhaps African Christianity—and the Christianity of the Third World generally—constitutes better reflections of the faith in its biblical forms than the historic Western patterns that, for centuries, the world has been made to accept as representing what Christianity was meant to be (Asamoah-Gyadu, *Sighs and Signs of the Spirit*, 104). However, consider also the warning of Carson about worldview confusion that can easily and unconsciously bedevil interpreting the Bible (Carson, *Exegetical Fallacies*, 103).

180. Originally, Pentecostals and charismatics did not mix in politics, like some Evangelicals. Their vision of the kingdom of God was defined in eschatological terms, as a future hope. While they drove out devils, their nations "went to the devil" (Shaw, *Kingdom of God in Africa*, 292). In many cases, however, this stance changed over time and they have become more involved in political and economic issues. Prophetic politics actualizes also in participation in politics; pentecostals were involved in the establishment of several political parties in African states and Zambia has had two pentecostal presidents (Anderson, "Deliverance and exorcism in Majority World pentecostalism," 104 and 108), with President Fredrick Chiluba declaring Zambia a Christian nation in 1991 and President Edgar Lungu's call to the nation to prayer, fasting, and reconciliation and a National Day of Prayer and Fasting Service in 2015 (see Chanda, "History of Pentecostalism in Zambia" and Munshya, "After We Have Said 'Amen'").

181. LeMarquand, "New Testament Exegesis in (Modern) Africa," 18.

exploited state.[182] Inculturation appropriates Christ's incarnation as paradigmatic for Christian theology; the incarnation serves as the principle and model of inculturation of Christianity.[183] Some of the proponents denied Christianity's legitimacy of inhabiting the spiritual universe of the African religious past.[184] Liberation theology is concerned with the relationship between the poor and the rich, the economic gap between Western countries and Africa, colonization and decolonization, existing inequalities between African societies, the brutalization and marginalization of women, and the superiority of Western nations who imposed their culture in Africa, including Western churches functioning in an African context. And while liberation theology opted for the poor, the poor have opted for Pentecostalism.[185]

The modern period of African biblical interpretation started in the 1990s from the comprehension that neither inculturation nor liberation had solved Africa's problems, leading to the refinement of a theology of reconstruction and renaissance that seeks to address in concrete ways the African reality of poverty, corruption, and political oppression that were effectively destroying parts of the continent, and to the recognition

182. See West and Dube, *Bible in Africa*, which defines the inculturation in regard to interpretive communities and an extensive range of interpretative methods such as historical critical studies, literary approaches, and new hermeneutics. Inculturation refers to "theologies of being" and liberation or "theologies of bread," which, in their opinion, constitute the most persuasive paradigms of African biblical scholarship (West, "Mapping African Biblical Interpretation," 34–35). Inculturation is related to the development of African reconstruction hermeneutics, rainbow hermeneutics, *ubuntu* hermeneutics, liberation hermeneutics, hermeneutics of engagement, Afrocentric hermeneutics, *Semoya* hermeneutics, womanist hermeneutics, development hermeneutics, storytelling hermeneutics, postcolonial hermeneutics, and many more (Loba-Mkole, "New Testament and Intercultural Exegesis," 9–10). Another development in the same tradition as West and Dube is Mugambi and Smit, *Text and Context in New Testament Hermeneutics.*

183. Quayesi-Amakye, "'Nativizing' the Gospel," 291.

184. Bediako, *Christianity in Africa*, 77.

185. Yong, "Reviews of Political Theologies," 158. West wonders whether pentecostal and charismatic Christianity ought to be included (along with AICs) in liberation hermeneutics because they provide sites in which liberation hermeneutics should be located—and even sites which have a contribution to make to liberation hermeneutics (West, "Locating 'Contextual Bible Study,'" 9). What should be remembered, however, is that Pentecostals' emphasis on liberation consists of a definition of "liberation" that differs from the one used by liberation hermeneutics, although it also comprises (and should comprise) issues like social justice and economic equality.

of the importance of including the community of ordinary readers[186] in the process of biblical interpretation, to serve the agenda of transformation.[187] "Ordinary readers" refers first to the literate African readers who remain poor and marginized (because that is the profile of the average African Bible reader) as well as the illiterate listener who listens to the reading of the Bible and discusses the meaning of the Bible in terms of their existential needs and challenges.[188] Even though these African readers lack formal training in biblical scholarship and approach the Bible pre-critically, they have unique and logical ways of interpreting biblical texts.[189] In Africa, the point of theology is not to talk about God or Chris-

186. In Africa, the vast majority of Bible readers are church members, believers who read the Bible with faith but also limited education. Their lack of critical skills keeps them from developing the skepticism about the supernatural interventions of God that characterize many Western Bible readers. Everyday hermeneutics or congregational hermeneutics concerns itself with how ordinary readers or nonspecialists work with biblical texts and how they are faithfully formed by and for their reading of Scripture (Green, "Modern and Postmodern Methods of Biblical Interpretation," 201). Theological schools, as such, mostly disregard untrained, illiterate, or semi-literate readers as important partners in the development of biblical hermeneutics (Kinyua, *Introducing Ordinary African Readers' Hermeneutics*, 6). Socially engaged scholars in Africa should commit to read the Bible from the experienced reality of societal margins, communally with each other, and critically, in a goal orientated manner (Kinyua, *Introducing Ordinary African Readers' Hermeneutics*, 330).

187. Ngong warns against endorsing the beliefs of ordinary people as though their reading of the Bible necessarily and always provides correct ways by which the world should be seen (Ngong, *Holy Spirit and Salvation*, 149). Their uncritical approach may not always be taken seriously. African theologians, he argues, should be philosophers who do not simply baptize the beliefs and practices of their people but critically reflect on them. Pentecostals do not agree. Every Spirit-filled Christian is able to hear the voice of God and proclaim God's message. For Pentecostals, the priesthood as well as the prophethood of all believers are imperative, leading to a democratic view of believers constituting the body of Christ, including both sexes. Although "ordinary" readers should be equipped with background information that helps them to unlock the meaning of Scripture, they should be listened to as the Spirit speaks through all those who are available. For that reason, 1 Corinthians states that, "When you come together, each one has a hymn, a lesson, a revelation, a tongue, or an interpretation. Let all things be done for building up" (1 Cor 14:26). Pentecostal theology is a theology of the ordinary people, rather than a narrowly text-focused theology (Cartledge, "Locating the Spirit," 253).

188. Kinyua, *Introducing Ordinary African Readers' Hermeneutics*, 1.

189. West and Zondi-Mabizela relate how the Institute for the Study of the Bible and Worker Ministry Project of the University of Kwa-Zulu Natal, South Africa created a contextual Bible study method that creates a "safe space" where grassroots communities can speak for themselves (West and Zondi-Mabizela, "Bible Story"). West details the depth of insight that was generated by women and men discussing the meaning of

tian truths in the abstract, as if God could be subject to human scrutiny or as if theology had nothing to do with the lived experience of human beings; in Africa, theology is practical. It is undertaken for the purpose of helping Christians to reflect on who they are called to be as followers of Christ in the unique cultural contexts where they live.[190]

Many scholars participated in the establishment of a *Theologia Africana* which sought to interpret Christ to Africans in such a way that they feel at home in their new faith.[191] This is possible because one of the basic characteristics of African biblical hermeneutics is that it is highly existential in its interpretation. African biblical interpreters bring real-life interest into the text, playing a major role in such interpretation. This life interest may be healing, provision, success, or protection, which are the major concerns of most Africans. When African biblical interpreters approach the text, the main question is not what is the historical, social and literary dimension of the text but rather, what does the text have to offer?[192]

The four sources identified by Emmanuel Martey for defining African theology are the Bible, Christian tradition, and theological heritage; African traditional religion, culture, and philosophy; African anthropology and other social sciences; and African Independent Churches.[193] The question should be asked, how should African theology present Christ to the African? African theology must meet the African at the sociopolitical level of poverty, racism and sexism, classism and colonialism, imperialism and injustice, political dictatorship and repression, rampant *coup d'etats* and the resultant displacement of thousands of migrants, hunger and drought, and incurable diseases that dehumanize the African personality.[194] A second emphasis is that African theology should meet the African at the religio-cultural level by offering a pneumatological supplement to the soteriological interests of the liberationist approach. This will require an image of Christ that can answer Africans' questions

---

Bible passages (West, "Reading the Bible," 4–5).

190. Jacobsen, *Global Gospel*, 61.

191. Quayesi-Amakye, "'Nativizing' the Gospel," 287.

192. Adamo, "Reading Psalm 23 in African Context," 2.

193. Martey, *African Theology*, 72.

194. Martey, *African Theology*, 84–86.

about the nature of the absent but yet present Christ who is willing and ready to promote African humanity.[195]

The positive side is that African biblical scholarship, according to LeMarquand, is characterized by several characteristics: it takes popular readings and the use of the Bible by ordinary people seriously (although this does not imply that scholars do not criticize some aspects of popular uses of the Bible); scholars, at times, utilize historical-critical tools—even though their emphasis is more on the readers than on the text, more on present and future than on the past, and their use of critical tools to reconstruct history has not been the major issue; women are beginning to emerge as a strong voice in the exegetical community, producing a different understanding of the role of African tradition than that found among male African scholars; and liberationist and inculturationist perspectives are combined in Bible reading practices, where liberation is seen as multi-faceted.[196]

Experience shows how the Bible-reading process can effectively transform the spiritual and social conditions of the poor people of Africa. The process has been called African biblical hermeneutics, African cultural hermeneutics, African biblical transformational hermeneutics, or African biblical studies, and Jesse N. K. Mugambi, Ka Mana, and Gerald O. West played leading roles in establishing it at grassroots level.[197] The hermeneutics consists of three essential elements. *Distantiation* follows from an understanding of the two realities, the Bible as a sacred text (not an ordinary document) that is normative for the faith community, and written for different people in a different context, struggling with issues that may be similar to (but not exactly the same as) ours.[198] This leads to the text speaking for itself, acknowledging the importance of listening to the text from its own historical, social, cultural, and economic context.

195. Quayesi-Amakye, "'Nativizing' the Gospel," 293.

196. LeMarquand, "New Testament Exegesis in (Modern) Africa," 21–22. Part of the debate is concerned with the abiding relevance of old religions in the transition to the new in Christianity. Another part is concerned with the primal religions of Africa as the background of the Christian profession by the vast majority of Christians of all generations and nations (Bediako, *Christianity in Africa*, 83).

197. Katho, "African Biblical Interpretation," 289.

198. Green concurs and suggests that those who want to read the Bible for its significance to the church must maintain two emphases from modern hermeneutics: *distantiation*, as the need to craft a mental space separating the contemporary reader from the ancient text, and *technique*, as the training necessary to interpret the text (Green, "Pentecostal Hermeneutics," 161).

The second step is *contextualization*, the acknowledgement that there is not absolute meaning in a text. Where the text was meticulously analyzed in the first step, now the details of the African contexts receive attention.[199] Vernacularization is one sure way of contextualizing the gospel for Africans, resulting in the fusion of horizons as recipients engage the Bible with their contextual experiences and questions.[200] Bediako is of the opinion that the existence of the Christian Bible in African languages was the single most important legacy of Western missionary activity, and in many instances the Bible became the foundation of a new literacy culture which did not exist previously, ensuring that an effectual rooting of the Christian faith in African consciousness would take place.[201] The interpretation of a text does not stop with what the text meant to its original hearers; the text must now help contemporary readers to discover themselves, confronted as they are by specific challenges in their own context. The highest level of interpretation is *appropriation*, where the Bible—now accepted as normative text for the community—leads to transforming the life or context of the contemporary reader. The interaction or dialogue between the biblical text and African context is determined by the vision of change that determines the questions that are asked of the text. The vision of change is determined by the tradition that the reader belongs to.

Pentecostalism as an expression of primal spirituality is also a measure of primal exegesis, where the significance of a passage for its readers is inherently of more interest to them than any meaning it might have had for others. African pentecostal spirituality consists of various features, such as a deepened awareness regarding Satan, demons, and evil in popular African Christianity; belief in libations, sacrificial objects, and incantations; a view that circumstances of life on earth are determined in the spiritual realm; belief in anointing oils, prophetic prayers, and seed sowing of money or material things; and the expectancy of miracles and the unexpected when people spend time in prayer.[202]

---

199. See, for example, Bediako, *Christianity in Africa*, 83–84. Bediako confronts three areas of religious meaning in African traditional life: the practice of sacrifice, priestly mediation, and ancestral function.

200. Quayesi-Amakye, "'Nativizing' the Gospel," 288–89. The vernacular Bible is also one of the major reasons for the fast growth of Pentecostalism, and the AICs, in Africa (Omenyo, "African Pentecostalism," 146).

201. Bediako, "Epilogue," 244.

202. Omenyo, "African Pentecostalism," 145–46.

In an African pentecostal context, it is meaningless to discuss the interpretation of the text by itself.[203] It only has value as it becomes personalized and directly related to the specific location of the reader, implying a phenomenological approach to Bible reading. Thus the Bible on the shelf is still God's word; it is not, however, God's word to me at that time. The practical result of reading the Bible in order to hear the voice of God is probably selective reading, with some passages containing meaning for a specific individual that receive most attention. This can lead to isolation from the message of the Bible, its metanarrative, and the production of a customized, individually-specified canon within the canon, of the texts that are most inspirational to an individual, serving as "the most inspired part" of the Bible.[204]

Much of African Christianity—and its own theological reflection—understands salvation in much the same way as it is understood in African Traditional Religions (ATR). For instance, Charles H. Mason (1866–1961), a pentecostal founding father, places value on the deep spirituality of African-American slave religion and spirituality, describing the continuity between African religions and African folk religion in terms of five points: the natural world is a religious universe, imbued with meaning; there are various objects and events that convey these religious meanings; certain persons are skilled in identifying religious objects and discerning God's word and will conveyed to them; signs are an indication that God is active and participating in nature and human life; and God judges human beings according to their regard or disregard for the truth conveyed by signs.[205]

It is a valid question whether it is possible to generalize when one speaks about African worldview and traditional religions. Although ample room should be left for diversity within Africa, it is also true that there is a certain unity of thought which appears to pervade Africa in a way that is quite unlike anything perceived in Europe, Asia, or the Americas. This makes it possible and viable to speak of "African traditional thought and religion" in a general way, without denying the particularism of different parts of Africa.[206]

---

203. Anderson, "Hermeneutical Processes," 1.

204. Davies, "What Does it Mean to Read?," 258.

205. Ware, "Use of Signs," 12.

206. See Anderson, *Moya*, 11.

Because the better part of traditional African cosmology is spiritualized, salvation is seen as freedom from the various spiritual powers that support or undermine the material, spiritual, economic, political, and psychological well-being of Africans. Kalu explains that African Christianity, specifically Pentecostalism, has produced a culture of continuity with ATR by mining primal worldviews and regaining a pneumatic and charismatic religiosity that existed in traditional society and that contemporary Africans can identify with.[207] Traditionally, mission churches, with their too-cerebral analytical "class-room religion," rejected the African worldview and primal vision and taught new believers that they need to formulate a new worldview—in accordance with the Bible—without acknowledging any connection between a biblical and African worldview.[208] Many Protestants still hold the same opinion. Kangwa represents the oppposite view; he believes that only by retrieving and applying values of African cultures and worldviews, African Christianity can help to diminish suffering in all facets of life, through a spirituality of holism and the integration of life representing a sacramental worldview in which salvation is mediated through all the channels of God's creation, and which can only be perceived and observed in a multi-sensory way.[209] In this way, by accepting the African worldview, it also changes in important respects in correlation with biblical perspectives. Ngong argues that ATR's *telos* differs from Christianity, which is true, although it should also be kept in mind that the ATR's salvific view contains holistic and this-worldly aspects that are utilized by African Pentecostalism, while parts of Western Christianity neglected these important aspects of the gospel.[210] Ukpong, writing from a Roman Catholic perspective, argues that the Christian church should respect African spirituality—a spirituality that Ukah depicts as liquid because of its ability to respond to the social context of the practice, to absorb external influences, rework indigenous cosmologies, and modify its self-understanding and practice accordingly.[211]

In African traditional life (and ATR) birth, illness, death, drought, and material challenges were explained as acts perpetuated by good or evil spirits. Human beings were vulnerable and open to both evil and

207. Kalu, *African Pentecostalism*, 186.

208. Taylor, *Primal Vision*, 21–22.

209. Kangwa, "African Democracy," 544.

210. Ngong, *Holy Spirit and Salvation*, 150.

211. Ukpong, "Charismatic Renewal," 336, and Ukah, "Deregulation of Piety in the Context," 372.

benevolent forces and the forefathers should be appeased because of their influence on the world of spiritual forces. The power of evil was perpetuated by bad witchcraft, ancestral spirits, and bad *muti* (or herbal medicines and potions made by *sangomas)*, which were believed to cause misfortune in the lives of people. The powers of evil caused illness, poverty, and broken relationships.[212] Because people were curious about their existential concerns, they explored sources of vital forces to change their destinies for the better; hence, the popularity and constancy of prophetism in Africa's religious climate.[213] Salvation consisted of freedom from evil powers that hinder human beings from achieving well-being,[214] implying that ancestor veneration is not godly and Christians should break with their extended families who practice ancestor veneration because Christians fight against the evil forces of ancestors, witchcraft, evil spirits, hobgoblins, and Satan.[215] Pentecostal prophetism appropriates the holistic African worldview[216] by focusing on how the spirit world impinges on the visible world to hinder or foster human flourishing because unemployment, poverty, the challenges of barrenness and an unhappy marriage, sickness, and death are problems that have their provenance in

212. Frahm-Arp, "Rise of the Megachurches," 271, and Quayesi-Amakye, *Christology and Evil in Ghana,* 51–85.

213. Quayesi-Amakye, "'Nativizing' the Gospel," 302.

214. Ndiokwere, *Prophecy and Revolution,* 239–43.

215. Frahm-Arp, "Rise of the Megachurches," 271–72. African Pentecostals are proud that they have not forsaken the spiritual customs their ancestors passed on to them before whites came to the continent, despite Western missionaries encouraging them to abandon the remnants of their superstition because of their intolerance of Christian patronage of traditional worship and practices (Quayesi-Amakye, "'Nativizing' the Gospel," 289). African Christians believe that God was already present in Africa before the Europeans arrived and that their way of worshiping is better than the ways the missionaries taught them, leading to a thoroughly Africanized version of Christianity (Cox, *Fire from Heaven,* 247). However, all African religious and cultural customs were not accepted uncritically. For instance, defetishisation was used to expose and denounce certain aspects of paganism controlled by evil spirits (Kärkkäinen, *Pneumatology,* 173).

216. Taylor describes the African worldview as a sense of cosmic oneness, where fundamentally all things share the same nature and the same interaction one upon another (Taylor, *Primal Vision,* 72). It is a hierarchy of power, but not of being—all are one, all are here, and all are now. No distinction is made between sacred and secular, natural and supernatural, for nature, human beings, and the unseen are inseparably involved with one another in a total community. Within the African worldview, African ideas of the Holy Spirit and the world are not far removed from the biblical revelation (Anderson, *Moya,* 5).

the spirit world—and not physical problems that need secular analysis, as viewed by Western society.[217] It is based on a primal vision with a sense of cosmic oneness, where fundamentally all things share the same nature and nature, humanity, and the unseen are inseparably involved in one another in a total community.[218] African exegetes take seriously the reality of cosmic powers and they treat these powers as some kind of organized disobedience to the will of God, which directly or indirectly affects the course of human history, while most educated Westerners probably look on demons as an outdated superstition and demon possession as a psychological malady to be treated in medical terms.[219] Another way that African Christians do battle with evil spirits is in the way they view and treat the Bible. Asamoah-Gyadu recounts the story of an African Christian who buried a copy of the Bible in the foundations of her new home, as the Christian equivalent of what her non-Christian compatriots buried in the foundations of their buildings, namely traditional charms, amulets, and medicines.[220] In the African universe, the supernatural can be hyperactive and against the background of a worldview that takes supernatural evils like the evil eye and witchcraft seriously. It is not uncommon for Christians to use protective medicines, charms, and amulets to secure them and their property against the presence of evil powers.[221] For many of them, the Bible carries the necessary supernatural power to protect them from evil. The primary use of the Bible is not talismanic, but there is a strong connection between the Bible's talismanic power and the

217. Ngong, "In Quest of Wholeness," 524.

218. Anderson, "Spirit and the African Spiritual World," 310.

219. LeMarquand, "New Testament Exegesis in (Modern) Africa," 20–21.

220. Asamoah-Gyadu, *Contemporary Pentecostal Christianity*, 169. Asamoah-Gyadu also recounts how a Bible is perpetually kept on the table from which a prophet in Ghana speaks (Asamoah-Gyadu, *Contemporary Pentecostal Christianity*, 171). The prophet does not read from the Bible; it simply lies there as a symbol of God's authority and presence of God's people as they gather in worship.

221. Adamo argues that mission Christianity encouraged the indigenous Africans to throw away all charms, medicines, incantations, forms of divination, sacrifices, and other cultural ways of protecting, healing, and liberating people from the evil powers that filled their lives: "They did not teach us how to use the Bible as a means of protecting, healing, and solving the problems of life, but by reading the Bible with our own eyes we have found ways of appropriating it for our context" (Adamo, "Use of Psalms," 339–40). For Africans, the Bible has come to be something more than a text to be read—it also has supernatural properties (Asamoah-Gyadu, *Contemporary Pentecostal Christianity*, 173). Like the Quran, it is viewed as a kratophany, a holy book with the ability to shed powerful influences either for good or for ill.

seriousness with which its contents are regarded.[222] The dynamism and growth of Christianity in contemporary Africa is due in part to the sacredness or supernatural character of the Bible that has been maintained in the African Christian imagination, as well as a view of salvation that is concerned with protection from spiritual powers that undermine the wellbeing of the African people. In this way, Ngong argues that the prevalent pneumatological soteriology in Africa simply baptizes the supposed African cosmology by way of inculturation.[223]

Pentecostal prophetism provides in what Sakupapa pejoratively calls "the prophetic craze among many Christians irrespective of church tradition or doctrine,"[224] and that Cox describes as an important ingredient of African Pentecostalism's recipe for success[225] (i.e., its ability to assimilate a wide variety of African indigenous religious practices while it links with the direct needs of ordinary people in the idiom that they understand and by emphasizing the power of the Holy Spirit to provide in any and all needs of contemporary believers, including childlessness and infertility, bodily and mental illness, drought and other natural catastrophes, accidents and bad luck, poverty, racism, sexism, classism, colonialism, neo-colonialism, imperialism, injustice, political dictatorship and repression, imprisonment without trial, and all that dehumanizes the African personality).[226] African pentecostal prophetism functions against the background of Spirit-possession that is familiar to the African custom of divination.[227] Pentecostalism, through its experience of the Spirit, often unconsciously taps into popular religious and cultural beliefs and draws from these sources while also using a biblical rationale for its practices.[228]

222. Asamoah-Gyadu, *Contemporary Pentecostal Christianity*, 169.

223. Ngong, *Holy Spirit and Salvation*, 121. Intercultural exegesis is grounded on the epistemological side on the philosophical hermeneutics of Gadamer and Ricoeur (Loba-Mkole, "New Testament and Intercultural Exegesis," 16). In the process of understanding the text, three steps have to be followed: pre-comprehension of the reader, fusion of the horizon of the reader and that of the text, and appropriation of the text by the reader.

224. Sakupapa, "Prophets in the Zambian/African context," 118.

225. Cox, *Fire From Heaven*, 247.

226. Quayesi-Amakye, "'Nativizing' the Gospel," 302. The quest for divine immediacy is vital to pentecostal spirituality, in opposition to many Protestant theologians' cessationism that limits supernatural intervention and the (so-called supernatural) *charismata* to the apostolic era.

227. Anderson, *Moya*, 31.

228. Anderson, "Spirit and the African Spiritual World," 304.

Pentecostal experience of the Spirit is grounded in the concept of the Bible as revelatory.[229] Some of these prophets enjoy widespread media coverage through online social media and digital television. That Pentecostalism attracts many Africans is not only related to its this-worldly perspective on salvation[230] but also to the affinity of their practices to certain ATR beliefs that underlie the African worldview.[231] Muindi argues that the *charism* of prophecy has a particular appeal because it echoes the traditional African prophetic spirituality, which accentuates "spirit possession," "divine seizure," and "supernatural revelations" concerning the spiritual causes of actual events among people.[232] Its fruit is in the personal, communal, and predictive nature, with the revelation of hidden sins, helping people overcome their traditional and deep-seated fear of witchcraft and sorcery, revealing the will of God in specific situations,

229. Neumann, "Spirituality," 198.

230. Pentecostals traditionally emphasized divine healing and based it on the connection between salvation, wholeness, and holiness. In demonstrating this connection, Maddocks defines health as a foretaste of the wholeness to come, when the kingdom will be established and creation healed (Maddocks, *Christian Healing Ministry*, 7). A Christian can never talk about healing without having Jesus in mind. The meaning of his name reflects the terms "save/heal" and speaks of the unleashing of power that brings the life of human beings (and society) back into a new spaciousness in which all the cells (or members) are released and delivered to perform their full and purposeful function (Maddocks, *Christian Healing Ministry*, 9). The shalom of the kingdom consists of prosperity, bodily health, contentedness, good relations between nations and human beings, and salvation, while holiness is a reflection of the holy God and the other-worldly equipment which equips human beings to be more whole in this world (Maddocks, *Christian Healing Ministry*, 12–14). African Pentecostals typify the *charismata* by the trinity of healing (health), predicting the future (prophecy), and promoting success (prosperity) (Ukah, "Deregulation of Piety," 366).

231. Bosch suggests that ATR's can be described by using three terms: Theism, or the belief in a supreme being (and sometimes lesser gods); spiritism, or the belief in spirits, including ancestors; and dynamism, or the belief in a life-force working through objects and available to some people to utilize for good or evil (Bosch, "Traditional Religions of Africa," 3). Traditional African concepts of God generally emphasize the transcendence of God, resulting in a *deus otiosus*, a withdrawn, distant supreme being who is not involved in the everyday affairs of people. This implies that it is necessary for the African to access some protection by the spirit world, which is done through witchcraft and magic (dynamism) (Anderson, *Moya*, 13).

232. Muindi, "Nature and Significance of Prophecy," 211. Cox suggests that for any religion to grow in Africa it must be able to include and transform at least certain elements of pre-existing religions which still retain a strong grip on the cultural subconscious. It must also equip people to live in rapidly changing societies. In Pentecostalism, these ingredients help people recover vital elements in their culture that are threatened by modernization (Cox, *Fire from Heaven*, 219–22).

revealing what is going to happen, revealing the cause of illness or misfortune and how to counteract it, and detecting wizardry, serving a distinct pastoral function of providing advice or exhortation.[233]

Ngong criticizes what he perceives to be much of African Christianity and theology buying uncritically into the dominant African worldview and argues that, to be theologically sound and conducive to the over-all well-being of the continent, it is imperative that Africa should not only dwell on the function of the Spirit but must also understand the person of the Spirit in trinitarian life.[234] It should also take into consideration that the Spirit is poured out on all flesh, necessitating their recognition that the Spirit not only operates in miraculous ways but also in the ordinary, rational, or scientific business of life, and that Africa today needs a revitalization of the Spirit of prophecy, qualified as the church's criticism of contemporary political, economic, and social trends.[235]

Pentecostals disagree with his viewpoint because they prefer to concentrate on the function of the Spirit and the experience of the Spirit's guidance and illumination. In their theological endeavors, they study the Bible with the express purpose to meet the one who is the truth and hear what God's will is for their situation, to then testify about their encounters with God before they theologize and develop their doctrines.[236] It should be kept in mind that the early church also concentrated on the function of the Spirit during the first three centuries before eventually attending to the doctrinal side of the person of the Spirit. As late as 325 CE, in the Nicene Creed, the church thought in binitarian terms, describing the Father and the Son in detail while only mentioning the Spirit in passing. Only at the end of the fourth century, in the Creed of Constantinople (381 CE), did the church elaborate on the place of the Spirit in the Trinity, leading to a formulation that would in the end alienate the Eastern Orthodox Church (with its *filioque* term).[237]

233. Anderson, *Moya*, 52.

234. Ngong, *Holy Spirit and Salvation*, 122.

235. This represents the Reformed and Roman Catholic perspective that the prophet is rather an engaged observer who, in solidarity with particular stakeholders, criticizes the actions and policies of other agents from outside, as an authentically Christian mode of moral discourse (De Villier, "Prophetic and Reformist Approaches," 154).

236. The criticism that Pentecostals emphasize the miraculous by viewing Spirit baptism in terms of an empowerment to do miracles at the cost of viewing Spirit baptism as an empowerment for effective witness (Ngong, *Holy Spirit and Salvation*, 128) may be valid in some cases, and African Pentecostalism need to do self-investigation.

237. Ngong's concern is that Pentecostals neglect the relational aspect of trinitarian

Another point of criticism that Ngong raises is that the pentecostal appropriation of the so-called African worldview led scholars to forget that this worldview contributed to the marginalization of the continent by promoting an imagination that did not critically engage the modern world or encourage the growth of science, which is a crucial element in the modernization of any society.[238] Instead of critiquing the African worldview, Ngong argues, Pentecostal churches baptize it; it assumes that reality can be explained spiritually, ignoring scientific and technological discoveries.[239] This, however, is a misrepresentation of African Pentecostalism that also allows room for natural causes and encourages believers to make use of medical treatment, including immunization.

Much has been written about the AICs, but almost no material on its biblical hermeneutics was published by the churches themselves, except for the booklet, *Speaking for Ourselves*. The leadership of AICs is indigenous African, and positions of leadership in these churches are not attained by either educational training or birth. It is rather a product of the election and anointing of the Spirit, as perceived by the faith community, and is rooted in a spiritual democracy where women bishops also play a prominent role, reflecting their role (at least in South

---

theology—with the Spirit manifesting the communion of the Father and the Son—by limiting the Spirit's role to that of a healer, anointer, baptizer, etc. Again, the pentecostal argument is that their experiential knowledge of the Spirit eventually leads to theological statements. The altar and the pulpit is where theology has primarily been done in pentecostal communities. The oral nature of pentecostal interpretive communities provided the experiential knowledge revealed by the Spirit, validated by Scripture, and confirmed by the community (Archer, *Pentecostal Hermeneutic*, 106). As mentioned previously, the early Pentecostals expected Christian unity to follow the outpouring of the Spirit that occurred throughout the world in response to the Azusa Street Revival. One never reads that Pentecostals thought that ecumenism was something that Pentecostals should pursue. However, they expected that it would follow as a natural result of the Spirit's work. They connected the Spirit with the answering of Jesus's prayer for unity in John 17 (Ngong, *Holy Spirit and Salvation*, 134). The expectation was carried by several elements. The most significant is the primitivist and restorationist impulse, the result of Pentecostals' interpretation of their experiences in continuity with the Early Church (Nel, "Pentecostal Movement's View," 2) as a form of criticism of mainline churches' apparent lack of charismatic practices. Their critical attitude contributed to their alienation from existing churches when they appreciated their own spiritual experiences as unique interventions by the Spirit in contradistinction to the older churches that they perceived to be caught up in a deadly web of tradition and doctrine with a sense of superiority that prohibited the possibility of any cooperation with existing churches (Faupel, *Everlasting Gospel*, 46).

238. Ngong, *Holy Spirit and Salvation*, 125.

239. Ngong, *Holy Spirit and Salvation*, 126.

Africa) as heads of households in the rural economy from which their men have been dislodged due to apartheid labor practices. These groups serve as "religious solidarity networks," growing from their origins in anti-colonial movements, representing a cultural subversion of official and "normal" Christianity and its structures and procedures.[240] Mosala investigates the Bible reading practices in Zion Apostolic churches, consisting of Africans whose African societal marital base and its culture have been eroded or even eradicated by colonialism and capitalism, and whose presence in capitalist society and culture is unwanted except as exploitable wage-slaves. Their members form an integral part of the black working class. They form a socio-religious sub-culture that lives in relation to the contradictions of monopoly capitalism in distinctive ways. As the commodityless, landless, and capitalless masses of African descent, the only commodity that they can manipulate is the Spirit (*Moya*). They cannot control the means of material production, but at least they can control the means of spiritual production.[241]

Among these churches, Mosala found that the Bible plays a crucial role. The AICs published a booklet, *Speaking for Ourselves*, in which they state that they read the Bible as a book that comes from God and take its every word seriously: "We do not have the same problems about the Bible as White people have with their Western scientific mentality."[242] Being Christian and believing in the Bible are inseparable. Members of the Zion Apostolic type of AICs utilize an oral knowledge of the Bible that they gained from listening to prayers and sermons.[243] Many of their leaders are semi-literate while a majority of members are illiterate. For them, the Bible as a written text makes no sense. They do not appropriate the Bible in terms of what it says but in terms of what it stands for, as a canonical authority. This stands in contrast to other groups who read the Bible in terms of its contents. AIC readers use a specifically black, working-class hermeneutics, drawing its conclusions largely from work place experiences, enabling them to negotiate their reality and resist the forces of brualization with which they are faced. Their interpretation of the Bible is also determined by the mystifications generated by the authority status of a basically unknown Bible. They appropriate the mysteries of the

240. Mosala, "Race, Class, and Gender," 8.

241. Mosala, "Race, Class, and Gender," 14.

242. Institute for Contextual Theology, *Speaking for Ourselves*, 26.

243. Mosala, "Race, Class, and Gender," 16.

An African oral pentecostal hermeneutics presumes textual impotence apart from the Bible's inspiration and application to the contemporary existential context. Verbalization of words from the Bible catalyzes interpersonal causality, activating other spirit-beings in the African imagination that populate the unseen dimensions of daily life.

Yong also illustrates the relation between biblical orality and African pentecostal hermeneutics, as explicated in the hermeneutical theory of the nascent African pentecostal scholarly discourse.[256] Pentecostal scriptural locutions extend in different pathways: at its foundational level, African pentecostal hermeneutics can be considered as a form of reader-reponse hermeneutics, with its emphasis on the world in front of the text, of contemporary listeners to the biblical world, rather than the world of (or behind) the text. The word of God is declared to realize and actualize prosperity, healing, deliverance, judgment on perceived enemies, and faith, empowering human responses to life's daily challenges.[257] It enables an encounter with the divine and provides guidance for decision-making. The truth of biblical accounts does not rest in the accurate recounting of what happened long ago but rather in the experience and actualization of the power of God that transforms the lives of contemporary listeners. For that reason, a message that does not challenge, invite, and convict its listeners is not perceived as Spirit-driven and effective. The word of God as a rule demands that choices and decisions be made and allegiances are shifted.

One of the results is that the Bible is at times divorced from its historical context to such an extent that its meaning is compromised. In most (or many) instances, however, the Bible's applicability to the holistic needs and challenges of its listeners is balanced by attention given to the historical. The result is that important elements of the biblical worldview—such as miracles, the spirit world and the *charismata* or work of the Spirit (which, at times, is ignored by Western believers whose scientific worldview excludes room for miraculous and supernatural interventions)—receives its due in African spirituality. For Africans, what happens on earth is directly interrelated with what happens in the spiritual dimension, agreeing with the cosmic principalities and powers that provide the mystical causality of a worldview found in the New Testament.

256. Yong, *Hermeneutical Spirit*, 53.

257. See Asamoah-Gyadu, *Contemporary Pentecostal Christianity*, 73–89, and Asamoah-Gyadu, *African Charismatics*, 164–200.

An African pentecostal hermeneutics also emphasizes the communal aspect of Bible reading, with the expectation that the liberative transformation described in the Bible not only happens in the lives of individuals but also at ecclesial and social levels, even influencing societies as a whole. While Western Pentecostalism might display an individualistic and personalized trend in its Bible reading practices, African Pentecostals emphasize the important role played by the prophet and pastor in the explication and application of the Bible. Communal pentecostal hermeneutics focuses on the relevance of the Bible for the faith community as well as for the individual.

Defining an African Pentecostal Hermeneutics

Yong argues that a framework for an African pentecostal hermeneutics could consist of three interrelated facets.[258] The first, orthopathy, relates to right affections and emotions; in religious language, it concerns the heart. On a foundational level, Pentecostalism arises from the affections rather than our intellectual abilities, with an emphasis on love, passion, desire, feeling, and emotion. It rejects the sole rule of the intellect while attempting to integrate the right affections with the right thinking and the right practices.[259] In an oral culture, affection is showed directly, without the need of description, in terms of joy, anger, desire, and other emotions that are communicated through facial expressions, sounds, and touch. This language is the portal that displays the results of the encounter between the human being and the Spirit of God. Orthopraxy is related to right action and behavior that follows on the words heard through performance or enactment. Language inspires practical implementation and invites participation in the ongoing mission of the Spirit. A last facet is orthodoxy, consisting of right beliefs and confessions. These three fac-

258. Yong, *Hermeneutical Spirit*, 57.

259. Vondey, *Pentecostalism*, 120. A significant part of pentecostal "thinking" happens at the affective, unconscious, and pre-deliberative level—aimed at witness and worship—before it enters the cognitive, deliberate world of understanding. As a result, Pentecostalism is dominated by the imagination rather than reason. It functions on an epistemological level that is aesthetic rather than noetic. The imagination is more improvisational and playful than the productivity, performance, and instrumentality demanded by established institutions, disciplines, and methodologies of the modern academy. Pentecostal "imagining of the world in otherwise terms" places less trust in purely cognitive knowledge than in participatory "action-reflection in the Spirit" (Land, *Pentecostal Spirituality*, 119).

ets are interrelated but the order is important among Pentecostals, so that an encounter with God leads to the right emotions and actions, resulting in the right beliefs. From an oral perspective, theology is embodied in proverbs, songs, narratives, and other genres of intersubjective interrelationality based on the experiential rather than the cognitive.

By noting and comprehending oral perspectives, one is better equipped to understand biblical textuality. African pentecostal hermeneutics is concerned with not only how the Bible is interpreted but also how the Bible is received and how it is used in relation to the mission of God.

All conferences of the Ecumenical Association of Third World Theologians (EATWOT) argued that Africa needs a new method of doing theology, and their proposed methodology is concerned with epistemology. An academic type of theology that is divorced from action should be rejected, needing a radical break in epistemology which makes commitment the first act of theology and engages in critical reflection on the praxis of the reality of the Third World and Global South. In this new methodology, the experiences of the marginalized and disenfranchised, of oppression and the struggle for liberation are fundamental, and the role of experience is the starting point for theological reflection. The stated goal of such reflection is the abolishment of the current unjust situation and the building of a different society, freer and more human. This theological paradigm is determined by a preferential option for the poor. In Western theology, the relation to the poor is usually an ethical question, not an epistemological question. Such a distinction does not do justice to the idea of the poor as interlocutors. Solidarity with the poor also has consequences for the perception of the social reality, as the epistemological privilege of the poor. Cognizance of the experience of those defined as poor is a necessary condition for theological reflection in Africa, since poverty is widely prevailing.[260]

This does not imply that traditional exegetical approaches—such as the historical, grammatical, linguistic, or literary—cannot make a contribution to the hermeneutics but rather that the significance of the Bible is only accomplished when orthopathic and orthopraxic perspectives accompany listening to the Bible because it results in encounters with the Spirit that transform listeners' lives, changing them into apostolic witnesses.

260. West, *Biblical Hermeneutics*, 85–87.

African pentecostal hermeneutics shows some level of literalism although it should be added that it is also characterized and supported by an awe for the Bible as a special book for believers. When Africans read it, they hear the message as if it were specifically written for them.[261] Omenyo and Arthur refer to several examples from their fieldwork, illustrating the level of literalism.[262] For instance, in referring to Matthew 11:12, that from the days of John the Baptist until now the kingdom of heaven suffers violence with the violent taking it by force, they found the conclusion among some African believers that if the exertion of violence is essential that their prayers would be answered. Hence the forceful, even violent way of praying for other people that one sometimes find among African church leaders. From Hebrews 4:12, that the word of God is quick, powerful and sharper than a two-edged sword, some conclude that the Bible needs to be viewed as a literal, physical weapon against the enemy, used in a magical manner by physically pointing it in the direction of the perceived enemy or even used as a sword to stab the enemy, be it human or spiritual. The teaching that Christians are children of the Creator who owns the world is also used by some to justify the expectation that the wealth of unbelievers is the Christians' for taking, with Deuteronomy 28 guaranteeing material and spiritual blessings to obedient believers, excluding non-believers in an obvious way.[263] Some African Pentecostals also teach that imprecatory prayers are the kind that demand divine retribution, vengeance, or evil against one's enemies. Using texts in the book of Psalms, some of them teach that one's enemy does not deserve to live.[264] It suggests literalness in reading these texts, ignoring the Christian view of enemies based on Jesus's clear teaching.[265]

African Pentecostalism functions in terms of the needs of those whose orientation to issues in life is rooted in the African primal worldview, including those newly empowered Africans who had experienced democracy and now form an influential middle class of political and economic rulers. Africans believe in a spirit world populated by godly and evil agents; hence the need for a more potent power to neutralize and ultimately overcome the evil ones. Part and parcel of the religious system

261. Kinyua, *Introducing Ordinary African Readers' Hermeneutics*, 293.

262. Omenyo and Arthur, "Bible Says!," 53–54.

263. See also Eccl 2:24–26; Job 27:13–19; Jas 5:1–3; Gen 12:14–16; 13:2–6; 26:3–30.

264. For example, see Ps 35:1–4; Ps 109:1–2, 5–10.

265. For example, see Matt 5:43–44; Luke 6:27, 35.

is belief in witchcraft as causative for the occurrence of some cases of death, barrenness, failure in life, and other misfortunes. Some Pentecostal churches revived and popularized a witchcraft mentality. Pentecostalism and African culture share the perception that things which are seen are representative of things which are not seen, and that events in the manifest world are first decided in the spirit world. This is in accordance with (some parts of) the worldview found in the New Testament and in apocalyptic literature, emphasizing that the enemy can only be attacked with weapons that are not carnal.[266]

If every negative event is believed to have a spiritual or metaphysical root, then one must look beyond physical events to their "actual causes." Traditionally, diviners provided help because they could decipher the past through their extra-sensitivity and extra-sensory abilities to perceive spiritual reality. Having identified the cause of the event, a sacrifice of some form was prescribed by them as a way of communicating with the world of spirits, to expiate sins, seek solutions, show gratitude, appease spiritual powers, or ask for their support.[267] Pentecostal prophets are expected to be able to perform a similar feat as the diviner by revealing the spiritual world to the believer or providing proof of their power by demonstrating signs and wonders. The difference is that the diviner relied on divinatory slabs, bones, spirits, or some other means, whereas the prophet invokes and speaks exclusively on behalf of the Holy Spirit. Both types of "divination" concentrate on the personal causation of illness or challenges, which forms the existential questions foremost in an African's mind.[268]

The vast majority of African Pentecostals read the Bible as ordinary readers rather than scholarly ones. Their African interpretation of the Bible is not concerned with understanding of the text for its own sake, or out of intellectual curiosity. It is need-driven and faith-oriented.[269] Their reading of the Bible is relevant to the extent that it speaks to their personal needs and serves to illumine their situation. A transcendent reality waits to be encountered and this is what happens when a believer reads the text, necessitating a distinction between believing and unbelieving readers. The biblical message is integrated into daily lives and appropri-

266. Kalu, *African Pentecostalism*, 179. See also the discussion about the apocalyptic character of pentecostal hermeneutic in chapter 4.

267. Omenyo and Arthur, "Bible Says!," 57–58.

268. Anderson, *Moya*, 54.

269. LeMarquand, "New Testament Exegesis," 93.

ated in terms of personal situations, while Bible reading is characterized by community-sharing as a hermeneutical process of learning, consistent with the African communal way of living. Groups read and share the biblical texts, especially in Bible study groups and prayer meetings, frequently with the aid of pamphlets and guides.[270]

African Pentecostals regularly distinguish between their own reading of the Bible and the practices of non-Pentecostals. They place a high premium on the Spirit's involvement in their reading of the Bible, by way of revealing Jesus Christ in and through passages. They look down on Bible reading practices of people who only acquire "book knowledge" without any spiritual complement. They believe that the "real" meaning of biblical passages is revealed to them by the Spirit, and they seldom leave room for multiple meanings.

By Way of Conclusion

The question was asked: Why do pentecostal people in many instances reach different conclusions or emphasize different aspects of the text when they read the Bible, compared to believers in other Christian traditions? And how does their hermeneutics inform Pentecostals' practice? It has been argued that a pentecostal hermeneutics emphasizes three elements: the interrelationship between the *Holy Spirit* as the One animating *Scriptures* and empowering the *believing community*. For them, the experience of an encounter with God through God's Spirit is imperative, and interpretation of the information contained in the Bible is determined by their praxis of such encounters.

The way ordinary classical Pentecostal Bible readers read and interpret the Bible can be summed up as: they view Scripture as the inspired word of God which is authoritative and reliable. As a result of Scripture's status as the objective, authoritative, and present word of God, Pentecostals do not recognize much of a historical distance between the text and themselves. They read the Bible at face value, without much of an appreciation for or understanding of its ancient context. They focus primarily on their own context, letting existential concerns determine what they read in the Bible. Their interpretation is theologically colored by their Christological "Full Gospel" pre-understanding, which, to a certain degree, is consistent with evangelical Christianity in general. Their

270. Omenyo and Arthur, "Bible Says!," 61.

doctrinal scopus and ethos produce stable and limited dimensions of meaning. The "Full Gospel" proclamation is also more than a catechism to be memorized; rather, it is a narrative way of life to be experienced and a metanarrative used to interpret what happens in life and thus it is "known."[271] This experiential narrative journey results in a transformation of the Pentecostal who comes to experience and know Jesus as savior, sanctifier, Spirit-baptizer, healer, and coming king.

In the local faith community of early Pentecostalism, the prime interpreter and preacher was the local assembly leader or pastor—mostly lay people who felt anointed by the Spirit to preach. The constitution of denominations that eventually developed acknowledged the anointing of the Spirit on their ministries. In some cases, they quit their work to give their full attention to the ministry. The essence of the movement was the emphasis upon the supernatural, with the omnipotent God breaking into the everyday life of the believer as in biblical times. They lived from the eschatological expectation that Christ might return at any moment, providing an urgency in their attempts to reach the ends of the earth with their pentecostal message.[272]

271. Thomas, "What the Spirit is Saying," 116.
272. Byrd, "Paul Ricoeur's Hermeneutical Theory," 209–11.

CHAPTER 3

The Centrality of the Holy Spirit
in Reading the Bible

Introduction

AS HAS BEEN ARGUED above, at the heart of Pentecostalism stands the
Bible as the inspired word of God, affirming that the (whole) Bible is a
reliable revelation of God, and that it states the exact truths the Holy
Spirit intends to convey.[1] One finds the way to reconciliation with one's
Creator explained and illustrated in the Bible, leading to a Spirit-filled
life in this world and eternal life in the world to come. The starting
point and foundation for pentecostal faith and praxis is the biblical text;
however, the distinctive nature and function of Scripture in the faith
community can only be realized in terms of the role of the Spirit.[2]

The previous chapter argues that, in reading the Bible, three main
elements influence the process: The interrelationship between the Holy
Spirit as the One animating Scriptures and empowering the believing
community in order to realize the Christ-event in the present, with the
purpose that members be equipped for ministry and witness in culturally appropriate ways. These three elements explain the emphasis on the
Spirit when Pentecostals read the Bible, or why they read the Bible from
the perspective of the day of Pentecost. The significant role of the Spirit in
reading, interpreting, and applying the Bible among Pentecostals will be
described before attention is given to the other two proposed distinctives

1. Arrington, "Use of the Bible by Pentecostals," 101.
2. Arrington, "Use of the Bible by Pentecostals," 107.

of a pentecostal hermeneutics, namely the eschatological lens defined by a pentecostal apocalyptic identity that is used to read Scriptures and the important notion of the faith community as normative for interpreting the Bible (as well as all other extra-biblical revelation).

The Holy Spirit is the One Who Realizes the Christ-event in the Present

The accusation has been leveled at Pentecostals that they emphasize the work of the Spirit at the cost of the Christocentric focus of the gospel.[3] However, Pentecostals teach that the experience of an encounter with Christ is the result of the Spirit revelation that never leaves a person neutral.[4] The center of the Christian message is Jesus Christ, Pentecostals confess; what is critical for them is the personal awareness and experiencing of the indwelling of the Spirit who sets Jesus present in the daily life of the believer.[5] The Spirit facilitates the encounter with Christ; the Spirit is Christ's Spirit (Rom 8:9; Phil 1:19).

The doctrine is upheld that the Holy Spirit dwells in some sense, to some extent, in every believer, but there is another gift that Pentecostals expect and wait for, entirely distinct and separate from conversion and acceptance of the forgiveness of sins. Christians need this gift in order to be empowered for service.[6] Möller describes this experience as a gift of grace based on the promise of Acts 1:5–8 that God would reveal Godself in a personal, immediate, intimate, and lasting way to believers by bringing humans under the control and fullness of God's Spirit, leading to their sensitized consciousness of the risen and glorified Christ in their lives, resulting in being more effective witnesses for Christ, having received a sanctified conscience that enables them to comprehend God's will in daily life, and worshiping God in a fuller dimension.[7] While Protestants emphasize orthodoxy (correctness in doctrine and confession as derived from Scripture), Pentecostals stress orthopraxy (correctness in practice and life style).[8] They do not deny the importance of doctrine

---

3. Möller, "Christ and Pentecostalism," 140.

4. Ma, "Full Circle Mission," 8.

5. Williams, "Pentecostal Reality," 1.

6. Daniels, *Moody*, 396–403, quoting Moody and Harper, "Waves," 105.

7. Möller, *Diskussie van die Charismata*, 43–44.

8. The result is that, in most conservative circles, Pentecostalism fails "the

being founded on the Bible but they seek validation of doctrinal truth in the dynamic activity of the Spirit. In their preaching, they do not primarily aim at communicating doctrinal truths but to minister to the spiritual, physical, psychological, and social needs of the people assembled to meet the word, Jesus Christ.[9] The liturgical implication is that worship services in Pentecostal churches generally allow for prayers for and ministry to people in need, changing the worship service into an experiential event for interested attendees.[10] Albrecht and Howard typify pentecostal worship services in terms of a threefold structure, revealing its "foundational rites" or "macro-rites," as worship in song, pastoral message(s), and the altar service.[11] Early Pentecostals participated in all three aspects, while current Pentecostals are, in a sense, excluded from participation in the pastoral message with the professional pastorate taking responsibility for the message, although ample space exists for believers to participate in the message by way of prophecy, interpretation of tongues, a word of wisdom or knowledge, a revelation in terms of a special insight, a testimony, or as the product of a vision or dream.[12]

---

breathalyzer test of established orthodoxy" (Ellington, "Pentecostalism and the Authority of Scriptures," 152).

9. Clark and Lederle, *What is Distinctive*, 64–65.

10. God's word cannot be confined to preaching. Barth discerns a threefold form of the one word of God—as the word preached, the written word, and the word revealed, which is Jesus Christ himself (Barth, *Kirchliche Dogmatik*, 1.1:61). The word facilitates God's address, which consists of words that transform listeners' lives in a radical manner.

11. Albrecht and Howard, "Pentecostal Spirituality," 238.

12. Maier refers to the program of pneumatic exegesis that arose at the end of the nineteenth and beginning of the twentieth centuries—the same time when the Pentecostal movement originated—but without any connection between the two (Maier, *Biblical Hermeneutics*, 308–11). Pneumatic exegesis functions with the supposition that it is necessary to engage in spiritual interpretation of a spiritual message as found in the Bible, qualifying the need for the Spirit's involvement in the interpretation process, while it serves as a rejection and acknowledgment of the "atheistic methods" of exegesis that were working incalculable woe in both academic theology and the church. The Bible seeks to be more than a document subject to historical-critical testing. It is reminiscent of Karl Barth's rejection of liberal theology, with the charge that it had lost the ability to penetrate "into the spirit of the Bible" (Barth, *Kirchliche Dogmatik*, 1.2:466). Pneumatic or neo-orthodox exegesis presupposes the spiritual rebirth or regeneration of the interpreter and the involvement of the Spirit, requiring the unity of doctrine and life. It is based on the principles of the *testimonium Spiritus Sancti internum* (inner witness of the Holy Spirit), the unity of Scriptures, and the equivalence of Scripture and Word of God (Maier, *Biblical Hermeneutics*, 310–11).

Ellington proposes that Pentecostals ask a different set of questions when it defines doctrine because modern rationalism, with its propositional character,[13] is limited by its very nature to a partial understanding of the nature and presence of God; it has reached boundaries in its speech about God beyond which it cannot pass.[14] For this reason, the divergence between conservative Christians and Pentecostals is primarily an epistemological one, involving a difference in the way in which they know, experience, and receive revelation from God.[15] To describe their perception of revelation, Pentecostals need a specific language because they experience God in relational terms.[16] Because their knowledge of God is relational—and not merely informational—their theology is better expressed orally, because that is the primary mode of relational communication among ordinary people in the faith community.[17]

Pentecostal experience functions in constant dialogue with the biblical story through the guidance of the Spirit, who introduces believers to God and God's actions, making the relationship with God a present and dynamic force. Dialogue does not refer to the merging of two or more voices into one; in genuine dialogue, each voice retains its integrity, yet

13. Pinnock, "Work of the Holy Spirit," 234. This model claims that the meaning of texts is discovered by using reason and the best scholarly tools, linguistic and otherwise. The implication is that the Spirit had fulfilled God's obligations to God's people millennia ago through inspiration, when the Spirit delivered the Bible to the church.

14. Ellington, "Pentecostalism and the Authority of Scriptures," 152. Modern rationalism functions within the narrow restrictions of a scientific worldview, which demands that all experience, including the descriptions of historical events, be challenged, subjected to, and measured according to a set of "objective" and "scientific" measures. Johns argues that the modern, rationalist, and scientific worldview is based on a Greek philosophical understanding of reality, which sees the "knower" as subject and the thing known as "object," creating a distinct and absolute barrier of separation between the knowing subject and the object of knowledge (see Johns, *Pentecostal Formation*). Johns reckons that this approach is both non-Hebrew and non-biblical. The biblical model for talking about knowledge of God is based on the Hebrew notion of *yada*`, a knowing which arises not by standing back from in order to look at an "object," but by active and intentional engagement in lived experience (Groome, *Christian Religious Education*, 141). On a pragmatic level, the rationalist worldview is rapidly becoming a minority view, with explosive growth in the Third World. Pentecostal movements are breaking the modernist monopoly on biblical studies from an exclusively Western perspective (Ellington, "Pentecostalism and the Authority of Scripture," 155).

15. The next paragraphs are based partly on Nel, "Pentecostal Talk about God."

16. Ellington, "Pentecostalism and the Authority of Scriptures," 19.

17. Ellington, "Pentecostalism and the Authority of Scriptures," 158.

each is also mutually enriched.[18] Pentecostals relate their story in light of the larger biblical metanarrative and the experiences of the faith community.[19] Because this process is decidedly oral and experiential, it also includes the uneducated and uninitiated, leading to Pentecostalism's success in reaching the impoverished and disenfranchised people of Africa (and other parts of the Global South), putting the "modern" person and church at a distinct disadvantage.[20] Oral expression and testimony lend themselves to understanding of God with whom they are in an active relationship, requiring no special knowledge or expertise in order to participate in the search to know God and to theologize about these experiences of encountering God. The result is that access to God is open to all, not only a few professionals trained to talk about knowledge of God. Each member of the faith community is encouraged to participate by sharing testimonies of the experiences, in dialogue with the Bible, the faith community, and the Spirit. The opportunity and responsibility to know God and mediate God's presence in the faith community is shared equally in a democratic manner by all. It is understandable that testimony functions at the heart of the speech about God in pentecostal circles.[21]

The nature of the Bible does not call readers into a passive acquiescence to the biblical text but, on the contrary, to take part in dispute and to engage with the text ethically.[22] "Rather than censoring and sanitizing out the undesirable parts, we are called by the text itself to learn to make ethical evaluations. Rather than being dependent on an authoritarian text, the very disputatious nature of the Hebrew canon invites us to engage with the text in the debate as morally responsible adults."[23] A challenging and revolutionary counter-reading is permitted, evoked, and

18. Vanhoozer, *Drama of Doctrine*, 290–91.

19. In dialogue, one must be ready to hear things you do not want to hear and, after listening carefully, to agree or disagree with what a given text or a fellow believer has to say (Cox, *How to Read the Bible*, 16).

20. Ellington, "Pentecostalism and the Authority of Scriptures," 159.

21. Ellington, "Pentecostalism and the Authority of Scriptures," 159.

22. In describing Pentecostals' long tradition of pacifism and quiescence, Smith describes their apolitical stance as an otherworldly uncomfortableness with relating to wider society and engaging in worldly issues such as politics (Smith, "Politics and Economics of Pentecost," 195). In fact, their pietism, eschatology, and evangelism contributed to their political quiescence (see Anderson, *Introduction to Pentecostalism*, 261 and Yong, "Pentecostalism and the Political," 333). What is necessary, then, is for Pentecostals to balance their dedication to God with their witness in the world.

23. Flood, *Disarming Scripture*, 96.

legitimated by the text.[24] Therefore, adopting the way that Jesus and Paul read the Hebrew Bible is about learning to think morally, for ourselves, to question and dispute with the aim to discern the will of God. When the Bible presents texts that challenge the ethical standards of Christians, the correct hermeneutical question is not, "How does this text function?" but rather, "How ought we function in light of the text?"[25] What is needed is not just that the interpretation of readers is shaped and transformed but that the readers themselves are shaped and transformed in the process of reading the text; the Spirit of God inspires the text by inspiring its readers. Not all of these texts are instructional, explanative, or encouraging, and they do not necessarily contain characters that should be viewed as role models. In order to not get trapped in a hermeneutical process that is constantly hinging on the capacity to explain away the limitations, tensions, complexities, dissonances, incoherencies, contradictions, obscurities, and ethical difficulties presented by some Scripture passages, Pentecostals cannot allow us to get limited to a hermeneutics of orthodoxy and/or orthopraxy. The assumption that what people did according to the descriptions found in the Old Testament must have been right "because it is in the Bible" is incorrect. They are not God's way of telling us, "That is good," but rather, "You need to know that this is how some people responded because things can go very wrong."[26]

Dunn[27] asserts that, of all Christians, Pentecostals should be the first to note that it was the experience of the Spirit which was seen to be sufficient to override previously hallowed Scripture and tradition. He refers to the Spirit coming upon the Galatians that made circumcision dispensable (Acts 10–11; 15:7–11; Gal 2:7–9; 3:2–5), in contradiction of the clear command in Genesis 17:9–14 that circumcision is an "eternal covenant": "The manifest grace of God evidently required of the first Christians a radical re-evaluation of what constitutes the law of God; that is, a radical evaluation of what the word of God is in unanticipated circumstances."[28] The Bible contains other examples as well of how Scripture in effect ceased to be the word of God for Christians of a later period. Paul even

24. Brueggemann, *Theology of the Old Testament*, 101.

25. Cole, "Taking Hermeneutics to Heart," 265.

26. Rowan Williams, the former Archbishop of Canterbury, quoted in Cole, "Taking Hermeneutics to Heart," 266.

27. Dunn, "Role of the Spirit," 155.

28. Dunn, "Role of the Spirit," 155.

amended the teaching of Jesus on divorce (compare 1 Cor 7:10–15 with Matt 5:31–32; 19:7–9).[29]

Their experience of God is based on and defined in terms of biblical accounts, leading to the question about the status of the Bible in pentecostal circles. They build their hermeneutics on the assumption that the Bible is infallible but at the same time recognize that they are neither able to demonstrate its infallibility nor do they take responsibility to do so.[30] Rather, they link the Bible's infallibility to its inspiration by God, who is infallible and argue that no further demonstration of its infallibility is either necessary or possible.[31] Any direct participation by God in biblical accounts falls outside the range of modern scientific investigation; God's speaking, acting, and revealing is not so much unscientific as ascientific. In other words, divine encounters are hardly accessible to examination using conventional historical methods, establishing an epistemology that challenges the fundamental scientific method, which is objectivity.[32] In sharing their testimonies, Pentecostals confess their subjective pre-understanding and make an objective claim when they evaluate their subjective experiences within the equally subjective faith community and in light of Scripture.

The fact is, scrutiny and testing of the interpretation of the Bible can never rely solely on an immediate interplay of Scripture and Spirit. Everyone's hearing of Scripture—as well as their interpretation of their own experience—have been shaped by their inheritance, education, upbringing, social conditioning, faith, etc. This can be called "tradition." Pentecostals should realize that they cannot short-circuit the Catholic/ Protestant debate about the relation between Scripture and tradition.

---

29. Dunn relates the different interpretation of biblical injunctions to new circumstances to two issues in the contemporary church that in his opinion require to be revisited, namely homosexual orientation, its practice by Christians and the local asssembly's pastoral care of homosexual couples; and the question of whether God's promises to Abraham of the promised land of Canaan/Israel can or should be regarded as a sufficient ground to justify present-day Israel's settlement policy in the West Bank (Dunn, "Role of the Spirit," 155). See Wansbrough, *Use and Abuse of the Bible*, 161–63, for a discussion of the biblical justification of Israel's occupation of the West Bank by drawing comparison between modern Jewish occupation and the entry of the Israelites under Joshua, with the myths of the lightning campaign, empty territory, and continuity or the denial of exile.

30. Van der Laan, "Theology of Gerrit Polman," 32n42.

31. Arrington, "Hermeneutics, Historical Perspectives," 382.

32. Ellington, "Pentecostalism and the Authority of Scriptures," 159.

They also have their own tradition through which they hear and understand the Bible.[33] Experience itself is an interpretation which cannot be taken for granted but needs to be critically evaluated.

Pentecostals view knowledge about God not as a cognitive recognition of a set of precepts and doctrines, as is the case in many other theological traditions, but rather as a relationship with the One who defined those precepts by which Christians tend to order their lives.[34] "Knowledge" is insight into divine truth, the gift which believers need to understand the Bible.[35] The precondition for participation in pentecostal theology, then, is belief in God and participation in God's current revelation to the faith community.[36]

Truth, in pentecostal practice, is located in the contribution of believers to the worship service and evangelization by way of testimonies, messages, and prayers that require the recalling of memory. This is based on what they perceive as the biblical precedent where truth is generated by the testimonies of witnesses. They find their precedent in the Bible. Brueggemann, for instance, states that the central truth-claims of Israel in the Old Testament are not a declaration of historical facts,

33. Dunn, "Role of the Spirit," 156.

34. Arrington, "Hermeneutics, Historical Perspectives," 382.

35. Taylor, "Spirit and the Bride," 64.

36. King, "Streams of Convergence," 73. Theology is defined here as a human construction of our reflection on God and God's relationship with human beings, based on the primary event of the revelation of God (recorded in the Bible) and on the secondary event of the Spirit's revelation of God (based on the appropriation of that primary event in the lives of contemporary believers). In this sense, pentecostal theology is a second-order reflection on the primary narrative of the revelation of God coordinated with the experience of that revelation by contemporary readers and their reflection about that experience (see Grenz, *Revisioning Evangelical Theology*, 73; Migliore, *Faith Seeking Understanding*, 9; Pinnock, *Tracking the Maze*, 182; and Railey and Aker, "Theological Foundations," 45). To state that theology is virtually absent from the Pentecostal movement—because their stress on the emotive stands in contrast to the intellectual—is not true, as can be seen by both the quantity and the quality of publications from pentecostal theologians. The popular stereotype is wrong (Jacobsen, *Reader in Pentecostal Theology*, 5). However, in many instances, pentecostal publications are characterized by their embodiment of the dramatic expressions of the charismatic life and the prophetic, spontaneous, and unadorned desire to let the Spirit speak through the work of the scholar. For this reason, it is in the form of testimony, exhortation, prayer, praise, and other elements not typical for scholarly conventions, with evangelistic, inspirational, expository, sermonic, and thematic emphases (Vondey, *Pentecostalism*, 127).

but is offered as a testimony by witnesses.[37] Biblical truth, for him, is not located in the historical events underlying the offered testimony, but in the testimony itself. When believers make theological constructions from the Old Testament, they only have access to the testimonies itself.[38] These testimonies are necessarily colored by the subjectivity of the witnesses.[39] The authority of the witnesses is based on nothing more and nothing less than the willingness of the community to credit, believe, trust, and take this testimony seriously.[40]

Today, the primary mode of appropriation by the faith community that reads those Scriptures which contain the truths proposed by biblical witnesses is not an ascension to the historical truthfulness of the information reflected in the biblical narratives but rather lies in the faith community perceiving the capacity of the text to generate, evoke, and articulate alternative images of reality[41] and, for Pentecostals, generate similar encounters with God.[42] Believers experience that God uses the text to create a new vision of how the world could and should be, inspiring them to campaign for the coming of the kingdom of God.[43] In this way, narratives in biblical narratives are tested against lived experience, an essential element of a Pentecostal community's appropriation of the truth-claims of Scripture. In other words, the text is re-experienced by contemporary readers as a precondition for interpreting it correctly and reappropriating its meaning.[44] Appropriation is only possible when the

37. Brueggemann, *Theology of the Old Testament*, 206.

38. Dela Cruz, "Preaching Among Filipino Pentecostals," 114.

39. See also Castelo, "Tarrying on the Lord," 53.

40. Brueggemann, *Theology of the Old Testament*, 68. It should be qualified that Pentecostals do not support ecclesiastical authority as such if it holds that the church itself must be the final authority in all matters of faith and practice and the interpretation by the church is limited to those who are specially trained and chosen for that task, whose labor is usually promulgated in creedlike statements that over time become authoritative (Railey and Aker, "Theological Foundations," 43). In the context of the pentecostal congregation, every believer is valued as a participant in realizing the Word of God.

41. Brueggemann, *Theology of the Old Testament*, 68.

42. Ukpong, "Current Theology," 523. In this regard, Pentecostals understand the mode of God's presence among God's people in conjunction with their use of Scripture, resulting in a pentecostal hermeneutic and theology that are different from an orthodox, non-pentecostal hermeneutic and theology at major points (McClean, "Toward a Pentecostal Hermeneutic," 50).

43. Ellington, "History, Story, and Testimony," 257.

44. Byrd, "Paul Ricoeur's Hermeneutical Theory," 210.

text is evaluated and interpreted in light of new experience; the congregants evaluate the message's explication and application of biblical truths on the same grounds.[45]

Pentecostal Talk about God

The implication is that Pentecostals have their own ethos to bring to the theological table.[46] Pinnock argues that they have the perfect ingredients for a theological recipe in their own worship and lives that allow them to speak authoritatively about God.[47] They have something important to share with others out of their own experience with God.[48] Because their

45. Goldingay, "Biblical Story and the Way," 7.

46. Cross, "Rich Feast of Theology," 29.

47. Pinnock, "Divine Relationality," 22.

48. In the past, pentecostal theology consisted mainly of using themes borrowed from evangelical theology and tacking on some issues emphasized by Pentecostals—like the Spirit, spiritual gifts, and fruit of the Spirit—which were viewed as distinctive (as demonstrated by the well-used text book of systematic theology prepared by lecturers of the American Assemblies of God, Horton, *Systematic Theology*). The motivation was that it is not necessary for Pentecostals to reinvent the theological wheel. Another tradition among Pentecostals is anti-intellectualist, suggesting that the free movement of the Spirit and theological enterprise exclude one another. Theological endeavors of some Protestant traditions were viewed as dry and lifeless because it was undertaken within what was perceived as a rationalist vacuum, devoid of the breath of the Spirit (Cross, "Rich Feast of Theology," 33). See Bowdle's remark that, "Pentecostals must make peace with the academy and understand that Jesus is Lord of learning, too (Bowdle, "Informed Pentecostalism," 10). Although early Pentecostals were classified as pre-modern, anti-intellectual, and anti-social, Archer believes they instead represented a paramodern, counter-culture movement (Archer, *Pentecostal Hermeneutic*, 18). His view is based on Robert Mapes Anderson's special deprivation theory. See also Poloma's remark that Pentecostalism may be understood as an "anthropological protest against modernity" as it provided a medium for encountering the supernatural (Poloma, *Assemblies of God*, 19). Vondey disagrees with Archer's viewpoint and states that at least the beginnings of modern-day Pentecostalism should be characterized as anti-intellectual, with its rejection of higher education and criticism of the academic world (Vondey, *Pentecostalism*, 116). This is also my conclusion (see Nel, "Development of Theological Training"). However, anti-intellectualism was not a general attitude and a more lenient perspective toward academic scholarship can also be found among some Pentecostals. It should also be kept in mind that the first generation of Pentecostals did not represent the intellectual elite; most of them only received a basic education and they could not engage in the challenges of academic discourse that characterized their day. Even today, pentecostal scholarship retains its counter-cultural stance, and speaking with tongues remains the most significant counter-cultural practice of Pentecostals. Tongues serve the critical function as a call for an affective and

spirituality is dynamic and not merely rationalist, they can see and appreciate the relationality of God, perhaps more than theologians from other traditions. And because they are "simple readers of the Scripture," they take the "natural" sense of the narrative and read the Bible as the story world of God interacting with humans. Archer argues that Pentecostals require a hermeneutical strategy that involves an interdependent tridactic dialogue between Scripture, the Spirit, and community, resulting in a creative negotiated meaning with the readers in the community, the story world of the text, and the leading of the Holy Spirit being participants in the tridactic negotiation for meaning.[49] They tend to engage with the narrative in a literal and existential sense.[50] An important part of their Bible reading practice is that they then expect that something in the same vein as described in the biblical narrative would happen to them in terms of God's ongoing interaction with human beings. They expect to encounter God as part of their reflection on Scripture, playing into an open, relational concept of God.[51] Their theology, then, follows their experience—and not the other way around, as in most other theological traditions.[52] They know and experience God in the existential reality of daily living and construct their theological understanding of God from this experiential reality. They do not get involved with philosophical speculation about the nature and will of God because their God is not devoid of existential meaning but teeming with life and interacting on a regular basis with God's children.[53] Their model allows for the God who intervenes and speaks in their lives in surprising ways rather than the God characterized by static perfection.

Pentecostal talk allows for God who interacts with God's creation by hearing and responding to prayers rather than God being a deistic force that is eternally distant from creation. They view God in this way because

---

embodied epistemology and a holistic spirituality (Yong, "Academic *Glossolalia*?," 64).

49. Archer, *Pentecostal Hermeneutic*, 189–91. "A person who is taught by the Spirit has an internal manifestation of an insight into the words of Jesus (John 14:26) and an external manifestation of wisdom, especially in regard to the Christ-life, and the hidden things of God" (Taylor, "Spirit and the Bride," 62).

50. Pinnock, "Divine Relationality," 9.

51. The Spirit is identified as the one who reveals God in relational terms, as supraspatial and supratemporal, yet intimately present with every Christian (Warrington, "Holy Spirit," 121). The Spirit also establishes a new community of relationships based on an alternative view of reality, determined by faith.

52. Johns, "Adolescence of Pentecostalism," 4.

53. Pinnock, "Divine Relationality," 21.

that is how they perceive God in Scriptures, and their experience of God verifies their developing theology.[54]

Pentecostals share many tenets in common with Christians from other traditions, but they have experienced God in ways that most others do not confess. While in the past they have viewed theology as a discussion of their distinctives, what is needed is for a perspective to be developed on the all-inclusive difference made by their experience of God in all areas of their lives. Their experience of God through God's Spirit shifts their *loci communes* and theological method.[55] They are not just Evangelicals who speak in tongues; they live and think in terms of their charismatic experience. In that sense, Menzies is not correct when he argues that pentecostal theology is based on the common truths found in evangelicalism with the addition that it emphasizes a place for the ministry of the Spirit.[56] The argument conducted here is that pentecostal theology should rethink every aspect of the theological enterprise through the lens of the reality of God's encounter with human beings as experienced in the faith community.

That this is not generally the case at the moment can be seen from a perusal of literature produced by pentecostal theologians. What is needed is the development of a theological method that would be commensurate with its experience of God, leading to serious reflection not only about the Spirit and the Spirit's work in believers but also of all aspects of theology. Land suggests that pentecostal spirituality is not merely emotional and non-cognitive, limiting experience to the realm of the affections (contra researchers like Spittler, Williams, and Hollenweger) but rather that affections and mind must be married in spirituality, forming the basis for pentecostal spirituality (contra other traditions that rely heavily or exclusively on the cognitive for theological endeavors).[57]

In his *Evangelical Theology*, Barth makes the same proposal that evangelical theology cannot be anything else but pneumatic, spiritual

---

54. Cross, "Rich Feast of Theology," 32.

55. Siekawitch, "Calvin, Spirit, Communion and the Supper," 23.

56. Menzies, "Synoptic Theology," 14–15. Pinnock describes the challenges raised for evangelical theology by a pentecostal hermeneutic: It challenges its nearly exclusive rationality, its disregard to a certain extent of experience, its spirituality, the clear distinction between theoretical knowledge and the application of such knowledge to practice, and the estrangement between eschatology and pneumatology within an ecclesiology (Pinnock, "Work of the Holy Spirit," 136–40).

57. Land, *Pentecostal Spirituality*, 25–27.

theology because it is only in the realm of the power of the Spirit that theology can be realized as a free, critical, and happy science of the God of the gospel: "Only in the courageous confidence that the Spirit is the truth does theology simultaneously pose and answer the question about truth."[58] Pentecostal theology should overcome the modernist split between reason and affections, cognition and experience, engaging the whole person within the communion of *charismata*, forming a worshiping, witnessing, and reflective whole, where the liturgical life lies at the heart of the community.[59]

This does not imply that theology should be relegated in order to be subordinate to spirituality. Then, theology is truncated to become a commentary on experience. But to argue that theology should be devoid of spirituality is unacceptable for Pentecostals because their encounter with God lies at the heart of their religious practice and its resultant reflection about it.[60] Spirituality consists of God and God's relationship with God's people, forming the heart of their theological endeavors.[61] How one experiences God influences the way one reflects on God.[62] For Pentecostals, experience is primary over theory and must, in all cases, inform cognitive packaging of theology, making pentecostal theology dynamic, not rationalistic.[63] Their theology should always be based upon Scripture as the original source but, at the same time, they believe God speaks to God's church through the gifts of the Spirit to correct, edify, and comfort.[64] Theology may not be a mere restatement of propositional

58. Barth, *Evangelical Theology*, 55.

59. Land, *Pentecostal Spirituality*, 34. Reason serves as a good servant of the revelation of God but is not a good master over that revelation (Railey and Aker, "Theological Foundations," 45). Pentecostalism is ideally situated to link rationality and affection because it moves preaching from the sterile pulpit and lecture hall of rationality and transforms it into prophetic witness in the untidy arena and marketplace of street level experience, characterized by powerful demonstrations and emotional responses (Anderson, "Pentecost, Scholarship, and Learning," 122). Whereas knowledge and rationality have traditionally been connected to the Word, Yong reminds us that there is a pneumatological dimension to knowing without which rationality itself is undermined (Yong, *Spirit-Word-Community*, 22). It refers to pneumatic encounters in terms of the experiences of the Spirit.

60. Plüss, "Religious Experience in Worship," 5.

61. Johnson, *Religious Experience*, 12.

62. Cross, "Rich Feast of Theology," 35.

63. Pinnock, "Divine Relationality," 4 and 10–11.

64. Railey and Aker, "Theological Foundations," 55.

truths, even though it appears so in contemporary idiomatic language. Rather, it should be a critical reflection on the primary truth of the biblical narrative, shaped by the language of the Bible (but not equated with it), because the truth should first be made real in the lives of contemporary readers by the witness of the Spirit before the biblical truth can be interpreted and appropriated.[65] Otherwise, philosopher Richard Rorty's complaint may become valid—that it is pictures rather than propositions, metaphors rather than statements, which determine most of our convictions, and language, then, no longer serves as a mirror of metaphysical reality but rather as a tool for edification and aesthetic enrichment.[66]

Pentecostal theology is experience-certified theology, a theology that, through faith and obedience, becomes a Bible-based "experience-reality."[67] Theology exists to serve the revelation of God to human beings and not the other way around.[68] It serves as the interpretation of biblical narrative to foster a response within the faith community to the revelation of God. For that reason, theology cannot be an enterprise taking place in the exclusive atmosphere of the proverbial ivory-tower but can only be the life-giving activity that defines it within the community of faith, providing believers with a coherent reflection on the revelation of God. Effective theology is measured in terms of the effects of the message, in people getting saved and healed, baptized in the Spirit, and encouraged through the specific Word of God.[69] The two elements conditional for good theology are the interpretation and appropriation of the biblical narrative and God's Spirit driving home the truth contained in that narrative. The Spirit confronts a person with the reality of God in the biblical narrative and in one's present situation, affecting a cognitive and emotive response to the event.[70]

---

65. Migliore, *Faith Seeking Understanding*, xii.

66. Rorty, quoted in Bloesch, *Theology of Word and Spirit*, 16–17.

67. Erickson, *Christian Theology*, 21.

68. Pinnock, *Tracking the Maze*, 182.

69. Compare with Byrd, "Paul Ricoeur's Hermeneutical Theory," 203–4.

70. Pinnock, "Divine Relationality," 26. A part of contemporary theology suffers from the uncertainty in stating anything with self-assurance as the truth as the direct result of postmodernism's disapproval of any form of unified knowledge and absolute truth. For a pentecostal attempt to define theology as an academic discipline, see Yong, "Whither Systematic Theology?"

Pentecostals and God

Pentecostals view God in trinitarian terms, however, they view the Trinity not as a doctrine about the abstract nature of God but rather about God's life with human beings and the resultant shift in relationships between human beings.[71] Trinitarian theology *per se* is a theology of relationships, concerned with communion and love, forgiveness and courtesy.[72] God is viewed as a being whose fundamental feature is loving relationality.[73] As the God who chooses to stand in relationship with human beings, God risks God's future and reputation with humanity as God becomes involved with the sordid detail of believers' (and non-believers') lives. As Father, Son, and Spirit relate lovingly among themselves as a personal, communicative God from all eternity, God also relates to humans.[74] The trinitarian relational model of God suits pentecostal experience and life,[75] providing a model for thinking about God and the personality of human beings with its source in the Trinity.[76] The faith community forming the church can also only be described in valid terms on the model of trinitarian relations.[77] At the same time, reason discovers a stumbling block when confronted with the paradoxical character of trinitarian theology but "since it is based on clear Scripture, reason must be silent at this point and we must believe."[78] The role of reason is ministerial—never magisterial or rationalistic—in relation to God and the Bible.[79]

Barth influenced pentecostal theology in a distinctive way, probably more than any other theologian of the twentieth century.[80] He states that we learn what it means to be a person and how to stand in relationships to other persons from Godself.[81] The absolute, immutable, changeless, timeless, and impassible God is also the personal God who answers prayers that seemingly (and incomprehensibly) change God's mind. For

71. LaCugna, *God For Us*, 1.

72. Yong, "Proclamation in/of the Spirit," 35.

73. Joubert, "Not by Order, Nor by Dialogue," 122.

74. McRoberts, "Holy Trinity," 161.

75. Zizioulas, *Being as Communion*, 12.

76. Schaeffer, *Trilogy*, 283.

77. Volf, *After Our Likeness*, 7.

78. Luther, quoted in Althaus, *Theology of Martin Luther*, 199.

79. McRoberts, "Holy Trinity," 140.

80. Becker, "Tener under Examination," 45.

81. Barth, *Church Dogmatics*, 2:284.

pentecostal thinking, the paradox contained in some biblical descriptions of God does not pose any problems because they experience God in dynamic, personal terms as the unknowable God who, in God's greatness, might, and majesty as Master of the universe, falls outside the frame of reference of human beings, who are the works of God's hands.[82] What is important in pentecostal theology is not to say much about God but to love God.[83] God is experienced as the God who engages in dialogue with God's children, a living person who responds to the adoration and worship of God's children's by encountering them with God's grace and provision.[84]

It falls outside Pentecostals' experience that God can be contained in absolutist and unchangeable philosophical categories (such as "unmoved mover," "cause of all being," "pure being," or "world soul") although they have to admit that philosophical terminology may be useful in describing their experience.[85] Theology can not only reiterate what the Bible states; it needs language to describe its object of investigation and reflection. It must be realized, however, that language can never adequately express the one that theology endeavors to picture.[86] Theology should be based on biblical language but it needs to remain relevant and faithful by utilizing philosophical mechanisms in its work.[87]

Barth argues that theology became nominalistic when the attributes of God were described as "names" given to describe God, or were human perceptions of God that do not correspond to any reality in God.[88] The

82. For the same reason, Pentecostals do not follow the Reformed practice of addressing prayer exclusively to the Father because, in Reformed theology, the unity of the one God is qualified by distinguishing between the three persons to such an extent that prayer should only be addressed to God as the Father. For Pentecostals, God is unknowable and unfathomable, and the doctrine of "Trinity" serves as a way to cover their embarrassment because they cannot say anything about God that God has not said about Godself. Their relationship with Jesus and the Spirit allows them to address them in worship and prayer along with the Father. This is confirmed by the fundamental principle of orthodox theology, *opera ad extra sunt indivisa*, that the external works of God in the world are undivided, and belong to all three persons of the Godhead together (see Yong, *Spirit-Word-Community*, 49).

83. Yong, *Spirit-Word-Community*, 23.

84. Pinnock, "Divine Relationality," 20.

85. McRoberts, "Holy Trinity," 143.

86. Tollefsen, "Morality and God," 59.

87. Tollefsen, "Morality and God," 60.

88. Barth, *Church Dogmatics*, 2:329.

essentia [essence] of God was viewed as the reality of God. The attributes or perfections of God seen in Scripture are then viewed as not proper to God. Something else behind this witness is essential to God, so that God's attributes lose their reality in favor of the essence. However, the Father of Jesus Christ has empathy with human beings, requiring that Jesus suffered and died in humans' stead in order to allow God to reconcile humans with God.[89] Instead of an immutable, perfect, and apathetic God—as Barth maintains traditional theism created when it pictured God in terms borrowed from ancient Stoicism and Neo-Platonism—what is needed is for God's attributes to be redefined through the lens of Jesus Christ and the work of the Spirit in the believer's life.[90] The power of God's almightiness, for instance, should be reflected through the lens of Christ's suffering on the cross, where the power of God becomes weakness, challenging and restructuring our ideas of power in a secularist sense.[91] Such redefinition is an essential task, which pentecostal theology should undertake as the basis of its God talk.

We cannot do anything else but talk of God in faithfulness to Scripture's witness about God and the reality of our contemporary experience, but it should be remembered that language can never encompass God, as argued already. Although God interacts with us, God's creatures, as Creator, the Lord is totally different from anything human beings can propose or devise. God enters space and time to encounter us in God's incarnation, yet God is beyond time and space—in eternity—a concept that does not make sense from our point of observation.[92] The transcendent God meets human beings in God's immanence, but God remains a mystery that our mind can never contain.

A further characteristic of pentecostal theology, it is suggested, is that it should use the philosophical language of dialectic, as has been intimated above in terms of the utility of paradoxical terms to describe God. From the start, pentecostal experience can only be called Christian if it draws its interpretation from the Bible as the word of God. In fact, it is the dialectic between the (given) narratives of the Bible and the liturgically celebrated (received) narratives of the church that brings meaning in the

89. Solivan, *Spirit, Pathos, and Liberation*, 47–48.

90. Migliore, *Power of God*, 74.

91. Moltmann, *Crucified God*, 12.

92. Noel, "Pentecostal and Postmodern Hermeneutics," 63.

here and now.[93] Dialectic allows one to speak of two or more (usually contradictory) truths while not negating either one. Barth and Brunner used this method to emphasize the qualitative difference between what can be said about God and who God really is.[94] Although dialectic intimidated the early Barth to say too little about God, later on he used it as a tool to describe the attributes of God in terms of their contradictions (mercy *vs.* justice, love *vs.* punishment, unity *vs.* omnipresence). God is the hidden one who reveals (something of) Godself. Dialectic, in describing what we can know about God, allows some glimpses of God, but, at the same time, it suggests that we can never exhaust God's being by what we say about God.[95] Speech about God can be nothing else but provisional and conditional because it is inadequate to encompass God with human words.[96] Words are often related to experience, but they are not the same thing. Words explain and describe experience and, in doing so, they provide models that can help people assess their own experience. Words situate experiences within a broader understanding of who God is, how the world is put together and what it means to be human. These uses of words taken together constitute the field of theology. Pentecostals also use theological words to make sense of their faith, but they are suspicious of words. The movement is, to some degree, a protest against too much reliance on words—rather, the use of religious words—without religious experience to back it up. Too many words, they suspect, might drain the power from their own experiences of the Spirit.[97] They would rather worship in tongues than perform theological monologues about God.

The living, interacting God is personal, as experienced in God's incarnation, where God stoops down and mingles with human beings.

93. Leoh, "Eschatology and Pneumatic Preaching," 103, and Plüss, "Religious Experience in Worship," 3.

94. Brunner, *Word and the World*, 6–7. Barth's and Brunner's dialectical theology is based on the view that there is neither an identity between thought and being (as in Platonic idealism) nor a direct correspondence (as in realism), but instead a cleavage, which is the result not of finitude *per se* but of sin. This cleavage is overcome in the paradoxical entry of eternity into time—that is, in the incarnation of the infinite God in Jesus of Nazareth. All contradictions in human thinking concerning God and God's relationship to us have their center in this absolute paradox (Kierkegaard), which is incomprehensible to human reason (Bloesch, *Theology of Word and Spirit*, 76).

95. Kärkkäinen, "Pentecostal Hermeneutics," 88.

96. Cross, "Rich Feast of Theology," 45.

97. Jacobsen, *Reader in Pentecostal Theology*, 5–6.

But God's works do not exhaust God's person. Therefore, Pentecostals worship the one living in a realm beyond human capacity to understand as the mighty God whose mere words create worlds.[98] Dialectic helps to view God more holistically as the indescribable reality that also exists outside creation.

Pentecostals worship the God of the Bible, the one who both is at hand and far away. No one can hide from God in secret because God fills both heaven and earth (Jer 23:23). God had chosen some human beings from the beginning for salvation (2 Thess 2:13b); before the foundation of the world, God predestined them to adoption as sons through Jesus Christ (Eph 1:4–5). At the same time, human beings may choose or reject salvation—if you confess with your mouth Jesus as Lord and believe in your heart that God raised him for the dead, you will be saved (Rom 10:9). The dialectic of election and free will together explains the mystery of salvation. On the one hand, the Bible clearly teaches monotheism, that there is one and only one God and that God is one (Deut 6:4). Yet, the Bible also teaches that the one God consists of three persons (Matt 28:19 and 2 Cor 13:14). Another paradox is the nature of Jesus Christ, with some passages clearly teaching that he is fully human (Rom 1:2–3), while other passages teach that Jesus is fully divine (Matt 1:23 and Col 2:9). These paradoxes need the logic of dialectic to make enough sense, that it encourages the student of the Bible to bow in worship before God. While pentecostal theologians strive for rationality in theological formulation, it is imperative that they must choose revelation over the finite restrictions of human logic.[99]

What is important in pentecostal theology is that abstract philosophical considerations of God are exchanged for the incarnation because through Christ, God grants eternal life.[100] The incarnation demonstrates that God desires a relationship with God's creatures, placing theology within the dynamic realm of relationality. However, God's transcendence may not be ignored and should also be considered—not in terms of abstractions but as the God beyond our language, the God before whom we stutter and stammer, requiring paradox to say something sensible about

98. Alvarsso, "Bible, Pentecostalism, and 'Magic,'" 193.

99. McRoberts, "Holy Trinity," 146.

100. Shaull, "What Can the Mainline Churches Learn," 8. Eternal life is defined in terms of a quality of life consisting of continuous fellowship with God that is experienced by the believer in a limited sense on earth and in an unlimited sense in eternity.

God.[101] The witness of Scripture and the testimony of the Spirit in our experience requires that both aspects are addressed.[102]

By way of conclusion, in bringing their own ethos to the theological table, Pentecostals regard the Bible as the inspired Word of God with authority for their lives. But they qualify that statement, determining that encounters with God within the faith community (in ways similar to those recorded in the Bible) are conditional for understanding and interpreting biblical accounts. I argued that Pentecostals need to develop a perspective on the all-inclusive difference made by their experience of God in all areas of their lives. The two elements conditional for good theology are the interpretation and appropriation of the biblical narrative and God's Spirit driving home the truth contained in that narrative. In talking about God, Pentecostals view God in trinitarian terms, as they experience God in God's interacting with human beings. Trinitarian theology is *per se* a theology of relationships, concerned with communion and love, forgiveness and courtesy. God is viewed as a being whose fundamental feature is loving relationality. God cannot be contained in absolutist and unchangeable categories, and language can never adequately express God. It is suggested that the philosophical language of dialectic be used to describe God. Dialectic allows one to speak of two or more (usually contradictory) truths while not negating either one. The living, interacting God is personal, as experienced in God's incarnation, where God stoops down and mingles with human beings until present times. God's works do not exhaust God's person and therefore Pentecostals worship the transcendent one living in a realm beyond human capacity to understand as the mighty God whose mere words create worlds. Dialectic helps to view God more holistically as the indescribable reality that also exists outside creation.

To a certain extent, the emphasis on experience of an encounter with Christ can be linked to postmodern thought—although postmodernism did not give rise to pentecostal experiential emphasis. In a sentiment shared by (cessasionist) fundamentalists, pentecostalism stands over against modernism's philosophical-scientific presuppositions and liberalism,[103] that only what can be proven to be historically and objec-

101. Holm, "Cadences of the Heart," 24.

102. Allowing Dela Cruz to speak of "testimonial hermeneutics" (Dela Cruz, "Preaching Among Filipino Pentecostals," 100).

103. Oliverio, "Introduction," 3. This liberalism was marked by a skepticism regarding biblical miracles, including rejection of the virgin birth of Christ, his bodily

tively true is meaningful.[104] Central to the pentecostal supernaturalistic worldview[105] is the confession that God speaks and acts today as God did as recorded in the Bible, leading to a high valuation of experience, non-rational epistemology,[106] and a resultant, unfortunate skepticism toward learning and higher education, as almost opposed to the (S) spirit.[107] Stronstad's[108] analysis of a pentecostal hermeneutics consists of three elements, that it is: experiential, at both levels of presupposition and verification; rational, by incorporating historical-grammatical principles of exegesis; and pneumatic, as it recognizes the Spirit as illuminator[109] and inspirer of Scripture, leading to a theology of biblical experience, or shared experience that expresses the charismatics' awareness of the similarity between their own experience and that of the prophets,

---

resurrection, and his literal second coming. Modernist eschatology fit well with postmillennialism, expecting that the world would be turned into an earthly paradise through education and social action. Liberalism was shaped by the teachings of Schleiermacher, Hegel, Kant, Ritschl, and Harnack, scholars from German universities in the nineteenth century (Menzies and Menzies, *Spirit and Power*, 197).

104. Cargal, "Beyond the Fundamentalist-Modernist Controversy," 168. Arrington argues that Pentecostals have traditionally sought to avoid two excesses. First, they have denied the liberal appraisal of the Bible as a document replete with human error—a view which undermines biblical authority—because it leaves the interpreter with the task of separating fact from fiction. Second, Pentecostals stopped short of the fundamentalist view of the Bible as a static deposit of truth that the interpreter approaches through human reason and logic alone (Arrington, "Pentecostal Identity and Interpretation of the Bible," 15).

105. A worldview that is the very reason for the overwhelming growth of the Pentecostal movement as an anthropological protest against modernity (Archer, "Pentecostal Hermeneutics," 132).

106. Genuinely Christian hermeneutics do not buy into the modern Enlightenment or other epistemologies which often seek to overcome the finitude and situatedness of humanity to attain some ideal state of knowledge and the quest for some meta-articulation of truth that can somehow move beyond cultures and traditions (an affirmation developed in Smith, *Fall of Interpretation* and supported by the pentecostal hermeneutic). Neither does pentecostal hermeneutic lead to a hermeneutic of suspicion or despair; it represents a Christian plurality of voices and interpretations—popularized as the "many tongues" principle of Amos Yong—as a reversal of Babel (Oliverio, "Book Review," 136).

107. Turnage, "Early Church and the Axis," 9.

108. Stronstad, "Pentecostal Experience and Hermeneutics," 25.

109. Anderson describes spiritual illumination in terms of the experiential immediacy of the Spirit who makes the Bible "alive" and therefore different from any other book (Anderson, *Introduction to Pentecostalism*, 223).

apostles and Jesus.[110] His proposal for pentecostal hermeneutics stresses the pneumatic in terms of an engagement with five elements: experiential presuppositions, a pneumatic aspect, the identification of literary genres, the use of human rationality in exegesis, and experiential verification.[111] However, his analysis is positivistic and limited to a segment of a diverse Pentecostal movement, where a majority (conservative) part devalues (with some justice) the second element consisting of rational forms of knowing.

Pentecostals emphasize re-experiencing the biblical text through preaching[112] as an immediate and continuationist meaning for Scripture, sometimes with little significance placed on the original context,[113] accompanied by the giving of testimonies that God is still working miracles in the present as found in biblical narratives.[114] Kinyua suggests that biblical narratives should also be re-enacted through storytelling with the main goal of enriching human freedom as the capacity to surpass the given and to help the readers to see themselves becoming different from

110. McKay, "When the Veil is Taken Away," 66. For Pentecostals, the prophets and the apostles are never merely objects for the study and assessment of later readers; they are living, speaking subjects on their own account (Bartholomew, *Introducing Biblical Hermeutics*, 524).

111. Stronstad, "Pentecostal Experience and Hermeneutics," 25–28.

112. In the first decade of pentecostal preaching, preaching was spontaneous and not relegated to professional clergy; it participated in the overall trajectory of worship services but was not necessarily the climax of the service (Byrd, "Paul Ricoeur's Hermeneutical Theory," 204–5). The congregation participated in the sermon in terms of responding, but the sermon also allowed for participation of the congregation more fully in the "altar call." The sermon reached for an immediate experience for the listeners, born from the expectation of the immediacy of God, and was not characterized by a hermeneutic that spent its time exegeting a text in a scientific manner. The preacher rather focused on the immediate meaning of the text and not upon what the text meant in its original context. It should be remembered that the use of the term "preaching" in terms of early pentecostal proclamation is anachronistic; early Pentecostals preferred to refer to "message from God" rather than "sermon," for the reasons explained above.

113. In their analysis of member's Bible reading practices, the AFM of SA found that 61 percent of participants are of the opinion that their pastor knows the Bible well, a worrying perception of AFM pastors' readiness to engage in theological endeavors. Only 58 percent are of the opinion that the Bible is taught well in their church while 52 percent think that their pastor's sermons are Bible-based. No less than 51 percent state that no reference is made to the Bible in sermons. This is in accordance with the remark that pentecostal preaching at times does not valuate the historical context. See Nel, "Bible Reading Practices in the AFM."

114. Fogarty, "Toward a Pentecostal Hermeneutic," 5.

what they have been.[115] Klaus speaks of believers' participating in Christ's continuing redemptive ministry, empowered by the Spirit before Christ's return.[116]

The risen Christ is a reality that believers experience on a continual basis through the working of the Spirit. The Spirit empowers the believing community by introducing them to Christ and by enriching them with the Spirit's gifts and fruit, bridging the gap between encounters that early disciples had with Jesus and present encounters with him, leading them in all truth (John 16:13).[117] The Spirit is the power through which the exalted Lord is present in the history of the cosmos as principle of a new history and a new world.[118] "The baptism into the Holy Spirit is not an encounter with the Spirit but with Christ, the baptizer. This means total surrender and absolute commitment to Jesus. Without this He cannot baptize you in the Spirit," writes David Du Plessis.[119]

Pentecostals interpret the description in Ezekiel 37 as the work of the Spirit to revive the dry bones in the age of the new covenant and Isaiah 44 as bringing seemingly dead people to new life and vitality.[120] As the rain brings the promise of new life and vitality, the outpouring of the Spirit promised in Joel 2 and 3 is interpreted as leading to a new dispensation, related to the Spirit.[121] Lochman describes the "new" element in terms of "*Vergegenwärtigung*" (making present of) and "*Teilhabe*" (gaining part of); the Spirit is the power through which God is made present in the Christ event, allowing God to be involved and partake directly in the life of the present-day church.[122] Christians live in the "relevant presence of God," changing their perspective on reality dramatically.[123]

Not only does the Spirit in the daily lives of believers introduce God but the Spirit also allows believers to partake in the life and work of the divine. People are not only the object of God's interest but are also addressed in their subjectivity, invited to become co-workers with God. The

---

115. Kinyua, *Introducing Ordinary African Readers' Hermeneutics*, 326.

116. Klaus, "Pentecostalism and Mission," 8.

117. Veenhof, "Holy Spirit and Hermeneutics," 115.

118. Gräbe, "Hermeneutical Reflections," 14.

119. Plessis, *Spirit Bade me Go*, 71.

120. Schafrot, "Exegetical Exploration of 'Spirit' References," 62–63.

121. Lochman, *Das Glaubensbekenntnis*, 149.

122. Lochman, *Das Glaubensbekenntnis*, 150.

123. Gräbe, "Hermeneutical Reflections," 16.

crucified and resurrected Lord is present in the midst of God's people. To understand in what way this is the case, it is necessary to know what the New Testament teaches about the Spirit, explaining pentecostal interest in the subject.[124] It should also be remembered that the worshiping, preaching, and teaching early church existed long before there was a New Testament and even before the books of the Old Testament were canonized. The church existed as a creation of the Spirit, proclaiming the saving and equipping word of God. The Spirit revealed Christ to the church, and eventually the church became the implied reader of the Bible (New Testament) it compiled. These books became canonized because the church saw the Spirit by which it lives also involved in these books or writings. Apart from the church, these writings wouould have no meaning or purpose.[125]

For Pentecostal people, the apostolic witness is crucial, as can be seen in their preference for the term to be incorporated in the early Pentecostal movement. For example, the Azusa Street Mission, where the Pentecostal movement originated, was called the "Apostolic Faith Mission"[126] and the earliest magazine published by the Mission was called "The Apostolic Faith."[127] Their preference for the term "Apostolic" is based on their perception of the apostles as the direct witnesses of Jesus's life and ministry and their message, therefore, is of primary importance. The New Testament as the result of their preaching sees an essential identity and continuity between Jesus of Galilee and the Lord who promises to be with them always—to the end of time (Matt 28:20).

The Holy Spirit is the One who Quickens and Animates Scriptures

Archer comments about Pentecostals' life with the Bible, stating that Pentecostals love their Bible.[128] Biblical themes, stories, and significant biblical numbers (e.g., three, seven, twelve, and forty) permeate pente-

---

124. De Beer, "Valence of Spirit Manifestation," 380.

125. Keegan, *Interpreting the Bible*, 158.

126. Burger and Nel, *Fire Falls in Africa*, 18.

127. McClung, *Azusa Street and Beyond*, 22, and Robeck, "Azusa Street Revival," 34.

128. Archer, *Pentecostal Hermeneutic*, 161. Oliverio groups Archer and Christopher Thomas together with others in the "Cleveland School" for charismatic-pentecostal hermeneutics (Oliverio, "Introduction," 8).

costal literature. More importantly, these things saturate pentecostal oral testimonies. In their narrated testimonies, one can clearly hear echoes of biblical stories, themes, and phrases. Pentecostals assimilated scriptural stories, verses, and concepts into their interpretation of reality.

The Bible speaks about God and claims to be God's word (2 Tim 3:16–17; Heb 4:12–13), a claim that results in Pentecostals' acknowledgement of the homiletical value of the Bible and the necessity of the Spirit's guidance in interpreting it. However, it is not doctrine or tradition that makes Pentecostalism what it is; it is the presence of God in and among God's people "in a manner which is readily evident to participator and bystander alike."[129] Pentecostal experience of the Spirit is, in pentecostal hermeneutics, the legitimate presupposition of biblical interpretation.[130] For this reason, the goal of studying Scripture is "knowledge of (not simply about) God."[131] Understanding Scripture serves the larger aim of knowing God. Pentecostals emphasize that the authority of the Spirit comes before the authority of Scripture. In this sense, their reading of the Bible may be called "agenda reading," reading with an intended result and a goal in mind.[132]

The same God who spoke and acted in the events of salvation-history and in the inspiration of Scriptures speaks and acts today. Pentecostals read the Bible in order to find the hermeneutical implications of God's

---

129. Clark and Lederle, *What is Distinctive*, 65.

130. Stronstad, "Pentecostal Experience and Hermeneutics," 18.

131. Autry, "Dimensions of Hermeneutics in Pentecostal Focus," 42. The Hebrew concept of *yada*ʾ is useful for describing this distinction. *Yada*ʾ refers to a knowing in active relationality. We do not simply know about God; rather, we "get to know" God experientially, in direct encounters. Such knowledge can never be absolutized into a theological system or reduced to a series of spiritual laws. It must always arise from a constant interaction with the known one (Ellington, "Pentecostalism and the Authority of Scriptures," 158).

132. Davies, "What Does it Mean to Read?," 256. The pentecostal reading of the Bible is creative, positive, and adversarial in that it approaches the text not in an objective sense—as a construct that might be understood and appreciated in its own right—but rather as a resource to be mined for specific treasures (Davies, "What Does it Mean to Read?," 256). According to Davies, Pentecostals ask three questions of the text, even if on an unconscious level: What did this mean to its original readers? What does this mean to me? What should I do about it? In responding to these questions, however, Pentecostals are much less interested in the first of the three, regarding original context, but the contextual pre-understanding (what does it mean to me?) and the enlarged meaning (what do I do about it?) are both of fundamental importance to them.

present activity in the faith community.[133] The Bible does not present itself as the word of God *per se*, but what we read in the Bible is mentioning of or references to the word of God.[134] Although God inspires the Bible, not everything in the Bible is of divine origins or a report of God's words and acts. Biblical writers utilized information available to their contemporaries and, at times, reported what they heard. The words of sinful and uninspired people were also written down. That the Bible is inspired implies that what is written down in the Bible is what God wanted to present to people and what is necessary for sinful humankind to know about God concerning how to live in the correct relationship with God.[135] The Bible is called the word of God when it contains something that Jesus revealed about God (John 14:24; 17:14–17), as a reference to the message of the gospel (Rev 1:2, 9), or what God revealed to the prophets and other individuals (Isa 2:3; Dan 9:2; Hos 1:1; 1 Thess 4:15).[136] McKay states that only prophetical persons can properly appreciate the records of prophetical figures, such as those found in the Old and New Testaments.[137] It is also true that Pentecostals treasure parts of the biblical record, specifically those that agree with their charismatic experiences, such as the miracle narratives in the Gospels, actions attributed to the Spirit in Acts, and the prophets' descriptions of the coming messiah.[138]

The word is God, but the Bible is not God. The Bible is the written witness about the word of God, a road sign indicating the way to God, containing everything needed by humans about God and God's will.[139] As a result, Scripture is viewed as the primal point of reference for encounters with God because to "encounter the Scriptures is to encounter God."[140] Reading Scripture should lead to affective transformation to be effective, although it does not exclude intellectual understanding as necessary in pentecostal understanding of truth based on Scriptures. McQueen argues that a distinctive pentecostal experiential pre-understanding determines how Pentecostals read the Bible, and experience plays a

---

133. McQueen, *Joel and the Spirit*, 3–4.

134. Möller, *Words of Light and Life*, 91.

135. Nelson and Wawire, *Bible Doctrines*, 14.

136. Möller, *Words of Light and Life*, 91.

137. McKay, "When the Veil is Taken Away," 64.

138. McKay, "When the Veil is Taken Away," 68.

139. Möller, *Words of Light and Life*, 93.

140. Johns, *Pentecostal Formation*, 14.

dialogical role in opening up the biblical text.[141] Although he adds that the communal nature of a pentecostal hermeneutics demands that the conclusions reached be viewed as one member's voice among the other members of the Christian community, he uses his pentecostal experience to interpret Joel in an invalid way.[142] He bases his reading of the Bible on Moore's suggestion that an implosion of "utter confession and utter criticism" occurs at the core of the pentecostal experience.[143] In those moments of intense encounter and communion of the believer with the Spirit, known in and expected by the Pentecostal community, confession is evoked by the claim of the Spirit. The believer is so claimed by the Spirit as "to be disclaimed, to be seized, taken captive and dispossessed of everything previously claimed," that these moments become critical. And even though it occurs outside the dialectic of text and reader, it opens up a different reading of reality and a different reading of the text.

To be a Pentecostal interpreter of Scriptures, one's confession about the text must agree with the previously evoked confession about the Spirit. The claim of the Spirit will be in agreement with the claim of the text, and one comes to know the claim of the text in the light of the claim of the Spirit.[144] This is where the danger of subjectivism looms, as McQueen illustrates, when he describes his experience of "a glorious encounter with the Spirit who filled me with rejoicing . . . Groans were replaced with glossolalia, and I was filled with a new sense of emotional and intellectual integration."[145] Emotional response is both highly subjective and contextual.[146] In this way, his conclusions in reading Joel is illuminated by pentecostal experience. His experience allows him to look "with new eyes intuitively focused" on the biblical book and three "confessions" arose out of the encounter: that the book of Joel enjoys literary and theological unity; that the theme of judgment in the book should not be subsumed under the theme of salvation (as happens in many commentaries) but rather should form a separate and third theme; and that the transition between the three movements of the book of Joel are found

---

141. McQueen, *Joel and the Spirit*, 5.

142. McQueen, *Joel and the Spirit*, 6 and 106–7.

143. Moore, "Deuteronomy and the Fire of God," 23.

144. Moore, "Deuteronomy and the Fire of God," 16.

145. McQueen, *Joel and the Spirit*, 107.

146. Baker, "Pentecostal Bible Reading," 97.

in the interaction of human cry and divine response.[147] It seems to me, however, that these conclusions are rather based on a rational reading of the book and to claim a pneumatological precedent for attaching authority to one's understanding of the biblical book (e.g., about its literary unity) is rather subjectivist and far-fetched. "Pentecostals do not found their understanding of the authority of Scripture on a bedrock of doctrine, but that, in fact, their doctrine is itself resting on something more fundamental, dynamic, and resilient; their experience of encountering a living God, directly and personally."[148]

Möller distinguishes between *fides humana* and *fides divina* at the hand of 1 Corinthians' reference to Paul's proclamation that was not "meant to convince by philosophical argument, but to demonstrate the convincing power of the Spirit, so that your faith should depend not on human wisdom but on the power of God" (1 Corinthians 2:4–5).[149] Pentecostal hermeneutics allows that a passage in Scripture may address an individual in certain circumstances while, at a later stage, in different circumstances, the passage does not address the same person or does not address another person in the same way[150]; the Spirit convinces the reader that the specific encounter with the Bible passage contains a unique revelation of God for them.[151] This, however, does not imply that the study of the Bible should not try to find out what the biblical writer intended as a message for the original listeners or readers (hermeneutics).

Pentecostals believe that the Bible contains not only the word of God for human beings but also a specific word applicable for their situation. What they need is the ability to hear with the ears of God, so that they can speak the word of God.[152] Scripture asks to be listened to, with ears of faith, as God's address to contemporary people.[153] Bartholomew emphasizes that the personal engagement of the reader to the text consists of silence.[154] The listener should stand openly before God, listening

147. McQueen, *Joel and the Spirit*, 107–8.

148. Ellington, "Pentecostals and the Authority of Scripture," 17. It should be kept in mind that pentecostal believers, both ancient and modern, are people of the Spirit and not people of the book alone (Pinnock, "Work of the Holy Spirit," 233).

149. Möller, *Words of Light and Life*, 97.

150. Van der Walt and Jordaan, "Kontekstualisering van die Nuwe Testament," 508.

151. Althouse, "Towards a Pentecostal Ecclesiology," 238.

152. Bonhoeffer, *Life Together*, 99.

153. Barth, *Kirchliche Dogmatik*, 1.1:51.

154. Bartholomew, *Introducing Biblical Hermeutics*, 19.

with patience, effort, work, and obedience, representing an art that has
been lost to a large extent in the contemporary logocratic culture. Even
our system of knowledge tends to ignore the listening processes; lack of
attention to listening has left us with a kind of epistemological benumb-
ment.[155] What is needed is the creation of an empty space or distance of
inner silence as crucial to inner listening. The analysis of texts will be
hindered and distorted if it does not begin with receptive listening.[156]

A result of reading the Bible prayerfully and with the belief that the
Spirit will reveal Christ (or the word) to them is that Pentecostals apply
promises from the Bible as though it is given to them when they experience that the Spirit highlights a specific passage for them. In this way,
they read the Bible from a promise-fulfilment scheme, applying certain
passages to their daily situation.[157] This may (and does) lead to the situation where the Bible is read ahistorically, as though the text has no history
or an underlying theology or ideology, allowing Pentecostals to find an
uncomplicated message directed to their present-day circumstances, a
kind of *lectio divina* borrowed from mystical theology. The working of
the Spirit (subjectively evaluated) is then supposed to guarantee that the
word becomes the truth of God for them in today's world. Pentecostals
agree with Karl Barth, who describes Scripture as "becoming" the word
of God to the reader or hearer through the action and participation of the
Spirit.[158] Barth insists on a single, thoroughgoing hermeneutics that applies not only to the Bible but to all acts of interpretation.[159] In conceptual
terms, this implies that all texts, things, and persons are only properly
understood when they are viewed in the light of God as revealed in Jesus
Christ. Barth also accentuates the spiritual dimensions of interpretation, suggesting that our disposition toward God, and God's disposition
toward us, determine whether and how well we understand the Bible,

155. Archer also emphasizes that hermeneutics cannot be reduced to rules; rather,
it is an art that affirms the necessity of human involvement, requiring the listener to
engage in active and reflective listening skills (Archer, "Hermeneutics," 108–9).

156. Bartholomew, *Introducing Biblical Hermeutics*, 22. Bartholomew refers to the
Shema (Deut 6:4–9) as the church's root metaphor for Scripture, as God's word or
address that calls for an attitude of reception in the form of respectful listening (Bartholomew, *Introducing Biblical Hermeutics*, 24).

157. Rance, "Fulfilling the Apostolic Mandate," 17.

158. Clark, "Investigation into the Nature," 57, and Fogarty, "Toward a Pentecostal
Hermeneutic," 7.

159. See Sparks, *God's Word in Human Words*, 177.

and everything else.[160] Lastly, Barth states that any account of biblical interpretation that neglects the role of the Spirit is bankrupt. The Holy Spirit is an essential animating presence in the reading of Scripture, so that readers of the biblical text cannot hear God speak without the Spirit's involvement.[161]

The danger is evident that the reader hears in the Bible what they wish to hear. It may also happen when Pentecostals allow for a directly inspired word from God functioning outside the narrow borders of the Bible, called prophecy, where one person feels inspired by the Spirit to speak a personal and individualized word to another or the assembly as they perceive it to be a word from God.

How can dangerous subjectivizing tendencies in a pentecostal hermeneutics be avoided? John Thomas suggests a holistic pentecostal hermeneutics that incorporates both Spirit and experience.[162] He deduces his paradigm from Acts 15, where Spirit and faith community play an important role in the interpretive approach regarding the issue of gentile or non-Jewish Christians. He observes that the interpretive process moves from the believing community's context to the biblical text. This reverses the order of exegetical processes, which normally starts from the text and then moves to the context. The Spirit enables the community that depends upon the Spirit to enlighten them in the interpretive process. This dependence goes far beyond evangelical claims to "illumination by the Spirit." The Spirit actually guides the community into a new understanding of God's will. The three primary components in the hermeneutical process are the community, the activity of the Spirit, and Scripture.[163]

160. See 1 Cor 2:14–15, which can be paraphrased as: "Some people don't have the Holy Spirit. They don't accept the things that come from the Spirit of God. Things like that are foolish to them. They can't understand them. In fact, such things can't be understood without the Spirit's help. Everyone who has the Spirit can judge all things. But no one can judge those who have the Spirit."

161. Sparks, God's Word in Human Words, 192. Zwiep emphasizes that Barth used the term "hermeneutics" only thirteen times in his monumental Kirchliche Dogmatik because, in his opinion, the question of a correct hermeneutics cannot be solved in discussions about exegetical method but rather only in exegesis itself (Zwiep, "Het Hermeneutische Vraagstuk," 3).

162. Thomas, "Women, Pentecostals, and the Bible," 43.

163. On the point of determining that circumcision was not a necessary hurdle for gentile converts, the council's reasoning was that the Spirit's activity and the church's willingness to "read" the Spirit allowed early Christians to interpret the Old Testament in this inclusive way (see Fowl, Engaging Scripture, and Sparks, God's Word in Human Words, 192).

These components are not static but in dialogue with each other. The community testifies to the experiences attributed to the Spirit and then engages Scripture to validate or repudiate the experience or issue, necessitating a dynamic balance between individual, Spirit, Scripture, and the faith community.[164] In this way, Scripture becomes authoritative and central to the rule and conduct of the church, forming the basic rule of faith and practice and supplying the corrective and interpretive authority for all religious experience because "what the Bible says" is identical with "what God says" in pentecostal theology.[165] Because an encounter with God is the essence of the religious experience, the unknowable and unfathomable are at the very heart of the experience.[166] Pinnock explains that the community needs the controlled liberty of the Spirit, where the Spirit takes what the inspired authors intended to say and discloses its significance for the contemporary community.[167] The original meaning is determinate and does not change, but God's Spirit in the Spirit's working out of salvation history uses this witness in new ways and in ever-new settings, creating significance for readers and hearers: "The Spirit is active in the life of the whole church to interpret the biblical message in the languages of today. He actualizes the word of God by helping us to restate the message in contemporary terminology and apply it to fresh situations. The result is that salvation history continues to take effect in us."[168]

In his quantitative research, Huckle finds that prophecy influences the contemporary American Pentecostal church to a large extent, that prophecy is understood in terms of personal and communal enlightenment and encouragement, and that nearly 95 percent of fellowships

164. Ellington, "Pentecostals and the Authority of Scripture," 28.

165. Ellington, "Pentecostals and the Authority of Scripture," 154.

166. Davies, "What Does it Mean to Read?," 253.

167. Pinnock, "Work of the Holy Spirit in Hermeneutics," 4. It is imperative to emphasize that the Holy Spirit cannot be tamed and domesticated. The Gospel of John explains that the Spirit is the living presence of the sovereign God. The Spirit bears witness to Jesus (John 15:26–27), convicts the world of sin, righteousness, and judgment (John 16:4–11), and guides the disciples in all truth by speaking what he receives from Christ and the Father (John 16:12–15). An epistemology informed by the Spirit will be responsive to God's critique of the individual and the church because the moving of the Spirit as agent of encounter with the holy God results in transformation. The Spirit exposes the individual and group for what they are, leaving them the choice of obedient response with its resulting transformation or denial of the truth with its resulting degeneration (Johns and Johns, "Yielding to the Spirit," 55).

168. Pinnock, "Work of the Holy Spirit in Hermeneutics," 4.

surveyed used Scriptures to judge prophecies, as doctrinal statements of these denominations require.[169] However, most respondents did not bring prophecy into relation with explication of Scriptures. Prophecy did help some to apply the Bible to a specific situation, or emphasize the blessings of God as expounded in Scriptures, but they realized that it should not be viewed as additions to the written Bible. Where they have been equated with Scripture, the danger of heretical doctrine became very real.

The Holy Spirit is Present Among God's People, the Community of Faith

What distinguishes pentecostal Bible reading from other traditions is not a different interpretive method but a distinct metanarrative that leads to a coherent and cohesive interpretive manner in which the Spirit plays the most important role and the community of faith and its story forms the influential hermeneutical filter as pre-understanding forming the condition for understanding.[170]

The use of any method is not objectively free from the social and cultural location of the person utilizing it; both method and person-in-community have been historically conditioned.[171] Comprehension is both discovery and creation of meaningful understanding.[172] McQueen also emphasizes that methodology can never be value-free.[173] There must be a correspondence between method and content, between formal and substantive matters. However, he concludes that a hermeneutics that embraces the critical claim of the Spirit simply cannot be fitted into a methodology that allows reason to be the final arbiter of truth, no matter how critical or creative the results.

Green remarks that pentecostal interpretation has moved beyond modern biblical studies and relocated the true home of scriptural

169. Huckle, "Contemporary Use of the Gift," 84.

170. Yong describes the role of the Spirit in the faith community and world in terms of several factors: the Spirit plays a relational role in and to the incarnation, the outpouring on the day of Pentecost, and the creation of the pentecostal body of Christ composed of many human members; the Spirit as rationality contributes to the fundamental notion of intelligibility itself; and the Spirit is the *dunamis* or the dynamic power of life (Yong, *Spirit-Word-Community*, 28–48).

171. Archer, *Pentecostal Hermeneutic*, 129.

172. Lategan, "Hermeneutics," 153–54.

173. McQueen, *Joel and the Spirit*, 109.

engagement, not in the faculty of theology of a university or seminary but in the church: "The Bible is the church's book, so the primary venue for biblical interpretation is the church's life: its worship, instruction, and mission."[174] The church understands theological interpretation not as reading the Bible as a historical or literary document, but as a source of divine revelation, and it is an essential partner in the task of theological reflection. Pentecostal theological interpretation is concerned with encountering the God who stands behind and is mediated in Scripture. Theological interpreters want to hear in the words of Scripture the word of God speaking in the present tense to their situation.

Although the Pentecostal community is part of the larger Christian community, it exists in distinction from the rest of the Christian world due to its distinct narrative tradition. The Pentecostal community is bound together by a shared pentecostal experience of the baptism with the Spirit, leading to a shared story based on the metanarrative of the general Christian story about the meaning of creation and God's role in creation as derived from the general narrative found in the Bible.[175] Pentecostals, however, concentrate specifically on the narratives found in the New Testament relating to encounters of early Christians with the Holy Spirit leading to an emphasis on the books of the synoptic Gospels (with a predilection for Luke)[176] and especially Acts of the Apostles.[177] Because the Pentecostal community understands itself to be a primitivistic[178] and restorationist movement, in many instances it also argues that it is the best representation of Christianity as an authentic continuation of the New Testament church.[179] Its conservative nature, however, also allows for operating legalistically when it succumbs to over-literal interpretations of Scriptures, leading it to become socially unhelpful, for instance, in the age of the earth debates, the role of women in leadership in the church and society, and the uncritical acceptance of the authority of governments.[180] Rather, Clark argues, the Bible should be used to provide

---

174. Green, "Pentecostal Hermeneutics," 163.

175. See Fackre, *Christian Story*, 8–9, and Nelson and Wawire, *Bible Doctrines*, 14.

176. Mittelstadt, *Reading Luke-Acts*, 2–3.

177. Hollenweger, *Pentecostals*, 336, and Mittelstadt, *Spirit and Suffering*, 2.

178. See Ngong, *Holy Spirit and Salvation*, 127.

179. Archer, *Pentecostal Hermeneutic*, 133.

180. Clark, "Pentecostalism and Philosophy of Religion," 3.

direction and boundaries to proclamation and experience, with "text" and "Spirit" proving balanced emphases.

Pentecostals regard their narrative tradition as synonymous with the New Testament narratives of experiences with baptism in the Spirit, and this narrative tradition provides the context for their search for meaning when they read the Bible. Penney[181] says that the experience of the day of Pentecost in Acts 2 becomes a "normative paradigm for every Christian to preach the gospel," and that Luke's "primary and pervasive interest is the working of the Holy Spirit in initiating, empowering, and directing the church in its eschatological worldwide mission."[182] Pentecostals read the Bible through a theological lens provided by Acts 2 and their own personal experience of Pentecost.[183] In this way, an experiential narrative forms the hermeneutical framework for interpreting Scripture, as well as experiencing reality, leading to a narrative theology that Scripture models.[184] Menzies describes the hermeneutics of the typical pentecostal believer as straightforward and simple—that the stories in Acts are *my* stories, stories that were written to serve as models for shaping my life and experience.[185] This narrative approach, contends Menzies, is one of the great strengths of the Pentecostal movement that enables the people in pre- or semi-literate cultures and people functioning in more experiential and less cognitive cultures to readily grasp the pentecostal message. Their narrative tradition allows for God's involvement in restoring the Spirit and its gifts to the Christian community. God's dramatic involvement in their reality and biblical events is interpreted to allow for the same miracles and interventions from the other side to happen in their world. They desire to live as the eschatological people of God, as part of the final drama of God's redemptive action, during the last of the last days. Keener makes the important observation that many

181. Penney, quoted in Anderson, "Towards a Pentecostal Missiology," 33.

182. Pentecostals argue from the unchangeableness of God that the nature of the apostolic church is normative for all time (Dayton, *Theological Roots of Pentecostalism*, 24).

183. Keener, *Spirit Hermeneutics*, 8.

184. Think of Paul and James using Abram's faith (Gen 14:6) as a model for believers (Rom 4:1–25 and Jas 2:21–23). James utilizes Job and the prophets as models for endurance (Jas 5:10–11). In 1 Cor 10, Paul cites the judgment experienced by Israel as a warning for Christians in his own day. The conclusion is that the apostolic church of the first century read the Bible as an inspired text that offers patters for God's continuing dealings with God's people (Keener, "Pentecostal Biblical Interpretation," 278).

185. Menzies, *Pentecost: This Story*, 23–24.

parts of the Bible also overtly invite experiential reading, like the Psalms, which are meant to be prayed and sung because they evoke feelings.[186] In the same manner, narratives invite readers into their world, facilitating reader identification.[187] Pentecostal hermeneutics affirms and attempts to practice what these genres naturally call forth.

All people read texts with interests and agendas, whether in terms of their social status or economic situation. It is impossible to read texts objectively, without the influence of larger and more personal contexts. Pentecostal hermeneutics is in a unique position to deconstruct the Enlightenment myth and ideal of critical and passionless objectivity by focusing on a balance between orthodoxy, orthopraxy, and orthopathy (or orthokardia).[188] Studying the Bible inductively should supplement reading the Bible exclusively with our own questions and challenges in mind in order to hear the Bible on its own terms. Ideally, the believer reading in faith should have a sound understanding of the orginal message as well

186. Keener, "Pentecostal Biblical Interpretation," 277, and *Spirit Hermeneutics*, 32–35. For instance, Stibbe, an Anglican charismatic theologian, identifies distinctive elements of a charismatic hermeneutic in Peter's Pentecost sermon (Acts 2:14–36) (interestingly enough, Acts 2:14 states that Peter did not act alone but stood up, indicating the action to preach, with the eleven). It is an experiential reading, an analogical reading, a communal reading, a christocentric reading, an eschatological reading, an emotional reading, and a practical reading (Stibbe, "This is That," 182–92). Archer shows how Keener's spirituality is more in tune with Wesleyan Pentecostalism and its concern to integrate the head and hands into the heart, which only an affective-narrative hermeneutic can provide (Archer, "Spirited Conversation about Hermeneutics," 186).

187. African slaves, for example, who heard about Moses leading an oppressed people out of slavery, lifted their voices in prayer to the God of the Israelites to do the same for them. The slave owners could not identify with Moses in the way the slaves did. They could not understand the biblical message of liberation as clearly as their slaves did. This is because the Bible is a book that resonates with the wounds of the oppressed. It tells of a God who cares for the oppressed. It tells of a God of justice, who is angry with hypocrites who twist the Bible into a book of injustice (Usry and Keener, *Black Man's Religion*, 108–9). It has been argued that those who favored slavery took verses out of context or simply appealed to the institutions that existed in biblical times without taking into account whether the Bible supported or resisted such institutions. Abolitionists, by contrast, took into account Scripture's historical situation and givenness and looked for broader principles in Scripture. Slaveholders' abuse of Scripture remains a textbook example of culturally insensitive hermeneutics and of a loveless application of biblical data, serving as a warning for contemporary Christians (Usry and Keener, *Black Man's Religion*, 187–88).

188. Cole, "Taking Hermeneutics to Heart," 269, and Baker, "Pentecostal Bible Reading," 96.

as insights into how it speaks to their settings because, when they hear the original message of the text, they can be assured that their experience of the text is relevant beyond them. In practice, experience shows that the Spirit can speak from the text, bringing insights that are directly relevant for our situation, even if it does not arise from sound exegesis of the text.[189] However, this is the exception; the rule is that Scripture and the Spirit provide believers with a more objective guide and framework for their personal experience of God.[190] To ignore the Bible as a historical and contextual document is to lay the table for reading the text with the purpose to find agreement with our own—at times distorted, and even heretical—ideas.

All reading is a transaction between the biblical text and the community, which results in the finding of meaning approximated by the reader.[191] Between the biblical text and the community is a dialectical encounter, made possible by a working plot within the biblical story that is recreated in the community. Hawk explains that a plot functions on the surface level of a tale as the framework of the story and as the arrangement of incidents and patterns as they relate to each other in a story[192]—but the abstract notion of plot also operates within the mind of the reader who organizes and makes connections between events, relating present-day experiences to the plot in the tale.[193]

The Pentecostal community reads Scripture in order to develop a praxis where biblical tales are placed into the cohesive pentecostal narrative tradition that interprets pentecostal existence in terms of the outpouring of the Spirit. Biblical tales challenge and reshape pentecostal tradition and provide the language to describe their praxis. In this way, the encounter between biblical text and community is dialogical as well as dialectical, and the search for an approximation of meaning takes

189. Keener, *Spirit Hermeneutics*, 32.

190. One often reads the objection that Pentecostals eisegete their experiences into the text—that is, they experience something and then find it in Scripture. Stronstad argues that the idea that personal experience should be assigned to a certification or verification function at the end of the hermeneutical process should be challenged since experience already enters the hermeneutical enterprise at the beginning of the hermeneutical process (Stronstad, "Pentecostal Experience and Hermeneutics," 16). Charismatic experiences provide an important pre-understanding for Scripture, supplementing a variety of cognitive elements.

191. Hart, *Faith Thinking*, 107.

192. Hawk, *Every Promise Fulfilled*, 19.

193. See Hart, *Faith Thinking*, 27.

place primarily within the community.[194] Pentecostal interpretation of the Bible includes an act of obedient response to the Scripture's meaning, as perceived by the Pentecostal community.[195] This leads Arrington to describe the three characteristics of pentecostal hermeneutics as an emphasis on pneumatic illumination, the dialogical role of experience, and biblical narrative.[196]

Stronstad challenges two standard evangelical principles of hermeneutics, using textual evidence. In the first place, he refers to Evangelicals' hermeneutical principle to use Paul to color all discussions of the Holy Spirit, arguing that Luke's and Paul's pneumatological lenses were different—with Paul using primarily salvation-initiation language and Luke using subsequent-empowerment language.[197] He suggests that Luke should be left to speak for himself, as this would demonstrate his uniqueness.[198] The second principle he challenges is that the didactic genre in the Bible should exclusively be used to define doctrine while the narrative genre should be used to reconstruct the history. Stronstad demonstrates the legitimacy of the narrative genre to carry theological intent, recognizing the legitimacy of the pentecostal nexus that shapes pentecostal mission and mission strategy.[199]

Two important differences between Pentecostals and many Evangelicals flow from Pentecostals' emphasis on the Spirit's involvement in explicating Scripture: they emphasize an immediate and experiential meaning for Scripture that does not necessarily equate with a historical-critical or grammatical-historical analysis of the text; and they believe that the Spirit can say more than Scripture, although never in contradiction to Scripture.[200] A hermeneutics that focuses only on what the original author meant (if it is possible to determine it) does not satisfy pentecostal sentiments, which assert that the spiritual and extraordinary supernatural experiences of biblical characters are to be replicated for contemporary believers. A pentecostal hermeneutics will always take into account the role of the Spirit and the impact of personal experience.

194. Fish, *Is There a Text in This Class?*, 34.

195. Archer, *Pentecostal Hermeneutic*, 136.

196. Arrington, "Hermeneutics, Historical Perspectives," 380.

197. Stronstad, *Charismatic Theology of St. Luke*, 49.

198. See also discussion in chapter 2.

199. See also Menzies, *Development*, and Penney, *Missionary Emphasis*, 87.

200. Fogarty, "Toward a Pentecostal Hermeneutic," 5–6.

A last argument is to be made from Jesus reading and interpreting the Hebrew Bible of his day. It cannot be doubted that Jesus regarded Scripture as inspired and authoritative. However, that does not imply that he considered every text as equally binding and relevant. For instance, according to Luke 4:18–19 (a quotation from Isaiah 61:1–2), Jesus omits the portion of the text that mentions any divine wrath because he knew the will of God in this matter and at this time.[201] Jesus blended the original prophetic word with its current significance for his hearers. In Matthew 5:38, he sets aside the "tooth for a tooth" maxim in order to state that his disciples are called to a higher level of ethical behavior. He did not deny that the text had been the word of God for previous times, but he changes its meaning to a radical injunction: to forgive one's enemies because one decides to love them. The conclusion can be made that Jesus took liberties when it came to the quotation and interpretation of texts, distinguishing between the original meaning and what the text means in the light of his incarnation. He also canceled the distinction between clean and unclean foods, disallowed divorce when Moses allowed it under certain conditions, and discouraged oaths that were permissible in his day. He did not see all texts as being on the same level or as having the same authority. He did not diminish Scripture but rather set it free—to function in new ways as the word of God for changing circumstances.

The church did the same in Acts 15:28–29, setting aside a significant element of the Torah. Peter changed the meaning of what is clean and unclean and taught that respect for holy days was a question of freedom. The Hebrew Bible prescribed circumcision for God's people, but the early church decided that it did not include non-Jewish believers. Jesus and the disciples were alive to the dynamic of their texts.[202]

By exalting the text as authoritative, one can choose the letter above the Spirit, giving the text too much respect. God, then, is made a prisoner of the Bible. The fact is, the word that was good for people in one situation may become destructive for people at another time. Scripture is a dynamic authority, a living guide, standing in life-transforming interaction with readers through the Spirit.

Most contemporary Pentecostals support the moral unacceptability of patriarchalism and androcentrism, slavery, anti-Semitism, violence against people, and such, even though these issues can be shown to be

201. Pinnock, "Work of the Holy Spirit," 235.
202. Pinnock, "Work of the Holy Spirit," 236.

supported by various passages in the Bible. The changes in moral sentiment were partly fuelled by a dialogue between the textual horizon and
the contemporary horizon from which meaning derives. Because the text
has a surplus of meaning, the dialogue never ends, allowing the generation of an effective history in interaction with the historical consciousness of the community.[203] All Bible readers need light from the Spirit for
their journey into love. In reading the texts about women in ministry or
homosexuality, the church should maintain its openness to the Spirit's
guidance, waiting for a consensus forming insight and a *sensus fidelium*.[204]

Synthesis

In this chapter, the first distinctive of pentecostal hermeneutics was described—that is, the necessity that Pentecostals experience the events and
truths described in the Bible first-hand, through the mediation of the
Holy Spirit (who inspired the Bible in the first place). It was important
to discuss this distinctive first because it serves as a precondition for the
next two distinctives. Pentecostals wait prayerfully to hear the voice of
and receive insights in their minds through the Spirit when they read
and meditate on Scripture. They read the text as *Scripture*, but that does
not make careful study of the Bible unnecessary. In order to counter unbridled subjectivism and popular charismatic excesses, the Bible should
not only be studied in all seriousness, but also, at the same time, with the
aim to live out biblical experience in the era of the Spirit.[205] The truth of
Scripture must become truth for them in encountering the word of God
because the Spirit is the one who realizes the Christ-event that the Bible
testifies of in the present. The Holy Spirit quickens and animates Scriptures, applying it to the contemporary situation and circumstances of
attentive readers. Their reading is Christ-centered—but not in an epistemological sense; rather, their experiential assessment is phenomenological in nature. The scopus that they use to evaluate what they read is the
Christ-event, including his teaching, ministry of healing and deliverance,
crucifixion and resurrection, and the outpouring of his Spirit on the day

203. Pinnock, "Work of the Holy Spirit," 243.

204. See Swartley, *Slavery, Sabbath, War, and Women*, for an illustration of this
principle.

205. Keener, "Pentecostal Biblical Interpretation," 282. See discussion in the first
chapter about challenging hermeneutical concerns in Africa for some of the charismatic excesses that damage the reputation of the Pentecostal movement.

of Pentecost. This also explains their emphasis on Luke-Acts as a primary resource in forming their experience, and the eventual formulating of their theology based on their experience of the Christ-event, utilizing the vocabulary provided in the Bible. In their faith life, pentecostals function within the context of the community of faith, and the Spirit is present among Christ's people, the body of Christ.

Waltke[206] relates how the Reformers balanced a "scholarly," objective, or analytical approach and a "spiritual" approach to hermeneutics,[207] in reference to writings by John Owen, Wesleyan scholars such as W. Mc-Cown and C. Michalson, Patrick Fairburn, Milton Terry, Daniel Fuller and Arthur W. Pink. However, he argues that there is a diminishing appreciation of spiritual factors in the present era. He shows how ten of the most widely used textbooks of the grammatico-historical method neglect the role of the Holy Spirit and the spiritual qualification of the interpreter due to what Carson calls the danger of a shift to a hermeneutical focus that would detract from the usefulness of the Bible as a practitioner's manual if the role of the Spirit in the exegetical task would be discussed in a sustained manner.[208] The result is that many seminarians are taught how to scrutinize a biblical text, but they are not expected to let the text speak for itself or to hear the voice of the Spirit. They are taught the sociology of ancient people, the theology of biblical authors, the mechanics of preaching, and the deciphering of Greek and Hebrew manuscripts, but not how to engage the hidden and mysterious God, who alone teaches, inspires, and gives the word that needs to be heard.[209]

While scientific exegetical methods like the grammatico-historical method are appropriate and necessary for understanding the text, they are inappropriate for the principal aim of Christian understanding of Scripture,[210] which is the knowledge of God, qualified in an experiential sense.[211] Immanuel Kant differentiated ways of knowing (*Erklärung*) per-

206. Waltke, *Dance between God and Humanity*, 301–4.

207. McKay, "When the Veil is Taken Away," 57.

208. Carson, *Exegetical Fallacies*, 73. Yong disagrees and describes how the Spirit was silenced by traditional Western theology but also how the once silent and "shy" member of the Trinity is silent and shy no more (Yong, *Spirit-Word-Community*, 28).

209. Virkler, *Hermeneutics*, 30.

210. Waltke, *Dance Between God and Humanity*, 305.

211. Waltke explains that it is as impossible to teach the Psalms—and its highly devotional content—to students without commitment to God as it is to know something about a person without knowing that person first-hand.

sonal objects that possess volition from knowing (*Verstehen*) impersonal objects that lack volition. We "explain" impersonal objects but "know" persons. To know impersonal objects, the scientific method is appropriate, and one distances onself from the object to be as detached and dispassionate as possible. The scientific method is inappropriate, however, for knowing persons. To know involves passion, affection, and a commitment to the other person.

A pentecostal hermeneutics can contribute to restoring the imbalance between a scientific study of the Bible and the spiritual engagement with the Bible as inspired word of God, leading Waltke to distinguish between adequate and perfect understanding.[212] The scientific method provides adequate understanding of the Bible on the condition that it is free from prejudices and preconveived opinions, except if they are declared, and engagements by secular advantages, false confidences, and authority of parties and societies. What is needed for perfect understanding includes walking in the Spirit and listening to insights developed by the Spirit in the mind of the prayerful reader. Because the Bible contains the revelation of God, even though it is in the form of historical events, described in a historical way, the nature of the Bible as revelation demands that the reader be led by the Spirit in the interpretation process.[213] The Bible is the revelation of God to humans about how to acquire salvation, and the process is by way of revelation, inspiration, and illumination, so that a modern reader can live in a relationship with the Creator.[214]

---

212. Waltke, *Dance Between God and Humanity*, 308.

213. It is acknowledged here that the historical narratives found in the Bible meet the contemporary requirements set for historical work in ancient times.

214. Waltke, *Dance Between God and Humanity*, 309.

CHAPTER 4

The Eschatological Lens that Pentecostals Use When They Read the Bible

Introduction

WILLIAM JOSEPH SEYMOUR (1870–1922) was born of parents who were former slaves in Centreville, Louisiana.[1] He was influenced by holiness teachings about the indwelling Christ. He had no formal education and taught himself to read. From the outset, he was a restless man. As a waiter in a hotel, he attended the local African Methodist Episcopal Church (AME Church) in Indianapolis, a black congregation in a predominantly white denomination. Later, he moved to Cincinnati, where he was saved and sanctified during services of the Evening Light Saints—a revivalist group who believed that human history was approaching the end and that Christ would soon appear to set up his kingdom on earth. Before the final denouement, God would refresh and equip believers with fresh gifts of the Spirit. It would be the "latter rain" that falls on spiritually parched ground, a bright light that would pierce the gathering darkness. Christians should urgently leave existing mainline established denominations because God is raising up a purified and racially inclusive church that will march through the earth. Later, Seymour moved to Houston, where he attended a black church and experienced something he had never seen before. He heard a woman praying aloud in a language that no one there understood. As a man

---

1. Alvarado, "Exploring Africanisms," 338.

who had spent much time in prayer, Seymour experienced that this woman's prayer showed a depth of spiritual intensity that he had long sought without avail. He also knew that, in holiness teaching, "speaking in tongues" was held to be a sure sign of the imminent coming of the last days that would inaugurate the events of the second coming of Christ.[2] The praying woman was Lucy Farrow, and Seymour interrogated her after the service about her experience. She introduced him to Charles Fox Parham, a white preacher, who managed a Bible school in the same city. At one stage, Lucy worked for Parham as a governess in Topeka, Kansas, where Parham had then managed a Bible school. Seymour begged Parham for permission to join his Bible school, but Parham was not keen, since integration of races was not encouraged in education and Parham held views sympathetic to British Israelism.[3] He could not get it over his heart to refuse Seymour, however, and compromised by allowing the black man to sit outside the classroom and listen to the lectures that the white students were attending. On rainy days, he was allowed to enter the building but not the classroom. He could sit in the hallway and listen at the door left ajar.

His exclusion from the classroom did not discourage Seymour. He listened to the lectures very ardently, praying for the experience of the baptism of the Spirit that Parham described to his students.[4] His "personal Pentecost," however, eluded him. Now, Seymour preached and witnessed about the experience of Spirit baptism, calling it the "second blessing" in language that holiness theology had taught him, although he had not experienced it himself. At a black church, he met Neely Terry from Los Angeles, who told him about a Sister Hutchins, who also spoke about the experience. When Terry returned to Los Angeles, she told Julia

2. Anderson, *Introduction to Pentecostalism*, 231.

3. Synan, *Holiness-Pentecostal Tradition*, 93.

4. Parham's doctrine of Spirit baptism with the initial evidence of tongues was significant in its influence on the resulting Pentecostal movement, but it was not the theme that held Parham's theology together (Jacobsen, *Thinking in the Spirit*, 19). Rather, his understanding of history as the grand narrative of time—from the original creation to the final consummation—that serves that role. He combined his view of history with an interconnected apocalyptic vision. His theology of Pentecost had three tenets: the miraculous ability of xenolalia as the "Bible evidence" for Spirit baptism; that those who received the Spirit baptism were the sealed bride of Christ, who will be raptured and avoid the tribulation of the eschaton; and that foreign tongues had the purpose of enabling missionary activity for an end-time revival (Goff, *Fields White Unto Harvest*, 132–33).

W. Hutchins about the young black preacher, and Hutchins invited him to take services at her small assembly. Seymour borrowed the train fare from Parham and set off to Los Angeles, eager to preach about an experience that he found in the Bible but had never experienced himself.[5]

His sermons in Los Angeles emphasized that speaking in tongues served as the sign that one had received the second baptism and sanctification, clashing with Hutchins's belief that tongue speaking may be one of the gifts of the Spirit but that it was not so central as Seymour believed. One day, when Seymour arrived at the storefront church, the doors were locked to keep him out. He was not welcome at Hutchins's church any longer. He did not have the necessary financial resources to return home.[6]

Seymour reacted to this rejection by hiring his own storefront, without any financial resources, and organized prayer meetings in the humble homes of black friends and sympathizers (such as the home of Richard and Ruth Asberry, at 216 North Bonnie Brae Street). Some of Hutchins's assembly supported his attempts; the members of the group were mainly domestic servants and washerwomen, coming from a poor section of the city. Seymour felt himself at home and carried on preaching the pentecostal message, even though he himself had not experienced the desired speaking in tongues. More and more people attended his house meetings. On April 9th, 1906, for the first time, people began praising God in unknown languages, among them the 35-year old Seymour. Shortly after, so many people started attending the house meeting that they could not fit into the house. Seymour's friends helped him to locate a two-story, white-washed, wooden-frame building that was vacant, at 312 Azusa Street, in the "colored," downtown section of town. The rent was $8 a month. Previously, the building served as a church for an African Methodist Episcopal congregation, and before that, it was used as a warehouse and a stable.[7] It smelled of horses and had no pews or pulpit; they placed timbers on upended nail kegs for benches and piled up shoeboxes for a pulpit. The benches faced each other in a square, so that believers looked at each other.

---

5. Anderson, "William Joseph Seymour," 186. Seymour arrived in Los Angeles on February 22nd, 1906, and started meetings at Santa Fe on February 24th (Robeck, "Azusa Street Revival," 32).

6. Robeck, "Azusa Street Revival," 32.

7. Anderson, "William Joseph Seymour," 187.

On April 14th, 1906, the building was occupied by the small band of believers. The worship services had no order; Seymour presided, but he left room for anyone who felt called to testify, bring a message, sing a song, or invite people for prayer. Seymour was not a charismatic leader. He was blind in one eye and had a scar on the right side of his forehead, the result of smallpox that he caught when a young child. He was an introvert with unassuming appearance. Nevertheless, he was the instrument that led to the revival.[8]

The services were long, characterized by spontaneity, joyous shouts, prayers, intercession, and the participation of those who attended, with people getting healed and baptized in the Spirit, and sinners getting saved.[9] They took up no collections; people could contribute to the rent of the building by placing some money in a small receptacle.[10]

From the start, the Azusa Street Mission was identified by its high eschatological fervor which identified the outpouring of the Spirit in apocalyptic terms. The recurrence of the experience of the day of Pentecost "in these last days" was interpreted as the sign that the end was imminent.[11] Spirit baptism was the preparation of the end-time church for the events that would inaugurate the second coming of Christ, with the rapture and the great tribulation (See Rev 7:14). The Holy Spirit was viewed as the eschatological Spirit, who bridges not only the past and the present but also the future, with God's presence. Pentecostal theology was less concerned with articulating a theology of transcendence than a theology of the end of the known order, the *telos*. The end had arrived in the person of the Spirit, introducing the "last days." The Spirit was bestowed by the eschatological and Spirit-endowed prophet of the last days, Jesus. Therefore, believers expect to see signs of the end within their midst, which is the ministry of the Spirit in the faith community, by way of *charismata*.[12]

The interraciality of the Azusa Street meetings, where black and white at times embraced in prayer and brotherly love, impressed visitors, and disgusted others.[13] One attendee, a white preacher from the south,

8. Anderson, *Vision of the Disinherited*, 60.

9. Robeck, "Azusa Street Revival," 33.

10. Cox, *Fire from Heaven*, 48–57.

11. Vásquez, "Past and Present Social Characteristics," 325.

12. Pinnock, "Work of the Holy Spirit," 140.

13. Anderson, "William Joseph Seymour," 188.

relates how he was at first offended and startled, but then inspired by the sign that "the color line was washed away by the blood."[14] The same happened in South Africa, where John G. Lake and Thomas Hezmalhalch held racially integrated services in Doornfontein, Johannesburg, in 1908. William F. P. Burton, a pioneer Pentecostal missionary in the Congo, reported that "all shades of colour and all degrees of the social scale mingled freely in their hunger after God."[15] The interracial fellowship was interpreted by early Pentecostals as a sign of the last days, of Christians who were united before the end would dawn with the judgment of all nations and people before the white throne of Christ (Rev 20:11).

On April 18th, 1906, San Francisco was shaken by an earthquake that almost completely destroyed the city—due to fires that started in the wake of the quake—representing the most spectacular and destructive natural disaster the United States had ever seen, and fueling urgent eschatological expectations of the end. Did not Jesus predict that earthquakes will occur as the beginning of the birth pangs that will introduce the end of the world (Mark 13:8; Matt 24:7; Luke 21:11)?

Combined with the natural catastrophe, the Azusa Street Revival persuaded participants that the last days had finally arrived and that they were the pivotal actors in the drama that God's Spirit was preparing to enact. The disenfranchised, marginalized, despised, and rejected were chosen by God to benefit from the Spirit baptism and to be the heralds of its occurrence to the rest of the world. As indicated, early Pentecostals interpreted the new tongues they received as equipment for spreading the pentecostal message across the globe.[16] Charles Parham had already believed and taught the same. For instance, he claimed that he had been specially gifted in Yiddish and anticipated that he would soon have a wonderful ministry among the Jews in Jerusalem. He suggested that the whole missionary enterprise should be reconfigured to have missionaries abstain from language study and instead base their mission plans on the language gifts they received as part of their baptism in the Spirit. All that was needed was that one discovers what language one had received as a gift from the Spirit before one departed to that country. The gift of tongues was interpreted in three senses: as the clearest evidence of Spirit baptism,

14. Cox, *Fire from Heaven*, 58.

15. Burton, quoted in De Wet, "Apostolic Faith Mission," 34.

16. Jacobsen, *Thinking in the Spirit*, 49.

equipment for mission work, and as a harbinger of the last days.[17] Seymour also viewed the interracial character of his Mission as a sign of the Spirit healing racial divisions within existing churches, introducing the end-time church inaugurated by the experience of Pentecost, and driven by the ecumenical impulse that would unite all born-again Christians.[18]

Seymour's teacher, Parham, visited Azusa Street by invitation of Seymour. Parham attended meetings in October, 1906, but judged it to be marked by emotional excess. Although he did not admit it, the interracial character of the early meetings also probably upset him. He wrote about his perceptions of Azusa Street: "Men and women, whites and blacks knelt together and fall across one another; frequently a white woman, perhaps of wealth and culture, could be seen thrown back into the arms of a 'buck nigger,' and held tightly thus as she shivered and shook in freak imitation of Pentecost. Horrible, awful shame!"[19] When Seymour invited Parham to preach, Parham preached about the outpouring of the Spirit before the end times and lambasted the Azusa Street members, denigrating their behavior as the result of "hypnotic influences, familiar-spirit influences, mesmeric influences, and all kinds of spells, spasms, falling in trances, etc." He judged that it did not represent the work of the Holy Spirit. Seymour and his elders responded by asking Parham to leave and never come back again; Parham responded by opening his own revival meetings across town, but only a few people attended. The split between Parham and Seymour was never healed.[20]

Hauerwas and Willimon make the important remark that the removal of eschatology from ethics within some parts of the Christian church may account for the suffocating moralism in the church.[21] Cox

17. Cox, *Fire from Heaven*, 63.

18. In 1907, Seymour wrote, "Pentecost . . . brings us all into one common family" (Seymour, quoted in Cox, *Fire from Heaven*, 297). Most of these expectations were never realized, such as the expected outcome that speaking in tongues is equipped with existing languages (*xenolalia*) and that the pentecostal experience would blur church boundaries and create a unified, end-time church. Charles Parham insisted to the end that missionary *xenoglossy* or *xenoglossia* (the phenomenon in which a person is able to speak or write a language he or she could not have acquired by natural means) should be the norm, even when it failed the empirical test, a view that some church fathers also held (Keener, *Spirit Hermeneutics*, 64). For a more extensive discussion of this topic, see Nel, "Pentecostal Ecumenical Impulses."

19. Cox, *Fire from Heaven*, 61.

20. Robeck, "Origins of Modern Pentecostalism," 19.

21. Hauerwas and Willimon, *Resident Aliens*, 90.

concurs, stating that, as a rule, the disappearance of eschatology within the church produces stagnation, comfort, and consumer religion.[22] Moralism is concerned with a list of acceptable virtues and suitable causes, the pursuit of which will give believers self-fulfilment. Without eschatology, they are left with only a baffling residue of strange commands. Such commands may seem impractical and ominous because it is not set within its proper context of an eschatological messianic community, which exists because it knows something that the world does not know, structuring its life accordingly. The pentecostal emphasis on an urgent, eschatological expectation urged members to lead holy, sanctified lives; their expectation of the imminent second coming encouraged them to be on the watch as they do not know when the time would be (Mark 13:33–37; 14:38; Matt 24:42; 26:41; Luke 21:36). Their expectation included an apocalyptic end of the world that would irreversibly change the destiny of all people. It is necessary to qualify the apocalyptic expectation of the Pentecostal movement, as well as the early Church.

Apocalypticism

"'Apocalyptic' and 'apocalypticism' are notoriously slippery words," concludes Philip Davies in his discussion of the subject.[23] We do not know who developed, read, or heard this genre at first or what the influence of apocalyptic literature on the Jewish community was. Modern researchers also find it difficult to describe the characteristics of apocalyptic texts as such because of the differences between the few extant texts. In trying to generalize, apocalypticism has been described by researchers in terms of the following characteristics: it consists of revelations by otherworldly mediators, speaking about salvation from the wretchedness of this world; it consists of an eschatological dualism with a clear differentiation between the present and future aeons—and the future seen

---

22. Cox, *Fire from Heaven*, 318.

23. Davies, *Daniel*, 66. Apocalyptic works circulating in Jewish circles during the first century CE professed to reveal (*apocalypto*) what would take place at the end of time, determined by the vivid expectation that the world was in its last age, the end would not be long delayed, and God would soon deliver God's chosen ones (Wansbrough, *Use and Abuse of the Bible*, 8). The New Testament letter of Jude (14–15) quotes from the book of Enoch, an important Jewish apocalyptic work, as prophecy—and thus seemingly as authoritative Scripture (Walton and Keener, *Cultural Backgrounds Study Bible*, 2214).

as predetermined; it is pseudonymous, as the authors need to earn credibility ('author-ity') by using the names of ancient, famous persons (like Enoch); it is secret; it is characterized by eschatological impatience; it contains careful calculations of the dates of future events and numbers have symbolic significance, applied to the present situation by the author; it contains phantasies; angels play a prominent part; and an expectation of life after death is expressed, an expectation that is first defined in the Hebrew Bible only at the very end of its theological development.[24]

As stated, Hanson remarks that the value of compiling such a list is limited because each apocalyptic work is characterized by unique features that do not fit the list, implying that the historical and social matrix of apocalypse cannot be explained satisfactorily.[25] Apocalypticism can be defined as a crisis phenomenon, illustrating the way that values and structures of a minority or disenfranchised group have become meaningless and require to be replaced by a new meaning system, displacing and alienating the minority group even further from the majority group—that is, those in power. For them, the only meaning in life consists in the revelation of a new world, when God will judge the majority group and punish them with eternal death, rewarding the disenfranchised with access to power. In the words of Larue: "The fundamental theological problem confronting the apocalypticist is theodicy. The struggle between good and evil experienced in human life is a microcosmic manifestation of a macrocosmic phenomenon."[26] Apocalypticism offers a solution to theodicy by way of the destruction of the known order that represents inexplicable suffering and the establishment of a new order of justice.

While Antiochus IV's oppression of Jews in the middle of the second century BCE was the catalyst for (or at least an important part of) apocalyptic thought patterns, its roots lie in Israel's sacral history. Antiochus's persecution led to "a failure of nerve, a despair of man's ability to effect the kingdom of God through his own efforts, and a conviction that the situation could only get worse until God himself broke in to terminate the present evil age and inaugurate the ideal."[27] The new expected

---

24. These paragraphs are partly based on Nel, "Daniel 9." See Davies, *Daniel*, 20; Hanson, *Dawn of Apocalyptic*, 9–12; LaCocque, *Daniel and His Time*, 88; Verhoef, *Profete en Profesie*, 83; Von Rad, *Old Testament*, 301–2; and Vorster, "Tekste Met 'n Apokaliptiese Perspektief," 158–59.

25. Hanson, *Dawn of Apocalyptic*, 6.

26. Larue, *Old Testament Life and Literature*, 3.

27. Larue, *Old Testament Life and Literature*, 3.

to be realized is incomparable with the known because "apocalyptic eschatology is the mode assumed by the prophetic tradition once it had been transferred to a new and radically altered setting in the post-exilic community."[28]

There is consensus among researchers that a distinction should be made between a literary genre (apocalypse), a social ideology (apocalypticism), and literary ideas and motifs (apocalyptic eschatology). Apocalypse refers to a specific text, while an apocalyptic perspective refers to a point of view from which reality is experienced and explained. An apocalyptic movement is a grouping within society, while apocalypticism refers to a phenomenon or ideology.[29] The distinction does not solve all related problems; for instance, García-Martínez[30] shows that the restriction of *apocalypticism* to a literary genre is too reductionist to give justice to the term's associations. Instead of trying to define the terms, it seems to be better to describe the phenomenon in terms of a specific document or text. In the end, one can compare the different descriptions in order to keep one from reading a text with *a priori* perceptions.

Where Did Apocalypticism Originate?

The question is: was apocalypticism an unfortunate turn-off from the prophetic tradition in the Hebrew Bible, or a linear and legitimate progression and development from prophecy? Is it a necessary or applicable development of the prophetic tradition? What is the distinction between prophetic and apocalyptic eschatology?

The distinguishing factor between prophecy and apocalypticism lies in the way the vision of the future is integrated with the events of daily life in prophecy, whilst the vision of the future needs a radical break with ordinary history in apocalypticism.[31] Prophecy is like an airplane, departing from the runway of history and flying into an eschatological future, while apocalypticism is like an airplane appearing in the clouds of the eschatological reality to land on the runway of the present.[32] While the historical situation is important for prophecy, apocalypticism comes

28. Hanson, *Isaiah 40–66*, 10.

29. See Vorster "Tekste Met 'n Apokaliptiese Perspektief," 158.

30. García-Martínez, "Encore l'Apocalyptique," 230.

31. Hanson, "Apocalypticism," 32.

32. Verhoef, *Profete en Profesie*, 83.

from God's distance to land in the situation he created, resulting in a new way of interpreting the present.

Von Rad is of the opinion that, to a certain degree, there is no connection between prophecy and apocalypticism, except in the fact that both are oriented towards the future.[33] The irreconcilability between prophecy and apocalypticism is found in the different views of history, with prophecy finding its roots in Israel's salvation history and the tradition of election, while apocalypticism never refers to the important traditions that defined Israelite identity, the patriarchal, exodus, Zion, or David traditions. The root from which apocalypticism grew was the wisdom tradition.[34] Koch, however, is correct when he states that wisdom literature does not show any form of critical agreement or parallels with apocalyptic literature, and wisdom literature of the second century does not show any interest in eschatological themes.[35] A relation between wisdom tradition and apocalypticism can be shown, but apocalypticism finds its other parent in prophecy.[36]

It is my tentative judgment that wisdom was wedded to the tradition of apocalyptic eschatology as part of the effort being made by visionary circles to establish their credentials in the third and second century BCE, at a time when prophetic figures were being regarded with a great deal of skepticism—and even animosity—by many religious leaders.[37]

Its View of History

Apocalypticism originated in a radical break with how the present and past is viewed, in order to reinterpret it in the light of a totally new future.[38] It is characterized by radical pessimism, where all human intervention is liquidated and the expectation is exclusively focused on the utopia of a new world with its new symbolic coherence. World history is in the process of being ended as a result of the nature of humankind and the kingdoms established by them. There is no expectation of salvation in the present; salvation is interpreted to be eschatological and in the

33. Von Rad, *Old Testament*, 303.

34. Von Rad, *Old Testament*, 303–5.

35. Koch, "Is Daniel Also Among the Prophets?," 240.

36. Baldwin, *Daniel*, 50.

37. Hanson, *Dawn of Apocalyptic*, 9.

38. Vorster, "Tekste Met 'n Apokaliptiese Perspektief," 160.

future.[39] Apocalyptic literature treats good and evil as timeless factors. The only interest lies with the last generation of Israel, who will experience the end of times. Apocalypticists paint history in a deterministic sense in the service of their view of the future. Human beings are seen as the victim of decisions made long ago without them having any say in it. Allegorical codes are utilized to summarize the whole historical process under a few denominators and objectify it conceptually, and history is schematized and unified by reducing it to the few primary powers that are determining it. In these events, humans are only agents in a limited sense, with limited power of choice.

Apocalypticism and the Christian Church

Only a fraction of apocalyptic texts probably survived, and these books represent a corpus that early Christians appreciated and utilized on a wide front.[40] That these books survived—although only in (primarily) Greek or Greek translation—is probably due to the interest shown by the Christian church. At the end of the first century CE, Christians had owned the apocalyptic elements in Jewish writings that originated during the inter-Testamental period. After 70 CE, partly due to Jews' perception of disloyalty of the Jewish Christians—who fled and left Jerusalem during the Roman siege (presumably in response to Jesus's warning in Mark 13:14–23; Matt 24:15–28; Luke 21:20–24)—but also their acceptance of apocalyptic ideas, Orthodox Judaism purposefully broke any ties with the Christian church, and, at the same time, they rejected apocalypticism, which had partly contributed to the Jewish Rebellion of 66–70 CE, leaving Jerusalem and the Temple being destroyed.[41] By 136 CE, apocalypticism was no longer a tenable outlook in Jewish (and a significant part of Christian) theology.[42]

The first converts of the Christian church were presumably from among the socially and financially disadvantaged Jews whose lives were

39. Von Rad, *Old Testament*, 303.

40. The discussion of apocalypticism in the Christian church is partly based on Nel, *Of that Day and Hour No One Knows*, 105–7.

41. Russell, *Method and Message of Jewish Apocalyptic*, 32. It was argued that this was also one of the important reasons for rejecting apocryphal books that previously influenced Jewish thinking but would now be left out of the Jewish canon (see chapter 2).

42. Frend, *Early Church*, 50, in reference to Grant, *Hellenistic Religions*, 33.

characterized by alienation, a battle to survive physically and emotionally, and their resultant despair and desperation. For them, Jesus's apocalyptic message of an imminent ending of a world characterized by injustice and the arrival of a new world, with new opportunities for the disadvantaged, had a revolutionary ring of hope. Initially, Jesus preached to rural Jews living in the small towns of Galilee. His followers viewed him as the expected messiah, the one their Scriptures promised would come to save them from a world of suffering and oppression defined by enemies among their kinfolk as well as foreign rulers.[43] Jesus served a political function in their view of the messiah. The Christian movement might have started as an apocalyptic sect within Judaism and it was initially contained within the mother religion.[44] Several similar sects probably functioned within the Jewish religious context, especially Galilee, as the region was well known for such expectations and revolutionary movements—at least some of which were marked by apocalyptic expectations.[45] In the second part of the first century CE, the Jewish component in the Christian church became marginalized with the majority of Jewish Christians emigrating and others assimilating with the customs of heathen Christians. A small group of Jewish Christians emigrated to Pella, a Greek town in Transjordan. They remained faithful to the Torah and survived as a sect of Ebionites, derived from the Hebrew word for "poor."[46] The non-Jewish part of the Christian church flourished after 70 CE and developed into a universal religion, available for people of all races and classes. Within forty years after the death of its founder, the message of the Christ was spread throughout the *oikoumene*, primarily due to the successful missionary work of apostles like Peter, Paul, Barnabas, and Silas. The Christian church, consisting of heathens, originated within the framework of Hellenistic Judaism, although it was also influenced by Palestinian Judaism. It accepted Jewish monotheism: the concept of one, personal God; a strict moral code deduced from the ethical requirements of the Torah; and the need for repentance, defined in terms

---

43. Vermes, *Story of the Scrolls*, 151–52.

44. Tripolitis, *Religions of the Hellenistic-Roman Age*, 92.

45. See Ehrman, *Lost Christianities*, 91–134.

46. Schröter, "Son of Man as the Representative," 37, and Nel, "Konteks(te) Waarbinne Apokaliptiese Geskrifte," 1327. This association with the "poor" may refer to their being part of the marginalized and disenfranchised, which the early Christians mostly represent, as argued above. However, the term may also relate to its use in Matt 5:3 and Luke 6:20.

of turning away from loyalty to other gods and accepting the Jewish God as the true God.[47] Another element of Hellenistic Judaism that was accepted was apocalypticism, with its expectation of an imminent *parousia* and the resultant end of the known order.[48] The Christian church was accepted by many Roman-Hellenistic people due to its message of hope that people will be saved from an evil world to be introduced into a world of justice and love, its practice of accepting all people within their *agape* community, and its pastoral functions to take care of the poor and disadvantaged.[49] Like the popular mystery cults, the Christian message satisfied the emotional and spiritual needs of a large group of people so that Christianity was established in all the important cities as well as rural districts by the end of the second century.[50]

Eschatological Identity

Instead of the more biblically accurate "already/not yet" eschatology of the kingdom of God that forms the central theme of Jesus's preaching, early Pentecostals typically read Scripture through the eschatologically determined narrative grid of the "latter rain," which they connected with the outpouring of the Spirit on the day of Pentecost and their current experience of Spirit baptism.[51] They also interpreted Scriptures through the interpretive grid of their social world and experience, including such factors as social environment, historical situation, ethnic and cultural identity, gender, worldview assumptions, and the like, implying that the text had (nearly) as many meanings as there were interpreters or interpretive communities.[52] They established an important part of their identity in terms of their eschatological expectations, and they read the

47. Keel, *Monotheismus im Alten Israel*, 65, and Tigay, *You Shall Have No Other Gods*, 75. Jewish exegetical methods also influenced Christians. Four kinds of interpretation were common in Jewish exegesis of the first century CE: literalist, midrashic, typological, and allegorical. The exegetical tradition rested on two pillars: the starting point of inspired words and the acceptance of a multiple sense of meaning in Scripture (which, in turn, was made possible by the conception of inspiration). These were also part of Jesus's use of Scripture and the example of the apostles' points in the same direction (Maier, *Biblical Hermeneutics*, 327).

48. Lang, *Der Einzige Gott*, 37.

49. DeSilva, *Introduction to the New Testament*, 362.

50. Ehrman, *New Testament*, 31.

51. Keener, *Spirit Hermeneutics*, 21.

52. Venema, "Interpreting the Bible," 25.

Bible through this identification. It also had important missiological implications, which determined their evangelistic strategies.[53] Because the task of reading the Bible can never be separated from the task of making sense of our experience—our observations of the world and of our lives—the question of the way our worldview influences our behavior is also relevant, including the reading patterns we use when we interpret an ancient text like the Bible.[54]

The eschatology of early Pentecostalism, consisting of dispensational premillennialism, passed through three different stages.[55] The earliest Pentecostals articulated a theology of the latter rain, which validated and justified their charismatic experiences related to Spirit baptism. The latter rain was supposed to prepare the world for the great harvest that immediately preceded the return of Christ in glory to establish God's kingdom on earth. As Pentecostals moved into the middle of the twentieth century, their eschatological understanding changed—along with their hermeneutical perspectives—also leading to a changed self-understanding.[56] They held to a fundamentalist-dispensational eschatology as part of evangelical doctrine as the price they paid for acceptance by mainline evangelicalism (as argued above), and its adoption created problems for their previous democratic ecclesiology, leading now to a professional pastorate and the change of members from democratic participants in the service and ministry to spectators and connoisseur consumers of the worship service. They were also embroiled in debates over pre-, mid-, and post-tribulation doctrine. Currently, a new wave of theological inquiry has called into question the role of dispensational premillennialism in pentecostal theology and has suggested a proleptic or inaugural eschatology that sees the eschatological kingdom as already being manifest in history, but not yet in its fullness. The already-but-not-yet tension of the coming kingdom is more in keeping with the charismatic center of Pentecostalism.[57] How-

53. For Pentecostals' self-understanding as eschatological, see Anderson, *Ends of the Earth*, 61–62.

54. Starling, *Hermeneutics as Apprenticeship*, 195.

55. Althouse, "Eschatology," 73–75.

56. This time also saw the emergence of the New Order of the Latter Rain, under the leadership of Herrick Holt and George Hawtin, in reaction to what was perceived as the waning of pentecostal spirituality. The New Order explained that Pentecostals had lapsed into a spiritual drought, requiring a new outpouring of the former rain given around 1906 in a new latter rain.

57. Althouse, "Eschatology," 74.

ever, parts of the charismatic movement and many independent neo-Pentecostals have again taken up the theology of the latter rain, using it to vindicate the continuing manifestation of charismatic experiences. They are not committed to the premillennial-dispensational eschatologies of Pentecostals of the middle of the twentieth century but rather opt for other eschatological forms, such as postmillennial social reconstruction (Kingdom Now Theology) or variations of realized eschatology.[58]

In the late nineteenth century, the Keswick movement[59]—with its "finished work" view of sanctification[60]—read Acts 2 as the divine empowerment for mission in light of what Luke considered Jesus's last words before his ascension: "[The apostles] will receive power when the Holy Spirit has come upon you; and you will be my witnesses in Jerusalem, in all Judea and Samaria, and to the ends of the earth" (Acts 1:8). Peter's rendering of Joel's "afterward" (Joel 3:1 in BHS) with "in the last days" is notable, with "last days" seen as a phrase associated with the expectation of Israel's promised restoration (in terms that remind us of Isa 2:2; Hos 3:5; Mic 4:1; Dan 2:28) that is now fixed in eschatological time. This eschatological period of restoration includes a period of great suffering just before the restoration (Jer 23:20; Jer 30:24; Ezek 38:16; Dan 10:14) and accompanying apostasy of the insincere. Early Christians also associated their eschatological expectations with suffering and apostasy (see Mark 13:9–13; Rom 8:22; 1 John 2:18), designated as the present and final period just before the end (1 Tim 4:1; 2 Tim 3:1; 2 Pet 3:3). "The last days" prefigured the final "day of the Lord" (Acts 2:20), indicating "the eschatological time."

Early Christians (and Pentecostals) consistently experienced this eschatological period as the time they were living in (Heb 1:2; Jas 5:3; 1 Pet 1:20). Luke emphasizes that this period is characterized by prophesying by sons and daughters, as well as male and female slaves. The eschatological time that believers lived in was characterized by prophetic empowerment, valid for all people. One never finds any suggestion in Acts that such empowerment would cease at any stage during the eschatological

---

58. Althouse, "Eschatology," 75.

59. The Keswick Convention began annual meetings in the Lake District in 1875 and influenced many Christian churches and movements (Anderson, "Keswick Movement," 128).

60. Menzies and Menzies, *Spirit and Power*, 328.

era. Moses's sign (Num 11:29) that all the Lord's people were prophets, and that God would put God's Spirit on them, is fulfilled in Acts 2.[61]

Pentecostals defined themselves in terms of and justified their existence at the hands of their identification with the early church's believers, who viewed themselves as continuing the biblical era and living in the last days. It is not tongues that distinguished Pentecostals but rather their perception that they belonged to the life of the church of the apostles, the church of Pentecost, with prophecy, healing, speaking in tongues, and deliverance as signs that they were living in the last days.[62] The restoration of the *charismata* was viewed as a sign of Christ's imminent return, providing an eschatological hope that drove the growth of Pentecostalism.[63] The present era was the era of the Spirit.[64]

61. Witherington, *Conflict and Community*, 286. In African Pentecostalism, prophets are appreciated as channels of encountering God and receiving God's blessing because prophets are perceived as possessing the authority of God (Magezi and Banda, "Competing with Christ?," 2–4). In the Zimbabwean context is, the prophets portray themselves to their believers in a manner that creates parallel soteriological structures, which ultimately undermines Christ's liberating, securing, and empowering lordship on the believer. This undermines Christ's deity and breeds practical atheism among prophetic pentecostal believers. The ripple effect is the undermining of Christ's soteriological work (Magezi and Banda, "Competing with Christ?," 6–7). It is clear that few Pentecostals would agree with this view.

62. Land, *Pentecostal Spirituality*, 62.

63. See, for example, Aimee Semple McPherson's argument that women preachers should be allowed to minister as a legitimate part of the end-time church due to the urgency of proclaiming the pentecostal gospel and the imminency of Christ's return (Blumhofer, *Aimee Semple McPherson*, 195).

64. Pentecostal scholars have an ongoing debate about the purposes of Spirit baptism. An interesting perspective on tongues is found in Macchia, "Babel and the Tongues of Pentecost," 43. Everts understands speaking in languages as the new spiritual language of the new community created by the Spirit when the Spirit removed long existing social, cultural, national, and linguistic barriers, allowing Jews, Gentiles, and followers of John the Baptist (see Acts 19) to become one community of faith (Everts, "Missionary Tongues?," 9). In this context, Shuman argues that *glossolalia* symbolizes new possibilities for social and political relationships in stark contrast to Babel-like violence (Shuman, "Pentecost and the End of Patriotism," 95–96). The import of *glossolalia* must not be restricted to utterance; rather, it is a community whose memory of its savior creates the miracle of being a people whose very differences contribute to their unity. Mittelstadt gives a summary of the debate, concluding that an early consensus shows the purposes of tongues speech as follows: it breaks down barriers between people, protests racism, models a culturally diverse yet a common witness to the gospel, presents a transformative experience, and (most significantlty) provides empowerment for witness (Mittelstadt, *Reading Luke-Acts*, 73–77).

Pentecostals' eschatological identity allows them to read the New Testament in a noncessationist, continuationist way, with biblical narrative serving as a model of how God works in our world, and to live in light of that narrative. Reading in this paradigm requires faith as a presupposition and invites an entirely new worldview or approach to reality around us in the expectation and awareness that God works actively in our world in the same way that the Bible depicts.[65]

Their apocalyptic vision resulted in a particular type of spirituality among early Pentecostals. They saw themselves as an eschatological community of universal mission in the power and demonstration of the Spirit.[66] The purpose of speaking in tongues was to facilitate the preaching of the gospel in all the languages of the earth, making it possible for Pentecostals to reach the ends of the earth with the pentecostal gospel.[67] The imminent return of Christ was the primary motivation for evangelism and world mission.[68] Many Pentecostals believed that the second coming of Christ would only occur when the gospel had been proclaimed to every nation (Matt 24:14), and so it was imperative to engage in the most rapid evangelization possible.[69] With reference to 2 Thessalonians 2:6–7, what is now restraining Christ's return was interpreted by many as the non-completion of the task to proclaim the gospel to all nations. The increase of false prophets, the expansion of Islam, theological liberalism (specifically "higher criticism"), and the spread of heterodox groups like Mormons and Jehovah's Witnesses were all seen and interpreted as signs of the impending doom. The expectation that Israel would reoccupy the "holy land," occupied by the Ottoman Turks until 1918, was also viewed as a sign of the imminency of the second coming.[70] Another sign of the

65. Keener, *Spirit Hermeneutics*, 55.

66. Land, *Pentecostal Spirituality*, 21–22.

67. "Pentecostal gospel" refers to the specific slant that Pentecostals held on the gospel—as the message of Christ as savior, healer, sanctifier, baptizer, and coming king (fivefold Full Gospel).

68. A distinction was historically made between evangelism (as reaching one's own cultural and ethnic group) and mission (as reaching people of other nationalities). It is a distinction that cannot be upheld because it is based on the assumption that people of color were inferior to white Caucasians.

69. Anderson, *Spreading Fires*, 221.

70. Many Pentecostals believed in an exclusive, God-given right belonging to the Jews concerning Palestine, a belief that persists in some pentecostal circles to this day. When British troops marched into Jerusalem in 1918, biblical prophecies seemed to have been fulfilled. Now, the final battle of Armageddon could start, when Palestine

imminency of the second coming was found in the First World War, further evidence that the world was coming to its end, leading to the battle of Armageddon and preceding the return of Christ.[71] Their mission was based on a particular eschatological view of salvation history.[72]

Early Pentecostals followed the futurist premillennial escapist[73] framework developed by John Nelson Darby (1800–1882) of the Plymouth Brethren, using the *Scofield Reference Bible* (1909) as their resource for dispensationalism, which provides an easily understood method of Bible study for laypeople,[74] including elaborate and often fanciful interpretations of both future and current world events in popular apocalyptic literature.[75] A monthly periodical, *The Prophetic Times*, commenced in 1863 and cooperated with prophetic conferences—like Dwight L. Moody's annual Prophecy Conference in Massachusetts—to advocate Darby's eschatological views.[76] Early Pentecostals embraced selected components of pre-existing nineteenth-century dispensationalist schemata because

---

would be invaded by Russia from the north. Before this final battle, the saints would be snatched away (rapture) from the world in the time of the great tribulation and the world would be left to its own fate of bloodshed, horror, and destruction. After this period, Christ would return and set up a thousand-year reign on earth, and Satan and his hordes would be confined to hell. At the end of the millennium, Satan would be released for a short period until his final destruction in the "lake of fire," and all people would appear before the judgment seat of Christ to receive their reward or punishment (Anderson, *Spreading Fires*, 223). This is the result of a premillennialist perspective used in reading the book of Revelation in a literalist fashion, a view that was widespread among early Pentecostals.

71. Many Pentecostals evaluated war as sinful and part of the evil world system, and they were pacifists in a Quaker way (see Nel, "Church and War," and Nel, *Pacifism and Pentecostals*).

72. Anderson, *Introduction to Pentecostalism*, 232.

73. Oliverio, *Theological Hermeneutics*, 28.

74. Menzies and Menzies, *Spirit and Power*, 221. See also discussion in chapter 2.

75. Anderson, *Introduction to Pentecostalism*, 233. Dayton remarks that those more Spirit-oriented movements in the history of the church have had a particular fascination with prophetic and apocalyptic themes (Dayton, *Theological Roots of Pentecostalism*, 144). The optimism of postmillennialism that prevailed in early nineteenth-century Protestantism was exchanged for a pessimistic, premillennialist secret rapture dispensationalism that swept through evangelical circles during the second half of the nineteenth century as a result of several factors, including a pessimistic reaction to theological liberalism and the "social gospel" that increasingly came to identify the main Protestant denominations (Anderson, *Spreading Fires*, 219). Its pessimism was related to its conviction that the world would get progressively worse until the return of Christ.

76. Anderson, *Spreading Fires*, 219.

of several influences, not least of all that of premillennialist dogma.[77] Darby and his predecessor, Charles Irving[78] (1792–1834), taught that the true church would be raptured to heaven before a seven-year tribulation period in which the Antichrist would rule the world. At the end of this great tribulation, Christ would come, defeat the Antichrist in the battle of Armageddon, and then rule for a thousand years (the millennium). At the end of the thousand years, Satan would be released and eventually defeated by the heavenly armies, and then the great white throne would be set up, all people would appear before Christ, and true believers ("sheep") would be separated from unbelievers ("goats") (Matt 25:32–33). Their destination would differ, with believers going to heaven and unbelievers to hell. This teaching is based on a literalist reading of the book of Revelation and other pasages in the New Testament presumably concerned with eschatology. Their expectation of the imminent second coming lent urgency to Pentecostals' task of world evangelization. For quite a long period, premillennialism was an essential part of Pentecostals' spirituality.[79] The church experienced itself as an apocalyptic construct of the Spirit, awaiting the return of its Lord with fervor, demonstrating the "already" of the kingdom of God because the present world order was inevitably doomed; their assignment was to rescue as many individuals from the coming disaster as they could.[80] It is still true of some African churches, who locate the establishment of the kingdom not in some distant land but in the present and tangible reality of Africa, accentuating a "realized eschatology" with their imagery of the New Jerusalem and Zion.[81] Even today, when earlier classical pentecostal fervor is being tempered as measured by a lessened eschatological urgency, there are still many refer-

77. Hunt, "Dispensationalism," 60. Oliverio refers to the theological core of premillennialist escapism as the socially deprived turned to an eschatological vision (Oliverio, *Theological Hermeneutics*, 28).

78. Irving made a compelling argument in favor of the legitimacy of the *charismata*, insisting that the spiritual power would only return to the church of the "last days," a church characterized by the restoration of the *charismata*. Darby did not agree with this submission (Hunt, "Dispensationalism," 61). Darby found advocates of his views in John Inglis (1913–1879), James H. Brookes (1830–1898), Dwight L. Moody (1837–1898), and John Alexander Dowie (1847–1898).

79. Land still considers that premillennialism determines pentecostal spirituality (Land, *Pentecostal Spirituality*, 222–23). However, that has changed when many denominations left out their previous emphasis on premillennialism.

80. Menzies and Menzies, *Spirit and Power*, 281.

81. Anderson, *Introduction to Pentecostalism*, 234.

ences to the expectation of the second coming of Christ. The lessening of eschatological fervor can be ascribed in sociological terms as the routinization and rationalization that attends all religious movements. It is also clear that insofar as that eschatological sensibilities impact missionary commitments and practices, the emergence of different eschatologies in contemporary pentecostal theology will have diverse missiological implications.[82]

Immersing themselves in Scripture and associating them with its eschatological worldview reinforces Pentecostals' confidence that the future lies in the hands of the sovereign Lord, who deserves their trust. A negative factor is that Pentecostalism's eschatology with its apocalyptic trends that determined its hermeneutics and theology also justifies its escapist mentality because it is based on a belief in the second coming of Jesus that will end the suffering experienced in this world, establishing an otherworldly theology that emphasizes escaping this current sinful and hurtful world, to the better one which is referred to as "home." This emphasis tends to disconnect its members from social engagement and a sense of belonging to the broader community.[83]

The global task to reach the ends of the earth with the gospel was so overwhelming that the church realized that it needed the Spirit's help.[84] The belief started among some radical Evangelicals that the missional task to preach the gospel to the nations could only be effectively realized when missionaries were baptized with the Spirit as in Acts 2, providing them with the ability to speak in the languages of the people they needed to reach without learning these languages first. They were praying for the second blessing, missionary tongues. And when some believers in holiness circles started speaking in tongues at the beginning of the twentieth century, it was believed that the tongues were existing languages.[85] The

82. Yong, "Instead of a Conclusion," 317.

83. Resane, "Pentecostals and Apartheid," 4.

84. A. J. Tomlinson at the 1912 General Assembly of the Church of God, Cleveland, Tennessee: "This is the time when everyone that can preach or conduct a prayer meeting ought to be out in the field. We speak in the fear of God, from a sincere heart, when we say that the world ought to be evangelized in our generation, and we should not dare to thrust this responsibility on a future generation. . . . The fields are before us and white unto harvest. It is time to push out into new territory. Foreign countries should be occupied, and the gospel given to them as rapidly as possible" (Tomlinson, quoted in Archer, *Pentecostal Hermeneutic*, 25).

85. See Anderson, *Introduction to Pentecostalism*, 33–34; Jacobsen, *Thinking in the Spirit*, 25, 49–50, 74–76, and 97; and Robeck, *Azusa Street Mission and Revival*, 41–42

first student to speak in tongues in Charles Parham's Bible School, Agnes Ozman, was supposed to speak in Chinese; for two days, she supposedly could not speak her own language again.[86] Before long, those baptized in the Spirit, supposing that they had received the ability to speak mission languages, discovered otherwise when the practice of the mission fields disillusioned them—but they kept their interest in mission.[87]

In the following century, Pentecostalism expanded throughout the world, faster than any other Christian movement.[88] However, the connection between speaking in tongues and the missional impulse, defining Luke's narrative use of tongues, was in time largely forgotten. Keener concludes that Luke's emphasis on the church as God's agents, inspired by the Spirit and worshiping God in the languages of other people, is still the greatest sign of cross-cultural prophetic empowerment.[89]

While many cessationist Evangelicals argue that it is not desirable to derive theology from biblical narrative, Pentecostals read Acts looking for clues to the signs of Spirit baptism. They argued that narratives communicated theological and moral perspectives, overcoming the dichotomy between theology and history that characterized a part of theology in the twentieth century.[90] Narrative is the most common genre in the Bible, and it provides the structure that gives context to most other parts of the canon. Pentecostals looked to the early church—depicted in Acts—as the model for their lifestyle and mission. Luke's narrative provides several descriptions of outpourings of the Spirit in different circumstances, suggesting patterns of God's activity.[91] Luke describes Spirit baptism in terms of prophetic empowerment (Acts 2:17–18), inspired speech (Acts 4:8; 4:31), visions (Acts 7:55), and worship (Acts 2:4; 10:46).

As already explained, Pentecostals read biblical narratives with faith, leading to academic theologians criticizing their utilization of Scripture as evidence of ignoring of the historical context. While it is true that a

---

and 236–37.

86. Synan, *Holiness-Pentecostal Tradition*, 91.

87. McGee, *People of the Spirit*, 77–78, and McGee, "Strategies for Global Mission," 204.

88. Lee, "Future of Global Christianity," 105.

89. Keener, *Acts*, 1:823–31.

90. See Keener, *Spirit Hermeneutics*, 22, for a discussion of ancient historians who utilized their writings for this purpose. For biblical writers also affirming this practice, see Rom 15:4; 1 Cor 10:11; 2 Tim 3:16–17.

91. Keener, *Spirit Hermeneutics*, 23.

reader who ignores the context may misinterpret the text, it is also true that a reader who understands the context and text but who does not apply the truths in the text to their daily lives, misses its function in Scripture. The implication is that hermeneutical distantiation, as proposed by African cultural hermeneutics,[92] does advantage biblical interpretation, but the danger should be avoided that it empowers the interpreter with knowledge about the text without necessarily requiring of the reader to attend to the historical context or live the text's message. Popular readers of the Bible, consisting of the majority of ordinary members of the church, should be equipped with information about the background of biblical texts, but many Pentecostals find themselves and their world in the Bible because they read the Bible in a serious manner, and their feeling for the tenor of texts in many instances reflects the first horizon of the text.[93] Academic theology that at times ignores the second horizon, of the present situation, may benefit by listening to ordinary readers, and contributes to popular interpretation by providing the necessary information about the first horizon, and ways to fuse the two horizons more effectively.[94]

When believers read the Bible with faith, they try to understand the text in order to embrace its message and theological worldview as true and applicable to the situation they find themselves in. When they do not understand a passage, they pray about it, also in tongues.[95] Their testimonies witness to the enlightenment they sometimes received when insights were revealed to them about the meaning of the text, as applied to their situation.[96] Some passages are difficult to make sense of in a cog-

92. See discussion in chapter 2.

93. Louw describes the three major sets of features that condition the reading of a text: extra-linguistic features, such as time and place, typography, format, background, and history of a text; para-linguistic features, such as punctuation, intonation, pause, speech act, genre, discourse types, and communication functions; and linguistic features, such as word order, embedding, normalization, levels of language, style, and the discrepancy between syntax and semantics. All of these features are part of the structure of a text and deserve attention in reading the text (Louw, "Reading a Text as Discourse," 18).

94. Archer, *Pentecostal Hermeneutic*, 167.

95. There are many problematic passages in the Bible that cannot be explained in a satisfactory exegetical way, as any honest exegete will accede.

96. John Wesley already urged Christians to pray about biblical passages that they do not understand; see Wesley, *Works*, 5:3 and 14:252–53. For a biblical precedent, see Dan 2:18–9; 9:2–3; 23.

nitive way; the Spirit's revealing its intention may provide the prayerful reader with a word applicable to the situation.[97] However, a Spirit-filled person reading the Bible in faith lingers prayerfully on each aspect of the text, especially those that are clear, because the purpose in reading the Bible is not primarily to understand the text but to hear from God (showing parallels with the practice of *lectio divina*). The hermeneutical lens includes the challenges and problems of daily living, and the reader listens to the voice of the Spirit in the light of Scripture as applied to those circumstances.[98] The process of reading Scripture in the light of our

97. Keener discusses authorial intention from the viewpoint of E. D. Hirsch (Keener, *Spirit Hermeneutics*, 133–40). He chooses to accept authorial intention as textual meaning, but avoids the Romantic hermeneutic consideration of authorial intention as psychological knowledge of the author in consonance with the interpreter's own psychology (see Zwiep, "Bible Hermeneutics from 1950," 970–71). Freed from the constraints of authorial intent, contemporary critics could now proclaim the autonomy of the text, downplaying the extraliterary, particularly the historical relevance of literary works. Here the text is cut off not only from the author but also from the extralinguistic reality to which it apparently refers (Kaiser and Silva, *Introduction to Biblical Hermeneutics*, 284–85). Keener underwrites Jürgen Habermas's consideration of texts as communicative actions, as does Kevin Vanhoozer's revision of E. D. Hirsch. Hirsch distinguished between meaning as the invariable sense intended by the writer and significance as the changeable application of a writing to different contexts. He believed he could preserve the crucial role of the original author against the attack of thinkers like Gadamer (Kaiser and Silva, *Introduction to Biblical Hermeneutics*, 280). Hirsch grants that authors' views change over time, but he contends that the meaning an author has invested in a text does not change, leading to their occasional need to qualify a view they previously expressed. He also acknowledges that not all attempts to communicate prove to be successful (Keener, *Spirit Hermeneutics*, 137). The originality of the text gravitates toward meaning but it does not entirely limit meaning (Oliverio, "Book Review," 138). Keener breaks with the thought of Gadamer in his estimation of the reality of the original text. Habermas states, "Writing is self-alienation," detaching the relationship between authorship and the otherness of texts. While Gadamer emphasizes that one experiences a text through a historically effected consciousness in a fusion of horizons, Keener affirms that history consists of memory of the past guiding our understanding for the future—like the memory of God's salvific acts in the Exodus narrative. Keener acknowledges a greater ontic existence to the past than in Gadamerian hermeneutics. For Keener, the past is there, communicated in and through presently experienced texts, and able to be differentiated from its history of effects. There is a correspondence between truth and the past, and we are joined to the original texts by the Spirit, who spoke in and through them then and is doing so now, again.

98. The goal of pentecostal hermeneutics is to hear the voice of God, which is *inter alia* the theological message of the word of God found through a careful and critically-discerning attendance to the canonical biblical text. Pentecostals study the Bible to "hear the voice of God," finding its precedent in the emphasis on divine speech as a vital element of the Old Testament concept of God. Pentecostals are attuned to the

circumstances, however, implies in practice that our own experience and our perspective on it is read and developed in light of Scripture.[99]

The objection may be levelled that it presents a purely subjective reading because it is determined by an experiential expectation, that reading the text is determined by a "feeling" about a text or a "deep" meaning that may be unrelated to the contextual meaning. The criticism sets up a cognitive, rational reading of the text against a "spiritual" reading. The rational reading then analyzes the text's grammar and context, while a spiritual reading listens for insights in the heart about the "deeper" meaning. Although a spiritual and rational reading may in some practices oppose each other, it is not necessary or valid to enforce such a distinction. In the vast majority of cases, ordinary readers interpret the text in a rational manner, and may even consult a resource about background information that provides help in understanding the context while prayerfully meditating about its message for the present situation.[100] Rational and spiritual

text that is foreign to modern literacy, because of their oral culture that shows affinities with postmodernity's secondary orality. "Hearing" is the most fundamental and most common biblical mode of encountering the word of God (Martin, "Hearing the Voice of God," 231).

99. John Wesley also emphasized the role of experience in reading and interpreting the Bible in his Wesleyan Quadrilateral (a term coined by the American Professor of Wesleyan Studies, Dr. Albert Outler), which emphasizes four elements: Scripture, Tradition, Reason, and Experience. These form the building blocks that can be placed in any order of priority, so that, depending on the issue, we can place one or the other at the top of the pile. The quadrilateral has been used to place a particular form of epistemology at the heart of Methodist understanding—the theory of how we know things to be true—which is deeply flawed, unconnected with Wesley, and can lead Christians and the church to make unwise decisions. See Methodist Evangelicals Together, "Wesleyan Quadrilateral."

100. Johns and Johns provide a useful approach to Bible study for ordinary readers from a pentecostal perspective, including four interactive movements: sharing their testimonies of encounters with God and revelations of the Spirit; searching the Scriptures in an effort to know the word of God by attending to the testimony of God's activity in human experience, the participation of each and every believer, involved in a corporate process of discernment that goes beyond individual perception and human reason, and bound to the eschatological mission of edifying the church and extending the gospel; yielding to the Spirit, consisting of the transforming encounter between the truth of Scripture and the truth found in our own selves; and responding to the call to know God and live in God's presence (Johns and Johns, "Yielding to the Spirit," 47–56). This represents an inductive approach to Bible study, in contrast to the mostly deductive approach followed by early Pentecostals. Searching the Scripture in the group study would be personal but also corporate and interactive. And the text must be approached in a manner consistent with its nature as the word of God, an avenue for personal and corporate engagement with God. It is an act of reason but it is

reading are combined, providing an experiential reading that emphasizes God's word for readers and their world.[101] What is important is that the text is read, heard, and interpreted in an engaged manner, resulting in transformed lives that reflect Christ. Zwiep emphasizes that it is impossible to not be (positively) prejudiced toward the object of investigation when believers read and interpret the Bible.[102] Their hermeneutics can never be objective; it will always be engaged because they believe that the text has something to tell them that will change their lives. In the words of 2 Timothy 3:16–17, Scripture should be useful to believers for teaching, for reproof, for correction, and for training in righteousness, so that everyone who belongs to God may be proficient, equipped for every good work.

Keener correctly warns against a wrong kind of experiential reading.[103] A sector of the church neglects personal spiritual experience while others highlight experiences to such an extent that they have to continually revise or harmonize their views as new claims of experiences come their way.[104] Experiences are not always self-interpreting and one's spiritual experience can easily be misinterpreted. For that reason, revival movements in the history of the church included elements of divine encounter and human frailty. It is true that radical subjectivity breeds mistakes—Keener refers to inaccurate prophecies, too much emotional intensity for "weaker human spirits," and misinterpretations about spiri-

---

not limited to reason (Johns and Johns, "Yielding to the Spirit," 52).

101. Experiential reading is based on the readers' participation in miracles, visions, prophecy, and other works of the Spirit, allowing them to read their experience in the light of Scripture rather than wrapping Scripture around their experiences (Spawn, "Interpretation of Scripture," 148). One can refer to Keener's compiling of miracles in all ages in two volumes (see Keener, *Miracles*).

102. Zwiep, "Het Hermeneutische Vraagstuk," 7.

103. Keener, *Spirit Hermeneutics*, 268–69.

104. This is highlighted by Van der Walt and Vorster, who state that the antirational trends in the church that focus on personal piety or on mindless devotions—singing the same words over and over as in a mantra—deprived many Christians from knowing what they believe, why they believe it, and the reasons why Christians throughout history have been willing to die for their faith (Van der Walt and Vorster, *Reformed Theology Today*, 50). The authors contend that the antirational and antidogmatic trends in Pentecostal churches are one of the important reasons why people leave the faith, as well as why extreme charismatic leaders and cults get others to believe many heresies and even to participate in atrocities. In their view, it is necessary for the human mind to be trained in its dogmatic understanding and apologetic defence of the truth. Without it, human beings can easily fall into the traps of cults and heresies.

tual authority as examples—that hurt people. What is critically important is that the subjective relationship with God should become anchored in objective study of God's word.[105] It is my contention that Classical Pentecostalism's most important contribution to the global church is the vision of the restoration of the *charismata*, as an experiential pre-understanding from which we read Scriptures and an impulse to missional living in the world.[106]

Their eschatological formation was the product of a restorationist urge among early Pentecostals, who viewed their revival as continuing or even completing the restoration of the church begun in the Reformation. They argued that the Reformation handed the Bible into the hands of ordinary believers; Pentecostalism restored the Spirit to the Spirit's rightful place among believers.[107] They emphasized a return to the lifestyle, spiritual experiences, and eschatological expectations of the early church. It may be argued that restorationism idealized the early church of which not much is known, but Pentecostals argue that they are going back to what Jesus affirms is God's word and what should be valued above any church doctrine.

Pentecostal spirituality affirms that God is present and active, working in the world to fulfill God's purpose with creation. The church plays a significant part in achieving God's goal with the world, and it expects the imminent return of Christ, supported by various texts in the New Testament.[108]

Cox suggests that Pentecostalism is not primarily a church or a religion, but a mood, consisting of a millennial sensibility; it is a feeling that a big change is under way, for the benefit of participants in the movement.[109] Early Pentecostals represented the people functioning at the periphery of society; their apocalyptic hopes included that when God would establish God's kingdom they would sit on thrones and help decide the destiny of the nations (Luke 22:30; Matt 19:28; Rev 20:4). Oliverio

---

105. Keener, "Biblical Fidelity," 38.

106. Keener, *Spirit Hermeneutics*, 26.

107. See the remark of the Catholic Keegan that the Reformation changed the status of the Bible into a weapon to be used against the Roman Catholic Church, driving a wedge between the Bible and the church (Keegan, *Interpreting the Bible*, 145). Previously, the (Western) church interpreted the Bible in terms of its tradition.

108. See, for example, John 11:17–27; 1 Thess 4:15–17; 5:1–9; 2 Thess 2:1–3; Tit 2:11–13; Heb 10:24–25; Jas 5:7–9; 1 Pet 4:7; 1 John 2:18; Rev 1:1.

109. Cox, *Fire from Heaven*, 116.

calls Pentecostalism a particular way of situating oneself in the world so that it is an embodied interpretive experience, which unconceals and lets be a pentecostal way of life, while Cox refers to the suggestion of Victor Turner that millennial movements are to a culture what rites of passage are to an individual, signaling moments of change and transition.[110] They enable a person or movement to touch base with the past and its deepest symbolic roots in order to be better prepared to take the next step into the future, which may be characterized by uncertainty and ambiguity. What is important is not to take the rhetoric of such movements literally; its use of language functions as a part of its mythic structure. Pentecostal expectations include a restorationist renaissance of what is past and a protest against the reigning assumptions of the time, posing a heavenly city as an alternative to the earthly city.

How Pentecostals process the challenge that their expectation of Christ's imminent second coming has not realized after a century is a valid question.[111] One might have expected that the radical millennial expectations would have been minimalized, but in fact the movement's future orientation still determines its theology to a large degree, even if in a slightly modified form.[112] Pentecostals still await the coming tidal change in world history, when Christ would appear in the clouds with great power and glory (Mark 13:26), and they still use the only language they know to describe their expectation, the "technicolor idiom of Christian apocalyptic imagery, with conflagrations, dragons, and beasts, and a New Jerusalem descending onto the smoking ruins of a world that God had judged and purified."[113] Perhaps as many as 87 percent of Pentecostals live below the world poverty line and the movement here (at least) still consists of the racially excluded, economically disinherited, and psychologically wounded. Like the early Pentecostals, they represent people who have little to lose in this world and much to gain in a radical hope of a new world order based on alternative power structures that includes

---

110. Oliverio, "Introduction," 7, and Cox, *Fire from Heaven*, 117.

111. Early Pentecostals adjusted and adapted their mission strategies, like other Evangelicals, when the second coming of Christ did not realize as imminently as they expected (Anderson, *Introduction to Pentecostalism*, 232).

112. For instance, the widespread premillennialism as part of its dispensationalist heritage has been changed, sometimes to an amillennialism, e.g., the British Assemblies of God and the Elim tradition (Cartledge, "Locating the Spirit," 261).

113. Cox, *Fire from Heaven*, 118.

them.[114] It also explains the appeal of an apocalyptic Pentecostalism for the impoverished majority rather than among the privileged few. Pentecostalism, however, does not only speak about a radical hope of a new world; it also facilitates the capacitation and empowerment of marginalized people, the community of the disregarded and dispossessed, through the presence and work of the Spirit. People are baptized in the Spirit for the purpose of equipping them for the task of being signs of the reign of God in the world.[115]

Empowerment for Mission

Luke 24:48–49 and Acts 1:8 explains that Jesus's promise to pour out the Spirit as promised by his Father was to empower his disciples for mission. Jesus's ascension and the pouring out of his Spirit is reminiscent of Elijah, who gives a double portion of his spirit on Elisha, his successor (2 Kgs 2:8–11; Acts 1:8–11).[116] The most prominent activity of the Spirit in Acts is empowerment for mission.[117] And Luke's programmatic texts (Luke 4:18–19; 24:45–49; Acts 1:8; 2:16–17) describe the Spirit's pivotal role in empowering disciples for their mission. The book of Acts describes the first part of the fulfilment of that mission, in the life of the early church. The most prominent description of that mission is found in Peter's message in Acts 2, which proclaims that the disciples now live in the "last days," when God will pour out God's Spirit on all people, leading to sons and daughters as well as male and female slaves prophesying, young men seeing visions, and old men dreaming. Even slaves, representing people without any corporate rights, will receive God's Spirit, accompanied by portents in the heavens above and signs on the earth below, such as blood, fire, and smoky mist, with the sun turned to darkness and the moon to blood. These signs will introduce the coming of the Lord's great and glorious day. Then everyone who calls on the name of the Lord shall be saved (Acts 2:17–21).

114. Cox, *Fire from Heaven*, 119.

115. Castelo, "*Diakrisis* Always *En Conjunto*," 206.

116. Moses also imparted the spirit to Joshua (Deut 34:9), providing a biblical model for Jesus's delegating prophetic empowerment to his disciples.

117. See Stronstad, *Charismatic Theology*; Shelton, *Mighty in Word and Deed*; and Penney, *Missionary Emphasis*.

Pentecostals believe they are in the last days, envisioning their own day as the "latter rain," corresponding to the "former rain" on the day of Pentecost (Acts 2:23).[118] Pentecostals are biblically correct in considering themselves as a part of the end-time church, a perspective they share with renewal movements of the Christian church through all the ages.

---

118. See Archer, *Pentecostal Hermeneutic*, 136–50, and Oliverio, *Theological Hermeneutics*, 114, from a dispensational perspective. Pentecostals' allegorical rendering of Israel's climate conditions misses Joel's point (Keener, *Spirit Hermeneutics*, 49).

CHAPTER 5

The Faith Community as Normative for the Interpretation of the Bible

Introduction

WHILE ONE CAN LEARN many things by taking a course or reading about a subject, some skills cannot be taught in an exclusively cerebral way. A brain surgeon needs not only to attend theoretical classes but also requires the acquisition of certain skills to perform surgery. These skills can only be taught by apprenticing with an experienced surgeon. Starling suggests that if one wants to learn how to interpret the Bible, there is no simple or single set of rules or techniques to learn and follow.[1] When believers accept the biblical text as the word of God, to be used as a benchmark to live by and make sense of the world, then it becomes important to establish the original meaning of the words, sentences, and books of the Bible for the first hearers. Believers are interested in understanding the text as being inspired by the Spirit, with the view to hear from Godself. That is why the Bible becomes important to them, and they spend time reading and meditating on it on a daily basis. Pentecostals, however, stand alone in their suspicion of treating the Bible as a book just to learn from. Instead, they engage with the text and utilize it as a resource for divine encounter. They do not read the Bible to grasp it, but so that God may grasp them through it.[2]

1. Starling, *Hermeneutics as Apprenticeship*, 16–21 and 205.
2. Davies, "What Does it Mean to Read?," 255.

As Christians can misinterpret the Bible for cultural and other reasons, Hauerwas and Willimon advised American Christians to stop reading their Bible if the church's primary social task has become the underwriting of American democracy; otherwise, the nation-state has taken the place of God.[3] Christian ethics are church-dependent; it only makes sense from the point of view of what we believe has happened in the life, death, and resurrection of Jesus of Nazareth.[4] To keep the church from practicing a civil religion, the church should be the most significant ethical unit, enabling ordinary members to do rather extraordinary (and perhaps even heroic) acts through its teaching, support, and worship.[5] Scripture and church are inseparable; only where the word is rightly proclaimed and the sacraments duly administered, a people are made present who are capable of acknowledging the authority of the Bible. The church should be the bridge where Scripture and people meet.[6]

In keeping with a strong sense of community, Pentecostals in the Majority World usually read (and, for the most part, hear) the Bible in the community of the faithful, during celebrations of communal worship—where it is often directly related to those real problems encountered by the community. The majority of these members are underprivileged workers, subsistence farmers, or are unemployed. Many of them are illiterate and dirt-poor. They hear the Bible in the context of an experiential interpretation enhanced by prayers, songs, dances, prophecies, and proclamation of messages. Their interpretation of the Bible comes from the underside of society, where people interpret the message of the Bible using the only tools they have at hand: their own lives, struggles, and experiences.[7] Many times, they hybridize their readings of biblical texts through retrieval and incorporation of the defunct, pre-colonial past. These hybridized readings and interpretations create interstices which become sites for assimilation, questioning, and resistance.[8] In Africa specifically, Christianity is about the community—and not the

3. Hauerwas and Willimon, *Resident Aliens*, 32. Reformers were concerned that the "laity" was not adequately able to understand the Bible apart from ministerial guidance (Smidt, *American Evangelicals Today*, 22). It should be kept in mind that illiteracy occurred widely during the Reformation.

4. Hauerwas and Willimon, *Resident Aliens*, 71.

5. Hauerwas and Willimon, *Resident Aliens*, 81.

6. Hauerwas and Willimon, *Resident Aliens*, 128–29.

7. Anderson, *Introduction to Pentecostalism*, 224.

8. Kinyua, *Introducing Ordinary African Readers' Hermeneutics*, 289.

individual—in a way that Western people can hardly imagine. To be an African Christian is to be enveloped in relation with others.[9] This interconnectedness can be described as *ubuntu*, and Jacobsen discusses the concept in terms of three theological expressions: that every human life has value, all human beings are interconnected, and that reconciliation should form an integral part of the agenda of the church (consisting of truthful confession, sorrowful repentance, and gracious forgiveness); that some of the deceased who lived their lives well on earth, who were morally upright, and who strengthened their families and communities receive the privilege of becoming ancestors, who continue to guide and protect their desendants in the present, and they should be venerated and looked upon for guidance, which they provide through dreams and divination; and the ancient understanding of God's universality and omnipresence that remains strong.[10]

The Essence of the Church

The church is the communion and mother of believers, says Bavinck.[11] It is the holy circle within which Christ communicates his benefits, especially through the proclamation of his word. He reigns as king over the kingdom of the church by his Spirit and word. Listening to his voice in the word has implications for all areas of life, including how one interprets the Bible.[12] To understand what the Bible is, it is necessary to understand what the church is.[13] The church is the continuation of the incarnation of Christ who revealed God to humankind. It lives by the Spirit of God. The Spirit of the church is the Spirit of Christ. And the Spirit makes the church the implied reader of the Bible, revealing God to them in encountering readers of the Bible. Apart from being read within the church, the Bible cannot be read. It may have historical or literary value for unbelievers but only reveals the saving God to believers.

9. The strength of a distinctive African sense of human connectedness is accompanied by a limitation and liability that a robust communal identity can sometimes blind individuals to their shared community with members of other groups or tribes, leading to the occurrence of *inter alia* homophobia and xenophobia (Jacobsen, *Global Gospel*, 62).

10. Jacobsen, *Global Gospel*, 63–72.

11. Bavinck, *Reformed Dogmatics*, 4:437.

12. Bartholomew, *Introducing Biblical Hermeutics*, 37.

13. Keegan, *Interpreting the Bible*, 161.

Contemporary society, however, to a lesser or greater degree, is characterized by a penetrating individualism that leads to a privatization of religion, reducing the *ecclesia* to a kind of leisurely activity, with little or no consequences for the way believers live, relate to each other, and interpret the Bible. The interpretive community can become paralyzed by believers who belong to the church on their own terms and conditions.[14] The church should co-determine the metanarrative that believers use to interpret their lives—where believers meet together and study the Bible in order to hear the word of God relating to their circumstances. Instead, many believers adopt an alternative, secular metanarrative within which they study the Bible, trading the ideological way of reading the Bible in a faithful manner, rejecting the witness of the Spirit to and through Scripture. Israel's *Shema* consequently stresses the need for the gathered faith community to listen to the word, and to extend it into the home because the family remains the domestic church.[15] The home as a place of listening to the word is one of the most important keys to recovering the word today, where the home becomes a barrier against the dromocratic, individualistic culture of the day, where speed has became the sole agent and measure of progress, to be shaped as a safe place of rest, relaxation, and renewal.[16] Exposure to Scripture is vital at every phase of a child's development; what is equally necessary is that each child learns the art of receptive listening. One is never too young to hear the voice of God; Jesus emphasizes that the children form an integral part of his kingdom and whosoever does not receive the kingdom as a little child would never enter it (Matt 19:14; Mark 10:14; Luke 18:16).

14. "Community" refers to the believing faithful or faith community at three levels: the immediate community of faith, that is, the local church; the larger community of faith, that is, the Christian community as such; and the historic Christian tradition, representing two millennia of history. Communities are complex networks of relationships interacting with and including others beyond their normally defined boundaries. Their experience of the transcendental changes them into a faith community, as the result of the dialogical aspect of community that includes the presence of God. A gathering of as few as two or three persons in relational conversation is sufficient to constitute a community (Yong, *Spirit-Word-Community*, 17).

15. Bartholomew, *Introducing Biblical Hermeutics*, 33.

16. Bartholomew, *Introducing Biblical Hermeutics*, 39. Although pentecostal spirituality is at times characterized as being individualistic, the fact that the communal worship service plays such a central role in pentecostal experience of the Spirit should not be overlooked. Pentecostal spirituality relies on this social dimension and even thrives on it (Neumann, "Spirituality," 199).

The Charismatic Community as an Interpretive Community

To safeguard them against misinterpreting the Bible, Christians should participate in the flesh-and-blood community of the church and learn from the imperfect examples of mothers, fathers, brothers, and sisters in the faith.[17] The best safeguard is the authority of the charismatic community, where the community as a whole is taught by God (1 Thess 4:9) and by apostolic authority in the community, referring to people who can speak with authority and protect the community when it comes under threat.[18] It also needs to include extending horizons of interpretation beyond the parochialism of the own particular faith community, denomination, and cultural group, to learn from others who have read the same Scriptures, even in previous generations. At the same time, primary attention should be given to the Bible and the guidance of the Spirit. Because pentecostal reading necessarily leads to the danger of subjectivistic interpretation, the faith community should serve as normative in the hermeneutical process. Believers should remain apprentices of the faith community that, through the Spirit, serves to teach, inspire, and help to distinguish between truth and heresy.

The solution to the problem of historical distance between the ancient and modern world, between the biblical text and the contemporary reader, lies in a recognition of the church as a continuing body throughout history.[19] The interpretation of the Bible is a communal task that belongs to the whole church. The church shares the identical location in redemptive history with the church since the day of Pentecost, guaranteeing a continuity throughout history. The Bible has been produced by the church, and the ongoing task of Scriptural interpretation is qualitatively indistinguishable from what took place when the church first produced the Bible and determined its canonical boundaries. At the same time, God has "elected" the Bible as a divinely-authored norm for the church's faith and praxis.[20]

Pentecostal interpretation of the Bible is and should be done within the context of the *charismatic* faith community and the act of proclamation. The gathered church is the primary context for the reception of the

17. Starling, *Hermeneutics as Apprenticeship*, 206.

18. Pinnock, "Work of the Holy Spirit," 244.

19. Venema, "Interpreting the Bible," 48.

20. Venema, "Interpreting the Bible," 50.

word, God's appointed place where God promises to meet with God's people.[21] The extraordinary potential of the act of proclamation is that God wants to and will address people through the exposition of Scripture.[22] Although much in the Bible is not clear, the doctrine of *claritas scripturae* teaches that the large landmarks of Scripture are clear, revealing how humankind can be reconciled with their Creator. The character of the Bible is kerygmatic. Scripture is not confined to one illocutionary force in its speech acts as kerygma. Kerygma can take many forms: the telling of a story or parable, sermons, letters, visionary forms, biographies, wisdom literature, and many more. It is true that a function of kerygma is to instruct and provide information; however, the knowledge that Scripture seeks to impart is more than that. Scripture becomes the means by which God gives Godself to us and draws us into God's very life. Proclamation of the kerygma of the Bible is never simply to illumine listeners; it is primarily to enable us to encounter, again and again, the living God who has come to us in Christ.[23] The concrete encounter of God and human beings finds a counterpart in the human event of proclamation.[24]

This high view of Scripture and the art of proclamation is based on the intention to usher in the presence of God. Such encounters can only be created by Godself, and the hermeneutics required will always be pneumatic and prayerful since it is the delight of the Spirit to use the word to bring people to God.[25] The act of proclamation can never only be a lecture or cerebral lesson, directed primarily to the head. The business of proclamation is to bring hearers face to face with Jesus Christ as savior, healer, sanctifier, baptizer, and coming king.[26]

Charismatic-Pentecostal communities have been born out of the desire for having experiences that align with what is taught and modeled in the New Testament.[27] They have established a prophetic, eschatological people grounded and formed by an interest in biblical texts, read not for what they teach about ancient history or ideas, but because Pentecos-

21. Bartholomew, *Introducing Biblical Hermeutics*, 33.

22. Barth, *Kirchliche Dogmatik*, 1.1:52.

23. Bartholomew, *Introducing Biblical Hermeutics*, 35.

24. Barth, *Kirchliche Dogmatik*, 1.1:59.

25. Barth, *Kirchliche Dogmatik*, 1.1:59.

26. Newbigin, *Good Shepherd*, 24.

27. Keener, *Spirit Hermeneutics*, 21–38.

tals expect to share the kind of spiritual experience and relationship with God described in the Bible.[28]

Clark distinguishes between a charismatic and non-charismatic community.[29] A charismatic community presupposes charismatic individuals, implying that they identify with certain gifts of the Spirit (*charismata*) that the Spirit equipped them with, and that they approach the text in a charismatic context at all times.[30] The implication is that, on the one hand, they read the Bible through the lens of their existential situation and, on the other, the expectation that the Spirit will speak to them the words of God that apply to their situation through their reading of and meditation on the Bible.[31] The role of the Spirit in the reading process is not merely limited to "illumination," the Spirit's contribution also includes the Spirit's leading, discerning, witnessing, and demonstrating of Christ as the living word of God in the pages of the Bible and the lives of contemporary believers. In the charismatic community, the interpreter is as relevant as the process of interpretation because they participate in the ministry of the Holy Spirit as the Spirit witnesses, guides, grants discernment, and more. The community, which provides both the filter and the criteria for evaluation of the interpretation, must also be charismatic in the sense that they are aware of and acquainted with the powerful pres-

---

28. Keener, *Spirit Hermeneutics*, 5.

29. Clark, "Investigation into the Nature," 182.

30. Bonhoeffer develops a model of "Christonomy," consisting of the community that is being established where the word of God is proclaimed by virtue of a divine mandate (Bonhoeffer, *Ethics*, 265). The community that comes into being around this word does not dominate the world but rather stands entirely in service of the fulfilment of the divine mandate. The church exists for the sake of the world, as the goal and center of all God's dealings with the world. The faith community stands where the world ought to be standing, before the face of God, and, to this extent, they serve as deputy for the world and exists for the sake of the world (Bonhoeffer, *Ethics*, 267). See also Bonhoeffer's remark that while Catholics are in danger of seeing the church as an end in itself, Protestants are in danger of neglecting the church as an entity, with consequent weak ecclesiastical organization.

31. Existential challenges such as illness, unemployment, childlessness, poverty, political violence, and xenophobia are perceived by Pentecostals as a kind of hermeneutical key with which they interpret the Bible (Anderson, "Hermeneutical Processes," 223), operating on the assumption that God wants to meet the needs of God's people in a direct manner. The "this-worldly" challenges then serve as the hermeneutical key to the interpretation of the Bible, at times, in a historicist way, where the social-historical background and horizon of the text is ignored and it is interpreted as though it was written exclusively for contemporary believers. The Bible is believed to contain answers for this-worldly needs (Anderson, *Introduction to Pentecostalism*, 224).

ence and working of God in their midst. The community searches the Scriptures and inspires its members to do the same.[32]

The Bible is only recognizable as Scripture, the word of God for believers within the faith community. Hauerwas's thesis that the Bible is not and should not be accessible to merely anyone, but rather should only be made available to those who have undergone the hard discipline of existing as part of God's people and that the church should take the Bible out of the hands of individual Christians should be understood in these terms.[33] Modern society has bred individualism and the threat of a destructive subjectivism in our interpretation of the Bible, making active participation in a reading faith community a prerequisite and safe-guard against subverting the text to the service of individual self-interest.[34] Biblical authority, then, incorporates the notion of believers' involvement in the faith community because the Bible is authoritative for that community. To place oneself outside of that community is to fail to recognize the Bible as authoritative. Any reading of Scripture which is devoid of experiences of encounters with God and which occurs in isolation from the faith community is an inadequate reading that fails to comprehend Scripture's origin, function, and essence. For the Bible to be truly authoritative, God must be experienced and encountered by that person and community in and through (but not confined to) Scripture.[35]

Pentecostals' skepticism and criticism of biblical interpretation in a non-charismatic context has earned them the accusation of gnosticism.[36] The potential for gross misunderstanding or manipulation of the text, however, is greater in proportion to the discrepancy between the realms of experience of the originating and interpreting communities. The early church represented a minority missionary movement rather than an established church, and the concerns of the Pentecostal movement against that of the established church presents a similarly significant difference between the interpretation made in a charismatic community and that made in a community in which charismatic phenomena are rare or resisted.

---

32. Clark, "Investigation into the Nature," 182.

33. Hauerwas, *Unleashing the Scripture*, 9.

34. Ellington, "Pentecostalism and the Authority of Scriptures," 161.

35. Ellington, "Pentecostalism and the Authority of Scriptures," 163.

36. See the discussion of this accusation in Clark and Lederle, *What is Distinctive*, 108–9.

A charismatic community is one in which the crucified and resurrected Christ is seen (by means of discernible phenomena such as the
gifts of the Spirit) to be dynamically and immediately present among
his disciples by the power of the Holy Spirit.[37] Although cultural differences characterize different Pentecostal groups, the demand to be charismatic distinguishes Pentecostals across diverse differences. Pentecostals
represent a community of prophets, as Luke describes the first-century
church, although they tend to identify themselves as people baptized in
the Spirit.[38] They should rather appropriate the gift of prophecy, argues
Stronstad, to fulfill their potential as a charismatic community of prophets to challenge believers and secular society alike, rather than selfishly
utilizing the *charismata* for narcissistic purposes, trivializing both the
phenomenon of prophecy and its content.[39] The presence of the Spirit
and the *charismata* should make the charismatic community a radical alternative community that changes its environment, expressed holistically
in physical and emotional ways, by way of tears and laughter, tongues
and prophecies, healings and deliverances, dancing and singing, shouting
and participation is testimonies, showing the affinity for oral expression
within pentecostal spirituality.[40]

Moore remarks that it is ironic that some Pentecostals are moving
away from their emphasis on the community's role in interpretation (and
on narrative theology and the preference of praxis above experience)
when certain cutting-edge trends in recent theology, driven by postmodern sentiments, are moving closer to these pentecostal emphases.[41] For
this reason, it is imperative that Pentecostals would revisit their hermeneutics to ensure that the foundational distinctives of the movement
be retained. The interpretive community serves as a safeguard against
excessive individualism, argues Grogan.[42] If believers reading the Bible
individually find themselves at variance with the hermeneutical tradition, then they need to be self-critical. As a divinely-established institution, the church represents the interpretive community, and although the
church stands under the direction of the Bible, its voice is more represen-

---

37. Clark and Lederle, *What is Distinctive*, 53–55.

38. See the argument in Stronstad, "Prophethood of All Believers."

39. Stronstad, "Prophethood of All Believers," 75–77.

40. Neumann, "Spirituality," 199.

41. Moore, "Pentecostal Approach to Scripture," 13.

42. Grogan, "Is the Bible Hermeneutically Self-Sufficient?," 210.

tative than that of the individual, argues Grogan. What is important to add is that all church tradition should always come under the judgment of Scripture. Church tradition provides helpful summaries of biblical truth, a salvation-historical metanarrative that serves as the framework to interpret the detail found in the Bible. Irenaeus refers to "the canon of the truth" and Tertullian to "the rule of faith" as a condensed summary setting out the key points of Christian revelation in the form of a *regula fidei*.[43] Lastly, it should be remembered that church tradition is always something of a mixed bag, in Grogan's terms, and the fact that doctrines, developed over centuries, had no clear warrant in Scripture should warn that the church's tradition is not above criticism. The Reformers, argues Berkouwer, saw that the the gospel itself, so clear in Scripture, could be obscured and even modified by church tradition.[44]

McQueen, on the other hand, argues that Pentecostals should revision themselves as an eschatological community, a perspective that the Spirit established in the earliest Pentecostal communities.[45] For them, the baptism in the Spirit signaled the beginning of the last days for the early church as well as the end of the last days in their day. McQueen reasons that pentecostal eschatology finds its source in the presence of the eschatological Spirit and that the waning of eschatological expectation in Pentecostalism is derived from a loss of the Spirit in these churches. He asserts that some Pentecostals have been quenching the Spirit through their cultural, moral, institutional, and theological accommodation; they have lost the drive for separation from the world that defined holiness for Pentecostals. In their worship services and lives, "the Spirit has become a domesticated helper who moves only within prescribed forms and at convenient occasions."[46] The rediscovery of its potential as a prophetic community can revitalize Pentecostals. McQueen represents the primitivist principle in Pentecostalism, in which a sincere desire to be linked to the dynamics of the earliest church is allied and paralleled with a present-day desire to rediscover the dynamic of the early twentieth-century Pentecostal movement.[47]

43. Grogan, "Is the Bible Hermeneutically Self-Sufficient?," 212.

44. Berkouwer, *Holy Scripture*, 303.

45. See McQueen, *Joel and the Spirit*.

46. McQueen, *Joel and the Spirit*, 97.

47. It should be kept in mind that Stronstad and McQueen represent North American Pentecostalism. In the Global South, however, Pentecostalism reveals many of the characteristics of the early church and early Pentecostal movement. It exists as an

Spirit and Community, and the Word

Thomas develops his model of the interaction between the faith community and the Spirit in the interpretation of Scripture by means of a close reading of Acts 15.[48] The missionary church of the first century discussed the critical issue of the validity of the *Torah* for the institution of life of the heathen part of the church. Only after listening to various testimonies of God's activity in accepting non-Jewish believers apart from circumcision did they appeal to Scripture. James quotes from Amos 9 in support of his argument, and, in doing so, he makes sense in light of Luke's already well-established interest in demonstrating from the Scriptures that God had fulfilled God's promises to David in Jesus and that those promises are therefore concerned with the nature of the church. From the reading of Acts 15, Thomas then identifies three primary components: Scripture,

---

apocalyptic movement, as argued in chapter 4, with a worldview that is highly spiritual—although these Pentecostals are less concerned with the schemas of dispensationalism (Hunt, "Dispensationalism," 64). A new wave of revivals in the 1960s, combined with the influence of the charismatic movement of the 1970s, led to a more optimistic postmillenarianism with its hope of a revival in the last days (Hunt, "Dispensationalism," 64). The working of spiritual powers in pagan religion requires African Pentecostals to depend on the continued revelation of the power of the Holy Spirit in their personal and communal lives. In the African context, pentecostal prophecy operates in the same context as the diviner in African Traditional Religion (ATR), focusing on diagnosing individual ailments and finding spiritual cures to all manner of challenges (Ngong, *Holy Spirit*, 143). The religious functionary's role includes diagnosis, healing, prophecy, and the reversal of unhappy destinies (Asamoah-Gyadu, *Sighs and Signs*, 87). The similarity between the diviner and prophet is that both have the task of uncovering the cause or root of a problem or felt need (Omenyo, "Man of God," 34); however, the similarity ends when the prophet interprets the problem in terms of a revelation of the Spirit. Pentecostal prophets are perceived as having a unique relationship with God, allowing them continuing access to supernatural knowledge of the seekers' problems as well as the power to bring about solutions to those problems. In many cases, the solution consists of something that the believer must do or stop doing. In their manner of operating, neo-Pentecostal prophets link with the phenomenon of prophecy within the African Indigenous Churches (AICs) rather than with the classical Pentecostal phenomenon of prophecy, so that neo-Pentecostalism may be viewed as the "AIC-ination" of African Pentecostalism (see Cox, *Fire from Heaven*, 250). Johnstone estimates that such "independent" churches will have grown from 1 percent in 1900 to a possible one-quarter of Christianity by 2050 (Johnstone, *Future of the Global Church*, 113). The notion of a "prophet" in Africa is particularly linked to the Old Testament prophets as figures of power and authority, contributing to the development of innumerable sects and groups based upon cultic devotion to individuals who set themselves up as prophets (Clark, "Investigation into the Nature," 200).

48. Thomas, "Reading the Bible," 109.

the interpretive community of faith, and the Holy Spirit, who prepares and equips the community to read the Bible. The three elements operate in concert. The community is the place of the Spirit's activity; they testify to the Spirit's activity in supplying them with the necessary insights to interpret the Bible and discuss and discern the Spirit's work in the forming of meaning of the Bible. The interpretive community model facilitates the uniting of a myriad of contrasting individualized, contextualized applications of meaning in an arena of mutual coherence and significance.[49] At the same time, in terms of its significance, the Bible is not static but dynamic. The Spirit's role in interpretation is not reduced to some vague talk of illumination of the cerebral facilities of the Christian reader; in pentecostal understanding, the Spirit creates the context for interpretation through the Spirit's actions and, as a result, guides the church in the determination of which texts are most relevant in a particular situation, clarifying how they might best be approached.[50] Since the church's experience is judged in relation to the Bible, a pentecostal hermeneutics prioritizes the authority of the Bible as guideline and criterion.

From the same triadic negotiation of Scripture, church, and Spirit, Archer posits a text-centered, reader-oriented approach that prioritizes Scripture, yet leaves the door open for the pneumatological convictions of the Pentecostal church.[51] Yong adds that the continuous interplay of Spirit, Word, and Community serves not only to clarify the hermeneutical activity of theological interpretation but also to locate the sources of theological inquiry.[52] This trinitarian relationship of Spirit, Word, and Community is also a movement—a hermeneutical trialectic—and such movement is sustained insofar as it proceeds from a pneumatological starting-point, in the methodology employed by Yong. The pneumatological framework is dependent upon a pneumatic intuition; pneumatology refers to the second-order discourse about what Christians experience as the Holy Spirit, and the experience itself can be understood in terms of a (hopefully ongoing) series of pneumatic encounters. Pentecostal hermeneutics rests on and is dependent upon such pre-theoretical encounters with and experiences of the Spirit of God. Yong's theological approach is fallibilistic, multiperspectival, self-critical, and dialogical, while it

49. Clines, "World Established on Water," 174.

50. Thomas, "Reading the Bible," 119.

51. Archer, *Pentecostal Hermeneutic*. See also Land, *Pentecostal Spirituality*, 28–34, and Thomas, "Women, Pentecostalism, and the Bible," 49–56.

52. Yong, *Spirit-Word-Community*, 7.

is also pneumatologically orientated and christologically focused.[53] Archer emphasizes that the Spirit's voice in the interpretive task is both in community discernment and in undergirding the clarity of Scripture, implying the dynamic presence and activity of the Spirit in both Scriptures and the faith community. Although the Spirit may have more to say than what is stated in Scripture, it will always be scripturally-based and determined by the spirit of biblical injunctions. In order to counteract the subjectivist nature of interpreting the Bible in a spiritual reading, the community must discern the signs and sound of the Spirit among the community in dialogical relationship with the Bible.[54] "Dialogical" (or dialectical) refers to the experience of the Spirit shaping the community's reading of the Bible while the Bible provides the lens through which the community perceives the Spirit's work. Theology is best undertaken *en conjuncto*, that is, "together" or "with others."[55] Castelo refers to John Donne's phrase, "No man is an island," suggesting that the interpreter of the Bible must also be genuinely and truly "involved" in humankind.[56] The faith community exists as a communitarian dynamic[57] because the Spirit has created a new community, making it one body, equipped to grow to the full stature of Christ.[58]

The core identity marker for Pentecostals is the person and work of the Spirit dynamically present among God's people.[59] At the same time, the Christian community stands central in a pentecostal hermeneutics of Scripture. The church is generated by the Spirit, who is active in the church, preparing the church to read the Bible and guide the church in its interpretation of the Bible. A prerequisite for pentecostal self-understanding is that they understand their hermeneutics better, enabling them to speak and be heard by the larger church.[60]

---

53. Cartledge, "Pentecostal Theology," 261.

54. Archer, *Gospel Revisited*, 132.

55. Castelo, "*Diakrisis* Always *En Conjunto*," 203.

56. This is contrasted to many Western exegetes' Lone Ranger approach with its survivalist and success-related connotations combined into a "sacred" individualism (Castelo, "*Diakrisis* Always *En Conjunto*," 203–4).

57. González, *Manana*, 28–30.

58. Castelo, "*Diakrisis* Always *En Conjunto*," 205.

59. Green, "Pentecostal Hermeneutics," 166.

60. Robeck, "Taking Stock of Pentecostalism," 60.

CHAPTER 6

Synthesis

SINCE THE 1980S, PENTECOSTAL scholarship[1] visited and revisited its hermeneutical angle, attempting to discern the implications of Spirit baptism, the exercise of the *charismata*, and the fivefold (or fourfold) Full Gospel for biblical interpretation.[2] What is needed is that a pentecostal hermeneutics be designed that is faithful to pentecostal praxis, theology, and ethos and that would be appropriate for the present context.[3] Menzies and Menzies makes the important remark that the future of Pentecostalism is uncertain because it does not have a strong theological base, which underlines the importance of the development of a pentecostal hermeneutics.[4] Pentecostals are known for their spiritual vitality—not their theological prowess or intellectual rigor. Theology gives direction to experience and praxis, and history shows that, without a strong theological base, enthusiastic movements dissipate

1. Vondey divides the history of pentecostal scholarship into five periods of development, each focusing on the formation of a particular vocation: missionaries, with the establishment of training schools and Bible institutes in the 1920s and 1930s; historians, following the work of Walter J. Hollenweger in the late 1960s; biblical scholarship, which, helped shape a distinctive pentecostal hermeneutic in response to both liberalism and fundamentalism in the 1970s; the emergence of constructive theological research in the 1990s; and, in the last twenty years, the expansion of pentecostal scholarship into the human and natural sciences, encouraging Pentecostals to enter scientific careers explicitly as Pentecostals (Vondey, *Pentecostalism*, 122–25).

2. In recent years, there has been an explosion of pentecostal theological scholarship, with various theological monograph series being published by important publishers as well as a number of journals (Cartledge, "Pentecostal Theology," 254).

3. See Martin, "Introduction to Pentecostal Biblical Hermeneutics," 8.

4. Menzies and Menzies, *Spirit and Power*, 50.

or evolve in other directions, including the acceptance of excesses and heresies.

At the moment, the common consensus existing among pentecostal scholars about a pentecostal hermeneutics can be described as: the agreement that Pentecostals' readings are narrative rather than propositional; that their readings are dynamic rather than static; that their readings are experience-based, using the existential situation as the hermeneutical lens to read the Bible and listen for/to its message (spiritual experience[5] is a significant factor in the interpretation of the Bible); that their readings are formed by their expectation of an encounter with the God that the Bible tells of, rather than mere cerebral understanding of biblical history, ideas, and context; that their readings are pragmatic, emphasizing the transformation of the reader and the application of the text to the present situation; that the work of the Spirit makes faithful interpretation possible, inspiring readers to make gospel sense of the texts; that it is reading the texts from the scopus of Jesus Christ—who is the reflection of God's glory, the exact imprint of God's very being, and who sustains all things by God's powerful word (Heb 1:3); that the Bible's final, canonical form has authority over the lives of believers and is sufficient to explain the way of salvation to all people; that the worshiping community, with an appreciation for its ethnic, linguistic, gender, national, and economic diversity, has a definitive role in the process of interpreting Scripture and discernment of spirits to evaluate what is presented as "revelation of the Spirit"; that Pentecostals need confessional, theological readings, determined by faith, to realize the Bible as God's address to God's people here and now; that the Bible contains an irreducible diversity of theological and literary "voices"[6]; that the overarching metanarrative of the history of salvation serves as a hermeneutical key—the overarching story of salvation is the theological context for arriving at the meaning of a particular text for the present faith community[7]; that narrative, literary readings of a text receive priority over against historical-critical readings; that the history of effects has significance for the contemporary interpretive process[8]; that the importance of Luke-Acts on pentecostal practice

5. Archer, "Pentecostal Biblical Interpretation," 173.

6. For a discussion of diverse biblical voices concerning violence and war, see Nel, "Church and War," and Nel, *Pacifism and Pentecostals*.

7. Anderson, *African Reformation*, 223, and Archer, "Pentecostal Biblical Interpretation," 173.

8. See Ellington, "Locating Pentecostals," and Green, *Toward a Pentecostal Theology*,

and theory be upheld; and that the significance of historic Christian traditions be emphasized for how Christians through the ages have understood a particular passage of the Bible with special attention given to the early Pentecostal readers.[9]

What is necessary is a method pluralism that serves the ethos of pentecostal hermeneutics, of an experiential, Spirit-driven reading of the Bible.[10] The object of hermeneutical reflection should prescribe the method needed to interpret it. Because it is the word of God, a consistent critical approach to its interpretation is not preferable but rather a receptive and positive attitude toward the Bible, in a prayerful and expectant attitude that the word of God (meaning, primarily, Jesus Christ) will be revealed in the process of reading the text. As part of the method pluralism it is important that the genre of the text should never be ignored. At the same time, the scopus of the text, as part of a salvation-historical approach, should define the boundaries of the readers' expectancy in reading the text. The "canon within the canon" for Pentecostals needs to stay Jesus, in terms of the fourfold or fivefold Full Gospel, and then Jesus as the means of living in a relationship with the Father. Their hermeneutics is to be tested in terms of the quality and effect of the revelation they receive when reading the Bible, in terms of the quality of positive life transformation experienced in the daily lives of Spirit-filled people. If interpreting the Bible does not accommodate the transforming of believers' lives in accordance with the gospel and Jesus's example, pentecostal hermeneutics would fail. What should always be realized is that the Spirit speaks as the Spirit wants to and when the Spirit wants to. The revelation of God and God's power to transform lives is the Spirit's prerogative. In the terms used by 2 Peter 1:19–21, believers have the prophetic message as something completely reliable and they need to be attentive to the message because no prophecy of Scripture is a matter of one's own interpretation; no prophecy ever came by human will, but men and women moved by the Holy Spirit (or carried along by the Spirit) spoke what they heard from God.

Pentecostal hermeneutics provides some decisive insights that can contribute to the Christian hermeneutical debate because Pentecostals bear witness to a reality and dimension of life in the Spirit out of which a

---

182–83.

9. Archer, "Pentecostal Biblical Interpretation," 173.

10. See Zwiep, "Het Hermeneutische Vraagstuk," 8.

uniquely pentecostal approach to Scripture emerges.[11] It has been argued that the most important of the distinctive marks of a pentecostal hermeneutics is that the Holy Spirit is central in reading the Bible. The Spirit addresses believers in ways which transcend human reason, by way of the *charismata* (1 Cor 12–14) and even more subtle ways (Rom 8:1–27). Pentecostal epistemology is not experience-based faith; it consists rather of the interplay between knowledge gained from reading the Bible and lived experience. Knowing about God and directly experiencing God perpetually informs and depends upon one another.[12] They share their knowledge of God, based upon encounters with God, through God's Spirit, in their testimonies. In their worship services, they do not expect only to be equipped with information about God but they believe that their lives will also be transformed when God speaks to them because of the creative power of God's words (as illustrated in the words that created the world, in Gen 1:1–27). In their worship services, they do not only have a "formal" sermon but also wait for a "message from the Lord," at times indicated by the prophetic announcement, "Thus says the Lord."[13]

A second mark of a pentecostal hermeneutics has been identified as Pentecostals' eschatology, which determines their identity and the way they interpret the Bible. A third mark is the importance that the faith community serves as normative for interpreting the Bible. Knowledge of truth is inseparable from active membership in the localized body of Christ. In Africa, neo-pentecostal prophets (or the phenomenon of neoprophets) may create the impression as if their words are always authoritative and to be obeyed; 1 Corinthians is adamant that all prophecies always have to be subjected to the discernment of the faith community to protect them from heresy and untruths.[14]

In a pluralistic world, the way forward for a pentecostal hermeneutics is not so much to develop a confessional approach founded on a genealogical connection with the Azusa Street Revival but rather to adopt the day of Pentecost apostolic charismatic experience as exemplary for biblical and theological interpretation.[15] Although the contemporary

11. Moore, "Pentecostal Approach to Scripture," 11.

12. Moore, "Pentecostal Approach to Scripture," 12.

13. Many Pentecostals discourage the use of similar pronouncements because it might bind the conscience of believers to accept the word as from the Lord even though they may not be convinced that it is a revelation of the Spirit.

14. See 1 Cor 12:10; 13:2; 14:1–5; 24–40.

15. Yong, *Hermeneutical Spirit*, 28.

Pentecostal community has much to learn from its origins, there are some aspects of the early experience that they cannot use to model their lives and practices on. Their restorationist urge to become conformed to the early church is much more valuable and meaningful. An apostolic hermeneutics implies that one reads the Bible as the apostles themselves read it—for instance, Acts 2 interprets the pentecostal experience scripturally, according to the prophecy of Joel, and Acts 15 explains how the early church took its significant decisions in council. What is important to note is the way apostolic meaning-making grasped the experience of the Spirit's outpouring via its appeal to the traditions in the Hebrew Bible. They interpreted their present experience with a this-is-that approach, according to their canonical heritage, with experiences compared to the prophecy of Joel as well as other Davidic, wisdom, and psalmic texts. They sought to understand present experience in terms of and in light of the established and accepted tradition. Further, an apostolic hermeneutics implies that it interprets the Bible following the established rules of post-apostolic traditions as received within the broad consensus of the church ecumenical. It includes the full scope of the Christian tradition after the apostolic generations, of patristic and medieval traditions, as well as modern hermeneutical traditions (such as historical and grammatical criticism and literary and canonical approaches developed since the early modern period). What is important to highlight is how there are a variety of approaches developed throughout Christian history that enable what Yong calls "living into the spirit of biblical texts" in subsequent ages and contexts. In the face of differences between disparate "spaces" of ecclesial and cultural inhabitation that characterize the enormous diversity of Pentecostalism, there is common categorical ground from which to engage the this-is-that instincts of apostolic interpretation.[16] What unites Pentecostal churches is not a doctrine but a religious experience.[17]

Such an understanding insists that understanding the Bible is also facilitated by engagement with pathos, consisting of the emotions, affections, feelings, sentiments, and passions embedded in the Bible's message. It invites contemporary readers into this world, to share the pathos in life-transforming ways. Since the Majority World is more oral, affectively attuned, and embodied than literary cultures, the orthopathic dimension should deliberately be developed in pentecostal hermeneutics. An

16. Yong, *Hermeneutical Spirit*, 37.
17. Hollenweger, "From Azusa Street to Toronto," 7.

embodied hermeneutics sings, worships, dances with joy, cries with lament, studies, and meditates. Pentecostal liturgy and worship become incubators that precipitate life in the Spirit, and this, in turn, nurtures hermeneutical instincts and dispositions.[18] What is discerned as the way the Spirit moved to encounter people in their needs in the Bible becomes the way contemporary believers expect the Spirit to move in their world, so that this helps interpret that (this-is-that approach).

Right thinking and right feeling are intertwined with right behavior and right acting, involving interpreting life in order to discharge in human acting, behaving, and living. The works of the Spirit are made manifest through human agents and their purposes, practices, and performances when the Bible is read in and through contemporary experiences ("this"), among the faith community as the fellowship of the Spirit (2 Cor 13:14). The Bible is read after Pentecost, but in and through the multicultural and intercultural witnesses ("that") that expect the divine reign of Christ. In this way, orthodoxy (right thinking), orthopathy (right feeling), and orthopraxy (right living) are intertwined in a pentecostal hermeneutics.

One implication is that the Bible is not and should not be treated as a magical book, as is the case in parts of African Christianity. There is no sense in burying a Bible in the foundation of a house or using it as a weapon to ward off evil spirits as it is only a book, manufactured like any other book. Its value lies in the Spirit's preference to use the Bible when the Spirit reveals the truth, Jesus Christ, to people.

Pentecostals believe and repeat that where two or three are gathered in Jesus's name, he is there among them (Matt 18:20). Pentecostal faith was born in a gathering of believers (Acts 2:1–4) and it is in the gathering of the faithful that their faith is nurtured and sustained (Acts 2:42–47). For that reason, it is important to them not to neglect to meet together but rather to encourage one another, and all the more as they see the day of Christ's coming approaching (Heb 10:25). When the local assembly is gathered, the body of Christ is realized, and each believer has a contribution to make in building up the body, whether it consists of a hymn, a lesson, a revelation, a tongue, or an interpretation (1 Cor 14:26). Believers are bound together in mutual interdependency and accountability. And the Spirit speaks here as nowhere else, using the gifts of members to edify the whole body (1 Cor 12:14; Eph 4; Rom 12).

---

18. Yong, *Hermeneutical Spirit*, 39.

Bibliography

Adamo, David T. "Reading Psalm 23 in African Context." *Verbum et Ecclesia* 39.1 (2018) 8.

———. "The Use of Psalms in African Indigenous Churches in Nigeria." In *The Bible in Africa: Transactions, Trajectories, and Trends*, edited by Gerald O. West and Musa W. Dube, 336–49. Leiden: Brill, 2000.

Adeseun, Anuoluwapo. "Tanzanian Pastor Arrested For Drowning Church Members During Baptism." *Nigerian Monitor*, 17 July 2017. http://www.nigerianmonitor. com/pastor-arrested-for-drowning-church-members-during-baptism-in-tanzania.

Albrecht, Daniel E. *Rites in the Spirit: A Ritual Approach to Pentecostal/Charismatic Spirituality*. Sheffield: Sheffield Academic, 1999.

Albrecht, Daniel E., and Evan B. Howard. "Pentecostal Spirituality." In *The Cambridge Companion to Pentecostalism*, edited by Cecil M. Robeck and Amos Young, 235–53. New York: Cambridge University Press, 2014.

Altany, Alan. "Biblical Criticism." In *Encyclopedia of Fundamentalism*, edited by Brenda E. Brasher, 64. New York: Routledge, 2001.

Althouse, Paul. *The Theology of Martin Luther*. Translated by R.C. Schultz. Philadelphia: Fortress, 1966.

Althouse, Peter. "Eschatology." In *Handbook of Pentecostal Christianity*, edited by Alan Stewart, 73–75. DeKalb: Northern Illinois University Press, 2012.

———. "Towards a Pentecostal Ecclesiology: Participation in the Missional Life of the Triune God." *Journal of Pentecostal Theology* 18 (2009) 230–45.

Alvarado, Johnathan E. "Exploring Africanisms in Latin American Pentecostalism." In *Latin America*, vol. 2 of *Global Renewal Christianity: Spirit-Empowered Movements Past, Present, and Future*. Edited by Vinson Synan and Miguel Álvarez, 337–53. Lake Mary, FL: Charisma House, 2016.

Alvarsso, J. Alvarez. "The Bible, Pentecostalism, and 'Magic.'" *Journal of the European Pentecostal Theological Association* 27.2 (2007) 183–96.

Ammerman, Nancy T. "North-American Protestant Fundamentalism." In *Media, Culture, and the Religious Right*, edited by Linda Kintz and Julia Lesage, 55–113. Minneapolis: University of Minneapolis Press, 1998.

Anderson, Allan H. "African Pentecostalism." In *Handbook of Pentecostal Christianity*, edited by Alan Stewart, 27–31. DeKalb: Northern Illinois University Press, 2012.

———. *African Reformation: African Initiated Christianity in the 20th Century*. Trenton, NJ: Africa World Press, 2001.

———. "Deliverance and Exorcism in Majority World Pentecostalism." In *Exorcism and Deliverance: Multi-Disciplinary Studies*, edited by William K. Kay and Robin Parry, 101–19. Milton Keynes: Paternoster, 2011.

———. "Global Pentecostalism in the New Millennium." In *Pentecostals After a Century: Global Perspectives on a Movement in Transition*, edited by Allan Anderson and Walter Hollenweger, 209–23. Sheffield: Sheffield Academic, 1999.

———. "The Hermeneutical Processes of Pentecostal-type African Initiated Churches in South Africa." *Missionalia* 24.2 (1996) 171–85.

———. *An Introduction to Pentecostalism.* 2nd ed. Cambridge: Cambridge University Press, 2013.

———. "Keswick Movement." In *Handbook of Pentecostal Christianity*, edited by Adam Stewart, 128–30. DeKalb: Northern Illinois University Press, 2012.

———. *Moya: The Holy Spirit in an African Context.* Manualia Didactica 13. Pretoria: Sigma, 1991.

———. "The Spirit and the African Spiritual World." In *Africa*, vol. 3 of *Global Renewal Christianity: Spirit-Empowered Movements Past, Present, and Future.* Edited by Vinson Synan, Amos Yong, and J. Kwabena Asamoah-Gyadu, 304–20. Lake Mary, FL: Charisma House, 2016.

———. "William Joseph Seymour." In *Handbook of Pentecostal Christianity*, edited by Adam Stewart, 186–89. DeKalb: Northern Illinois University Press, 2012.

Anderson, Allan H., and Gerald J. Pillay. "The Segregated Spirit: The Pentecostals." In *Christianity in South Africa: A Political, Social, and Cultural History*, edited by Richard Elphick and Rodney Davenport, 227–41. Berkeley: University of California Press, 1997.

Anderson, Gordon. "Pentecost, Scholarship, and Learning in a Postmodern World." *Pneuma* 27.1 (2005) 115–23.

Anderson, Ray S. "Fundamentalism." In *The Blackwell Encyclopedia of Modern Christian Thought*, edited by Alister E. McGrath, 229–33. Oxford: Basil Blackwell, 1993.

Anderson, Robert M. *Vision of the Disinherited: The Making of American Pentecostalism.* New York: Oxford University Press, 1979.

Ansberry, Christopher B., and Christopher M. Hays. "Faithful Criticism and a Critical Faith." In *Evangelical Faith and the Challenge of Historical Criticism*, edited by Christopher M. Hays and Christopher B. Ansberry, 204–22. Grand Rapids: Baker Academic, 2013.

Archer, Kenneth J. "Full Gospel." In *Handbook of Pentecostal Christianity*, edited by Adam Stewart, 89–91. DeKalb: Northern Illinois University Press, 2012.

———. *The Gospel Revisited: Towards a Pentecostal Theology of Worship.* Eugene, OR: Pickwick, 2011.

———. "Hermeneutics." In *Handbook of Pentecostal Christianity*, edited by Alan Stewart, 108–16. DeKalb: Northern Illinois University Press, 2012.

———. "Pentecostal Biblical Interpretation." In *Issues in Contemporary Pentecostalism*, edited by R. Keith Witt and French L. Arrington, 167–83. Cleveland, TN: Pathway, 2012.

———. *A Pentecostal Hermeneutic for the Twenty-First Century: Spirit, Scripture, and Community.* London: T&T Clark, 2004.

———. *A Pentecostal Hermeneutic: Spirit, Scripture, and Community.* Cleveland, TN: CPT, 2009.

———. "Pentecostal Hermeneutics: Retrospect and Prospect." In *Pentecostal Hermeneutics: A Reader*, edited by Lee Roy Martin, 131–48. Leiden: Brill, 2013.

———. "Spirited Conversation about Hermeneutics: A Pentecostal Hermeneut's Response to Craig Keener's *Spirit Hermeneutics*." *Pneuma* 39 (2017) 179–97.

Arrington, French L. "Hermeneutics, Historical Perspectives on Pentecostal and Charismatic." In *Dictionary of Pentecostal and Charismatic Movements*, edited by Stanley M. Burgess and Gary B. McGee, 376–89. Grand Rapids: Zondervan, 1988.

———. "Pentecostal Identity and Interpretation of the Bible." In *Issues in Contemporary Pentecostalism*, edited by R. Keith Witt and French L. Arrington, 10–20. Cleveland, TN: Pathway, 2012.

———. "The Use of the Bible by Pentecostals." *Pneuma* 16.10 (1994) 101–7.

Asamoah-Gyadu, J. Kwabena. *African Charismatics: Current Developments Within Independent Indigenous Pentecostalism in Ghana*. Studies of Religion in Africa 27. Leiden: Brill, 2005.

———. *Contemporary Pentecostal Christianity: Interpretations from an African Context*. Eugene, OR: Wipf & Stock, 2013.

———. *Sighs and Signs of the Spirit: Ghanaian Perspectives on Pentecostalism and Renewal in Africa*. Oxford: Regnum, 2015.

———. *Spreading Fires: The Missionary Nature of Early Pentecostalism*. Maryknoll, NY: Orbis, 2007.

———. *To the Ends of the Earth: Pentecostalism and the Transformation of World Christianity*. New York: Oxford University Press, 2013.

———. "Towards a Pentecostal Missiology for the Majority World." *Asian Journal of Pentecostal Studies* 8.1 (2005) 28–47.

Atkinson, William. "Angels and the Spirit in Luke-Acts." *Journal of the European Pentecostal Association* 26.1 (2006) 76–90.

Autry, Arden C. "Dimensions of Hermeneutics in Pentecostal Focus." *Journal of Pentecostal Theology* 1.3 (1993) 29–50.

Baker, Robert O. "Pentecostal Bible Reading: Toward a Model of Reading for the Formation of the Affections." In *Pentecostal Hermeneutics: A Reader*, edited by Lee Roy Martin, 95–108. Leiden: Brill, 2013.

Baldwin, Joyce G. *Daniel*. Tyndale Old Testament Commentaries. Leicester: Inter-Varsity, 1978.

Banjo, Temi. "Aftermath Of Eating Grass: Pastor Lesego Daniel's Church Members Fall Sick." *Nigerian Monitor*, 16 Jan 2014. http://www.nigerianmonitor.com/photos-aftermath-of-eating-grass-pastor-lesego-daniels-church-members-fall-sick.

———. "Pastor Orders Female Congregants To Come To Church Without Underwear For Christ To Enter Their Lives." *Nigerian Monitor*, 3 March 2014. http://www.nigerianmonitor.com/endtime-pastor-orders-female-congregants-to-come-to-church-without-underwear-for-christ-to-enter-their-lives.

Barr, James. "Fundamentalism." In *The Encyclopedia of Christianity*, vol. 2, edited by Erwin Fahlbusch et al., 363–65. Grand Rapids: Eerdmans, 2001.

———. *The Semantics of Biblical Language*. London: Oxford University Press, 1961.

Barrett, David B. "AD 2000: 350 Million Christians in Africa?" *International Review of Mission* 59 (1970) 39–54.

———. "Appendix: A Chronology of Renewal in the Holy Spirit." In *The Century of the Holy Spirit: 100 Years of Pentecostal and Charismatic Renewal*, edited by Vinson Synan, 415–52. Nashville: Thomas Nelson, 2001.

—. "The Worldwide Holy Spirit Renewal." In *The Century of the Holy Spirit: 100 Years of Pentecostal and Charismatic Renewal*, edited by Vinson Synan, 381–414. Nashville: Thomas Nelson, 2001.

Barth, Karl. *Die Lehre vom Wort Gottes*, vol. 1 of *Die Kirchliche Dogmatik*. Freudenstadt: Heesen, 1947.

—. *Die Offenbarung Gottes*, vol. 2 of *Die Kirchliche Dogmatik*. Zollikon-Zürich: Theologischer Verlag Zürich, 1948.

—. *The Doctrine of God*, vol. 2 of *Church Dogmatics*. Translated by G.W. Bromiley. Edinburgh: T&T Clark, 1957.

—. *Evangelical Theology*. Translated by Grover Foley. Warfield Lectures. Zürich: EVZ-Verlag, 1979.

Bartholomew, Craig C. *Introducing Biblical Hermeneutics: A Comprehensive Framework for Hearing God in Scripture*. Grand Rapids: Eerdmans, 2015.

Bavinck, Herman. *Reformed Dogmatics*. Translated by John Vriend. 4 vols. Grand Rapids: Eerdmans, 2003–2008.

Bebbington, David W. *Evangelicalism in Modern Britain: A History from the 1730s to the 1980s*. London: Routledge, 2002.

Becker, Matthias. "A Tenet Under Examination: Reflections on the Pentecostal Hermeneutical Approach." *Journal of the European Pentecostal Theological Association* 24 (2004) 30–48.

Bediako, Kwame. *Christianity in Africa: The Renewal of a Non-Western Religion*. Edinburgh: Edinburgh University Press, 1995.

—. "Epilogue." In *On Their Way Rejoicing: The History and Role of the Bible in Africa*, edited by Ype Schaaf, 243–54. African Challenge series of the AACC 5. Akropong: Regnum Africa, 2002.

Berger, Peter L. "Four Faces of Global Culture." In *Globalization and the Challenges of a New Century: A Reader*, edited by Patrick O'Meara, Howard D. Melinger, and Matthew Krain, 419–27. Bloomington: Indiana University Press, 2000.

—. *A Rumour of Angels: Modern Society and the Rediscovery of the Supernatural*. New York: Doubleday, 1969.

Berkouwer, G. C. *Holy Scripture*. Studies in Dogmatics. Grand Rapids: Eerdmans, 1975.

Bernard, Robert W. "The Hermeneutics of the Early Church Fathers." In *Biblical Hermeneutics*, edited by Bruce Corley, Steve W. Lemke, and Grant I. Lovejoy, 90–100. 2nd ed. Nashville: Broadman & Holman, 2002.

Bezuidenhout, Marthinus E. J. "Pauliniese Kriteria ten opsigte van die Beoefening van die Charismata: 'n Eksegetiese Studie van 1 Kor 12–14." DD diss., University of Pretoria, 1980.

Bloesch, Donald G. *A Theology of Word and Spirit: Authority and Method in Theology*. Downers Grove, IL: InterVarsity, 2005.

Blumhofer, Edith L. *Aimee Semple McPherson: Everybody's Sister*. Grand Rapids: Eerdmans, 1993.

—. *To 1941*. Vol. 1 of *The Assemblies of God: A Chapter in the Story of American Pentecostalism*. Springfield, MO: Gospel, 1989.

Bonhoeffer, Dietrich. *Ethics*. Translated by Reinhard Krauss. New York: Macmillan, 1955.

—. *Life Together: The Classic Exploration of Christian Community*. Translated by Gerhard Ludwig Müller and Albrecht Schönherr. Dietrich Bonhoeffer Works 5. Minneapolis: Fortress, 1996.

Boone, Kathleen C. *The Bible Tells Them So: The Discourse of Protestant Fundamentalism.* Albany: State University of New York Press, 1989.

Bosch, David J. "The Traditional Religions of Africa: Study Guide for MSR203." Pretoria: University of South Africa, 1975.

Bowdle, Donald N. "Informed Pentecostalism: An Alternative Paradigm." In *The Spirit and the Mind: Essays in Informed Pentecostalism,* edited by Terry L. Cross and Emerson B. Powery, 9–19. Lanham, MD: University Press of America, 2000.

Brookes, James H. "Studying the Bible." *Truth* 5 (1879) 5–6.

Brueggemann, Walter. *Theology of the Old Testament: Testimony, Dispute, Advocacy.* Minneapolis: Fortress, 1997.

Brunner, Emil. *The Word and the World.* New York: Scribner's Sons, 1931.

Bruns, Gerald L. "Midrash and Allegory: The Beginnings of Scriptural Interpretation." In *The Literary Guide to the Bible,* edited by Robert Alter and Frank Kermode, 625–46. Cambridge, MA: Harvard University Press, 1987.

Bultmann, Rudolph. "The Problem of Hermeneutics." In *New Testament Mythology and Other Basic Writings,* edited by Schubert M. Ogden, 69–93. Philadelphia: Fortress, 1984.

Burger, Isak, and Marius Nel. *The Fire Falls in Africa: A History of the Apostolic Faith Mission of South Africa.* Vereeniging: Christian Art, 2006.

Burgess, Stanley M., ed. *Christian Peoples of the Spirit: A Documentary History of Pentecostal Spirituality from the Early Church to the Present.* New York: New York University Press, 2011.

Byrd, Joseph. "Paul Ricoeur's Hermeneutical Theory and Pentecostal Proclamation." *Pneuma* 15.1 (1993) 203–14.

Cargal, Timothy B. "Beyond the Fundamentalist-Modernist Controversy: Pentecostals and Hermeneutics in a Postmodern Era." *Pneuma* 15.2 (1993) 163–87.

Carson, D. A. *Exegetical Fallacies.* Grand Rapids: Baker, 1984.

Cartledge, Mark J. "Locating the Spirit in Meaningful Experience: Empirical Theology and Pentecostal Hermeneutics." In *Constructive Pneumatological Hermeneutics in Pentecostal Christianity,* edited by Kenneth J. Archer and L. William Oliverio, 251–66. New York: Palgrave Macmillan, 2016.

———. "Pentecostal Theology." In *The Cambridge Companion to Pentecostalism,* edited by Cecil M. Robeck and Amos Young, 254–72. New York: Cambridge University Press, 2014.

———. "Text-Community-Spirit: The Challenges Posed by Pentecostal Theological Method to Evangelical Theology." In *Spirit and Scripture: Exploring a Pneumatic Hermeneutic,* edited by Kevin L. Spawn and Archie T. Wright, 130–43. New York: Bloomsbury, 2012.

Castelo, Daniel. "*Diakrisis* Always *En Conjunto*: First Theology Understood from a Latino/a Context." In *Constructive Pneumatological Hermeneutics in Pentecostal Christianity,* edited by Kenneth J. Archer and L. William Oliverio, 197–210. New York: Palgrave Macmillan, 2016.

———. "Tarrying on the Lord: Affections, Virtues, and Theological Ethics in Pentecostal Perspective." *Journal of Pentecostal Theology* 13.1 (2004) 31–56.

Chance, J. Bradley. *Acts.* Macon: Smyth & Helwys, 2007.

Chanda, Davies. "History of Pentecostalism in Zambia." *Times of Zambia,* 2 September 2015. http://www.times.co.zm/?p=66547.

Chapman, Mark E. "The Spirit and the Magisterium: Authority in the Community of Freedom." *The Ecumenical Review* 42.4 (1990) 268–78.

Cherok, Richard J. "Common Sense Philosophy." In *Encyclopedia of Fundamentalism*, edited by Brenda E. Brasher, 107. New York: Routledge, 2001.

Chinappan, M. *In Covenant Bible College, Durban*. Brochure 1983–1993.

Christian Action. "Threats to Freedom of Speech in South Africa." https://www.christianaction.org.za/index.php/articles/religious-freedom/878-threats-to-freedom-of-speech-in-south-africa.

"Church Members Defend Pastor Who Sprays Them With Insecticide." *Punch*, 28 November 2016. http://www.punchng.com/church-members-defend-pastor-spray-insecticide.

Clark, Matthew. "Contemporary Pentecostal Leadership: The Apostolic Faith Mission of South Africa as Case Study." *Asian Journal of Pentecostal Studies* 10.1 (2007) 42–61.

———. "An Investigation into the Nature of a Viable Pentecostal Hermeneutic." DTh diss., University of South Africa, 1997.

———. "Pentecostalism and Philosophy of Religion." Philosophy and Religious Practices Workshop, 9 May 2013, University of Liverpool. https://philosophyreligion.wordpress.com/2013/05/19/mathew-clark-pentecostalism-and-philosophy-of-religion.

Clark, Mathew S., and Henry I. Lederle. *What Is Distinctive about Pentecostal Theology?* Miscellanea Specialia 1, UNISA. Pretoria: University of South Africa, 1989.

Clines, David J. A. "A World Established on Water (Psalm 24): Reader-Response, Deconstruction and Bespoke Interpretation." In *Interested Parties: The Ideology of Writers and Readers of the Hebrew Bible*, edited by David J. A. Clines, 172–86. JSOT Supp 205. Gender, Culture, Theory 1. Sheffield: Sheffield Academic, 1995.

Cole, Casey S. "Taking Hermeneutics to Heart: Proposing an Orthopathic Reading for Texts of Terror Via the Rape of Tamar Narrative." *Pneuma* 39.3 (2017) 264–74.

Collins, James. "Deliverance and Exorcism in the Twentieth Century." In *Exorcism & Deliverance: Multi-Disciplinary Studies*, edited by William K. Kay and Robin Parry, 69–85. Milton Keynes: Paternoster, 2011.

Collins, John J. *Introduction to the Hebrew Bible*. Minneapolis: Fortress, 2004.

Cone, James H. *A Black Theology of Liberation*. Maryknoll, NY: Orbis, 2012.

Conzelmann, Hans. *The Theology of St Luke*. Translated by Geoffrey Bushwell. 2nd ed. New York: Harper & Row, 1961.

Cox, Harvey. *Fire From Heaven: The Rise of Pentecostal Spirituality and the Reshaping of Religion in the Twenty-First Century*. New York: Addison-Wesley, 1995.

———. *How to Read the Bible*. San Francisco: HarperOne, 2016.

Craven, Patrick. "Beware All Prophets of Doom." *Daily Maverick*, 8 February 2017. https://www.dailymaverick.co.za/opinionista/2017-02-08-beware-all-prophets-of-doom.

Croatto, Severino. *Biblical Hermeneutics: Toward a Theory of Reading as the Production of Meaning*. Translated by R. R. Barr. Maryknoll, NY: Orbis, 1987.

Cronjé, Frank H. J. "Die AGS Teologiese Kollege." In *AGS Werkersraadverslagbundel*. Johannesburg: AGS Drukkers, 1979.

Cross, Terry L. "The Rich Feast of Theology: Can Pentecostals Bring the Main Course or Only the Relish?" *Journal for Pentecostal Theology* 16 (2000) 27–47.

Dabney, D. Lyle. "Why Should the Last Be First? The Priority of Pneumatology in Recent Theological Discussion." In *Advents of the Spirit: An Introduction to the Current Study of Pneumatology*, edited by Bradford E. Hinze and D. Lyle Dabney, 240–61. Milwaukee: Marquette University Press, 2001.

Dados, Nour, and Raewyn Connell. "The Global South." *Jargon* 11.1 (2012) 12–13. http://journals.sagepub.com/doi/pdf/10.1177/1536504212436479

Daneel, Marthinus L. *Quest for Belonging*. Gweru: Mambo, 1987.

Daniels, David D. "Everyone Bids You Welcome: A Multicultural Approach to North American Pentecostalism." In *Globalization of Pentecostalism*, edited by Murray W. Dempster, Byron D. Klaus, and Douglas Petersen, 222–52. Irvine: Regnum, 1999.

Daniels, William H., ed. *Moody: His Words, Works, and Workers*. New York: Nelson and Phillips, 1877.

Daunton-Fear, Andrew. "Deliverance and Exorcism in the Early Church." In *Exorcism & Deliverance: Multi-Disciplinary Studies*, edited by William K. Kay and Robin Parry, 69–85. Milton Keynes: Paternoster, 2011.

Dayton, Donald W. "Holiness Movement, American." In *The New International Dictionary of the Christian Church*, edited by J. D. Douglas, 475. Grand Rapids: Zondervan, 1974.

Dayton, Donald W. *Theological Roots of Pentecostalism*. Peabody, MA: Hendrickson, 1987.

Davies, Andrew. "What Does It Mean to Read the Bible as a Pentecostal?" In *Pentecostal Hermeneutics: A Reader*, edited by Lee Roy Martin, 249–62. Leiden: Brill, 2013.

Davies, Philip R. *Daniel*. Old Testament Guides. Sheffield: JSOT Press, 1985.

De Beer, Frederic J. "The Valence of Spirit Manifestation, and its Influence on the Transformation of the Mind and Redemption of the Body and Flesh according to Romans 8 and 12 and its Application in a Secular Society." DLitt et Phil diss., University of Johannesburg, 2013.

Dela Cruz, Roli G. "Preaching Among Filipino Pentecostals and Exposition Through Testimonial Hermeneutics: A Positive Contribution of the PGCAG to Evangelicalism in the Philippines." *Asian Journal for Pentecostal Studies* 31.1 (2010) 98–123.

Dempster, Murray W. "The Search for Pentecostal Identity." *Pneuma* 15.1 (1993) 1–8.

DeSilva, David A. *An Introduction to the New Testament: Contexts, Methods & Ministry Formation*. Downers Grove: InterVarsity, 2004.

Detel, Wolfgang. *Geist und Verstehen*. Frankfurt am Main: Vittorio Klostermann, 2011.

De Villiers, Etienne. "Do the Prophetic and Reformist Approaches in Christian Ethics Exclude One Another? A Responsibility Ethics Attempt at Reconciliation." In *Prophecy Today: Reflections From a Southern African Context*, edited by Hermen Kroesbergen, 148–62. Special Edition of Word and Context Journal. Wellington: Christian Literature Fund, 2016.

De Wet, Christiaan R. "The Apostolic Faith Mission in Africa: 1908–1980: A Case Study in Church Growth in a Segregated Society." PhD diss., University of Cape Town, 1989.

"Dispensationalism." *Theopedia*. https://www.theopedia.com/dispensationalism.

Dunn, James D. G. *Baptism in the Holy Spirit: A Re-Examination of the New Testament Teaching on the Gift of the Spirit in Relation to Pentecostalism Today*. Studies in Biblical Theology 15. London: SCM, 1970.

———. "The Role of the Spirit in Biblical Hermeneutics." In *Spirit and Scripture: Exploring a Pneumatic Hermeneutic*, edited by Kevin L. Spawn and Archie T. Wright, 154–59. New York: Bloomsbury, 2012.

Du Plessis, David J. *The Spirit Bade Me Go*. Rev. ed. California: Self-published, 1963.

Efird, James M. *How to Interpret the Bible*. Eugene, OR: Wipf and Stock, 1984.

Ehrman, Bart. *Lost Christianities: The Battle for Scripture and the Faiths We Never Knew*. Oxford: Oxford University Press, 2003.

———. *The New Testament: A Historical Introduction to the Early Christian Writings*. 4th ed. New York: Oxford University Press, 2008.

Ellington, Mark. *The Evangelical Movement*. Minneapolis: Augsburg, 1988.

Ellington, Scott A. "History, Story, and Testimony: Locating Truth in a Pentecostal Hermeneutic." *Pneuma* 23.2 (2001) 245–63.

———. "Locating Pentecostals at the Hermeneutical Round Table." *Journal of Pentecostal Theology* 22.2 (2013) 206–25.

———. "Pentecostals and the Authority of Scriptures." *Journal of Pentecostal Theology* 4.9 (1996) 16–38.

———. "Pentecostalism and the Authority of Scriptures." In *Pentecostal Hermeneutics: A Reader*, edited by Lee Roy Martin, 149–70. Leiden: Brill, 2013.

Erasmus, Nelie. "Judge Extends Ruling on 'Doom' Pastor." *Polokwane Observer*, 23 March 2017. http://www.observer.co.za/judge-extends-ruling-on-doom-pastor-2.

Erickson, Millard J. *Christian Theology*. Grand Rapids: Baker, 1985.

Ervin, Howard M. "Hermeneutics: A Pentecostal Option." *Pneuma* 2.2 (1981) 11–25.

Everts, Janet. "Missionary Tongues?" Annual Meeting of the Society for Pentecostal Studies, 11–13 November 1993, Guadalajara, Mexico.

Fackre, Gabriele. *The Christian Story: A Narrative of Basic Christian Doctrine*. 3rd ed. Grand Rapids: Eerdmans, 1996.

———. "Narrative Theology: An Overview." *Interpretation* 37 (1983) 340–52.

Faeza. "Pastor Sprays Congregants With Doom to Drive Away Demons." *Move!Mag*, 21 November 2016. https://www.news24.com/MoveMag/Archive/pastor-sprays-congregants-with-doom-to-drive-away-demons-20170728.

Falwell, Jerry. *The Fundamentalist Phenomenon: The Resurgence of Conservative Christianity*. Grand Rapids: Baker, 1986.

Farrell, Frank. "Outburst of Tongues: The New Penetration. *Christianity Today* 13.5 (1963) 4–5.

Faupel, David W. *The Everlasting Gospel: The Significance of Eschatology in the Development of Pentecostal Thought*. Sheffield: Sheffield Academic, 1996.

Fee, Gordon D. *God's Empowering Presence: The Holy Spirit in the Letters of Paul*. Peabody, MA: Hendrickson, 1994.

———. *Gospel and Spirit: Issues in New Testament Hermeneutics*. Grand Rapids: Baker Academic, 1991.

———. *To What End Exegesis?: Essays Textual, Exegetical, and Theological*. Grand Rapids: Eerdmans, 2001.

Fee, Gordon D., and Douglas Stuart. *How to Read the Bible for All It's Worth*. 3rd ed. Grand Rapids: Zondervan, 2003.

Fish, Stanley. *Is There a Text In This Class? The Authority of Interpretive Communities*. Cambridge: Harvard University Press, 1980.

"Five Policemen Dead in Attack on Station." *ENCA*, 21 February 2018. https://www.enca.com/south-africa/five-police-dead-in-attack-on-station.

Flood, Derek. *Disarming Scripture: Cherry-Picking Liberals, Violence-Loving Conservatives, and Why We All Need to Learn to Read the Bible Like Jesus Did.* San Francisco: Metanoia, 2014.

Fogarty, Stephen. "Toward a Pentecostal Hermeneutic." *Pentecostal Charismatic Bible Colleges* 5.2 (2015). http://webjournals.ac.edu.au/journals/PCBC/vol5-no2/toward-a-pentecostalhermeneutic.

Forrester, Duncan B. "Christianity in Europe." In *Religion in Europe: Contemporary Perspectives*, edited by Sean Gill, Gavin da Costa, and Ursula King, 34–45. Kampen: Kok Pharos, 1994.

Fowl, Stephen E. *Engaging Scripture: A Model for Theological Interpretation.* Oxford: Blackwell, 1998.

Frahm-Arp, Maria. "The Rise of the Megachurches in South Africa." In *Africa*, vol. 3 of *Global Renewal Christianity: Spirit-Empowered Movements Past, Present, and Future*, edited by Vinson Synan, Amos Yong, and J. Kwabena Asamoah-Gyadu, 263–84. Lake Mary, FL: Charisma House, 2016.

Frei, Hans W. *The Eclipse of Biblical Narrative: A Study in Eighteenth and Nineteenth Century Hermeneutics.* New Haven: Yale University Press, 1974.

Frend, W. H. C. *The Early Church: From the Beginnings to 461.* 2nd ed. London: SCM, 1982.

Gadamer, Hans-Georg. *Philosophical Hermeneutics.* Translated by David E. Linge. Berkeley: University of California Press, 1976.

———. *Truth and Method.* Translated by William Glen-Doepel. London: Sheed and Ward, 1979.

———. *Wahrheit und Methode: Grundzüge Einer Philosophischen Hermeneutik.* 2nd ed. Tübingen: Mohr, 1965.

García-Martínez, Florentino. "Encore l'Apocalyptique." *Journal of Scientific Studies* 17 (1987) 230.

Gasque, W. W. *A History of the Criticism of the Acts of the Apostles.* Grand Rapids: Eerdmans, 1975.

Gee, Donald. *Pentecost.* Springfield, MO: Gospel, 1932.

Gerlach, L. P. "Pentecostalism: Revolution or Counter-Revolution?" In *Religious Movements in Contemporary America*, edited by I. I. Zaretsky and M. P. Leone, 669–99. Princeton: Princeton University Press, 1974.

González, Justo L. *Mañana: Christian Theology from a Hispanic Perspective.* Nashville: Abingdon, 1990.

Goff, Christopher W. *Measuring the Clergy/Laity Gap and its Effect on Church Health and Outreach.* Eisenhower: ProQuest, 2008.

Goldingay, John. "Biblical Story and the Way It Shapes our Story." *Journal of the European Pentecostal Theological Association* 17 (1997) 5–15.

———. *Models for Scripture.* Grand Rapids: Eerdmans, 1994.

Goff, James R. *Fields White unto Harvest: Charles F. Parham and the Missionary Origins of Pentecostalism.* Fayetteville, AR: University of Arkansas Press, 1988.

Gräbe, Peter J. "Hermeneutical Reflections on the Interpretation of the New Testament with Special Reference to the Holy Spirit and Faith." In *The Reality of the Holy Spirit in the Church: In Honour of F. P. Möller*, edited by Peter J. Gräbe and Willem J. Hattingh, 14–26. Pretoria: JL van Schaik, 1997.

Grady, J. Lee. "Five Ways Prosperity Gospel Is Hurting Africa." *Charisma*. 13 November 2011. http://www.charismamag.com/blogs/fire-in-my-bones/19113-5-ways-the-prosperity-gospel-is-hurting-africa.

Grant, Frederick C. *Hellenistic Religions: The Age of Syncretism*. New York: Liberal Arts, 1953.

"Grass-eating Pastor Now Has Congregation Drinking Petrol." *ENCA*, 24 September 2014. https://www.enca.com/shock-scenes-grass-pastor-giving-his-congregation-petrol-drink.

Green, Chris E. W. *Toward a Pentecostal Theology of the Lord's Supper: Foretasting the Kingdom*. Cleveland, TN: CPT, 2012.

———. "'Treasures Old and New': Reading the Old Testament with Early Pentecostal Mothers and Fathers." *41st Annual Meeting of the Society for Pentecostal Studies*, 29 March–3 April 2015, Virginia Beach, VA, 1–20.

Green, Joel B. "Modern and Postmodern Methods of Biblical Interpretation." In *Scripture and Its Interpretation: A Global, Ecumenical Introduction to the Bible*, edited by Michael J. Horman, 187–204. Grand Rapids: Baker Academic, 2017.

———. "Pentecostal Hermeneutics: A Wesleyan Perspective." In *Constructive Pneumatological Hermeneutics in Pentecostal Christianity*, edited by Kenneth J. Archer and L. William Oliverio, 159–74. New York: Palgrave Macmillan, 2016.

Green, Michael. *I Believe in the Holy Spirit*. Grand Rapids: Eerdmans, 1975.

Grenz, Stanley J. *Revisioning Evangelical Theology: A Fresh Agenda for the 21st Century*. Downers Grove: InterVarsity, 1993.

Grogan, Geoffrey. "Is the Bible Hermeneutically Self-Sufficient?" In *Interpreting the Bible: Historical and Theological Studies in Honour of David F. Wright*, edited by A. N. S. Lane, 205–21. Leicester: Apollos, 1997.

Groome, Thomas H. *Christian Religious Education*. San Francisco: Harper & Row, 1980.

Hanson, P. D. "Apocalypticism." In *The Interpreter's One-Volume Commentary on the Bible*, edited by C. M. Layman, 27–28. London: Collins, 1976.

———. *The Dawn of Apocalyptic. The Historical and Sociological Roots of Jewish Apocalyptic Eschatology*. Rev. ed. Philadelphia: Fortress, 1979.

———. *Isaiah 40–66*. Louisville: John Knox, 1995.

Harper, Michael. "The Waves Keep Coming In." *Journal of the European Pentecostal Theological Association* 28.2 (2008) 102–17.

Harrison, Roland K. *Introduction to the Old Testament*. Grand Rapids: Eerdmans, 1969.

Hart, Trevor. *Faith Thinking: The Dynamics of Christian Theology*. London: SPCK, 1995.

Hastings, Adrian. *African Christianity*. London: Geoffrey Chapman, 1976.

Hauerwas, Stanley. *Unleashing the Scripture: Freeing the Bible from Captivity to America*. Nashville: Abingdon, 1993.

Hauerwas, Stanley, and William H. Willimon. *Resident Aliens: A Provocative Christian Assessment of Culture and Ministry for People Who Know that Something Is Wrong*. Nashville: Abingdon, 2014.

Hawk, L. Daniel. *Every Promise Fulfilled: Contesting Plots in Joshua*. Louisville: Westminster John Knox, 1991.

Healey, Joseph, and Donald Sybertz. *Towards an African Narrative Theology*. Maryknoll, NY: Orbis, 1996.

Hebner, Christine. "Introduction: Multivalence in Biblical Theology." In *The Multivalence of Biblical Texts and Theological Meanings*, edited by Christine Helmer and Charlene T. Higbe, 1–10. Atlanta: Society of Biblical Theology, 2006.

Hine, Virginia H. "The Deprivation and Disorganization Theories of Social Movements." In *Religious Movements in Contemporary America*, edited by Irving I. Zaretsky and Mark P. Leone, 646–61. Princeton: Princeton University Press, 1974.

Holdcroft, L. Thomas. *The Holy Spirit: A Pentecostal Interpretation.* Springfield, MO: Gospel, 1979.

Hollenweger, Walter J. "After Twenty Years' Research on Pentecostalism." *International Review of Missions* 75.297 (1986) 3–12.

———. "From Azusa Street to Toronto Phenomenon: Historical Roots of the Pentecostal Movement." *Concilium* 3.6 (1993) 3–14.

———. *The Pentecostals.* London: SCM, 1988.

———. *Pentecostalism: Origins and Developments Worldwide.* Peabody, MA: Hendrickson, 1997.

Holm, R. "Cadences of the Heart: A Walkabout in Search of Pentecostal Preaching." *Didaskalia* 7.1 (2003) 3–27.

Horton, Stanley M., ed. *Systematic Theology.* Springfield, IL: Logion, 1994.

Huckle, John S. "The Contemporary Use of the Gift of Prophecy in Gatherings of Christians in Comparison with their Use in the 20th Century." *Journal of the European Pentecostal Theological Association* 29.1 (2009) 73–86.

Hunt, Stephen J. "Dispensationalism." In *Handbook of Pentecostal Christianity*, edited by Alan Stewart, 60–64. DeKalb: Northern Illinois University Press, 2012.

Institute for Contextual Theology. *Speaking for Ourselves.* Braamfontein: ICT, 1985.

Jacobsen, Douglas. "The Ambivalent Ecumenical Impulses in Early Pentecostal Theology in North America." In *Pentecostalism and Christian Unity: Ecumenical Documents and Critical Assessments*, edited by Wolfgang Vondey, 3–19. Eugene, OR: Pickwick, 2010.

———. *Global Gospel: An Introduction to Christianity on Five Continents.* Grand Rapids: Baker, 2015.

———. "Knowing the Doctrines of Pentecostals: The Scholastic Theology of the Assemblies of God, 1930–55." In *Pentecostal Currents in American Protestantism*, edited by Edith L. Blumhofer, Russell L. Spittler, and Grant Wacker, 90–107. Urbana: University of Illinois Press, 1999.

———. ed. *A Reader in Pentecostal Theology: Voices from the First Generation.* Bloomington: Indiana University Press, 2006.

———. *Thinking in the Spirit: Theologies of the Early Pentecostal Movement.* Bloomington: Indiana University Press, 2003.

———. *The World's Christians: Who They Are, Where They Are, and How They Got There.* West Sussex, UK: Wiley-Blackwell, 2011.

Jeanrond, Werner G. "Biblical Interpretation as Appropriation of Texts: The Need for a Closer Cooperation Between Biblical Exegetes and Systematic Theologians." *Proceedings of the Irish Biblical Association* 6 (1982) 1–18.

———. *Text Und Interpretation als Kategorien Theologischen Denkens.* Hermeneutische Untersuchungen zur Theologie 23. Tübingen: JCB Mohr, 1986.

Jerome. *St. Jerome: Commentary on Galatians.* Translated by Andrew Cain. Washington, DC: Catholic University of America Press, 2010.

John C. Hutchison, "Bible Study." In *Encyclopedia of Fundamentalism*, edited by Brenda E. Brasher, 63–64. New York: Routledge, 2001.

Johns, Cheryl B. "The Adolescence of Pentecostalism: In Search of a Legitimate Sectarian Identity." *Pneuma* 17 (1995) 3–17.

————. *Pentecostal Formation: A Pedagogy among the Suppressed.* JPT Supp 2. Sheffield: Sheffield Academic, 1993.

Johns, Jackie David. "Pentecostalism and the Postmodern Worldview." *Journal for Pentecostal Theology* 7 (1995) 73–96.

Johns, Jackie David, and Cheryl Bridges Johns. "Yielding to the Spirit: A Pentecostal Approach to Group Bible Study." In *Pentecostal Hermeneutics: A Reader,* edited by Lee Roy Martin, 33–56. Leiden: Brill, 2013.

Johns, Kenneth D. *The Pentecostal Paradigm: A Seductive Paradise.* Xlibris: Privately published, 2007.

Johnson, Luke T. *Religious Experience in Earliest Christianity: A Missing Dimension in New Testament Studies.* Minneapolis: Fortress, 1998.

Johnson, Todd M., David B. Barrett, and Peter F. Crossing. "Christianity 2010: A View from the *New Atlas of Global Christianity.*" *International Bulletin of Missionary Research* 34.1 (2010) 29–36.

Johnstone, Patrick. *The Future of the Global Church: History, Trends, and Possibilities.* Downers Grove: InterVarsity, 2011.

Joubert, Stephan. "Not by Order, Nor by Dialogue: The *Metanoetic* Presence of the Kingdom of God in a Fluid New World and Church." *Acta Theologica* 33.1 (2013) 114–34.

Kaiser, Walter C., and Moisés Silva. *Introduction to Biblical Hermeneutics: The Search for Meaning.* Rev. ed. Grand Rapids: Zondervan, 1994.

Kasper, Walter. "Prolegomena zur Erneuerung der Geistlichen Schriftauslegung." In *Vom Urchristentum zu Jesus: Für Joachim Gnilka,* edited by Hubert Frankemölle and Karl Kertelge, 508–52. Freiburg: Herder, 1989.

Kalu, Ogbu. *African Pentecostalism: An Introduction.* New York: Oxford University Press, 2008.

Kangwa, Jonathan. "African Democracy and Political Exploitation: An Appraisal of Xenophobia and the Removal of the Rhodes Statue in South Africa." *The Expository Times* 127.11 (2016) 534–45.

Kanyoro, Musimbi R. A. *Introducing Feminist Cultural Hermeneutics: An African Perspective.* Cleveland: Pilgrim, 2002.

Kärkkäinen, Veli-Matti. "Anonymous Ecumenists? Pentecostals and the Struggle for Christian Unity." *Journal of Ecumenical Studies* 37.1 (2000) 13–27.

————. "Pentecostal Hermeneutics in the Making: On the Way from Fundamentalism to Postmodernism." *Journal of the European Theological Association* 18 (1998) 76–115.

————. *Pneumatology: The Holy Spirit in Ecumenical, International, and Contextual Perspective.* Grand Rapids: Baker Academic, 2002.

————. *Spiritus Ubi Vult Spirat: Pneumatology in Roman Catholic-Pentecostal Dialogue (1972–1989).* Schriften der Luther-Agricola-Gesellschaft 42. Helsinki: Luther-Agricola Society, 1998.

Katho, Bungishabaku. "African Biblical Interpretation." In *Scripture and Its Interpretation: A Global, Ecumenical Introduction to the Bible,* edited by Michael J. Horman, 284–97. Grand Rapids: Baker Academic, 2017.

Keegan, Terence J. *Interpreting the Bible: A Popular Introduction to Biblical Hermeneutics.* New York: Paulist, 1985.

Keel, Othmar, ed. *Monotheismus im Alten Israel und Seiner Umwelt.* Oxford, UK: Blackwell, 1980.

Keener, Craig S. *Acts: An Exegetical Commentary.* 4 vols. Grand Rapids: Baker Academic, 2012–2015.

———. "Biblical Fidelity as an Evangelical Commitment." In *Following Jesus: Journeys in Radical Discipleship: Essays in Honor of Ronald J. Sider,* edited by Paul Alexander and Al Tizon, 29–41. Regnum Studies in Global Christianity. Oxford: Regnum, 2013.

———. *Mind of the Spirit: Paul's Approach to Transformed Thinking.* Grand Rapids: Baker Academic, 2016.

———. *Miracles: The Credibility of the New Testament Accounts.* 2 vols. Grand Rapids: Baker Academic, 2011.

———. "Pentecostal Biblical Interpretation/Spirit Hermeneutics." In *Scripture and Its Interpretation: A Global, Ecumenical Introduction to the Bible,* edited by Michael J. Horman, 270–83. Grand Rapids: Baker Academic, 2017.

———. *Spirit Hermeneutics: Reading Scripture in Light of Pentecost.* Grand Rapids: Eerdmans, 2016.

Keener, Craig S. and M. Daniel Carroll. "Introduction." In *Global Voices: Reading the Bible in the Majority World,* edited by Craig Keener and M. Daniel Carroll, 1–4. Peabody, MA: Hendrickson, 2013.

Kennedy, Philip. *A Modern Introduction to Theology: New Questions for Old Beliefs.* London: IB Tauris, 2006.

Kenyon, Esek W. *Identification: A Romance in Redemption.* Seattle, WA: Kenyon's Gospel Publishing Society, 1968.

King, J. D. *Salvation Healing through Third Wave.* Vol. 2 of *Regeneration: A Complete History of Healing in the Christian Church.* Lee's Summit, MO: Christos, 2017.

King, Gerald W. "Streams of Convergence: The Pentecostal-Fundamentalist Response to Modernism." *PentecoStudies* 7.2 (2008) 64–84.

Kingsolver, Barbara. *The Poisonwood Bible.* New York: HarperCollins, 1998.

Kinyua, Johnson K. *Introducing Ordinary African Readers' Hermeneutics: A Case Study of the Agikuyu Encounter with the Bible.* Religions and Discourse 54. Oxford: Peter Lang, 2011.

Klaus, Byron D. "Pentecostalism and Mission." *Missiology* 35.1 (2007) 39–54.

Klein, William W., Craig L. Blomberg, and Robert L. Hubbard. *Introduction to Biblical Interpretation.* 3rd ed. Grand Rapids: Zondervan, 2017.

Koch, Klaus. "Is Daniel Also Among the Prophets?" In *Interpreting the Prophets,* edited by James L. Mays and Paul J. Achtemeier, 237–48. Philadelphia: Fortress, 1987.

Kombo, James H. *The Doctrine of God in African Christian Thought: The Holy Trinity, Theological Hermeneutics and the African Intellectual Climate.* Studies in Reformed Theology 14. Leiden: Brill, 2007.

Kraus, C. N. "The Great Evangelical Coalition: Pentecostals and Fundamentals." In *Evangelicalism and Anabaptism,* edited by C. N. Kraus, 39–62. Scottdale, PA: Herald, 1979.

Kroesbergen-Kamps, Johanneke. "Prophetic Struggles: Zambian Pastors' Diverse Views on Prophecy." In *Prophecy Today: Reflections from a Southern African Context,* edited by Hermen Kroesbergen, 28–40. Special Edition of Word and Context Journal. Wellington: Christian Literature Fund, 2016.

Kruger, Michael J. *The Question of Canon: Challenging the Status Quo in the New Testament Debate.* Downers Grove: InterVarsity, 2013.

LaCocque, André. *Daniel and His Time.* Studies of Personalities of the Old Testament. Columbia: University of South Carolina Press, 1988.

LaCugna, Catherine M. *God for Us: The Trinity and Christian Life.* San Francisco: HarperSanFrancisco, 1993.

Laing, Mark. "The Changing Face of Mission: Implications for the Southern Shift in Christianity." *Missiology* 34.2 (2006) 165–77.

Land, Steven J. *Pentecostal Spirituality: A Passion for the Kingdom.* Cleveland, TN: CPT, 1993.

Lang, Bernhard, ed. *Der Einzige Gott: Die Geburt die Biblischen Monotheismus.* Münich: Kosel, 1981.

Larue, Gerald A. *Old Testament Life and Literature.* Boston: Allyn and Beacon, 1970.

Lategan, Bernard. "Hermeneutics." In *Anchor Bible Dictionary,* edited by David N. Freedman, 153–4. 6 vols. New York: Doubleday, 1992.

———. "New Testament Hermeneutics (Part I): Defining Moments in the Development of Biblical Hermeneutics." In *Focusing on the Message: New Testament Hermeneutics, Exegesis and Methods,* edited by Andri du Toit, 13–63. Pretoria: Protea, 2009.

———. "New Testament Hermeneutics (Part II): Mapping the Biblical Hermeneutics." In *Focusing on the Message: New Testament Hermeneutics, Exegesis and Methods,* edited by Andri du Toit, 65–105. Pretoria: Protea, 2009.

Lederle, Henry. *Treasures Old and New: Interpretation of the Spirit Baptism in the Charismatic Renewal Movement.* Peabody, MA: Hendrickson, 1988.

Lee, Moonyang. "Future of Global Christianity." In *Atlas of Global Christianity, 1910–2010,* edited by Todd M. Johnson and Kenneth R. Ross, 104–5. Edinburgh: Center for the Study of Global Christianity, 2009.

LeMarquand, Grant. "New Testament Exegesis in (Modern) Africa." *Journal for the Study of the New Testament* 30.1 (2007) 7–28.

Leoh, Vincent. "Eschatology and Pneumatic Preaching with a Case of David Yonggi Cho." *Asian Journal for Pentecostal Studies* 10.1 (2007) 101–11.

Lewis, Paul W. "Reflections of a Hundred Years of Pentecostal Theology." *Cyberjournal for Pentecostal-Charismatic Research* 12 (2003) 1–25. http://www.pctii.org/cyberj/cyberj12/lewis.htm#_ftn1.

Liddell, Henry G. *A Lexicon: Abridged from Liddell and Scott's Greek-English Lexicon.* Oak Harbor, WA: Logos Research Systems, 1996.

Loba-Mkole, Jean-Claude. "The New Testament and Intercultural Exegesis in Africa." *Journal for the Study of the New Testament* 30.1 (2007) 7–28.

Lochmann, Jan M. *Das Glaubensbekenntnis: Grundriss der Dogmatik im Anschluss an das Credo.* Gütersloh: Gütersloher Verlagshaus Gerd Mohn, 1982.

Louw, Johannes P. "Reading a Text as Discourse." In *Linguistics and New Interpretation: Essays on Discourse Analysis,* edited by David Alan Black, 17–30. Nashville: Broadman, 1992.

Ma, Wonsuk. "Full Circle Mission: A Possibility of Pentecostal Missiology." *Asian Journal of Pentecostal Studies* 8.1 (2005) 5–27.

Macchia, Frank. "Babel and the Tongues of Pentecost: Reversal or Fulfilment? A Theological Perspective." In *Speaking in Tongues: Multidisciplinary Approaches,* edited by Mark J. Cartledge, 34–51. Studies in Pentecostal and Charismatic Issues. Paternoster: Waynesboro, 2006.

———. *Baptized in the Spirit: A Global Pentecostal Theology.* Grand Rapids: Zondervan, 2006.

MacRoberts, Iain. *The Black Roots and White Racism of Early Pentecostalism in the USA.* Basingstoke: Macmillan, 1988.

Maddocks, Morris. *The Christian Healing Ministry,* 2nd ed. London: SPCK, 1990.

Magezi, Vhumani, and Collium Banda. "Competing with Christ? A Critical Christological Analysis of the Reliance on Pentecostal Prophets in Zimbabwe." *In die Skriflig* 51.2 (2017) 10.

Maier, Gerhard. *Biblical Hermeneutics.* Translated by Robert W. Yarbrough. Wheaton, IL: Crossway, 1994.

Marsden, George M. "Everyone One's Own Interpreter? The Bible, Science, and Authority in Mid-Nineteenth-Century America." In *The Bible in America: Essays in Cultural History,* edited by Nathan O. Hatch and Mark Noll, 79–100. New York: Oxford University Press, 1982.

———. *Fundamentalism and American Culture.* New York: Oxford University Press, 2006.

———. *Reforming Fundamentalism: Fuller Seminary and the New Evangelicalism.* Grand Rapids: Eerdmans, 1987.

———. *Understanding Fundamentalism and Evangelicalism.* Grand Rapids: Eerdmans, 1991.

Marshall, I. Howard. *Luke: Historian and Theologian.* Contemporary Evangelical Perspectives. Grand Rapids: Zondervan, 1970.

Martey, Emmanuel. *African Theology: Inculturation and Liberation.* Maryknoll, NY: Orbis, 1993.

Martin, David. "Pentecostalism: An Alternate Form of Modernity and Modernization?" In *Global Pentecostalism in the 21st Century,* edited by Robert W. Hefner, 37–62. Bloomington: Indiana University Press, 2013.

Martin, Francis. "Spirit and Flesh in the Doing of Theology." *Journal of Pentecostal Theology* 18 (2001) 5–31.

Martin, Lee Roy. "Hearing the Voice of God: Pentecostal Hermeneutics and the Book of Judges." In *Pentecostal Hermeneutics: A Reader,* edited by Lee Roy Martin, 205–32. Leiden: Brill, 2013.

———. "Introduction to Pentecostal Biblical Hermeneutics." In *Pentecostal Hermeneutics: A Reader,* edited by Lee Roy Martin, 1–9. Leiden: Brill, 2013.

Marty, Martin. *Religion and Republic: The American Circumstance.* Boston: Beacon, 1987.

Masenya, Madipoane. "Foreign on Own Home Front? Ruminations from an African-South African Pentecostal Biblical Scholar." In *Africa,* vol. 3 of *Global Renewal Christianity: Spirit-Empowered Movements Past, Present, and Future,* edited by Vinson Synan, Amos Yong, and J. Kwabena Asamoah-Gyadu, 380–94. Lake Mary, FL: Charisma House, 2016.

Maxwell, David. "Social Mobility and Politics in African Pentecostal Modernity." In *Global Pentecostalism in the 21st century,* edited by Robert W. Hefner, 91–114. Bloomington: Indiana University Press, 2013.

Mbiti, John S. *African Religions and Philosophy.* London: Heinemann, 1969.

———. "The Biblical Basis in Present Trends of African Theology." *International Bulletin of Mission Research* 4.3 (1980) 119–24.

McClean, Mark D. "Toward a Pentecostal Hermeneutics." *Pneuma* 6.2 (1984) 35–55.

McClung, Grant, ed. *Azusa Street and Beyond: Pentecostal Missions and Church Growth in the Twentieth Century*. South Plainfield: Bridge, 1986.

———. "Introduction: 'Try to Get People Saved': Azusa Street Missiology." In *Azusa Street & Beyond: Missional Commentary on the Global Pentecostal/Charismatic Movement*, edited by Grant McClung, 1–22. 2nd ed. Alachua: Bridge-Logos, 2012.

McDonnell, Kilian. "The Holy Spirit and Christian Initiation." In *The Holy Spirit and Power: The Catholic Charismatic Renewal*, edited by Kilian McDonnell, 57–85. Garden City: Doubleday, 1975.

McGee, Gary B. *People of the Spirit: The Assemblies of God*. Springfield, MO: Gospel, 2004.

———. "Strategies for Global Mission." In *Called and Empowered: Global Mission in Pentecostal Perspectives*, edited by Murray A. Dempster, Byron D. Klaus, and Douglas Petersen, 203–24. Peabody, MA: Hendrickson, 1991.

McKay, John W. "When the Veil Is Taken Away: The Impact of Prophetic Experience on Biblical Interpretation." In *Pentecostal Hermeneutics: A Reader*, edited by Lee Roy Martin, 57–80. Leiden: Brill, 2013.

McQueen, Larry R. *Joel and the Spirit: The Cry of a Prophetic Hermeneutic*. Rev. ed. Cleveland, TN: CPT, 2009.

McRoberts, Kerry D. "The Holy Trinity." In *Systematic Theology*, edited by Stanley M. Horton, 140–72. Rev. ed. Springfield, IL: Logion, 2007.

Menzies, Robert P. *The Development of Early Christian Pneumatology with Special Reference to Luke-Acts*. JSNT Supp 54. Sheffield: JSOT, 1991.

———. "Luke's Understanding of Baptism in the Holy Spirit: A Pentecostal Perspective." *Penteco Studies* 6.1 (2007) 108–26.

———. *Pentecost: This Story Is our Story*. Springfield: GPH, 2013.

Menzies, William. "Synoptic Theology: An Essay on Pentecostal Hermeneutics." *Paraclete* 13.1 (1979) 14–21.

———. "The Methodology of Pentecostal Theology: An Essay on Hermeneutics." In *Essays on Apostolic Themes*, edited by P. Elbert, 1–14. Peabody, MA: Hendrickson, 1985.

Menzies, William W., and Robert P. Menzies. *Spirit and Power: Foundations of Pentecostal Experience*. Grand Rapids: Zondervan, 2000.

Merrick, James, Stephen M. Garrett, and Stanley N. Gundry. *Five Views on Biblical Inerrancy*. Counterpoints. Grand Rapids: Zondervan, 2013.

Mesters, Carlos. "The Use of the Bible in Christian Communities of the Common People." In *The Bible and Liberation*, edited by Norman K. Gottwald and Richard A. Horsley, 119–33. Maryknoll, NY: Orbis, 1993.

Methodist Evangelicals Together. "The Wesleyan Quadrilateral." http://methodistevangelicals.org.uk/resources/wesleyan-quadrilateral.

Metzger, Bruce M. "Seventy or Seventy-Two Disciples?" *New Testament Studies* 5 (1959) 299–321.

———. *The Text of the New Testament: Its Transmission, Corruption, and Restoration*. 2nd ed. Oxford: Clarendon, 1968.

Middlemiss, David. *Interpreting Charismatic Experience*. London: SCM, 1996.

Migliore, Daniel. *Faith Seeking Understanding: An Introduction to Christian Theology*. Grand Rapids: Eerdmans, 1991.

———. *The Power of God*. Philadelphia: Westminster, 1983.

Miller, Aaron G. "Pentecostalism as a Social Movement: Beyond the Theory of Deprivation." *Journal of Pentecostal Theology* 4.9 (1996) 98–119.

Minear, Paul S. "Luke's Use of the Birth Stories." In *Studies in Luke-Acts: Essays Presented in Honor of Paul Schubert*, edited by Leander E. Keck and J. Louis Martyn, 111–30. Nashville: Abingdon, 1966.

Mittelstadt, Martin W. "Latter Rain Movement." In *Handbook of Pentecostal Christianity*, edited by Adam Stewart, 135–38. DeKalb: Northern Illinois University Press, 2012.

———. *Reading Luke-Acts in the Pentecostal Tradition*. Cleveland, TN: CPT, 2010.

———. *The Spirit and Suffering in Luke-Acts: Implications for a Pentecostal Theology*. London: T&T Clark, 2004.

Moberly, R. Walter L. "Pneumatic Biblical Hermeneutics: A Response." In *Spirit and Scripture: Exploring a Pneumatic Hermeneutic*, edited by Kevin L. Spawn and Archie T. Wright, 160–65. New York: Bloomsbury, 2012.

Mofokeng, Takatso A. "Black Christians, the Bible and Liberation." *The Journal of Black Theology* 2 (1988) 34–42.

Möller, Francois P. "Christ and Pentecostalism." In *The Reality of the Holy Spirit in the Church: In Honour of F. P. Möller*, edited by Peter J. Gräbe and Willem J. Hattingh, 140–44. Pretoria: Van Schaik, 1997.

———. *Die Diskussie van die Charismata soos wat dit in die Pinksterbeweging Geleer en Beoefen word*. Braamfontein: Evangelie, 1975.

———. *Words of Light and Life: Part 1*. Westdene: AGS, 1991.

Molobi, Stephens. "Pastor: Grass to Flowers!" *Daily Sun*, 4 July 2017. https://www.dailysun.co.za/News/National/pastor-grass-to-flowers-20170704.

Moltmann, Jürgen. *The Crucified God: The Cross of Christ as the Foundation and Criticism of Christian Theology*. Translated by R. A. Wilson and John Bowden. New York: Harper & Row, 1974.

Moore, Rickie D. "Altar Hermeneutics: Reflections of Pentecostal Biblical Interpretation." *Pneuma* 38.2 (2016) 148–59.

———. "Deuteronomy and the Fire of God: A Critical Charismatic Interpretation." *Journal of Pentecostal Theology* 3.7 (1995) 11–33.

———. "A Pentecostal Approach to Scripture." *Seminary Viewpoint* 8.1 (1987) 12–13.

———. "A Pentecostal Approach to Scripture." In *Pentecostal Hermeneutics: A Reader*, edited by Lee R. Martin, 11–13. Leiden: Brill, 2013.

———. "Canon and Charisma in the Book of Deuteronomy." In *Pentecostal Hermeneutics: A Reader*, edited by Lee R. Martin, 15–31. Leiden: Brill, 2013.

Mosala, Itumeleng J. *Biblical Hermeneutics and Black Theology in South Africa*. Grand Rapids: Eerdmans, 1989.

———. "Race, Class, and Gender as Hermeneutical Factors in the African Independent Churches' Appropriation of the Bible." Unpublished Report for the Human Sciences Research Council, Pretoria, 1989.

Mueller-Vollmer, Kurt. "Introduction: Language, Mind, and Artefact: An Outline of Hermeneutic Theory Since the Enlightenment." In *The Hermeneutics Reader*, edited by Kurt Mueller-Vollmer, 1–53. New York: Continuum, 2006.

Mugambi, J. N. K. and Johannes A. Smit. *Text and Context in New Testament Hermeneutics*. Nairobi: Actor, 2004.

Muindi, Samuel W. "The Nature and Significance of Prophecy in Pentecostal-Charismatic Experience: An Empirical-Biblical Study." PhD diss., University of Birmingham, 2012.

Mullin, Robert B. *A Short World History of Christianity.* Louisville: Westminster John Knox, 2008.

Munshya, Elias. "After We Have Said 'Amen': Towards A Pentecostal Theology of Politics in Zambia." *Elias Munshya,* 15 October 2015. https://eliasmunshya.org/2015/10/15/after-we-have-said-amen-towards-a-pentecostal-theology-of-politics-in-zambia.

Myland, D. Wesley. *The Latter Rain Covenant and Pentecostal Power.* Chicago: Evangel, 1910.

Ndiokwere, Nathaniel. *Prophecy and Revolution: The Role of Prophets in the African Churches and in Biblical Tradition.* London: SPCK, 1981.

Nel, Marius. "Attempting to Define a Pentecostal Hermeneutics." *Scriptura* 114 (2015) 1–21.

———. "Bible Reading Practices in the AFM." 31 Aug 2017. https://issuu.com/afm_ags/docs/bible_reading.

———. "Church and War: A Change in Hermeneutical Stance among Pentecostals." *Verbum et Ecclesia* 38.1 (2017) 1–8.

———. "Daniel 9 as Part of an Apocalyptic Book?" *Verbum et Ecclesia* 34.1 (2013) 8.

———. "Development of Theological Training and Hermeneutics in Pentecostalism: A Historical Perspective." *Studia Historiae Ecclesiasticae* 422 (2016) 191–207. https://upjournals.co.za/index.php/SHe

———. "Fundamentalism and Pentecostalism: Blood Nephews?" *Journal of Theology for Southern Africa* 158 (2017) 57–71.

———. 'He Changes Times and Seasons': Narratological-Historical Investigation of Daniel 1 and 2. Theology in Africa 8. Zürich: LIT, 2017.

———. "A Hundred Years of Theological Training in the Apostolic Faith Mission of South Africa." *Acta Theologica* 34.1 (2014) 108–26.

———. "Konteks(te) Waarbinne Apokaliptiese Geskrifte Gedurende die Intertestamentêre Periode Floreer Het." *HTS Teologiese Studies* 64.3 (2008) 1327–45.

———. *Of That Day and Hour No One Knows: Mark 13 as an Apocalypse.* Theology in Africa 3. Zürich: LIT, 2014.

———. *Pacifism and Pentecostals in South Africa: A New Hermeneutic of Nonviolence.* Routledge New Critical Thinking in Religion, Theology, and Biblical Studies. Abingdon: Routledge, 2018.

———. "Pentecostal Ecumenical Impulses: Past and Present Challenges." *In die Skriflig* 52.1 (2018) 8.

———. "Pentecostalism and the Early Church: On Living Distinctively from the World." *Journal of Theology for Southern Africa* 153 (2016) 141–59.

———. "The Pentecostal Movement's View of the Continuity of Tongues in Acts and 1 Corinthians." *In die Skriflig* 51.1 (2017) 7.

———. "Pentecostals' Reading of the Old Testament." *Verbum et Ecclesia* 282 (2007) 524–41.

———. "Pentecostal Talk about God: Attempting to Speak from Experience." *HTS Teologiese Studies* 73.3 (2017) 8.

Nel, Marius, and Fika Janse Van Rensburg. "Integrating Spirituality and Rationality: The Long and Arduous Journey of the Historical Development of Theological Training in the Apostolic Faith Mission of South Africa." *In die Skriflig* 50.2 (2016) 10.

Nelson, P. C., and Pius Wawire. *Bible Doctrines*. Africa's Hope Discovery Series. Springfield, MO: Gospel, 2004.

Neumann, Peter D. "Spirituality." In *Handbook of Pentecostal Christianity*, edited by Alan Stewart, 195–201. DeKalb: Northern Illinois University Press, 2012.

Newbigin, Lesslie. *The Good Shepherd: Meditations on Christian Ministry in Today's World*. Oxford: Mowbray, 1977.

Ngong, David T. *The Holy Spirit and Salvation in African Christian Theology: Imagining a New Hopeful Future for Africa*. Bible and Theology in Africa. Oxford: Peter Lang, 2010.

———. "In Quest of Wholeness: African Christians in the New Christianity." *Review & Expositor* 103.3 (2006) 519–40.

Noel, Bradley T. "Pentecostal and Postmodern Hermeneutics: Comparisons and Contemporary Impact." DTh Diss., University of South Africa, 2007.

"Notorious Pastor Penuel Mnguni of South Africa, Beaten, Tied Up, and His Church Burnt Down." *Bummyla*, 17 November 2015. https://bummyla.com/2015/11/17/notorious-pastor-penuel-mnguni-of-south-africa-beaten-tied-up-and-his-church-burnt-down.

O'Day, Gail R. "'Today this Word Is Fulfilled in your Hearing': A Scriptural Hermeneutic of Biblical Authority." *Word and World* 26.4 (2006) 357–64.

Ogbeche, Danielle "Youths Burn Down Church of South African Pastor Who Makes Members Swallow Live Snakes, Eat Grass." *Daily Post*, 18 November 2015 http://dailypost.ng/2015/11/18/youths-burn-down-church-of-south-african-pastor-who-makes-members-swallow-live-snakes-eat-grass.

Oliverio, L. William. "Book Review: Reading Craig Keener: On *Spirit Hermeneutics: Reading Scripture in Light of Pentecost*." *Pneuma* 39 (2017) 126–45.

———. "Book Review: Theological Hermeneutics in the Classical Pentecostal Tradition: A Typological Account." *E-Publications@Marquette* 2018. https://epublications.marquette.edu/dissertations/AAI3357966.

———. "Introduction: Pentecostal Hermeneutics and the Hermeneutical Tradition." In *Constructive Pneumatological Hermeneutics in Pentecostal Christianity*, edited by Kenneth J. Archer and L. William Oliverio, 1–14. New York: Palgrave Macmillan, 2016.

———. *Theological Hermeneutics in the Classical Pentecostal Tradition: A Typological Account*. Global and Pentecostal Studies 12. Leiden: Brill, 2012.

Olivier, Bert. "Kingsolver's Narrative Indictment of Colonisation: The Poisonwood Bible." *Thought Leader*, 15 May 2018. http://thoughtleader.co.za/bertolivier/2018/05/15/kingsolvers-narrative-indictment-of-colonisation-the-poisonwood-bible.

Omenyo, Cephas. "African Pentecostalism." In *The Cambridge Companion to Pentecostalism*, edited by Cecil M. Robeck and Amos Young, 132–51. New York: Cambridge University Press, 2014.

———. "Man of God, Prophesy unto Me: The Prophetic Phenomenon in African Christianity." *Studies of World Christianity* 17.1 (2011) 30–49.

Omenyo, Cephas, and Abamfo Atiemo. "Claiming Religious Space: The Case of Neo-Prophetism in Ghana." *Ghana Bulletin of Theology* New Series 1.1 (2006) 55–68.

Omenyo, Cephas N., and Wonderful Adjei Arthur. "The Bible Says! Neo-Prophetic Hermeneutics in Africa." *Studies in World Christianity* 19.1 (2013) 50–70.

Oosthuizen, Gerhardus C. *The Healer-Prophet in Afro-Christian Churches.* Leiden: Brill, 1992.

Osborne, Grant R. *The Hermeneutical Spiral: A Comprehensive Introduction to Biblical Interpretation.* 2nd ed. Downers Grove: InterVarsity, 2006.

Otto, Rudolf. *The Idea of the Holy: An Inquiry into the Non-Rational Factor in the Idea of the Divine and its Relation to the Rational.* 2nd ed. London: Oxford University Press, 1950.

Paas, Steven. *Christianity in Eurafrica: A History of the Church in Europe and Africa.* Washington, DC: New Academia, 2017.

Packer, James I. *Fundamentalism and the Word of God: Some Evangelical Principles.* Grand Rapids: Eerdmans, 1958.

Palmer, Richard E. *Hermeneutics: Interpretation Theory in Scheleiermacher, Dilthey, Heidegger, and Gadamer.* Evanston, IL: Northwestern University Press, 1969.

Parham, Charles F. *Kol Kare Bemidbar: A Voice Crying in the Wilderness.* Baxter Springs: Robert L. Parham, 1902.

"Parliament Slams CRL Chair's Comment on eNgcobo." *ENCA,* 25 February 2018. http://www.enca.com/south-africa/parliament-slams-crl-chairs-comment-on-engcobo.

"Pastor Banned From Using Doom on Congregants." *ENCA,* 21 March 2017. https://www.enca.com/south-africa/pastor-banned-from-using-doom-on-congregants.

"Pastor Makes Congregation Strip." *ENCA,* 23 May 2015. http://www.enca.com/south-africa/shocking-pictures-pastor-makes-congregration-strip-and-jumps-top-them.

"Pastor Penuel Mnguni Makes Congregation Strip." *Citizen,* 22 May 2015. https://citizen.co.za/news/387857/pastor-makes-congregation-strip.

Peel, John D. Y. "Post-Socialism, Post-Colonialism, Pentecostalism." In *Conversion After Socialism: Disruptions, Modernities, and the Technologies of Faith,* edited by Mathijs Pelkmans, 183–201. Oxford: Berghahn, 2009.

Peerbolte, Bert J. L. "'Do not Quench the Spirit!' The Discourse of the Holy Spirit in Earliest Christianity." *HTS Teologiese Studies* 71.1 (2015) 1–9.

Penney, John M. *The Missionary Emphasis of Lukan Pneumatology.* Sheffield: Sheffield Academic, 1997.

Pinnock, Clark H. "Divine Relationality: A Pentecostal Contribution to the Doctrine of God." *Journal for Pentecostal Theology* 16 (2000) 2–26.

———. *Tracking the Maze: Finding Our Way Through Modern Theology from an Evangelical Perspective.* San Francisco: Harper, 1990.

———. "The Work of the Holy Spirit in Hermeneutics." *Journal of Pentecostal Theology* 1.2 (1993) 3–23.

———. "The Work of the Holy Spirit in the Interpretation of Holy Scripture from the Perspective of a Charismatic Biblical Theologian." In *Pentecostal Hermeneutics: A Reader,* edited by Lee Roy Martin, 233–48. Leiden: Brill, 2013.

Plüss, Jean-Daniel. "Azusa and Other Myths: The Long and Winding Road from Experience to Stated Belief and Back Again." *Pneuma* 15.2 (1993) 189–201.

———. "Religious Experience in Worship: A Pentecostal Perspective." *PentecoStudies* 2.1 (2003) 1–21.

Pollman, Karla. "Einführung." In *Handbuch der Bibelhermeneutiken: Von Origenes bis zur Gegenwart*, edited by Oda Wischmeyer, 9–11. Berlin: De Gruyter, 2016.

Poloma, Margaret M. *The Assemblies of God at the Crossroads: Charisma and Institutional Dilemmas*. Knoxville: University of Tennessee Press, 1989.

Porter, Stanley E., and Beth M. Stovell. *Biblical Hermeneutics: Five Views*. Downers Grove: InterVarsity, 2012.

Poythress, Vern S. *Understanding Dispensationalism*. Grand Rapids: Eerdmans, 1987.

Pretorius, Stephanus P. "The Toronto Blessing: An Expression of Christian Spirituality in the Charismatic Movement?" DTh diss., University of South Africa, 2002.

Purdy, Harlyn G. *A Distinct Twenty-First Century Pentecostal Hermeneutic*. Eugene, OR: Wipf & Stock, 2015.

Quayesi-Amakye, Joseph. *Christology and Evil in Ghana: Towards a Pentecostal Public Theology*. Amsterdam: Rodopi, 2013.

———. "'Nativizing' the Gospel: Pentecostalism and Theology in Africa." In *Africa*, vol. 3 of *Global Renewal Christianity: Spirit-Empowered Movements Past, Present, and Future*, edited by Vinson Synan, Amos Yong, and J. Kwabena Asamoah-Gyadu, 287–303. Lake Mary, FL: Charisma House, 2016.

Raeesa, Kimmie. "Court Orders Pastor to Stop Spraying Doom." *Weekend Bosveld Review*, 20 March 2017. https://reviewonline.co.za/200327/court-orders-pastor-stop-spraying-doom.

Railey, James H., and Benny C. Aker. "Theological Foundations." In *Systematic Theology*, edited by Stanley M. Horton, 39–60. Rev. ed. Springfield, MO: Logion, 2007.

Rance, DeLonn L. "Fulfilling the Apostolic Mandate in Apostolic Power: Seeking a Spirit-Driven Missiology and Praxis." *Encounter: Journal for Pentecostal Ministry* 5 (2008). http://legacy.agts.edu/encounter/articles/2008_winter/rance.pdf.

Reddy, Dean C. "The Apostolic Faith Mission of South Africa with Special Reference to its Rise and Development in the 'Indian' Community." MTh Diss., University of Durban-Westville, 1992.

Reese, Robert. "The Surprising Relevance of the Three-Self Formula." *Mission Frontiers* (2007) 25–27.

Reilly, Jill. "Lawn Again Christians: South African Preacher Makes Congregation Eat Grass to 'Be Closer to God.'" *Daily Mail,* 10 January 2014. http://www.dailymail.co.uk/news/article-2537053/Lawn-Christians-South-African-preacher-makes-congregation-eat-GRASS-closer-God.html.

Resane, Kelebogile T. "Pentecostals and Apartheid: Has the Wheel Turned Around Since 1994?" *In die Skriflig* 521 (2018) 8.

Rice, Monte Lee. "Book Review: Oliverio: *Theological Hermeneutics in the Classical Pentecostal Tradition*." *Pneuma* (2018). http://pneumareview.com/bill-oliverio-theological-hermeneutics-in-the-classical-pentecostal-tradition.

Ricoeur, Paul. "Philosophical Hermeneutics and Theological Hermeneutics." *Studies in Religion* 5 (1975) 14–33.

Robeck, Cecil M. "The Assemblies of God and Ecumenical Cooperation: 1920–65." In *Pentecostalism in Context*, edited by Wonsuk Ma and Robert Menzies, 107–50. JPT Supp 11. Sheffield: Sheffield Academic, 1997.

———. *The Azusa Street Mission and Revival: The Birth of the Global Pentecostal Movement*. Nashville: Nelson, 2006.

———. "Azusa Street Revival." In *Dictionary of Pentecostal and Charismatic Movements*, edited by Stanley M. Burgess and Gary B. McGee, 31–36. Grand Rapids: Zondervan, 1988.

———. "National Association of Evangelicals." In *Dictionary of Pentecostal and Charismatic Movements*, edited by Stanley M. Burgess and Gary B. McGee, 634–36. Grand Rapids: Zondervan, 1988.

———. "The Origins of Modern Pentecostalism." In *The Cambridge Companion to Pentecostalism*, edited by Cecil M. Robeck and Amos Yong, 13–30. New York: Cambridge University Press, 2014.

———. "Pentecostals and Ecumenism: An Expanding Frontier." In *Crossing Borders*, edited by Jean-Daniel Plüss, 1–17. Conference on Pentecostal and Charismatic Research, 3–6 July 1991, Kappel, Switzerland.

———. "Pentecostals and the Apostolic Faith: Implications for Ecumenism." *Pneuma* 9.1 (1986) 61–84.

———. "Taking Stock of Pentecostalism: The Personal Reflections of a Retiring Editor." *Pneuma* 15.1 (1993) 35–60.

Russell, Colin A. "Biological Science and Christian Thought." In *The Blackwell Encyclopedia of Modern Christian Thought*, edited by Alister E. McGrath, 51–56. Oxford: Basil Blackwell, 1993.

Russell, D. S. *The Method and Message of Jewish Apocalyptic: 200 BC–100 AD*. Philadelphia: Westminster, 1964.

Ryrie, Charles C., ed. *The Ryrie KJV Study Bible*. Chicago: Moody Press, 1978.

Sakupapa, Teddy. "Prophets in the Zambian/African Context: A Survey from an Ecumenical Perspective." In *Prophecy Today: Reflections from a Southern African Context*, edited by Hermen Kroesbergen, 113–28. Special Edition of Word and Context Journal. Wellington: Christian Literature Fund, 2016.

Sandidge, Jerry L. *Roman Catholic-Pentecostal Dialogue (1977–1982): A Study in Developing Ecumenism*. Studien zur interkulturellen Geschichte des Christentums 144. Frankfurt am Main: Peter Lang, 1987.

Schaeffer, Francis. *The Trilogy*. Wheaton, IL: Crossway, 1990.

Schafroth, Verena. "An Exegetical Exploration of 'Spirit' References in Ezekiel 36 and 37." *Journal of the European Theological Association* 29.2 (2009) 61–77.

Schröter, Jens. "The Son of Man as the Representative of God's Kingdom: On the Interpretation of Jesus in Mark and Q." In *Jesus, Mark, and Q: The Teaching of Jesus and Its Earliest Records*, edited by Michael Labahn and Andreas Schmidt, 34–68. JSNT Supp 214. Sheffield: Sheffield Academic, 2001.

Schnabel, Eckhard J. *Acts*. Zondervan Exegetical Commentary on the New Testament. Grand Rapids: Zondervan, 2012.

Schnackenburg, Rudolf. *Belief in the New Testament*. Translated by J. Moiser. New York: Paulist, 1974.

Schofield, C. I., ed. *Schofield Reference Bible*. Oxford: Oxford University Press, 1909.

———. *The New Schofield Reference Bible*. Oxford: Oxford University Press, 1967.

Fiorenza, Elizabeth Schüssler. *Bread not Stone: The Challenge of Feminist Biblical Interpretation*. Boston: Beacon, 1995.

Schütz, Christian. *Einführung in die Pneumatologie*. Darmstadt: Wissenschaftliche Buchgesellschaft, 1985.

Seaman, M. X. *Illumination and Interpretation: The Holy Spirit's Role in Hermeneutics*. Eugene, OR: Wipf & Stock, 2013.

Sethusa, Pheladi, and Austil Mathebula. "Pastor's Supporter Drinks Petrol as Part of 'Miracle.'" *Citizen*, 25 September 2014. https://citizen.co.za/news/south-africa/247788/pastor-daniel-can-now-turn-petrol-juice.

Shaull, Richard. "What Can the Mainline Churches Learn from Pentecostals about Pentecost Preaching?" *Journal for Preachers* 21.4 (1998) 8–14.

Shaw, Mark R. *The Kingdom of God in Africa: A Short History of African Christianity.* Grand Rapids: Baker, 1997.

Shelton, James B. *Mighty in Word and Deed: The Role of the Holy Spirit in Luke-Acts.* Peabody, MA: Hendrickson, 1991.

Shuman, Joel. "Pentecost and the End of Patriotism: A Call for the Restoration of Pacifism Among Pentecostal Christians." *Journal for Pentecostal Theology* 9 (1996) 70–96.

Siekawitch, Larry D. "Calvin, Spirit, Communion, and the Supper." *Journal of the European Pentecostal Theological Association* 2 (2009) 14–35.

Smidt, Corwin E. *American Evangelicals Today.* Lanham, MD: Rowman & Littlefield, 2013.

Smit, Peter-Ben. *From Canonical Criticism to Ecumenical Exegesis? A Study in Biblical Hermeneutics.* Studies in Reformed Theology 30. Leiden: Brill, 2015.

Smith, Christian. *The Bible Made Impossible: Why Biblicism Is not a Truly Evangelical Reading of Scripture.* Grand Rapids: Brazos, 2011.

Smith, Calvin L. "The Politics and Economics of Pentecostalism: A Global Survey." In *The Cambridge Companion to Pentecostalism*, edited by Cecil M. Robeck and Amos Yong, 175–94. New York: Cambridge University Press, 2014.

Smith, James K. A. *The Fall of Interpretation: Philosophical Foundations for a Creational Hermeneutic.* 2nd ed. Grand Rapids: Eerdmans, 2012.

Solivan, Samuel. "Sources of a Hispanic/Latino American Theology: A Pentecostal Perspective." In *Hispanic/Latino Theology: Challenge and Promise*, edited by José David Rodríguez and Loida I. Martell-Otero, 137–48. Louisville: Westminster John Knox, 1997.

———. *The Spirit, Pathos, and Liberation: Toward an Hispanic Pentecostal Theology.* JTP Supp 14. Sheffield: Sheffield Academic, 1998.

Soulen, Richard N. *Sacred Scripture: A Short History of Interpretation.* Louisville: Westminster John Knox, 2009.

Sparks, Kenton L. *God's Word in Human Words: An Evangelical Appropriation of Critical Biblical Scholarship.* Grand Rapids: Baker Academic, 2008.

Spawn, Kevin L. "The Interpretation of Scripture: An Examination of Craig S. Keener's *Spirit Hermeneutics.*" *Pneuma* 39 (2017) 146–52.

Spawn, Kevin L., and Archie L. Wright. "The Emergence of a Pneumatic Hermeneutic in the Renewal Tradition." In *Spirit and Scripture: Exploring a Pneumatic Hermeneutic*, edited by Kevin L. Spawn and Archie T. Wright, 3–23. New York: Bloomsbury, 2012.

Spittler, Russell J. "Scripture and the Theological Enterprise: A View from the Big Canoe." In *The Use of the Bible*, edited by Robert K. Johnston, 75–77. Atlanta: John Knox, 1985.

Spurling, Richard G. *The Lost Link.* Turtletown, TN: R. G. Spurling, 1920.

Starling, David I. *Hermeneutics as Apprenticeship: How the Bible Shapes Our Intepretive Habits and Practices.* Grand Rapids: Baker Academic, 2016.

Stibbe, Mark. "This Is That: Some Thoughts concerning Charismatic Hermeneutics." *Anvil: An Anglican Evangelical Journal for Theology and Mission* 15.3 (1998) 181–93.

Stott, John R. W. *Baptism and Fullness: The Work of the Holy Spirit Today.* 2nd ed. Downers Grove: InterVarsity, 1976.

Stronstad, Roger. *The Charismatic Theology of St. Luke.* Peabody, MA: Hendrickson, 1984.

———. "Pentecostal Experience and Hermeneutics." *Paraclete* 26.1 (1992) 14–30.

———. "The Prophethood of All Believers: A Study in Luke's Charismatic Theology." In *Pentecostalism in Context: Essays in Honor of William W. Menzies*, edited by Wonsuk Ma and Robert P. Menzies, 60–77. Sheffield: Sheffield Academic, 1997.

Studebaker, Steven M. "Book Review: Oliverio, William L. *Theological Hermeneutics in the Classical Pentecostal Tradition: A Typological Account.*" *Themelios* 39.2 (2014) 375–77.

Stuhlmacher, Peter. *Vom Verstehen des Neuen Testaments: Eine Hermeneutik.* Grundrisse zum Neuen Testament NTD Ergänzungsreihe 6. Göttingen: Vandenhoeck & Ruprecht, 1979.

Swartley, William M. *Slavery, Sabbath, War, and Women: Core Issues in Biblical Interpretation.* Scottdale, PA: Herald, 1983.

Synan, Vinson. "Fundamentalism." in *Dictionary of Pentecostal and Charismatic Movements*, edited by Stanley M. Burgess and Gary B. McGee, 324–5. Grand Rapids: Zondervan, 1988.

———. *The Holiness-Pentecostal Movement in the United States.* Grand Rapids: Eerdmans, 1971.

———. *The Holiness-Pentecostal Tradition: Charismatic Movements in the Twentieth Century.* 2nd ed. Grand Rapids: Eerdmans, 1997.

Taylor, Charles. *A Secular Age.* Cambridge: Belknap, 2007.

Taylor, George Floyd. "The Spirit and the Bride." In *A Reader in Pentecostal Theology: Voices From the First Generation*, edited by Douglas Jacobsen, 58–66. Bloomington: Indiana University Press, 2006.

Taylor, John V. *The Primal Vision: Christian Presence and African Religion.* London: SCM, 1963.

Tenney, Merrill C. *New Testament Survey.* Grand Rapids: Eerdmans, 1961.

Thiselton, Anthony C. *Hermeneutics: An Introduction.* Grand Rapids: Eerdman, 2009.

———. *New Horizons in Hermeneutics.* Grand Rapids: Zondervan, 1992.

Thomas, John C. "'What the Spirit Is Saying to the Church': The Testimony of a Pentecostal in New Testament Studies." In *Spirit and Scripture: Exploring a Pneumatic Hermeneutic*, edited by Kevin L. Spawn and Archie T. Wright, 115–29. New York: Bloomsbury, 2012.

Tolar, William B. "The Grammatical-Historical Method." In *Biblical Hermeneutics*, edited by Bruce Corley, Steve W. Lemke, and Grant I. Lovejoy, 21–38. 2nd ed. Nashville: Broadman & Holman, 2002.

Tollefsen, Christopher. "Morality and God." *Quaestiones Disputatae* 5.1 (2014) 7–60.

Thomas, Derek. *Acts.* Reformed Expository Commentary. Phillipsburg, NJ: P&R, 2011.

Thomas, John C. "Reading the Bible From Within Our Traditions: A Pentecostal Hermeneutic as Test Case." In *Between Two Horizons: Spanning New Testament Studies and Systematic Theology*, edited by Joel B. Green and Max Turner, 108–22. Grand Rapids: Eerdmans, 2000.

———. "Women, Pentecostals and the Bible: An Experiment in Pentecostal Hermeneutics." *Journal of Pentecostal Studies* 5 (1994) 41–56.

Tigay, Jeffrey H. *You Shall Have No Other Gods*. Atlanta: Scholars, 1986.

Tomberlin, Daniel. *Pentecostal Sacraments: Encountering God at the Altar*. Cleveland, OH: Center for Pentecostal Leadership and Care, 2010.

Topping, Richard A. *Revelation, Scripture, and Church: Theological Hermeneutic Thought of James Barr, Paul Ricoeur and Hans Frei*. Hampshire: Ashgate, 1988.

Torrey, Reuben A. et al., eds. *The Fundamentals: Testimony to the Truth*. Los Angeles: The Bible Institute of Los Angeles, 1895.

Tripolitis, Antonia. *Religions of the Hellenistic-Roman Age*. Grand Rapids: Eerdmans, 2002.

Turnage, Marc. "The Early Church and the Axis of History and Pentecostalism: Facing the 21st Century: Some Reflections." *Journal of the European Pentecostal Theological Association* 23 (2003) 4–29.

———. "Does Luke Believe Reception of the 'Spirit of Prophecy' Makes All 'Prophets'? Inviting Dialogue with Roger Stronstad." *Journal of the European Pentecostal Association* 20 (2000) 3–24.

Twelftree, Graham H. *People of the Spirit: Exploring Luke's View of the Church*. Grand Rapids: Baker, 2009.

Ukah, Asonzeh. "The Deregulation of Piety in the Context of Neoliberal Globalization: African Pentecostalisms in the Twenty-First Century." In *Africa*, vol. 3 of *Global Renewal Christianity: Spirit-Empowered Movements Past, Present, and Future*, edited by Vinson Synan, Amos Yong, and J. Kwabena Asamoah-Gyadu, 362–78. Lake Mary, FL: Charisma House, 2016.

Ukpong, Donatus. P. "Charismatic Renewal and Roman Catholicism in Africa: Challenges and Prospects of Pentecostalism." In *Africa*, vol. 3 of *Global Renewal Christianity: Spirit-Empowered Movements Past, Present, and Future*, edited by Vinson Synan, Amos Yong, and J. Kwabena Asamoah-Gyadu, 321–37. Lake Mary, FL: Charisma House, 2016.

Ukpong, Justin S. "Current Theology: The Emergence of African Theologies." *HTS Teologiese Studies* 45 (1984) 501–36.

Usry, Glenn, and Craig S. Keener. *Black Man's Religion: Can Christianity be Afrocentric?* Downers Grove, IL: InterVarsity, 1996.

Vásquez, Oscar C. "Past and Present Social Characteristics of Pentecostal Churches in South America." In *Latin America*, vol. 2 of *Global Renewal Christianity: Spirit-Empowered Movements Past, Present, and Future*, edited by Vinson Synan and Miguel Álvarez, 315–36. Lake Mary, FL: Charisma House, 2016.

Van der Geest, Sjaak. "Participant Observation in Demographic Research: Fieldwork Experiences in a Ghanaian Community." In *The Methods and Uses of Anthropological Demography*, edited by A. M. Basu and P. Aaby, 39–56. Oxford: Clarendon, 1998.

Van der Laan, Cornelis. "Theology of Gerrit Polman: Dutch Pentecostal Pioneer." Annual Meeting of the Society for Pentecostal Studies, 10–12 November 1988, Wilmore, Kentucky.

Van der Walt, Sarel J., and Gert J. C. Jordaan. "Die Kontekstualisering van die Nuwe Testament Binne 'n Postmodernistiese Paradigma: Die Skep van Betekenis of die Toepas van Betekenis." *In die Skriflig* 38.4 (2004) 495–517.

Van der Walt, Sarel J., and Nico Vorster. *Reformed Theology Today: Practical-Theological, Missiological and Ethical Perspectives*. Pretoria: AOSIS, 2017.

Vanhoozer, Kevin J. *The Drama of Doctrine: A Canonical Linguistic Approach to Christian Theology*. Louisville: Westminster John Knox, 2005.

———. *Is There a Meaning in this Text? The Bible, the Reader, and the Morality of Literary Knowledge*. Leicester: Apollos, 1998.

Veenhof, Jan. "The Holy Spirit and Hermeneutics." *Scottish Bulletin of Evangelical Theology* 5 (1987) 105–22.

Venema, Cornelis P. "Interpreting the Bible In and With the Church: An Evaluation of 'Post-Liberal' or 'Post-Critical' Hermeneutics." In *Correctly Handling the Word of Truth*, edited by Mees te Velde and Gerhard H. Visscher, 24–55. Eugene, OR: Wipf & Stock, 2014.

Verhoef, Pieter A. *Profete en Profesie*. Cape Town: Lux Verbi, 1993.

Vermes, Geza. *The Story of the Scrolls*. London: Penguin, 2010.

Virkler, Henry A. *Hermeneutics: Principles and Processes of Biblical Interpretation*. Grand Rapids: Baker, 1981.

Volf, Miroslav. *After Our Likeness: The Church as the Image of the Trinity*. Grand Rapids: Eerdmans, 1998.

Vondey, Wolfgang. *Pentecostalism: A Guide for the Perplexed*. London: Bloomsbury, 2013.

Von Rad, Gerhard. *The Theology of Israel's Prophetic Tradition*, vol. 2 of *Old Testament*. Translated by D. M. G. Stalker. London: SCM, 1965.

Vorster, Willem S. "Tekste Met 'n Apokaliptiese Perspektief." In *Woorde Wat Ver Kom: Die Literatuur van die Ou Testament*, edited by Ferdinand Deist and Willem Vorster, 158–76. Deel 1. Cape Town: Tafelberg, 1986.

Wacker, Grant. "The Functions of Faith in Primitive Pentecostalism." *Harvard Theological Review* 77.3–4 (2011) 353–375.

———. *Heaven Below: Early Pentecostals and American Culture*. Cambridge: Harvard University Press, 2001.

Waddell, Robby. *The Spirit of the Book of Revelation*. JOST Supp 30. Blandford Forum: Deo, 2006.

Waldvogel, Edith. "The Overcoming Life: A Study in the Reformed Evangelical Origins of Pentecostalism." PhD diss., Harvard University, 1977.

Waltke, Bruce K. *The Dance between God and Humanity: Reading the Bible Today as the People of God*. Grand Rapids: Eerdmans, 2013.

Walton, John H., and Craig S. Keener. *Cultural Backgrounds Study Bible NIV*. Grand Rapids: Zondervan, 2016.

Wansbrough, Henry. *The Use and Abuse of the Bible: A Brief History of Biblical Interpretation*. London: T&T Clark, 2010.

Ware, Frederick L. "The Use of Signs in the Preaching of Charles Harrison Mason." 34th Meeting of the Society for Pentecostal Studies, 10–12 March 2005, Virginia Beach, VA. https://www.umbrasearch.org/catalog/fc801b108762ac9848c387a0c769b85cb17b12a5.

Warrington, Keith. "Holy Spirit." In *Handbook of Pentecostal Christianity*, edited by Alan Stewart, 121–25. DeKalb: Northern Illinois University Press, 2012.

Weber, Max. *The Sociology of Religion*. Boston: Beacon, 1962.

Welker, Michael. "Word and Spirit, Spirit and Word: A Protestant Response." *Concilium* 3 (1996) 52–79.

Wepener, Cas J. "Liturgical 'Reform' in Sub-Saharan Africa: Some Observations on Worship, Language and Culture." *Studia Liturgica* 44.1–2 (2014) 82–95.

Wesley, John. *The Works of John Wesley.* 14 vols. 3rd ed. London: Wesley Methodist Book Room, 1872.

West, Gerald O. "The Bible Story That Became a Campaign: The Tamar Campaign in South Africa (and Beyond)." *Ministerial Formation* (2004) 4–12.

———. *Biblical Hermeneutics of Liberation: Modes of Reading the Bible in the South African Context.* 2nd ed. Maryknoll, NY: Orbis, 1995.

———. "Locating 'Contextual Bible Study' Within Biblical Liberation Hermeneutics and Intercultural Biblical Hermeneutics." *HTS Teologiese Studies* 70.1 (2014) 1–10.

———. "Mapping African Biblical Interpretation: A Tentative Sketch." In *The Bible in Africa: Transactions, Trajectories, and Trends,* edited by Gerald O. West and M. W. Dube, 29–53. Leiden: Brill, 2000.

———. "Reading the Bible with the Marginalised: The Value/s of Contextual Bible Reading." *Stellenbosch Theological Journal* 1.2 (2015) 1–7.

West, Gerald O., and M. W. Dube, eds. *The Bible in Africa: Transactions, Trajectories, and Trends.* Leiden: Brill, 2000.

Whalen, Robert K. "Literalism." In *Encyclopedia of Fundamentalism,* edited by Brenda E. Brasher, 280–81. New York: Routledge, 2001.

Wilkinson, Michael. "Pentecostals and the World: Theoretical and Methodological Issues for Studying Global Pentecostalism." *Pneuma* 38.4 (2016) 373–93.

Williams, Daniel H. *Tradition, Scripture, and Interpretation: A Sourcebook of the Ancient Church.* Grand Rapids: Baker Academic, 2006.

Williams, Joseph J. *Hebrewism of West Africa: From Nile to Niger with the Jews.* London: George Allen & Unwin, 1930.

———. "The Pentecostal Reality." (2015) http://www.cbn.com/spirituallife/biblestudyandtheology/drwilliams/bk-pentacostal-ch03.aspx

Wink, Walter. *The Bible in Human Transformation: Toward a New Paradigm for Biblical Study.* Philadelphia: Fortress, 1973.

Witherington, Ben. *Conflict and Community in Corinth: A Socio-Rhetorical Commentary on 1 and 2 Corinthians.* Grand Rapids: Eerdmans, 1995.

Wright, N. T. "How Can the Bible Be Authoritative?" The Laing Lecture, 1989; Griffith Thomas Lecture, 1989. *Vox Evangelica* 21 (1991) 7–32.

Wyckoff, John W. *Pneuma and Logos: The Role of the Spirit in Biblical Hermeneutics.* Eugene, OR: Wipf & Stock, 2010.

———. "The Relationship of the Holy Spirit to Biblical Hermeneutics." PhD diss., Baylor University, 1990.

Yong, Amos. "Academic Glossolalia? Pentecostal Scholarship, Multi-Disciplinarity, and the Science-Religion Conversation." *Journal of Pentecostal Theology* 14.1 (2005) 61–80.

———. *The Hermeneutical Spirit: Theological Interpretation and Scriptural Imagination for the 21st Century.* Eugene, OR: Cascade, 2017.

———. "Instead of a Conclusion: A Theologian's Interdisciplinary Musings on the Future of Global Pentecostalism and Its Scholarship." In *The Cambridge Companion to Pentecostalism,* edited by Cecil M. Robeck and Amos Young, 313–20. New York: Cambridge University Press, 2014.

———. "Pentecostalism and the Political: Trajectories in its Second Century." *Pneuma* 32.3 (2010) 333–36.

———. "Proclamation in/of the Spirit: Toward a Pneumatological Theology of Preaching." *The Living Pulpit* (2015) 34–8.

———. "Reviews of Political Theologies: Public Religions in a Post-Secular World; Controversies in Political Theology; Being the Church in the Midst of Empire: Trinitarian Reflections." *Pneuma* 31 (2009) 157–58.

———. *Spirit-Word-Community: Theological Hermeneutics in Trinitarian Perspective.* Ashgate New Critical Thinking in Religion, Theology, and Biblical Studies. Aldershot: Ashgate, 2002.

———. "Whither Systematic Theology? A Systematician Chimes in on a Scandalous Conversation." *Pneuma* 29 (1998) 89–93.

Zaimov, Stoyan. "Doom-Spraying Pastor Backed by Church Members Claiming to Be 'Healed.'" *Christian Post*, 28 November 2016. https://www.christianpost.com/news/pastor-spraying-doom-peoples-faces-backed-members-who-claim-to-be-healed-171767.

Zizioulas, John. *Being as Communion: Studies in Personhood and the Church.* Crestwood, NY: St Vladimir's Seminary Press, 1997.

Zwiep, Arie W. "Bible Hermeneutics from 1950 to the Present: Trends and Developments." In *Handbuch der Bibelhermeneutiken: Von Origenes bis zur Gegenwart*, edited by Oda Wischmeyer, 933–1008. Berlin: De Gruyter, 2016.

———. "Het Hermeneutische Vraagstuk: Een Verkenning en een Stellingname." *Soteria* 14.1 (1997) 3–13.

———. "Luke's Understanding of Baptism in the Holy Spirit: An Evangelical Perspective." *Penteco Studies* 6.2 (2007) 127–49.

Zylstra, Sarah E. "The Most Popular and Fastest Growing Bible Translation Isn't What You Think It Is." *Christianity Today* (2014) 1. http://www.christianitytoday.com/gleanings/2014/march/most-popular-and-fastest-growing-bible-translation-niv-kjv.html.

Index